"Ricks knocks it out of the park with this jewel of a book. On every page I learned something new. Read it every night if you want to restore your faith in our country."

—General James Mattis, United States Marine Corps (Ret.), and twenty-sixth secretary of defense

"One of my favorite works of history in a very long time. I grew up revering Jefferson. I found him loathsome here, but still recognize that like Churchill in 1940, a flawed man can move future events dramatically. Madison's reach was remarkable. Poor Adams remained as miserable as I had always viewed him. But Washington was my revelation here. I have never been able to put flesh on those bones, but Ricks has done it."

—Joe Scarborough

"A rich compendium of the ancient wisdom that Washington, Adams, Jefferson, and Madison believed they were gleaning from Aristotle or Tacitus, and the formation of 'classically shaped behavior' in the early republic. . . . Antiquity mattered, Ricks suggests, because it formed the intellectual foundation for the revolutionary generation. Knowing the source of the values they claimed to espouse and the historical comparisons they took as obvious, we can know more about the founders themselves—and perhaps something of how the country we now have measures up to the one they envisioned."

—*Washington Post*

"Ricks masterfully documents how examples of city states like Athens and the Roman Republic informed the four aforementioned Founding Fathers and their fellow travelers. . . . So the question lurking in the shadows throughout this engaging political peregrination is the one the author asks in the epilogue: Did the founders anticipate Donald Trump? . . . Ricks points out that even iconic political figures oftentimes behaved in disturbing ways, just like politicians do today. . . . It seems the document was eminently more perfect than the men who created it."

—*USA Today*

"[An] extraordinarily timely book. . . . If classical culture helped the new nation coalesce, what serves the same function today? Money? Pop culture? Political activism? And what about virtue? Does it still have a place in our society, and if so how might one define it? Interestingly, Mr. Ricks points out that for the Revolutionary generation, 'silent virtue almost always would be valued more than loud eloquence.' Of course the opposite is true now."

—*Wall Street Journal*

"In this instructive new book, [Ricks] offers a judicious account of the equivocal inheritance left to modern Americans by their eighteenth-century forebears. . . . [He] urges Americans to fix their government so that it protects citizens from the inevitable lapses of a fallible people and, perhaps, even more fallible leaders."

—*New York Times Book Review*

"*First Principles* is a fascinating and erudite look at how Greek and Roman writers influenced members of the founding generation. From the Harvard-educated John Adams to the largely self-taught George Washington, the most well-known of American revolutionaries turned statesmen, looked to the classical world to answer critical questions about the nature of power and the nature of government."

—Annette Gordon-Reed, Charles Warren Professor of American Legal History, Harvard Law School, and Pulitzer Prize–winning author of *The Hemingses of Monticello*

"Ricks knows his subject well, and, equally important, he writes about it lucidly."

—Gordon Wood, Alva O. Way University Professor and Professor of History Emeritus, Brown University, and author of *The Radicalism of the American Revolution* and *Empire of Liberty: A History of the Early Republic*

"Thomas Ricks's deeply personal, patriotic quest to recover and renew the principles that animated America's founders testifies eloquently to the value of historical understanding in these troubled times. Steeped in the classics, the founders could not have imagined our world and we are now, more than ever, acutely conscious of their failure to engage with the fundamental problem of racial slavery and its enduring legacies. But Ricks offers us a timely reminder of what the first four, nation-making presidents *could* imagine and did struggle to achieve."

—Peter S. Onuf, Thomas Jefferson Memorial Foundation Professor, Emeritus, University of Virginia, and coauthor of *Most Blessed of the Patriarchs: Thomas Jefferson and the Empire of the Imagination*

"An immersive and enlightening look at how the classical educations of the first four U.S. presidents (George Washington, John Adams, Thomas Jefferson, and James Madison) influenced their thinking and the shape of American democracy. . . . With incisive selections from primary sources and astute cultural and political analysis, this lucid and entertaining account is a valuable take on American history." —*Publishers Weekly* (starred review)

"Ricks does something quite remarkable: he takes a seemingly academic topic—the Greco-Roman education of the Founding Fathers—and makes it resonate with grand relevance. . . . Offering a look at the Founders rarely glimpsed, Ricks successfully argues that America needs to rediscover its classical roots."

—*Library Journal* (starred review)

"An elegantly written celebration of two men who faced an existential crisis to their way of life with moral courage—and demonstrated that an individual can make a difference."

—*San Francisco Chronicle*

"Readers of this book will realize, if they needed reminding, that the struggle to preserve and tell the truth is a very long game."

—*Los Angeles Times*

"In *First Principles*, Ricks provides us the reading list we would have to undertake to get close to the framers' worldview. Ricks is not squeamish about their collective blindness to the evil of slavery, or its cruelty and brutality. . . . What the flawed Framers gifted us was a blueprint of genius that we have since improved upon greatly because of Lincoln, the suffragists, the Reverend Martin Luther King Jr. and the many other civil rights leaders of that era. . . . Ricks reminds us of our purpose."  —Hugh Hewitt, *Washington Post*

"The Pulitzer Prize–winning author offers a new interpretation of the individuals who shaped our constitution and government. You'll find new insights into the past from the first page to the last."  —*Detroit Free Press*

"In *First Principles*, a lively and accessible synthesis of the work of generations of historians and his own reading of the letters, speeches, and pamphlets of Washington, Adams, Jefferson, and Madison, Ricks assesses the influence of classical public philosophy and practice on politics in America in the late eighteenth and early nineteenth centuries—and draws conclusions about the country we have become."  —*Psychology Today*

"Penetrating history with a modest dollop of optimism."

—*Kirkus Reviews*

"*First Principles* stands alone as an important work on the Revolutionary period."  —*Journal of the American Revolution*

"Well informed, gracefully written and brimming with contemporary relevance."  —Bookreporter.com

# FIRST
# *Principles*

# FIRST
# *Principles*

WHAT AMERICA'S

FOUNDERS LEARNED

*from the* GREEKS

*and* ROMANS *and*

HOW THAT SHAPED

OUR COUNTRY

## THOMAS E. RICKS

HARPER ● PERENNIAL

NEW YORK ● LONDON ● TORONTO ● SYDNEY ● NEW DELHI ● AUCKLAND

HARPER ● PERENNIAL

A hardcover edition of this book was published in 2020 by HarperCollins Publishers.

HarperCollins books may be purchased for educational, business, or sales promotional use. For information, please email the Special Markets Department at SPsales @harpercollins.com.

FIRST HARPER PERENNIAL EDITION PUBLISHED 2021.

Designed by Leah Carlson-Stanisic

Map on p. xvi by Gene Thorpe

Library of Congress Cataloging-in-Publication Data has been applied for.

ISBN 978-0-06-299746-3 (pbk.)

24 25 26 27 28 LBC 8 7 6 5 4

For the dissenters, who conceived this nation,

and improve it still

Unless we can return a little more to first principles,
& act a little more upon patriotic ground, I do not
know . . . what may be the issue of the contest.

——*George Washington to James Warren,*
*March 31, 1779*

# Contents

# A Note on Language

I HAVE QUOTED THE WORDS OF THE REVOLUTIONARY GENERATION as faithfully as possible, including their unusual spellings and surprising capitalizations. I did this because I think it puts us nearer their world, and also out of respect: I wouldn't change their words when quoting them, so why change their spellings? For some reason, I am fond of George Washington's apoplectic denunciation of an "ananominous" letter written by a mutinous officer during the Revolutionary War. Seeing this reinforces our need to understand that the past really is "a foreign country" where they did things differently, and where words sometimes carried different meanings. The one point where I nearly broke this rule is with the variant spellings of the Roman conspirator Catiline, sometimes spelled as Cataline. But I decided to preserve their variations after realizing that this is necessary to enable readers to search for a given quotation in *Founders Online*, the National Archives' wonderful digital compilation of the papers of the leaders of the early United States. Along the same lines, I have where possible quoted from the eighteenth-century editions of books that they might have used, including Greek and Roman authors in translation. The only alteration I have consistently made is to capitalize the first letter of sentences, because I found that leaving them in lowercase made their words more difficult to comprehend.

\*　　\*　　\*

I also have chosen to use the term "First Peoples" rather than "Indian" or "Native American." In researching this issue, I was struck by a statement by a group of musicians that "We do not call ourselves 'Native American,' because our blood and people were here long before this land was called the Americas. We are older than America can ever be and do not know the borders."

# Chronology

1732 —— Birth of George Washington

1735 —— Birth of John Adams

1743 —— Birth of Thomas Jefferson

1751 —— Birth of James Madison

1754 — 1763 —— Seven Years' War, called by Americans the French and Indian War

1755 —— Washington witnesses Braddock's Defeat

—— Adams graduates from Harvard

1762 —— Jefferson, considered graduated from William & Mary, begins to study law under George Wythe

1765 —— Stamp Act passed by Parliament to assert British authority over the colonies and to raise revenue to pay for the French and Indian War

1768 —— British troops are stationed in Boston for the first time

1770 —— Boston Massacre

1771 —— Madison graduates from College of New Jersey (Princeton)

1772 —— Boston town meeting creates a "Committee of Correspondence" to communicate about the political situation with other towns and colonies

1773 —— Boston Tea Party

1774 —— Massachusetts government suspended; colony is placed under British military rule

—— First Continental Congress convenes

1775 —— FEBRUARY —— Parliament declares Massachusetts to be in a state of rebellion

APRIL —— Battles of Lexington and Concord

JUNE——Battle of Bunker Hill

JUNE——Washington appointed to command the Continental Army

AUGUST——Parliament declares most of the American colonies to be in a state of rebellion

OCTOBER——British shell and burn Falmouth, Massachusetts (now Portland, Maine)

1776——JANUARY——British fleet bombards Norfolk, Virginia, for three hours, destroying most of the city

JULY——Second Continental Congress issues Declaration of Independence

1777——SEPTEMBER AND OCTOBER——American forces win two battles at Saratoga, comprising the most important victory in the war. Washington fights two battles near Philadelphia, at Brandywine and Germantown, then withdraws to encamp for the winter at Valley Forge

1778——FEBRUARY——France formally allies with the American rebels

——JUNE——The British withdraw from Philadelphia, the rebel capital

1779—1780——The American effort almost collapses

1781——Articles of Confederation take effect

——Battle of Yorktown signals the end of the war

1783——Peace treaty formally ends the war

1786—87——Shays' Rebellion challenges the postwar distribution of power in Massachusetts

1787——Constitutional Convention devises new plan of government for the United States

1789——Washington becomes first president under the new government created by the Constitution

——French Revolution begins

1793—94——Reign of Terror in France; Louis XVI and his queen executed

1794——The Whiskey Rebellion in western Pennsylvania poses another major challenge to the postwar distribution of American power and wealth

1796——Adams elected president

1798——Alien and Sedition Acts crack down on newspaper editors and other critics of Adams administration

1799——Washington dies

1801——Jefferson becomes president after the outcome is decided by the House of Representatives

1804——Aaron Burr, Jefferson's alienated vice president, shoots and kills Alexander Hamilton

1808——Madison elected president

1820——Missouri Compromise formalizes geographic division of country along the lines of slavery

1826——Jefferson and Adams die on the same day, fifty years to the day after July 4, 1776

1836——Madison dies

1861——American Civil War begins

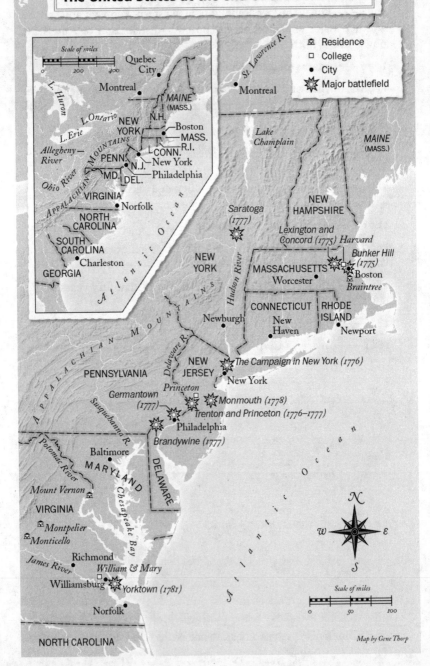

# The United States at the end of the Revolution

**Residence** 🏠
**College** ▢
**City** ●
**Major battlefield** ✷

*Scale of miles*
0    200    400

Quebec City
Montreal
*MAINE (MASS.)*
N.H.
NEW YORK
Boston
MASS.
R.I.
CONN.
New York
PENN.
N.J.
MD. DEL.
Philadelphia
*Ohio River*
*Allegheny River*
*APPALACHIAN MOUNTAINS*
L. Huron
L. Erie
L. Ontario
VIRGINIA
Norfolk
NORTH CAROLINA
SOUTH CAROLINA
Charleston
GEORGIA

*St. Lawrence R.*
Montreal
*Lake Champlain*
*MAINE (MASS.)*

Saratoga (1777)

NEW HAMPSHIRE

Lexington and Concord (1775) *Harvard*
Bunker Hill (1775)

NEW YORK

*Hudson River*

MASSACHUSETTS
Worcester
Boston
*Braintree*

CONNECTICUT
New Haven

RHODE ISLAND

Newburgh

Newport

*APPALACHIAN MOUNTAINS*

*Delaware R.*

PENNSYLVANIA

NEW JERSEY

The Campaign in New York (1776)

*Princeton*
New York

Germantown (1777)

Monmouth (1778)

Trenton and Princeton (1776–1777)

Philadelphia

Brandywine (1777)

*Susquehanna R.*

Baltimore

*Potomac River*

MARYLAND

DELAWARE

*Mount Vernon*

VIRGINIA

*Montpelier*
*Monticello*

*James River*

Richmond

*William & Mary*

Williamsburg

Yorktown (1781)

Norfolk

*Chesapeake Bay*

*Atlantic Ocean*

NORTH CAROLINA

N
W    E
S

*Scale of miles*
0    50    100

*Map by Gene Thorp*

# Prologue

## *What Is America?*

THE AMERICAN NOVELIST AND LITERARY CRITIC RALPH ELLISON once remarked that, "Whenever we as Americans have faced serious crises we have returned to fundamentals; this, in brief, is what I have tried to do." Me too. On that gray Wednesday morning after the presidential election of 2016, I woke up with a series of questions: What just happened? What kind of nation do we now have? Is this what was designed or intended by the nation's founders?

Recalling that the people who made the Revolution and wrote the Constitution had been influenced by the thinkers of the ancient world, I decided to go back to fundamentals. I went to my library and took down Aristotle's *Politics*, not knowing I was embarking on an intellectual journey that would last four years. Aristotle led me to other political thinkers, and eventually I found myself rereading the Declaration of Independence and other foundational documents.

Before that Tuesday night in November 2016, I had thought I understood my country. But the result of that election shocked me. Clearly, many of my fellow citizens had an understanding of our nation profoundly different from mine. Foremost among them was the new president-elect. I found myself examining my assumptions about this country and its design, not only questioning what the founders had thought but wondering what had shaped their thinking. What did they read, what did they think, what resonated with them? How different were their intellectual influences from today's? What were they thinking as they constructed this nation? How did we get from there to here? And where are we going on this ship they designed?

In recent years dozens of wonderful biographies of members of the Revolutionary generation have been published, but they tend to gloss over the educations of those people. The biographers would mention where these people went to college (or didn't go, as in the case of George Washington) and the names of their tutors, and sometimes would list some of the books they read. But I couldn't find what they took away from those tutors and books. Who were the men who taught them, and where did they come from? What books influenced them? Where did they get their political ideas, their political vocabularies? What ideas and attitudes would they take from college to adulthood and into the public arenas of Revolutionary America? What ancient works were in their minds as they drafted the Declaration of Independence or debated the Constitution? How does their reliance on Greco-Roman history affect how we live now?

In other words, I embarked on an intellectual quest to try to find my way toward answering a question: *What is America supposed to be, anyway?*

So I read the books they read and the letters they wrote to one another about those books. While much attention has been paid to the influence of Enlightenment thinking on the founders—in particular the writings of John Locke—the fact is that these men did not study Locke as much as they did the writings of the ancient world, Greek and Roman philosophy and literature: the *Iliad*, *Plutarch's Lives*; the philosophical explorations of Xenophon, Epicurus, Aristotle; and the political speeches and commentaries of Cato and Cicero. In the course of this I revisited writers I had not considered since I was in high school and college four decades ago, and read some other things I had not encountered back then.

This journey took me a long way in time and space and to unexpected corners, as with the Scottish invention of geology in the late eighteenth century, and into some historical curiosities, such as the importance of Aristotle to the redoubled Southern defense of slavery in the first half of the nineteenth century. Along the way I learned many things to help me better understand my country, both its past and its present. Some of what I learned had been subjects of debate and discussion among scholars for decades. But some of it has been neglected, lying long in a letter or diary here, a military order there, and an obscure academic journal way over there.

I've been changed by this journey and seek in this book to share what I've learned. Not everyone has the time, opportunity, or inclination to spend several years in the basements of college libraries reading ancient Roman political speeches or minor Greek philosophers, and then comparing them to the wartime letters of George Washington and the essays of James Madison and Alexander Hamilton. But I did, and I loved every day of it. As I burrowed through the library shelves, I also found my own views of the first four presidents began to shift. George Washington's ability to observe and learn seems to me underappreciated. James Madison's contributions, especially his designing gridlock into the American system, also seem to me to be undervalued. John Adams, by contrast, began to strike me as having an inflated reputation in recent years, with insufficient attention paid to his unhelpful commentary during the War for Independence and also his disastrous presidency. Likewise, though raised by my parents to revere Thomas Jefferson, I increasingly found myself disturbed by his habitual avoidance of reality.

Throughout, I marveled at what a rich and paradoxical history this country possesses. We are a nation fundamentally dedicated to equal standing before the law, yet also have developed a political system in which one of the two major parties always seems to have offered a home to white supremacists, up to the present day.

I dwell in these pages on the faults of the founders in part so we can better understand our own. Thus we can try to live up to their aspirations while perhaps avoiding some of their shortcomings. If there is one thing a reader should take away from this book, it is that there is little certain about our nation except that it remains an experiment that requires our serious and sustained attention to thrive.

\*     \*     \*

To my knowledge, no one has written a book addressing these questions before, examining and comparing the educations of George Washington, John Adams, Thomas Jefferson, and James Madison. There have been many books about the early lives of each of these men, and there even have been specialized studies of the educations of Washington and Madison. Historians also have produced several illuminating biographical pairings—Jefferson and Adams, Jefferson and Madison, Jefferson and Washington, and so on. But as far as I can tell, there does not exist a study of what our first four presidents learned, where they learned it, who they learned it from, and what they did with that knowledge. That is what I endeavor to explore in this work.

Thus the first part of the book will look at their early lives and educations. The second section will show how they used what they learned in their political deliberations as they sought independence and designed a new nation. The final chapters explore how the neoclassical culture that shaped them was altered by the powerful forces that emerged in the 1790s and the early nineteenth century, mainly the democratization of American politics and culture, but also the coming of the Industrial Revolution.

I examine them chronologically. I begin with George Washington, who managed to become the exemplar of the classical Roman values that meant so much to elite colonial society. I next turn to John Adams, who cast himself as a modern Cicero, a significant association because the parable of Cicero's triumph over the Catilinarian conspiracy in 63 BC was the essential political narrative for the Revolutionary generation. I proceed to Thomas Jefferson, the only one in this quartet who favored the Greeks over the Romans, and look at how Jefferson's Greek-inflected classicism steered him away from Federalism and also provided the philosophy embedded in the Declaration of Independence. Finally I examine James Madison, whose classicism was leavened by a greater cosmopolitanism and an understanding of the limits to which one could rely on what the Romans called virtue, by which they meant public-mindedness.

In the second part of the book, I look at how their classical perspectives were challenged as the American Revolution unfolded. Washington, despite his lack of a classical education, came at different times to embody three of the great Roman role models—Cato, Fabius, and Cincinnatus—while avoiding the temptation of becoming an American version of Julius Caesar. I'll then show how the paradigm shifted away from virtue at the moment of the maximum classical influence during the writing of the Constitution, and then began to decline along with the Federalist party it inspired, bottoming out with Adams' failed presidency. Finally I'll explore the moral and intellectual void that opened as classical ideals yielded in the nineteenth to the rise of religious evangelism and commercial culture, and consider if we might develop a new sense of public-spiritedness in our own time.

This approach leads to some new observations. By looking at the first four presidents collectively and placing them in the classical context, we can see illuminating new patterns and contrasts. For example, it is one thing to read that Jefferson and Madison as young men were influenced by a Scottish tutor, but another to see that Scots again and again played a major role in colonial American education. In fact, those young Scots transmitted to America the intellectual skepticism and dynamism of the Scottish Enlightenment, which was firmly rooted in classicism, and came even as the English universities of the time were mired in the intellectual doldrums and in fact sat out the Enlightenment. Likewise, Scottish legal thinking was far more rooted in Roman philosophy than was English law, which was more oriented toward local precedent and tradition.

Another case is Madison's decision to leave Virginia for a college in New Jersey, which becomes more significant when contrasted with the fact that Adams and Jefferson, like most wealthy young men of the time, went to college in their home colonies. Madison chose to travel weeks to attend the most politically radical college in the country, one with a new, explicitly "continental" approach to recruiting its students—and one that was led by a politicized Scottish minister. Understanding the influence of classicism also helps us understand why, for example, George Washington placed such faith in "virtue," why John Adams held such a fear of "faction," and why Thomas Jefferson was so determined to give the official buildings of Washington, DC, a feel of ancient Rome.

"Synthesis demands regard for complexity," Peter Gay cautioned in his colossal two-volume history of the Enlightenment. It is a useful admonition. As I wrote this work of synthesis, roaming across political, cultural, and intellectual aspects of history and literature both in the ancient world and in the eighteenth and nineteenth centuries, I tried to respect the complexities of the matter. So while this book emphasizes the classicism of the Revolutionary generation of Americans, it is not meant to suggest that other narratives—such as the influence of English liberal thought—are incorrect, only that the classical dimension has been underappreciated, especially outside academia. This is important because the more we grasp the influence of the Greco-Roman world on the Revolutionary generation, the better we will understand them and their goals, problems, fears, and mistakes.

I also have tried to hold in mind the ambiguities and to acknowledge the unknowns and the mysteries. There are still aspects of this story that defy explanation. Most notable is that the starting point for the United States is the fundamental contradiction of a slaveholder's declaring that the basic fact of public life is that all people are created equal. One of the more powerful commentaries on America was the arch question Samuel Johnson posed in 1777: "How is it that we hear the loudest *yelps* for liberty among the drivers of negroes?" It is a question that still hangs in the air more than two centuries later.

The differences between these men ran deep. Washington absorbed classicism mainly secondhand, from the elite culture of his day. Adams focused on the laws and rhetoric of Rome, especially on the speeches of Cicero, the self-made orator of the first century BC who became a personal model for him as he scrabbled out of a depressing post-college job as a schoolteacher in a Massachusetts backwater. Jefferson delved deeper into classical philosophy than the others did, especially Epicureanism, the philosophy of pursuing happiness and avoiding pain, which (as we shall see) pervades the most significant sections of his Declaration of Independence. Madison was the most academic in his approach, studying the ancient world almost as a political scientist.

They grew into distinctly dissimilar men: Washington a stiff-necked soldier; Adams a brilliant, honest, self-absorbed crank; Jefferson a dreamer of liberty who lived in hypocritical luxury off the sweat of captive humans; Madison already with one foot in the next generation, perhaps more of an American than a Virginian, and an unapologetic politician. Like Alexander Hamilton, he was more skeptical than his elders of the verities of the Enlightenment, with its core faith in human improvement.

And of course each would play an essential role in the formation of the new nation—Washington, above all, in winning the war for independence and becoming the first president; but also Adams, who was a key member of the Continental Congress and then was the first president to carry out a peaceful transfer of power to the political opposition; Jefferson, whose Declaration is one of the nation's two fundamental documents, and the more inspirational of the two; and Madison, the chief driver of the other foundational document, the Constitution, which not only put forth a set of ideals but was flexible and strong enough to survive as the supreme law of the land for more than 225 years—so far.

Their concentration on the classical world does not decline with each man, but actually intensifies from Washington to Adams to Jefferson to Madison. Washington, as was said, learned about the ancient world mainly by osmosis. It was for him, as for the others, a major part of the intellectual climate of the day, part of daily conversation and writing. Adams delved into classicism intensely but narrowly, mainly because of his ambition to become a great lawyer. Jefferson was broadly interested in classical philosophy and politics, but not always deeply. Madison, in order to prepare for the drafting of the American Constitution, would spend years engaged in a methodical study of ancient political systems, especially the histories of Greek republics. He was aided greatly by the trunkloads of books shipped to him from Paris by Jefferson. It was partly because of him that the writing of the Constitution became the high-water mark of classical republicanism in America—but also because of him that the pursuit of virtue, the very core of the old viewpoint, was abandoned.

Emphatically, they were not detached philosophers. They were statesmen and revolutionaries, looking to the ancient world for the help it could give them in illuminating their situation. There was an abiding practicality in their approaches. "Their reading in the classics was highly purposeful, adaptive and selective," notes Meyer Reinhold, one of the pioneer scholars of this topic. Before them, he writes, the classical world was important mainly to colonial Americans preparing to be clergymen. After them, it was used to train members of the elite, especially in law and oratory. But during the middle and later parts of the eighteenth century, the thoughts and stories of the ancient Greeks and Romans stood front and center in American political and intellectual life as the founders grappled with the questions of how to gain independence and then how to form a new nation.

*Part I*

# ACQUISITION

If on a spring morning in May 1778 following that hard
winter at Valley Forge, we could approach a soldier warming himself by a fire and ask him his opinion of the great
Roman orator Cato, he probably would not find the inquiry
odd. Rather, he might respond with great enthusiasm that
he had in fact seen a play about Cato just the previous evening, when it was staged, by some accounts, in the camp's
bakery. He might even have played a role in it. Joseph Addison's *Cato* was, after all, one of the most popular plays in
pre-Revolutionary America, and indeed the favorite dramatic
work of the camp's commander, General George Washington.
This was a time when live drama was one of the few forms of
public art. Our soldier might even be able to quote from the
play——maybe that striking line about choosing between
liberty or death, or perhaps the passage in which a character regrets that he has only one life to give for his country.

◄────►

## Chapter I

# The Power of
# Colonial Classicism

THE CLASSICAL WORLD WAS FAR CLOSER TO THE MAKERS OF THE American Revolution and the founders of the United States than it is to us today. Nowadays the Greeks and Romans are remote to us, their works studied by a few in college and then largely forgotten even by most of those readers. But Greco-Roman antiquity was not distant to the leaders of the American Revolution. It was present in their lives, as part of their political vocabulary and as the foundation of their personal values. In short, it shaped their view of the world in a way that most Americans now are not taught and so don't see.

Colonial classicism was not just about ideas. It was part of the culture, a way of looking at the world and a set of values. The more one looks around early America for the influence of ancient Greek and Roman history and literature, the more one finds. Classicism wafted even in the air of colonial romance. When John Adams and Abigail Smith courted, they used classical pseudonyms in their letters—Lysander for him, Diana for her. James Madison kept a bust of Athena on the mantelpiece of his drawing room at Montpelier, and a small head of Homer hanging over that room's doorway—this last probably a nod to the figure of the Greek bard that during Madison's college days looked down from atop the center door of Princeton's Nassau Hall. Thomas Jefferson's front hall at Monticello greeted visitors with, among other things, a marble statue of Ariadne, the princess of Crete who led Theseus out of the minotaur's labyrinth. He designed that room to reflect the Ionic style of classical architecture, while adjoining ones are imprinted with the marks of the Tuscan, Doric, and Corinthian styles.

The colonials named their horses and their enslaved humans after classical figures. A bit down the hill from Jefferson's house, a stable housed Caractacus, Tarquin, Arcturus, and Diomede. This naming habit resulted in asides in correspondence such as one in which Adams instructed his wife that "Cleopatra ought not to be fed too high—she should have no Grain." Among the enslaved, one who worked on contract for Madison was called Plato, while Jefferson held title to Jupiter, Caesar, and Hercules, and Washington to Neptune and Cupid. Even people such as Washington who had not attended college were familiar with the names and stories of the Romans, especially of the heroes whose lives and values were seen as worthy of emulation. Many decades later, after Emancipation, one of the grievances listed by freedmen was that they had not been allowed even to keep their own names.

The ancient world was present in their lives in ways that, because they gave the country its shape, echo down the corridors of time, mainly in ghostly ways that people today tend not to notice. Our "Senate" meets in "The Capitol"—both references to ancient Rome. Most of its members are either "Republicans," a name derived from Latin, or "Democrats," a word of Greek origin. Just east of the Capitol building, our Supreme Court convenes in a marbled 1935 imitation of a Roman temple, with great bronze doors at the entrance weighing twenty-six thousand pounds apiece. To the west in the Federal City stands the Lincoln Memorial, which resembles the Parthenon of Athens, turned sideways, and the Jefferson Memorial, which borrows from Rome's Pantheon. Reach into your wallet, take out a one-dollar bill, and on the reverse side you will see three Latin phrases: On the left, *annuit coeptis* (more or less, "our undertakings are favored") and *novus ordo seclorum* ("new order of the ages"), and on the right, the more familiar *E pluribus unum* ("Out of many, one"). Ironically, on the obverse side is the image of George Washington, the only one of our first four presidents not to read Latin.

The proverbs offered in Benjamin Franklin's *Poor Richard's Almanack* often were updated versions of Greek and Roman sayings. "He does not possess Wealth, it possesses him," for example, comes from the Greek philosopher Aristippus. *The Moral Sayings of Publius Syrus*, a collection of about a thousand aphorisms that appeared in the first century BC, particularly influenced Franklin. Among them was one that Franklin quoted, a saying that lives even today in the names of a pop culture magazine and a rock music group—"A rolling stone gathers no moss."

The early Americans also nodded to the ancient world in naming their settlements. In upstate New York, it is possible to drive in one day from Troy to Utica to Rome to Syracuse to Ithaca, while passing through Cicero, Hector, Ovid, Solon, Scipio Center, Cincinnatus, Camillus, Romulus, Marcellus, and even Sempronius, who didn't exist—he was a fictional character in Addison's *Cato*. Downstate, overlooking New York City's great harbor, towers a statue of a Roman goddess, though few today might recognize Miss Liberty, or *Libertas*, as such. Her upheld torch soars 305 feet above the saltwater lapping her little island.

## The Pursuit of Virtue

THE BEST PLACE TO BEGIN TO UNDERSTAND THE VIEWS OF THE REVOLU-tionary generation is with a look at the word "virtue." This word was powerfully meaningful during the eighteenth century. Today it is a mere synonym for morality, and also, anachronistically, a signifier of female chastity or the lack of it, as in the euphemistic phrase "a woman of easy virtue." But for the Revolutionary generation, virtue was the essential element of public life. Back then, it actually was masculine. It meant putting the common good before one's own interests. Virtue, writes the historian Joyce Appleby, was the "lynchpin" of public life—that is, the fastener that held together the structure.

It is worth dwelling on the word for a moment, because it runs like a bright thread through the entire period of the Revolution and the first decades of the new nation. The founders used it incessantly in their public statements. The word "virtue" appears about six thousand times in the collected correspondence and other writings of the Revolutionary generation, compiled in the U.S. National Archives' database, *Founders Online (FO)*, totaling some 120,000 documents. That's more often than "freedom." The practice of virtue was paramount, which is one reason George Washington, not an articulate man, loomed so large over the post-Revolutionary era.

## A Different Ancient World

IN RECOGNIZING THE IMPACT OF CLASSICISM ON THE FOUNDERS, WE also need to see that their conception of the ancient world was not the one we have now. They favored different subjects and people than we do in the modern era. One good cultural marker is the Harvard Universal Classics, a collection of essential works of world literature, designed to offer the basic building blocks of a liberal education. Published in 1909, it selected works from twice as many Greeks (Homer, Herodotus, Plato, Epictetus, Aeschylus, Sophocles, Euripides, Aristophanes) as Romans (Virgil, Cicero, Marcus Aurelius, and Pliny the Younger). It also included Plutarch, who had a foot in both worlds. A similar project, Great Books of the Western World, which grew out of the University of Chicago in the 1940s, emphasizes the Greeks even more heavily, with four times as many of them as Romans.

But for the Revolutionary generation, Rome stood well in front of Athens, with the Greek world pushed to the background, seen sometimes as a bit obscure and impractical. "It is impossible to read in Thucydides, his account of the factions and confusions throughout all Greece, . . . without horror," John Adams wrote.

They did on occasion look with admiration on the Greeks, but when they did, it was more often toward Sparta than Athens.

They saw the Spartans as plainspoken, simple, free, and stable, while they disparaged the Athenians as turbulent, factionalized, and flighty. They knew that the Greek historian Polybius had criticized the people of Athens for being like a ship without a commander. "The history of Athens abounds with instances of the levity and inconstancy of that unsteady people," Edward Wortley Montagu warned in 1759. By contrast, John Dickinson, in his influential pre-Revolutionary *Letters from a Farmer in Pennsylvania*, called the Spartans "as brave and as free a people as ever existed." John Adams reported that the two ancient republics he most admired were Sparta and Rome. His second cousin, the determined revolutionary Samuel Adams (Harvard, 1740), desired that their city of Boston would become a "Christian Sparta."

The founders' conception of ancient literature was also unlike ours. Here again, the Romans stood in the forefront. Sallust and Tacitus were their preferred historians. The Epicurean poet and philosopher Lucretius was far more popular then. Most of all, the Roman orator Cicero enjoyed a far higher profile in their world than he does in ours. His luster has faded in modern times, to the point where he is seen, if at all, as a kind of pompous ass. Not so in the eighteenth century. Edward Gibbon, that era's great chronicler of Rome's decline, recommended that any young scholar begin with "Cicero in Latin, and Xenophon in Greek." The hierarchy was different then; the founders refer to Cicero in their correspondence and diaries about five times as often as they do to Aristotle. The Roman's prominence was noted at the time by the Scottish Enlightenment philosopher David Hume, who observed in 1748 that, "The Fame of Cicero flourishes at present; but that of Aristotle is utterly decay'd." These preferences extended across national and cultural boundaries—the generation that made the French Revolution owned a remarkably similar bookshelf, with Cicero again in the lead.

The great Greek tragedians stood far in the background of the colonial view, with Jefferson as an exception, especially in his reading of Euripides. Appreciation of the Greek dramatists as major figures in world literature would come only in the nineteenth century, spurred generally by the rise of Romanticism, and specifically by German academics and critics.

The sole ancient dramatist widely read in early America was not a Greek. Rather, it was Terence, a Roman comic playwright who is little read today. Thucydides also did not figure largely in their commentaries, although John Adams liked him. There were other exceptions to the general disregard for the Greeks. One whose reputation loomed larger at the time was the philosopher and military memoirist Xenophon. Adams, for example, saluted him as "my favourite author." Jefferson also was a fan.

Their attention to Rome was itself uneven, focused heavily on the demise of the Republic in the first century BC. Their readings ranged over more than a thousand years of ancient history, all the way from the *Iliad* to Justinian's *Codex*, but came back again and again to that crucial period of the decline of the Republic. That decades-long process of republican erosion provided their political context, their point of reference, and much of their civic language. "What gripped their minds, what they knew in detail, and what formed their view of the whole of the ancient world," the historian Bernard Bailyn concludes in his classic study of *The Ideological Origins of the American Revolution*, "was the political history of Rome from the conquests in the east and the civil wars in the early first century BC to the establishment of the empire on the ruins of the republic at the end of the second century AD." It was not just their core narrative, it was their lodestar. Alexander Hamilton, for instance, flatly asserted in the thirty-fourth of the Federalist Papers that "the Roman Republic attained to the utmost height of human greatness."

And so they focused on just a few texts by a handful of key authors about the Roman Republic—Livy, Sallust, Plutarch, Tacitus, and, most of all, Cicero. Their heroes were the orators portrayed in those books defending the Republic, led by Cato and Cicero. Their villains were those who brought it down, especially Catiline and Julius Caesar. John Adams considered Caesar a destructive tyrant, the man who "made himself perpetual dictator."

This conception of the classical world seeped into the popular culture of eighteenth-century America, as with that play about Cato. Two of the most influential English political commentators of the era, John Trenchard and Thomas Gordon, published their weekly essays under the title *Cato's Letters*. One of their major themes was the necessity of being skeptical of the exercise of state power. Their articles became central to the political debate in mid-century America, says Bailyn, who found in his study of the pamphlets of the time that they were "the most frequently cited authority on matters of principle and theory." In 1722 in one of those *Letters*, notes another historian, they "first gave unreserved endorsement to free speech as being indispensable to 'Liberty, Property, true Religion, Arts, Sciences, Learning, Knowledge.'" Later in life, Gordon went on to produce popular translations of Cicero and the historians Sallust and Tacitus.

## The Colonial Colleges

WHO WERE THESE COLONIAL MEN, PROFICIENT IN THE LITERATURE OF late Republican Rome, who would go on to design and lead a new republic? They were an economic elite, but a new one. They were emphatically not products of a long-standing aristocracy. Of the ninety-nine men who would sign the Declaration of Independence or the Constitution, only eight had fathers who themselves were college-educated.

The colleges they attended were hardly the sprawling factories of mass higher education we see today. Rather, they were tiny outposts of learning, having more in common with medieval seminaries. In the early eighteenth century, there were just three of them—William & Mary in Virginia, Harvard in Massachusetts, and Yale in Connecticut. In 1746 they were joined by the College of New Jersey, later known as Princeton, and then in 1754 by King's College, later known as Columbia, established by New Yorkers in conservative reaction to the radical politics of Princeton. Each had just a few score of students and a handful of faculty members. Many of the students were in their late teens; many of their teachers were just a few years older. At William & Mary, Jefferson wrote, they lived in brick buildings, "rude, mis-shapen piles" that provided "an indifferent accommodation." Their academic diet consisted mainly of the best-known works of Latin literature, history, and philosophy, with some Greek works thrown in, usually for the more advanced students.

These campuses also could be surprisingly rowdy, with college life interrupted by riots that involved not just students but some of the younger, more outspoken faculty members. Many of those teaching were recent graduates of Scottish universities, educated there in the new skeptical, probing way of thinking coming out of Edinburgh and Glasgow. Jefferson and Madison were the most influenced by these young Scots, Adams somewhat, and Washington least. Even in Puritanical New England, Adams picked up the disruptive new attitudes about freedom of religion and expression emanating from this remarkable new generation of Scottish intellectuals. Here they developed their ideas of liberty, of freedom, and of the proper ("natural") relationship of government to man.

## Where Classical Republicanism Went Wrong

FINALLY, AND CRUCIALLY, IT IS ESSENTIAL TO NOTE THAT THEIR CLASsical knowledge ultimately steered the founders wrong on three crucial issues:

- First, on whether the new nation could subsist on "public virtue," relying on the self-restraint of those in power to act for the common good and not their personal interest, a proposition that would be tested almost instantly during the War for Independence.
- Second, on party politics, which the classical writers taught them to regard as unnatural and abhorrent. Their

misunderstanding of partisanship, or "faction," as they tended to call it, nearly wrecked the new republic in the 1790s.

⊙  Third, and most troubling, was their acceptance of human bondage, which would prove disastrous to the nation they designed. Often seeing it a natural part of the social order, they wrote it into the fundamental law of the nation, and so sustained a system that was deeply inhumane and rested on a foundation of physical and sexual abuse, including torture.

On this last, it is vital to remember that, despite the Southern images of moonlight and magnolias, of gracious living and mint juleps on the porch, Washington, Jefferson, and Madison all came from what the historian Annette Gordon-Reed calls "a society built on and sustained by violence, actual and threatened." For example, one of the penalties an owner legally could impose on an enslaved person who ran away and then was captured was cutting off that person's toes. The Virginia planter Robert Carter reported that "I have cured many a Negro of running away by this means." Some punishments were explicitly designed to intensify pain, with those who were flogged sometimes then "pickled" with brine, to inject salt into their wounds. Six years before James Madison was born, his great-uncle burned a woman at the stake for attempting to poison her owner. Madison's own grandfather, Ambrose Madison, was supposedly murdered in 1732 with poison by three enslaved people. One of them, Pompey, from a neighboring estate, was executed. Some of George Washington's "famous false teeth," notes the historian Henry Wiencek, came from enslaved humans, and had been pulled from their living jaws. At Jefferson's Monticello, Wiencek adds, "A small boy being horsewhipped by a visitor was just part of the background of the bustling plantation scene." When Jefferson was president, he received a report from his son-in-law that the output in the plantation's lucrative nail-making shop had improved after "the small ones" working there, boys aged ten to twelve, had been whipped.

Americans, and especially Southerners, were fond of noting that both the Greeks and Romans embraced systems of slavery.

But in leaning on classical justifications, they neglected the fact that their system of slavery tended to be harsher than ancient forms. A particularly malign aspect of this was the racial justification for American slavery. The Greeks and Romans held that being enslaved was a matter of misfortune. The people they owned had a variety of colors and nationalities. "Roman slavery was a nonracist and fluid system where the places from which slaves came varied considerably from one period to another," concludes one historian. Roman slavery could be very cruel, but generally, states legal historian David Bederman, it was "not as harsh and exploitative as its modern analogues." Indeed, under Roman law, slaves had the right to petition the emperor for help against abusive owners, while freed slaves could become citizens and their offspring could hold public office.

In the New World, slavery became more pernicious, with those enslaved defined as less than human. The U.S. Supreme Court ruled in 1857, in the Dred Scott decision, that black people, whether enslaved or free, were social outcasts who were not citizens and in fact could *never* become so. Chief Justice Roger Taney wrote that they were "beings of an inferior order" who "had no rights which the white man was bound to respect." Because the founders failed to find a way to address the entire issue of race-based chattel slavery, less than a century later the nation they built would fracture into civil war and undergo a long and halting reconstruction that continues even today.

◆━━━◆

## Chapter 2

# Washington Studies
# How to Rise in Colonial
# Society

B ECAUSE CLASSICISM WAS THE CULTURAL CONTEXT OF UPPER-CRUST colonial America, acting in a Roman manner was the clearest way to rise in that part of society. The best example of this is George Washington, which is surprising, because he was the least learned of the first four American presidents. But because he was not bookish and instead learned by observation and experience, he was perhaps more sensitive to the markers of status in his society. Classically shaped behavior was the road to respectability.

Washington was not a learned man, and he knew it. "I am conscious of a defective education," he once confessed to an aide-de-camp, David Humphreys, himself a 1771 graduate of Yale. He did not have a classical education, nor even a good education of any kind. He spoke only English, and was not widely read even in that language, mainly favoring books about farming, military affairs, and political pamphlets. He never traveled to Europe.

Washington's peers were conscious of this deficit. One evening in Philadelphia in 1791, John Adams (Harvard, 1755) debated with Timothy Pickering (Harvard, 1763) about whether their president was illiterate, or close to it. Pickering, who that year became postmaster general, contended that Washington "was So ignorant, that he had never read any Thing, not even on military Affairs: he could not write A Sentence of Grammar, nor Spell his Words." And so on.

Adams, then Washington's vice president, objected. "I had been in Congress with Washington in 1774 and in May and part of June 1775 and had heard and read all his Letters to Congress in 1775. 1776. 1777, and had formed a very different Opinion of his litterary Talent. His Letters were well written and well Spelled."

You are mistaken, Pickering countered: "He did not write them, he only copied them."

Well then, Adams asked, who did write them? Pickering said, "His Secretaries and Aids." (Pickering, who had held two major administrative posts in the Army during the War for Independence, later would serve as secretary of state under Washington and then Adams himself.)

Adams' own conclusion was that "Washington was not a Schollar is certain. That he was too illiterate, unlearned, unread, for his Station and reputation is equally past dispute." But he added insightfully that "He was indeed a thoughtful Man."

Thomas Jefferson also was long perplexed by Washington's ability to make his way in the world without having the sort of education then considered essential for a public life. He recognized that there was something unusual in the man. "His mind was great and powerful, without being of the very first order; . . . and as far as he saw, no judgment was ever sounder. It was slow in operation, being little aided by invention or imagination, but sure in conclusion."

Jefferson was many things, but he was never a soldier, so he probably did not grasp that in military life, a mind "slow in operation" tends to be not a fault but a strength. Indeed, it was a skill Washington had acquired rather painfully in his two wars. In leading combat operations, slow and steady thinking, followed with energetic execution, often is more effective than a series of hasty moves that tend to exhaust a force and expose it to attack. One of the more thoughtful commentators on Washington, Adrienne Harrison, herself a former Army officer, observes that early in his military career, Washington had a "propensity for rashness." He had to learn the hard way to operate more deliberately.

As to his education, Jefferson continued, Washington was no

great shakes. Jefferson was at once laudatory and condescending in sketching his predecessor's intellectual qualities:

> *Altho' in the circle of his friends, where he might be unreserved with safety, he took a free share in conversation, his colloquial talents were not above mediocrity, possessing neither copiousness of ideas, nor fluency of words. In public when called on for a sudden opinion, he was unready, short, and embarrassed. Yet he wrote readily, rather diffusely, in an easy & correct style. This he had acquired by conversation with the world for his education was merely reading, writing, and common arithmetic, to which he added surveying at a later day. His time was employed in action chiefly, reading little, and that only in Agriculture and English history.*

Yet, despite all his ambivalence, Jefferson ultimately found Washington had figured out how to become an exemplar of the classical standard. "Perhaps the strongest feature in his character was prudence, never acting until every circumstance, every consideration was maturely weighed; refraining if he saw a doubt, but, when once decided, going through with his purpose whatever obstacles opposed. His integrity was most pure, his justice the most inflexible I have ever known." *Prudent, considerate, careful, determined, honest,* and *inflexible*: Jefferson did not quite say so, but he was describing Washington as the American Cato, the eighteenth century's embodiment of virtue, the very ideal of what a public man should be. Even people who might not know anything about Cato would recognize these as the traits expected of great public men.

Indeed, Washington came closer to the Roman example than his peers precisely because he was a man of deeds, not of words. Adams, Jefferson, and Madison were articulate men of ideas—they wrote essays and letters, gave speeches, made arguments. Reading the comments of his two successors as president, one can only have a bit of sympathy for Washington. They were world-class talkers. He emphatically was not.

At times he must have felt his patience tried by them and by

Hamilton and his wordy peers. A proud, ambitious, and thin-skinned man, Washington also must have sensed their occasional condescensions. To be fair, these voluble civilians appear quite respectful in their treatment of Washington when compared to some of the generals around him during the war, such as Thomas Conway, Charles Lee, and Horatio Gates, who schemed to replace him as senior commander, and Benedict Arnold, who proved a traitor to Washington and to the American cause.

## The Real George Washington

ALMOST EVERY BIOGRAPHER OF WASHINGTON SETS OUT DETERMINED to show us the real man, to bring that stiff image to life. In the nineteenth century, Paul Leicester Ford wrote at the outset of *The True George Washington* that "if the present work succeeds in humanizing Washington, and making him a man rather than a historical figure, its purpose will have been fulfilled." In the twentieth, another biographer subtitled his work "George Washington as a Human Being," which begs the question of what sort of creature other authors had studied. James Thomas Flexner, returning from a four-volume expedition into Washington's life, reported that he discovered "a fallible human being made of flesh and blood and spirit—not a statue of marble and wood." In our own century, Ron Chernow, in a fine study of Washington, states that "the goal of the present biography is to create a fresh portrait of Washington that will make him real, credible, and charismatic in the same way that he was perceived by his contemporaries."

But his chroniclers, in pursuing this humanizing mission, in fact seek to undo Washington's work of a lifetime, which was to discipline his turbulent emotions, build an image of lofty distance, and most of all, establish a reputation for valiant leadership, unselfish virtue, and unyielding honor—that is, someone with the makings of a great man. Washington would spend decades in erecting and polishing that statue of himself. Nathaniel Hawthorne was not just being humorous when he mused that Washington was "born with his clothes on, and his hair powdered, and made a stately bow on his first appearance in the world." Rather, the novelist was putting his finger on the essence of the man.

One anecdote from the Constitutional Convention gives a sense of the effort Washington put into developing and preserving this potent public persona. Alexander Hamilton remarked to Gouverneur Morris (Columbia, 1768) on the general's social reserve, noting that even with close friends, he "allowed no one to be familiar with him." Morris disputed that. Hamilton challenged Morris, the next time he saw Washington, to slap him on the back in hearty greeting. Try that, Hamilton said, and I will reward you with a good, wine-filled dinner for a dozen friends. So it was that Morris, the next time he encountered Washington, shook the man's hand while grasping his shoulder. According to an account attributed to Hamilton, Washington "withdrew his hand, stepped suddenly back, fixed his eye on Morris for several minutes with an angry frown, until the latter retreated abashed, and sought refuge in the crowd. The company looked on in silence." Morris stated ruefully at the subsequent meal paid for by Hamilton that "nothing could induce me to repeat it."

## Washington's Pursuit of Virtue

WASHINGTON DID NOT RECEIVE A FORMAL EDUCATION BECAUSE HIS FAther died when he was just eleven years old and then, when he was twenty, he lost his surrogate father, his older half brother Lawrence. In his lack of schooling, he grew up like most Americans of his time. In the America of 1775, there were only nine colleges, and out of a population of 2.5 million, there were just three thousand college graduates.

In colonial America, the typical young white boy got at best a year or two of schooling from four to six hours a day, which was enough to learn to read a bit and to add and subtract. After that brush with learning he was set to farming with his family or to an apprenticeship. Most instruction consisted of oral repetition, mainly because paper was expensive. Girls, blacks, and First Peoples* generally received even less education. There was a major regional difference here. In New England, the Puritans were trying to make a new society, their "city upon a hill," and so established publicly supported "town schools," in part to enable people to read the Bible. But Virginians, and to a lesser extent other Southerners, were trying as much as possible to replicate existing English society, and so were less interested in educating the vast majority of children.

Washington never attended college, nor did he pick up Latin or French on his own, as the autodidact Benjamin Franklin did. As a youth, Washington read Caesar's *Commentaries* in translation, which indicates some curiosity about military affairs, but there is no record that he followed up on this by reading other Roman histories. This interest in Caesar was a bit unusual, because in the republican atmosphere of the eighteenth century, the Roman dictator was "conspicuous by his absence from most secondary curricula." Yet Washington remained an admirer. When he was sprucing up his house after marrying Martha Custis, among the decorations he ordered from London was a small bust of Caesar. However, his English buying agent was unable to find a Caesar of the size he wanted, and offered instead a list of the busts readily available: "Homer, Virgil, Horace, Cicero, Plato, Aristotle, Seneca, Galens, Vestall Virgin Faustina Chaucer, Spencer, Johnson, Shakespear, Beaumont Fletcher, Milton, Prior, Pope, Congreve, Swift, Addison, Dryden, Locke, Newton." Washington apparently let the idea drop.

It is no surprise that *Cato* was his favorite play. The drama is as stiff as Washington strove to be, almost unreadable to us today. But, writes one specialist in the history of American theater, eighteenth-century audiences expected lengthy declamations and

---

* Please see this book's introductory note on this usage.

were not put off by predictable plots. They came primed to enjoy the play's "crisp and quotable epigrams and the beautiful expression of worthy sentiments." We do not know how old Washington was when he first saw the play, which was performed in Charleston, South Carolina, in 1735; a year later at the College of William & Mary; and in 1749 in Philadelphia.

During the eighteenth century, Cato was the very embodiment of virtue. "Think Cato sees thee," was one of Franklin's sayings in his "almanacks." It was natural that the Roman would become Washington's ideal. He would know about the orator from the play, and also perhaps from listening to conversations about the portrayal of the man in *Plutarch's Lives*, which was enormously popular with eighteenth-century American elites. This is how Plutarch describes Cato:

> *It is said of Cato that even from his infancy, in his speech, his countenance, and all his childish pastimes, he discovered an inflexible temper, unmoved by any passion, and firm in everything. He was resolute in his purposes, much beyond the strength of his age, to go through with whatever he undertook. . . . It was difficult to excite him to laughter,—his countenance seldom relaxed even into a smile.*

Born to an aristocratic Roman family in 95 BC, Cato was considered remarkable even in his youth for his strict rejection of corruption and luxury. He possessed wealth, yet lived and dressed simply. Aside from that, he had a typical life for a successful Roman notable, first achieving military recognition by commanding a legion in Macedon, where he lived as his soldiers did, eschewing special food and lodging. He then began climbing the rungs of the Republican government. Plutarch states that "he undertook the service of the state as the proper business of an honest man." But in politics as in war, he stood out for his self-denying, hardworking approach. By learning accounting and studying the records of the treasury, he was able to detect and stop kickbacks, embezzlement, and a variety of other shady financial dealings by the office's senior functionaries.

Cato's first great political confrontation came in 63 BC, when Cicero, who had been elected consul the previous year, exposed the conspiracy of Catiline, a populist patrician who had stood for consul three times, only to be rejected each time. After the third such rebuff, Catiline and his followers apparently planned a violent takeover of the city. Cicero responded by calling for their execution. He was opposed in this by Julius Caesar, who was just beginning his own rise to political prominence. "Caesar at this time had not done much in the Roman world except fall greatly into debt," Anthony Trollope, a historian as well as a novelist, notes tartly. Caesar argued that the conspirators instead should simply be exiled. Cato denounced Caesar as pleading for false mercy that endangered the state. For the next two decades, the men would be relentless enemies as Cato struggled to preserve the Republic against Caesar's dictatorial ambitions. A few years later, Caesar proposed a law that would reward his veterans with government-owned land but in doing so would diminish the state's tax base. Cato spoke vigorously against this, provoking Caesar to have him dragged away. Cato continued to speak the entire time.

In January of 49 BC, Caesar led his troops into Italy, effectively declaring war on the Senate and provoking a civil war. Cato fled across the Adriatic to join Pompey, Caesar's former ally but now his enemy. When Caesar defeated Pompey, Cato led a remnant force across the Mediterranean to Africa. In April of 46 BC, facing capture, Cato committed suicide in Utica, a Roman town in what is now Tunisia, preferring death to submitting to Caesar. Julius Caesar himself was of course assassinated just two years later.

To become an American Cato, Washington would need to become a man of recognized great virtue. Despite his lack of education, he understood that for someone of his time and place, attainment of public virtue was the highest goal one could have in life. He also may have sensed that eighteenth-century "virtue" was essentially male—the root of the word is *vir*, the Latin word for man. To be virtuous was to be a public man with a reputation for selflessness. Washington likely never read the definition by Montesquieu, the eighteenth-century French political philosopher, of "virtue" as "the love of the laws and of our country," but many of his peers did.

Young George Washington wove together these cultural strands when he wrote a letter in 1756, at the age of twenty-four, stating that in his life he would pursue "Honor and Reputation." In other words, he would judge his own actions by how they might affect those two things, and he would measure his peers the same way. Eventually he would come to personify them for his fellow Americans.

Today, that approach to life may seem profoundly conservative. But in the eighteenth century, it carried a whiff of egalitarianism. Aristocrats had little need to show public virtue—they held power and position by birth, and their rank would be unaffected by public esteem. Washington, the fatherless adolescent and third son for the purposes of inheritance, enjoyed no such advantage. "Justifying by virtue is a way of escaping hereditary control," observes Gordon Wood. Young George Washington had something to prove, and he saw how to do it.

## Washington's American Education

JOHN ADAMS HAD IT RIGHT. WASHINGTON WAS NOT A PHILOSOPHER, BUT he was a sturdy practical thinker. By that, Adams seems to have meant that Washington was capable of observing and learning. He read all his life, but mainly about surveying and agriculture. His library consisted of books on those subjects, plus some history, law, and religion. There was little philosophy, and even less fiction or poetry.

So how did Washington acquire the ability to think critically, as he would do during the American Revolution?

Any answer is necessarily speculative. It appears that his consciousness of the gaps in his education made him a studious observer. On top of that, his early military defeats provided compelling incentives to make him want to learn from his experiences. More than almost all his peers, he became able to study a situation, evaluate its facts, decide which ones were meaningful, develop a course of action in response to work toward a desired outcome, and verbalize the orders that needed to be issued.

Those are the basic steps in critical thinking, but the military commander's task is especially difficult because he or she must take one additional step, often the hardest one of all: ensuring that one's orders are implemented. It is one thing to know what to do, but quite another to get other people to do it. New presidents often make the mistake, for example, of paying too much attention to formulating policy and not enough to implementing it. Washington knew he needed help putting his thoughts into words. He would never become a strong writer, but he learned to compensate by finding helpers who possessed potent verbal skills, most notably Alexander Hamilton, who attended King's College (later Columbia) in New York City.

But all that was to come. The first question Washington faced as a youth was what to do with his life. He was of uncertain promise in the eyes of others. He hunted, danced, played cards and billiards, and tried to see how he might make his way in society. He did not appear to make much of an impression on anyone. Indeed, he appears almost interchangeable with the amiable but thick-tongued bachelors who people the background in Jane Austen's novels.

But Washington seemed to know he was destined for bigger things. He threw himself into life, quickly learning a trade as a surveyor and making a living at it while still a teenager. By November 1750, at the age of eighteen, he felt confident enough in his judgment and finances to make his first land purchase, a parcel of fine pastureland just west of the northern Shenandoah River. Within two years he owned a total of 2,315 acres in that verdant valley, which even now, some 270 years later, remains one of the most beautiful parts of the country. Even more significant, he was learning how to read the land, especially on the frontier, a skill that would serve him all his life, but most notably as a military commander.

His first appearance in public life came in the fall of 1753, when the royal governor of Virginia, Robert Dinwiddie, selected the twenty-one-year-old Washington for a difficult and perhaps dangerous mission: Carry a provocative diplomatic message from Virginia through the deep woods of the First Peoples country to the French officers moving into the headwaters of the Ohio Valley, around today's Pittsburgh, and tell them to withdraw. Then come back, again through the snow-covered wilds, with the French response, and deliver it to the governor in Williamsburg.

## A Frontier Tutor

FOR ADAMS, WE WILL LOOK AT HIS TIME AT HARVARD AND THEN AS A schoolteacher as formative. For Madison, that would be his Princeton years. And for Jefferson, the crucial years probably were his time spent learning the law and then his sojourn in Paris. But the parallel for Washington was far from American colleges or French salons. Like many colonial Americans, he was educated in the frontier of his time, a much harder course of study. His prep school was surveying the Shenandoah Valley. His finishing school would be the backwoods of western Pennsylvania. And his graduate education, a few years later, would be witnessing the British military disaster in the same area, under the arrogant General Edward Braddock.

His tutor in the deep woods was Christopher Gist, a tough pioneer in his late forties who a few years earlier had paddled well down the Ohio River. This is how Washington's most thorough biographer, Douglas Southall Freeman, describes Gist:

*No frontiersman understood the Indians better or had greater patience in dealing with them. Gist was a good shot, a fine hunter who seldom went hungry if there was any game in the woods, and he had a quick eye for good land. Few could excel him in making himself comfortable in the wilderness, as, for example, when he*

*drove a panther from its lair under an overhanging rock and slept*
*cheerfully there on a January night in 1752. . . . More than any other*
*man, Gist was to be George's teacher in the art of the frontiersman.*

Washington received his formal orders on October 31, 1753. The
trip northwestward in the mild November weather went well. By
mid-December he reached the French fort at Venango, in today's
far northwestern Pennsylvania. They received him cordially. The
wine flowed copiously over dinner and his French hosts began to
speak freely, he reported. The French at Venango may have been
in their cups, but there was *veritas* in their *vino*:

> *The Wine, as they dos'd themselves pretty plentifully with it, soon*
> *banish'd the restraint which at first appear'd in their Conversation,*
> *& gave license to their Tongues to reveal their Sentiments more*
> *freely. They told me it was their absolute Design to take Posses-*
> *sion of the Ohio, & by G——they wou'd do it, for tho' they were*
> *sensible, that the English cou'd raise two Men for their one; yet*
> *they knew their Motions were too slow & dilatory to prevent any*
> *Undertaking of theirs.*

There is a lot going on in that intelligence report. It includes
what the enemy intended to do and why they thought they could
achieve it, as well as their view that the British were dawdlers and
their assessment of the relative strength of each side.

Washington's next stop was at Fort Le Boeuf, a new outpost
just sixteen miles south of the shore of Lake Erie. It was a strategic location, one of the most important forts on the continent,
anchoring the French line of communication in North America,
which ran in a great arc from the St. Lawrence River through the
Great Lakes to the Ohio and Mississippi Rivers, and so to the Gulf
of Mexico. While Washington talked there to the regional French
commander, Captain Jacques Legardeur de Saint-Pierre, his com-
panions outside scouted the French encampment, noted their
heavy weapons—some nine cannons—and counted some 220 canoes already built and ready, and others being prepared. This last

was a clear sign that the French were preparing to launch a riverine armada to enforce their claim to the upper Ohio Valley—that is, today's western Pennsylvania and a bit of western Maryland. Legardeur gave him a letter of response to pass to the governor of Virginia.

Washington perceived that it was essential to get word back to Williamsburg as quickly as possible that the French were preparing for war, which, given their strong relationships with First Peoples tribes, would wreak havoc on the western line of British settlements along the eastern slope of the Appalachians. He set out with haste, but December brought two weeks of rain and snow and then a severe cold snap. Washington's homeward-bound party sometimes had to carry their canoes when the creeks were frozen over. Next, their mounts began to falter. "The Horses grew less able to travel every Day. The Cold increas'd very fast, & the Roads were geting much worse by a deep Snow continually Freezing," he wrote.

As the horses began to fail, Washington decided that he should proceed through the snowy woods on foot. Few physical activities are as taxing as breaking a trail through deep, crusted snow, which is probably what he and Gist faced. Each step requires an effort, and the footing is constantly uncertain, as one's boots break through the crusty top and sink onto unseen rocks and snag on branches under the snow. In normal walking, as one foot is planted, the other swings forward. But in deep snow, a planted boot cannot swing forward in turn through the snow, but instead must be lifted up from the hole it has just made and then moved forward over the snow and placed down again, requiring twice the effort for half the progress, with each step. And so on, endlessly.

Gist, who was far more experienced in the wilderness, objected to Washington's plan for the two of them to move on foot, but Washington insisted—and despite his youth, he was the commander of their tiny expedition. His enormous force of will, perhaps his most significant quality as an adult, was beginning to emerge. As Plutarch wrote of Cato, "He was resolute in his purposes, much beyond the strength of his age, to go through with whatever he undertook."

As they hiked through the snow they met a First Peoples tribesman who claimed to know of a shortcut he could show them. But as the tribesman led them suspiciously to the northeast, Gist grew wary. A few miles later, the man, leading the way, turned and fired on them with his musket. While he was reloading, they grabbed and bound him. Gist wanted to kill him. Washington disagreed and set him loose, perhaps not wanting to stir up the man's comrades. They made a campfire, warmed themselves, and then after sunset moved off, walking all night.

When they finally reached the Allegheny River, they found it not completely frozen over. They used their sole hatchet to cut wood to build a raft—slow, draining work. At sundown they set off. In the middle of the stream, an ice jam built up against the upriver side of the raft, tumbling Washington into the freezing water. They spent a miserable night on an island in midstream, Washington partly encased in ice and Gist suffering frostbite. "The Cold was so extream severe, that Mr. Gist got all his Fingers, & some of his Toes Froze," Washington noted in his report to the governor.

The arctic conditions did them one favor: In the morning, the remainder of the river was frozen from their island to the far shore. They walked across that ice and then the remaining ten miles to the welcome food and fire of a trading post. Washington purchased a horse and rode hard to Williamsburg, where on January 16, 1754, he presented the French response. "Precisely one month had passed from the day George had left Fort Le Boeuf— season considered, a splendid achievement," in the judgment of his biographer Freeman.

The letter to the governor from the French, signed by Captain Legardeur, was both polite and clear. The key sentence came in the fourth paragraph: "As for the summons you send me to retire, I do not think myself obliged to obey it."

Washington learned a lot from this journey, but not all of it was correct. From this first encounter, he took away a mistaken impression of the French. "The shabby and ragged appearance the French common Soldiers make affords great matter for ridicule amongst the Indians and I really believe is the chief motive why they hate and despise them as they do," he informed the governor. In fact, the French tended to be superior fighters, seasoned in the ways of North American warfare. And contrary to what Washington believed, the First Peoples were inclined to support the French more than the British, because they had observed that the French were interested solely in trade, but that when the British built a fort, English settlers followed and cleared woods for farming, and then the land grew crowded and game became scarcer.

## Fort Necessity and British Disrespect

THE BRITISH COUNTER-RESPONSE WOULD BE IN THE FORM OF A MILI-tary expedition. Less than two weeks after making his report, Washington, still just aged twenty-one, applied to be the lieutenant colonel of the Virginia Regiment—that is, the unit's deputy commander. Despite his youth, he was a natural choice, having demonstrated his stamina and dedication in his recent journey, during which he had become familiar with the lands in dispute.

But almost from the beginning, he would be torn between the honor of being chosen and the insult of Virginia troops being treated (and paid) worse than militiamen sent from other colonies. Aggravating the situation, the captain who commanded one of those state militia detachments held a British commission and so would decline to come under Washington's command, on the grounds that a British officer could not take orders from a colonial officer, even if the colonial held a higher rank.

Soon another promotion came Washington's way, when the chosen commander fell from his horse and died two days later, leaving Washington in charge at the front. He was now twenty-two, and he had his hands full. At almost the same time, the disgruntlement of his subordinate officers over their unequal treatment by the British government began to boil over. They were particularly upset that they were ordered to build a road into the Ohio country that other soldiers would use later, as reinforcements arrived from other colonies, but that they were being paid less than those men. They handed him a written protest. He essentially agreed with their views, yet as the commander in the field could hardly join their cause.

He came close. "I am heartily concerned, that the officers have such real cause to complain," he wrote to Governor Dinwiddie. "I really do not see why the lives of his Majesty's subjects in Virginia should be of less value, than of those in other parts of his American dominions; especially when it is well known, that we must undergo double their hardship. I could enumerate a thousand difficulties that we have met with, and must expect to meet with, more than other officers who have almost double our pay."

Even more galling was the disrespect inherent in this unequal treatment. If it were not for the imminent danger presented by the French, Washington warned, the officers might well quit. "Nothing prevents their throwing down their commissions . . . but the approaching danger, which has too far engaged their honor to recede till other officers are sent in their room, or an alteration made regarding their pay," he told the governor.

That danger was genuine, and moving closer. Early on the morning of May 27, Gist rode into Washington's camp in Great Meadows, a grassy spot atop the last big ridge on the west slope of the Alleghenies. He carried crucial information. The previous day about fifty Frenchmen had walked into Gist's frontier settlement in a surly mood. Unobserved by them, Gist rode off to warn Washington. En route, he observed the tracks of a smaller French party that was hovering nearby, just five miles northwest of Great Meadows.

Iroquois scouts working for Washington located, about half a mile from a major trail, the hiding place of that French advance patrol, in a sheltered pocket of the forest tucked into the base of a cliff on one side and shielded by a field of boulders, some as high as fifteen feet. Washington and the tribal chief the British called

Half King led an ambush party there, through groves of maple, beech, and oak trees, their leaves still bearing the bright green of late spring. The Americans fired down from the top of the cliff, on the west, and from the upper slope of the glen, to the south. Tribal warriors blocked the natural escape route downhill in the glen, northward. The skirmish was short and shocking. Soon ten Frenchmen lay dead or dying. One fled, while the surviving twenty-one surrendered. Among the dead was Joseph Coulon de Jumonville, the leader of the French party. "The Indians scalped the Dead," Washington noted in his diary. Washington's party suffered just one dead and two or three wounded.

The fight lasted just fifteen minutes, yet marked the start of a conflict that would last almost a decade and flare around the world—the French and Indian War. The French would claim that Jumonville was on a diplomatic mission to tell the British to withdraw, but this seems doubtful given the large and armed nature of their party, and their aggressive behavior at Gist's settlement.

Washington seems to have been almost elated afterward. "I heard Bulletts whistle and believe me there was something charming in the sound," he wrote to his half brother John Augustine Washington. When his letter was published later that year in both Virginia and London, that line raised some eyebrows. To some readers, Washington was engaging in youthful bravado. "He would not say so, if he had been used to hear many," King George II reportedly remarked. But such sneers probably did the young man an injustice. He had just led men into combat and emerged the victor, a heady combination. He also may have been pleased to find that he enjoyed doing so.

Washington pulled back a few miles from the ambush site to Great Meadows, one of the only places in the dense forests where there was grass available for horses and cattle, as well as room for the reinforcements he knew would soon arrive. He oversaw the building of a small palisaded fort and hunkered down for the inevitable French counterattack. He and his men also waited for food and other supplies, which were slow to arrive.

The French assault came a few weeks later, and was led by Louis

Coulon de Villiers—significantly, the elder half brother of the slain Jumonville. Coulon, unlike the newly blooded Washington, was a seasoned veteran of fighting in French North America, having ranged across a huge area, from what is now Michigan and Wisconsin to Louisiana and northern New York.

Bracing for the French reaction, the British and colonial troops under Washington were hungry, demoralized, and outnumbered. Their Iroquois allies, no fools, saw the probable outcome and began slipping away, forcing Washington to rely solely on white scouts, far less adept in reading the woods. When the battle began at about eleven in the morning on July 3, 1754, Washington had fewer than three hundred soldiers rated capable of fighting.

The fight was as one-sided as the May ambush had been, but this time in favor of the French. Most of it took place in a drenching rain, making firing weapons increasingly difficult. By the dismal twilight, Washington's force had suffered about a hundred dead or wounded. French losses were just three dead and seventeen wounded. The French offered to parley. Washington had never learned French and had only one unwounded officer who could speak the language. That was Jacob van Braam, a Dutchman who claimed to have been an officer in Europe and whose English was faulty. Amid the mud and blood, the wounded and the dead, in the impending darkness, van Braam translated for Washington a proffered document of surrender. It isn't clear whether Washington knew that in signing his name to the damp paper, he was confessing to what the document termed the "assassination" of Jumonville.

Coulon that night became the only officer to whom Washington would surrender in his entire life. He allowed the Virginians to leave in the morning with their light arms and also some gunpowder to defend themselves on the march through the forested ridges back to British-held territory.

Washington's woes were just beginning, though. The following spring, the British mounted an expedition to go west of the Appalachians and eject the French. Washington was desperate to be part of it, but not if he had to take orders from lower-ranking officers who held British commissions. "This was too degrading for G. W. to submit to," he later explained to his first biographer. Plainly he felt his honor to be at stake.

## Braddock's Defeat

NEXT CAME THE SERIES OF EVENTS THAT, WHILE DISASTROUS, MAY have molded Washington for the future. Certainly without them he would have been less prepared to weather the troubles of the War for Independence.

He had at this time the negative but instructive example of General Edward Braddock, commander of the British force. Braddock took on Washington as one of his personal aides without rank or pay—but with something more desirable to Washington, public honor. The young Virginian found the old general "generous & disinterested—but plain and blunt in his manner even to rudeness." Reading that last phrase, one might wonder if at some point the general had wearied of Washington's griping about his lack of a British commission and told the young man to drop it.

Yet others found Braddock dangerously arrogant. Benjamin Franklin wrote in his *Autobiography* years later that when he met with Braddock about getting the government of Pennsylvania to send wagons and supplies, "he had too much self-confidence, too high an Opinion of the Validity of Regular Troops, and too mean a One of both Americans and Indians." George Croghan, a veteran frontier trader working as a guide for the expedition, appears to have confided in Franklin that Braddock "slighted & neglected" the tribal scouts, "and they gradually left him." When Franklin expressed some doubts to Braddock himself, he added, the general responded dismissively that "these Savages may indeed be a formidable Enemy to your raw America Militia; but, upon the King's regular & disciplin'd Troops, Sir, it is impossible they should make any Impression."

Braddock was not shy about denigrating his Americans. He

reported to London that "the greatest part [were] Virginians, very indifferent Men, this country affording no better."

And so at the end of May 1755, full of unwarranted self-confidence, the self-assured British marched westward toward the Ohio headwaters. The force consisted of an advance guard, a party just behind them cutting trees and moving rocks, a main body with the baggage and big guns, and finally a rear guard. Moving on the mile-long column's sides, about one hundred yards out, were flankers to screen any attack. It was slow, hard movement, up dozens of high ridges and then down them to cross rivers and streams.

Not far beyond those flankers sometimes lurked hostile First Peoples warriors. They were there less to impede the British force than to gather intelligence on its composition and procedures. They did this mainly by conducting probing attacks. On June 25, three soldiers, probably sent out to round up grazing horses, were shot and scalped, and a wagoneer was also killed.

After a few weeks the tribal scouts had developed a good understanding of the British mode of warfare. At Fort Duquesne, as the French called their outpost at what is now Pittsburgh, a Delaware tribesman boasted to an English prisoner about how the warriors were scouting the British and would eventually attack them. "Shoot um down all one pigeon," he declared confidently. The Delaware may have been not just boasting, but describing with some precision an ambush plan based on how passenger pigeons typically were hunted back when great clouds of them still flew through the acorn-laden forests around the Great Lakes. First, make a loud noise to scare the roosting flock into the air, and then, in the moment while they are still clustered, have a group of shooters quickly fire multiple volleys, downing many birds before they have time to scatter.

As the British expedition moved westward, Washington fell violently ill and was left behind in the Maryland hills to recover. When he was slightly better but still weak, he rode forward, sitting on pillows tied to his saddle, to catch up with Braddock. Washington was bothered mentally as well as physically, terribly anxious that he might miss any action in the biggest European military operation on North American soil to date. He pushed himself hard and rejoined the British force.

Around midday on July 9, 1755, the two elite grenadier companies at the head of Braddock's mile-long column forded the winding Monongahela River twice, the water reaching to their knees. At both crossings there were indications that tribal warriors were in the area—fresh footprints in the mud, sightings in the forest. The grenadiers began ascending a path that slanted up across the face of a hill. They were heading for a trail that soon would lead them to Fort Duquesne, just a few miles away. Their caps displayed the phrase *"Nec Aspera Terrent"*—that is, "not frightened by difficulties." They arrived at a point where their trail crossed a ravine.

"The Indians are upon us," shouted one of the soldiers at the front. The enemy force consisted of roughly seven hundred tribal warriors—mainly Hurons, Shawnees, Miamis, and Senecas—and about two hundred French and Canadians. Some even were Osage, who had traveled from west of the Mississippi specifically to participate in the battle, a sign of good long-term planning and wide-ranging diplomacy on the part of the French. It was, writes military historian David Preston, author of the most authoritative account of the battle, the largest First Peoples force ever assembled on behalf of the French to that point.

The tribal warriors rippled out along both British flanks, forming a semicircle, more on the uphill side than on the downhill. "As soon as the Enemys Indians perceiv'd our Grenadiers, they divided themselves & Run along our right & Left flanks," wrote Captain Harry Gordon, an engineering officer.

British flankers, who had been protecting the column, fled before them, running back toward the main body. In the noise, confusion, shouting, and smoke, the flankers' own comrades began to fire on them. The warriors, knowing from their time tracking Braddock's force in the forest that most of the cannons were in the center of the column, focused their fire there, understanding it was key to silence the cannons quickly. They were demonstrating how dangerous it had been for Braddock to underestimate their ability to plan and wage war.

The British force collapsed on itself, the advance guard falling back even as the rear kept moving up. It degenerated into a huge knot of terrified men. "Nothing afterwards was to Be Seen Amongst the Men But Confusion & Panick," recalled Captain Gordon. "They form'd Altogether, the Advanced & Main Body in Most places from 12 to 20 Deep." Packed so tightly, few soldiers could actually fire at the foe, greatly reducing their combat effectiveness.

This was the pivotal moment in the battle. The tribesmen were operating with a speed and precision that outstripped the British ability to react. As Preston puts it, "Experienced [tribal] war captains led their men along the flanks of Braddock's column with great efficacy, seeking opportune places to strike as well as cover that offered security to their men. Native squads functioned like modern fire teams as they extended the killing zone." They particularly targeted the officers, conspicuous on horseback, effectively destroying the British ability to command and control their force.

Washington, riding about the battlefield to try to bring some order to the chaotic scene, had several shots pass through his clothes but was not wounded. He thought that many of the soldiers were firing indiscriminately, without knowing whether they were hitting friend or foe. "Our own cowardly . . . regulars . . . gatherd themselves into a body contrary to orders 10 or 12 deep, woud then level, Fire, & shoot down the Men before them." The British troops "broke and run as Sheep before Hounds," he wrote with disdain nine days later. These were serious allegations, but if the British were going to degrade his honor, he would do the same when they faltered in their duty.

The British force lost all combat cohesion. When the tribal fighters had silenced the British cannons, "the whole Body gave way," Gordon, the engineering officer wrote. General Braddock took a round through a shoulder and lung but remained in command. He eventually gave the order to fall back and then to retreat. Riding across the Monongahela, Gordon turned to see warriors on the bank behind him "tomohocking some of our Women & wounded people." Already shot in the right arm, he took a second bullet through the right shoulder.

In all, of a total British force of about 1,200, about two-thirds were killed or wounded, an extraordinary toll. The numbers differ in various histories because some reports included the casualties suffered by wagoneers and other civilians. The British officers were especially hard hit, with about sixty of eight-five killed or wounded, leaving the force almost decapitated. A small number of the British were taken prisoners. Their First Peoples captors marched them back to Fort Duquesne and burned some of them at the stake.

Any large-scale military movement can be difficult. Retreating after a defeat is always hard, and often is the point when a force suffers some of its heaviest personnel losses through attacks from pursuers or simple desertion. But perhaps the most challenging of all retreats is withdrawing at night through hostile, wooded, mountainous territory after a severe setback. The harrowing experience can easily shatter an army. Washington saw it all that night as he rode with two escorts the sixty miles through the wilderness to deliver an order from Braddock to a rear camp to bring up food and medical articles. As he moved through the gloom, his horse occasionally would halt and then gingerly step over the wounded and dead lying in the mud, some of them crying out for help. Decades later, Washington would recall that painful night with revulsion:

*The shocking Scenes which presented themselves in this Nights March are not to be described—The dead—the dying—the groans—lamentation—and crys along the Road of the wounded for help . . . were enough to pierce a heart of adamant. the gloom & horror of which was not a little encreased by the impervious darkness occasioned by the close shade of thick wood.*

Braddock, having been carried dozens of miles in a makeshift litter, perished on July 13. Washington, having rejoined the remains of the column, presided over interring the general, wrapped in a blanket, in an unmarked grave in the road the army had built, the better to hide the body from any pursuing warriors seeking his scalp.

The British had abandoned so much equipment on the battle-field, the French and tribesmen were kept busy going through it. Their force had suffered about twenty-five dead and an equal num-ber wounded. Among the gear they carried off were at least six cannons, four howitzers, and four mortars. Some of those pieces would resurface for years as the war continued, employed with great effect by the French in subsequent sieges of British forts.

The experience of his second battlefield defeat in two years did not bolster Washington's health. "I am still in a weak and Feeble condn which induces me to halt here 2 or 3 Days in hopes of re-covg a little Strength, to enable me to proceed homewards," he wrote to his mother from a stop on the road back east.

## Washington Mulls His Situation

IN THE DAYS AND WEEKS AFTERWARD, RECUPERATING AT HIS HOME AT Mount Vernon, Virginia, which he would inherit after the deaths of his brother Lawrence and Lawrence's widow and son, Wash-ington began to wonder if it was all worth it. He marveled at the magnitude of the defeat: "When this story comes to be Related in future Annals, it will meet with unbelief and indignation; for had I not been witness to the act on that fatal Day, I should scarce have given credit to it even now." He again took the trouble to pin blame on the British regulars for a shameful performance.

The same day, he glumly summarized his military career in a melancholy letter to his half brother Augustine. First, "I was em-ploy'd to go a journey in the Winter (when I believe few or none woud have undertaken it) and what did I get by it? my expences borne!" Next, "after putting myself to a considerable expence in equipping and providing Necessarys for the Campaigne—I went out, was soundly beaten, lost them all." That wasn't all, he added, "I then went out a Volunteer with Genl Braddock and lost all my Horses." In truth, he had little to show for it.

What he wanted in life, he told the governor plainly, was "Honor and Reputation in the Service"—the noblest of goals from a classical perspective, which he had absorbed as an aspiring member of Virginia's ruling class. And he still deeply resented being treated by the British as a second-class officer. "We want nothing but Commissions from His Majesty to make us as regular a Corps as any upon the Continent."

In command of an outpost on the receding frontier, he fretted over the disorder and indiscipline of the surviving troops. "I see the growing Insolence of the Soldiers, the Indolence, and Inactivity of the Officers," he warned the governor. When panicked reports arrived of a tribal raid a few miles away, leaving "horrid Murders" in its wake, he marched out with a party of forty-one men, only to find that the disturbance was actually caused by "3 drunken Soldiers of the Light Horse carousing, firing their Pistols, and uttering the most unheard off Imprecation's." This was another unhappy lesson in holding an army together.

Desertions became a major problem. He ordered the building of a huge gallows, towering nearly forty feet, as a warning to his men. "I am determined, if I can be justified in the proceeding, to hang two or three on it, as an example to others," he wrote. Two weeks later, he did just that, ordering the executions of two deserters—William Smith, a twenty-year-old saddler, and Ignatius Edwards, twenty-five, a carpenter described as "a great Dancer & Fidler." He pardoned twelve others who were convicted with them, with some of those reprieved being flogged instead. "They were proper objects to suffer: Edwards had deserted twice before, and Smith was accounted one of the greatest villains upon the continent," Washington reported to the governor.

The war continued. In the summer of 1758, the British severed the French line of communication across Lake Ontario, effectively isolating the French contingent in the Ohio headwaters area and forcing them to retreat. Washington, in the British force once again, arrived to see the smoldering ruins of the abandoned French fort, with the French paddling away down the Ohio. On the ashes the British began building the replacement they would name Fort Pitt. The French and Indian War would continue, but its focus moved elsewhere, to the northeastern colonies and to Canada. Eventually the French would be utterly routed, but not without great financial cost to the British.

The departure of the French from the Ohio headwaters presented a timely moment for Washington to resign his position, go home to his plantation, and get on with his life—and that is precisely what he did. One can only wonder if he was familiar with a comment of Cicero's, in an echo of Xenophon, that "of all sources of wealth, farming is the best, the most agreeable, the most profitable, the most noble."

There were two final touches in his basic education in life. First, in January 1759, he married a wealthy widow, Martha Custis. He also won election as a delegate to Virginia's House of Burgesses, the colony's elected legislative body. He took his seat a month after his wedding, on his twenty-seventh birthday, and served there for fifteen years. He would not do much as a member, but it is significant that he repeatedly stood for public office and was consistently reelected, and then he was chosen to be part of Virginia's delegation to the First Continental Congress in the fall of 1774. Yes, he later would be a general who became president. But before that, he was an officer who became a local politician. He was a member of the House of Burgesses far longer than he was a general at war. And after being a general, of course, he again would be a politician—and a notably successful one.

## Born in Defeat

MORE THAN ANY OF THE OTHER EARLY PRESIDENTS, GEORGE WASHINGTON learned in early life the pain of loss, humiliation, and hardship. It is axiomatic among military historians that commanders learn more from defeat than from victory, but this is especially true of Washington. He had been taught many hard lessons and would have two decades in which to mull them over before he fought again. Reviewing his experiences, he could have distilled them into some general maxims along these lines:

- Know yourself, and know those you are fighting. This is a more complex proposition than it may seem, as it requires introspection, strategic thinking, and reliable intelligence.
- Study the terrain and make it your friend.
- As circumstances change, be ready to change views and abandon assumptions. Listen to dissenters and know how to weigh alternatives.

He also had absorbed some specific lessons about waging war in eighteenth-century North America. He had worked with indigenous allies. He had developed an appreciation of the military and diplomatic resourcefulness of the French. Long before Adams and Jefferson would treat with the great powers in Europe, Washington had engaged in diplomacy with tribes in the watershed of the Ohio—and with the French there, too.

He would carry this knowledge with him all his life. He had developed a new appreciation for the French, warning a comrade that "the policy of the French is so subtle, that not a friendly Indian will we have on the continent, if we do not soon dislodge them from the Ohio." This was a matter not just of manpower but also of military intelligence—a European force in the dense forests of North America that moved without having local allies to act as scouts was operating almost blind.

In addition, he had learned that his lack of tribesmen to operate as a screening force gave the French and their allies an opening to move freely in the forests and so closely observe British movements. "We cannot suppose the French, who have their Scouts constantly out, can be so difficult in point of Intelligence, as to be unacquainted with our Motions when we are advancing by slow degrees towards them."

In strategic terms, he had seen events that would resonate with him decades later during the War for Independence. First, he had seen the French appear to be on the cusp of victory in the war, only to lose years later. Second, he had witnessed an army of British regulars shattered in a battle with people born in North America. Third, he had seen in Braddock's spectacular failure what can happen to a general who disregards informed advice and fails to adapt his approach to the circumstances.

Most of all, he had seen that he himself could recover from stinging personal defeat—and also, perhaps, that the key goal of a general is sometimes not to win but merely to keep his army alive. His conclusion as a commander, he wrote in 1757, was that "Discipline is the soul of an army." This was a crucial lesson, not just for his command of troops, but for his command of himself.

Which would prove more influential in American history, Washington's practical education on the frontier or the study by Adams, Jefferson, and Madison of classical history, philosophy, and rhetoric? It is impossible to say. The answer is probably that both were essential. His college-educated comrades learned what was needed to found and design a new kind of nation; Washington, in a different but equally daunting school, learned what was necessary to liberate it and lead it toward stability. More than any other founder, concludes Gordon Wood, Washington "always understood power and how to use it." What could be more Roman than the prudent exercise of power?

## Chapter 3

# John Adams
# Aims to Become an
# American Cicero

THE DOMINANT POLITICAL NARRATIVE OF COLONIAL AMERICAN elites was the story of how the Roman orator Cicero put down the Catiline conspiracy to take over Rome. John Adams aspired to be the Cicero of his time—that is, the key political figure in late-eighteenth-century America.

He would come very close to achieving that vaulting ambition, which is surprising, because he was in many ways the odd man out among the first four presidents. He was the only one who spent time as a schoolteacher, working for wages. The other three were emotionally reserved, while he wore his feelings on his sleeve and tended to wallow in them all his life. They were Virginians, while he was a son of Massachusetts, a colony founded by Puritans in 1628. He was also the only one of the four never to own an enslaved human being.

Most significant of all, Adams also was the first of the four men to move toward revolt. He was entertaining radical notions while still an adolescent—and while George Washington was striving to achieve rank and standing in the structure of the British empire. Indeed, long before the adolescent Adams crossed the Charles River to Harvard, he was full of thoughts about how to better resist British authority. It helped that he was both bright and naturally irascible. He had been questioning authority for years. More than most men, he was born to do so.

## The Education of John Adams

BORN IN 1735, JOHN ADAMS WAS SMART ENOUGH AS A YOUNG BOY TO learn to read at home. But when he went to the local Latin grammar school, he took a dislike to his teacher, Joseph Cleverly (Harvard, 1732 or 1733—accounts differ), whom he found "the most indolent Man I ever knew." Classes with Cleverly consisted of hours of reading and reciting Latin classics. Young Adams preferred hunting to the classroom, often skipping school to fish and to hunt ducks and geese in the nearby sea marshes. "I did not love my Books half so well as my fowling-piece, my paddles, my Skates or my Kite," he later recalled.

He knew his father was determined to send him to college, so young John took him aside and set him straight, telling him that he would rather be a farmer. His father took him the next day to the dirty work of gathering thatch in the knee-deep muck of the salt marsh. Adams that night told his father that "though the Labour had been very hard and very muddy . . . I like it very well Sir." Adams' father nonetheless sent him back to school, where the boy became angry with his teacher over not being included in the "Arithmetick" class. "I resented it," Adams wrote, so he obtained the textbook and taught himself the subject.

Nearing the age of fourteen, Adams again asked his father to let him leave school and become a farmer. "Sir," he recalled responding, "I don't like my schoolmaster. He is so negligent and cross that I can never learn any thing under him." Adams then cut a deal with his father: If his father would send him to another teacher, Joseph Marsh (Harvard, 1728), he would study hard and go to college.

Adams' assessment of his teachers, for all its brashness, likely was correct. He thrived under Marsh, even spending some of his own meager money to buy a book by Cicero. A year later Marsh declared him ready to apply to the local college.

That institution, Harvard College, had been in existence for over a century when John Adams enrolled there in 1751. It was the first American college, and the one most connected to English traditions. By the mid-seventeenth century, some 140 graduates of British universities lived in New England, the majority of them alumni of Cambridge. Indeed, a quarter of them came from a single Puritanical college at Cambridge, Emmanuel.

When John Adams started at Harvard, students there and at Yale were still ranked by their social standing—that is, by the public distinction of their fathers and families. This arrangement was manifested in writing, in the published list of members of a given class, and also physically, by where students sat in the chapel on Sundays and on other formal occasions, ensuring that they were elbow to elbow with gentlemen of similar status.

Adams was placed in the middle of his class, ranked fourteen of twenty-five. Adams' father worked with his hands as a farmer and cobbler, but also had good standing in his community of Braintree, just south of Boston, having been a selectman and deacon for many years, as well as a tax collector and militia officer. Charles Francis Adams, in his biography of his grandfather, asserts that John Adams' class rank probably had more to do with the status of the family of his mother, a Boylston. In his preface, Charles Francis Adams attributes authorship of the chapter in question, as well as the following one, to his father, President John Quincy Adams. Zabdiel Boylston, uncle to John's mother, Susanna, was one of the most prominent physicians in colonial America, the first to perform some kinds of surgeries, and also the first to perform a smallpox inoculation—using a technique apparently learned from an African who was enslaved. He also was a member of the Royal Society.

Rank determined, among other things, where one sat in the Commons for meals. Those at the top of the table had the right to get their food first. Their repasts were simple but hearty. Breakfast was two hunks of bread with butter and a half pint of beer. The college had its own brewhouse to keep the students' mugs filled. Noon brought a dinner with meat, baked or boiled, except on Saturdays, when it was salted fish. Supper was either a meat pie or a pint of milk and a big biscuit. Students brought their own knives and forks to meals, cleaning them on the tablecloth.

As it happened, Adams' tutor—his sole teacher—at Harvard was Joseph Mayhew. Born in 1709, Mayhew had graduated from Harvard in 1730. Nine years later, after spending some time as a missionary among the First Peoples of Martha's Vineyard, where he had been born, he returned to Harvard to become a tutor. He may have found the atmosphere at the college less civilized than that on the island. A history of the college records:

> In the years which followed his appointment he grew accustomed to being greeted in the yard with "Contemptuous Noise & Hallowing" and to being subjected to "Heinous Insults." He was defied by drunken students and his orders were resisted with physical violence. Logs were rolled down the stairs by his study door, his door knob was broken off, and his cellar was broken open and his beer and brandy stolen.

Given this treatment, it may not be a surprise that in 1755 he resigned his position and returned to live on his family's island farm. The studious Adams was not distracted by such undergraduate shenanigans. Harvard awakened him intellectually, he later wrote. "I soon perceived a growing Curiosity, a Love of Books and a fondness for Study, which dissipated all my Inclination for Sports, and even for the Society of the Ladies. I read forever, but without much method, and with very little Choice."

## The Centrality of Cicero

AT THE END OF HIS FIRST YEAR AT HARVARD, ADAMS WAS AWARDED A Detur Prize, then awarded to freshmen showing academic achievement in their first year at the college. Winners could choose a book as their reward, and Adams selected Conyers Middleton's popular *Life of Cicero*, first published in 1741. Adams idolized Cicero, the great Roman orator. As an old man, he would write that, "I have read him, for almost 70 years and seeme to have him almost by heart."

It is essential to take a look at Cicero's life to understand how much he meant to Adams and to other colonial Americans. His words and his actions often provided the context for their own. Adams would write later that "the Period in the History of the World, the best understood, is that of Rome from the time of Marius to the Death of Cicero, and this distinction is entirely owing to Ciceros Letters and Orations."

Cicero was born in 106 BC in Arpinum, a small town in the hills about seventy-five miles southeast of Rome, a bit short of Monte Cassino. There was little indication that he was destined for greatness. He was a plebian, the son of a rustic "nobody," as Trollope puts it. Cicero would become what the Romans called a "new man," one who would become ennobled by eventually holding high office. As a boy he was shipped off to Rome to be educated and there he was noticed for his talent, so much so that Plutarch says the fathers of other students came to witness his "quickness and readiness in learning." Late in his teens he became a soldier for a brief time. He then turned to the study of philosophy and law. In 81 BC he began practicing law, soon becoming one of Rome's most prominent lawyers, noted for the quiet intensity of his oratory. He also steadily moved up the ladder of Roman politics.

In 63 BC he reached the top rung, becoming one of Rome's two consuls for the year. In that same year he would confront the Catilinarian conspiracy, which was at least in part the product of tensions between the aristocracy and the common people over political power. To Adams, Cicero's life must have looked like a career plan. Here was a man who, lacking wealth, noble birth, or military glory, rose to the top of Roman society through his powerful rhetorical skills.

Plutarch always balances his praise of great men by emphasizing one great shortcoming. In Cicero's case, this was vanity. "He was always excessively pleased with his own praise, and continued to the very last to be passionately fond of glory; which often interfered with the prosecution of his wisest resolutions." Adams would also exhibit this flaw.

Most young men of privilege were introduced to Cicero's works in secondary school, so they arrived at college already familiar with his four speeches against Catiline, which was part of the standard curriculum in college preparatory courses. These orations were the powerful denunciations Cicero delivered against Catiline in 63 BC. The students would know from reading Plutarch that "Catiline has plotted a dreadful and entire subversion of the Roman state by sedition and open war, but being convicted by Cicero, was forced to flee the city." The fact that Catiline was a charismatic populist, calling for land reform and cancellation of debts, received less attention.

The first of Cicero's four great orations was delivered on November 7, 63 BC, the day after Catiline's plan to assassinate Cicero failed. Cicero was consul, and as the city was under martial law because of the political tumult, he held the powers of a dictator.

Cicero famously began his first speech against Catiline with striking urgency: "How far wilt thou, O Catiline! abuse our patience?" There was no throat clearing here, none of the customary preliminaries. He grabbed his audience by beginning almost with the climax of a speech. "How long shall thy Madness outbrave our justice?"

What kind of country had Rome become? Cicero asked. "There are here, among our fellow-senators, my lords, . . . men who are meditating the destruction of us all, the total ruin of this city and in fact of the civilised world."

Cicero then showed he knew much more about the attempted coup d'etat than Catiline realized—where the man had been, in what house he had met with other conspirators, and how they planned to burn Rome, massacre their opponents, and divide Italy between themselves. He said he knew that Catiline had sent two men to murder Cicero in his own bed—and in fact Cicero had alerted friends about their identity before those men arrived at his door. "You cannot possibly remain in our society any longer," he admonished.

But, Cicero added, he would not order Catiline's execution. That, he explained, would eliminate only one conspirator and perhaps leave Rome in even more danger, with the other conspirators still in place. Rather, he said, he wanted Catiline to leave the city, along with his followers. "Let the disloyal then withdraw, let them separate themselves from the loyal. . . . get you gone to your unholy and abominable campaign."

Catiline stood in the Senate and attempted to respond to this blast. An aristocrat himself, he attacked Cicero's relatively low birth, calling him "an immigrant citizen" (that is, born outside Rome). He accused Cicero of being jealous of his own noble standing. He argued that Cicero long had been his enemy and thus should not be believed too quickly. But he was shouted down and left Rome that night. He pretended that he was going into exile in Massalia, the city that is now Marseille, France. But Cicero knew that Catiline in fact was going to join and lead a rebel army gathering north of Rome.

The next day Cicero went to the Forum to tell the people this, to defend his Senate speech, and to rally them for civil war. "He is gone, he is vanished, he is escaped, he is sallyed out," he began in this second oration. There are those who say I forced him into banishment, but that is not so, Cicero argued. "Did I drive into exile the man who I already saw has entered upon Hostilities?"

He also warned that those conspirators who had remained behind in the city would not receive the indulgence he had shown Catiline. "There is not any longer room for lenity; the business itself demands severity." He described Catiline and his accomplices not as friends of the poor and the debt-laden, but as drunks and whoremongers acting only in their own interests:

*For on the one side are fighting modesty, on the other wantonness; on the one chastity, on the other uncleanness; on the one honesty, on the other fraud; on the one piety, on the other wickedness; on the one consistency, on the other insanity; on the one honour, on the other baseness; on the one continence, on the other lust; in short, equity, temperance, fortitude, prudence, all the virtues contend*

*against iniquity with luxury, against indolence, against rashness,
against all the vices.*

During the ensuing weeks, some of the conspirators who were
still in Rome approached a Gaulish embassy, seeking their aid.
The ambassadors, who themselves had come to ask for tax relief,
at first were intrigued, but then grew fearful of retribution, so
they went to a patron, who in turn notified Cicero. He encouraged the envoys to draw out the conspirators on their plans and
to get pledges in writing. They did. The Gauls prepared to leave
Rome, along with a Roman who was carrying conspirators' letters to Catiline. On December 3, as they departed the city, Cicero
sprang the trap and had them captured and brought to the Senate,
where their Roman fellow traveler told all, including Catiline's
plan to incite a slave revolt, set fire to the city, and massacre an
untold number of political opponents. Fear of a slave uprising was
genuine, as the famous one led by Spartacus in southern Italy had
ended only eight years earlier.

After the Senate concluded its business, Cicero summoned the
people to the Forum to hear his third blast against Catiline and
his group. He related how the conspirators had been confronted
with the incriminating letters about the contemplated attacks. He
reported that the Senate had thanked him for saving the city from
fire, the citizens from murder, and Italy from war. He then took a
rhetorical victory lap, noting his skill at drawing out the conspiracy and getting evidence of it in writing. But, he quickly added,
his effort had worked so well that it really must have been the
work of the gods. "Jupiter resisted them," Cicero said. "He saved
these temples, he saved this city, he saved all of you."

On December 5, the Senate met to consider the fate of their
prisoners. But Cicero, surprisingly, began his fourth and final
oration instead by talking about his own demise. "If anything
does happen to me, I shall fall with a contented and prepared
mind; and, indeed, death cannot be disgraceful to a brave man,
nor premature to one of consular rank, nor miserable to a wise
man." But, he added, don't worry about me. Look instead to your

wives and children, and "attend to the safety of the republic; look round upon all the storms which are impending." He never quite called for execution in this speech. Rather, he argued that showing leniency to the conspirators would be cruel to their intended victims—you and your families. The duty of the Senate is not to be kind, but to do what is best for the Republic, he counseled. He concluded that, "You have a Consul, who, without Hesitation, will Obey your orders, and while he breathes, will, in his own Person, charge himself, with the Execution and Defense of whatever you shall decree."

As was noted earlier, Julius Caesar called for mercy, saying that the Senate should not yield to anger. Rather, he said, the conspirators should be stripped of their wealth and exiled to provincial cities. Otherwise, he warned, the Senate would set a precedent of giving a consul powers that would be difficult to restrain. Cato rose in indignant response. These men conspired to burn the city, summoned the Gauls to make war on Rome, and still have an army in the field, he said, and then asked, almost incredulously, "Do you, then, still hesitate and doubt what to do with the enemies caught inside the walls?"

The conspirators were strangled to death the same day. When that news reached Catiline's army, his soldiers began to desert. His force soon shrank to a quarter of its size, easily outnumbered by the three Roman legions pursuing it. When the confrontation came, it was utterly destroyed, with Catiline among the battlefield dead.

This story of Catiline fascinated post-Renaissance Europe, whose artists explored it in drama, poetry, and opera. Ben Jonson tried his hand at it early in the seventeenth century. In the 1730s, Alexander Pope pondered in his *Essay on Man* how a passionate spirit can go either very right or spectacularly wrong:

*The fiery Soul abhor'd in Catiline*
*In Decius charms, in Curtius is divine,*
*The same Ambition can destroy or save,*
*And makes a Patriot as it makes a Knave.*

In eighteenth-century France, there were two notable plays about the Catiline war, both patriotically highlighting the pivotal role played by the Gaulish envoys. A drama by Prosper Jolyot de Crébillon, staged in 1748, provoked a response two years later from Voltaire titled *Rome Sauvée*—that is, *Rome Saved*. In some private performances, Voltaire played the role of Cicero. A few decades later Mozart's rival Antonio Salieri wrote an opera about the Catiline war.

## Cicero and Adams

———

ADAMS LOVED THE SPEECHES OF CICERO, READING THEM ALOUD TO himself at night. He wrote in his diary that

> The Sweetness and Grandeur of his sounds, and the Harmony of his Numbers give Pleasure enough to reward the Reading if one understood none of his meaning. Besides I find it, a noble Exercise. It exercises my Lungs, raises my Spirits, opens my Porr, quickens the Circulations, and so contributes much to Health.

Among all the founders, it was Adams who seems most to have consciously used Cicero as a model for his life. "Cicero, it may be said, was the one man, above all others, who made the Romans feel how great a charm eloquence lends to what is good, and how invincible justice is, if it be well spoken," writes Plutarch. Also, he taught Romans "to prefer that which is honest before that which is popular." He was so successful in office as consul that Cato, in a speech, extolled him as "the father of his country."

Like the great Roman, Adams was a largely self-made man who through his own efforts and eloquence would rise to the pinnacle of power. Both first came to public notice as lawyers. Both strove mightily, exhausting themselves at times and withdrawing from public life for a spell in order to recover their health. Both grieved at the loss of a beloved adult daughter. One major difference is that Cicero in the course of his legal career became a wealthy man, ultimately owning at least nine villas and other properties. Adams always lived modestly, especially when compared to the other three presidents. He was accustomed to chopping his own firewood.

Cicero's faults and failings were also those of Adams, to a surprising and even alarming degree. Plutarch tells us that the Roman was known for his sharp wit and sarcasm, "but his using it to excess offended many, and gave him a repute of ill-nature." In addition, Cicero was "always excessively pleased with his own praise" and "lauding and magnifying himself." Today we would call Cicero's self-promotion efforts over the top—for example, writing to beg a historian to write an account extolling how well he put down the Catiline's conspiracy: "I have a very strong, and, I trust, a very pardonable passion, of being celebrated in your writings. . . . I hope you will excuse my impatience. . . . [I have] the most ardent desire of being immediately distinguished in your glorious annals."

Adams throughout his life would indulge his own egotism while faulting it in others. He also would nurse petty grievances, sometimes for years. He told his diary that "Bob Paine is conceited and pretends to more Knowledge and Genius than he has." It didn't help matters that Adams had been told that at a social event, Robert Paine had called him "a Numbskull and a Blunder Buss before all the Superiour Judges."

Adams was conscious of his great pride, writing in his diary in May 1756, at the age of thirty, that "Vanity I am sensible, is my cardinal Vice and cardinal Folly, and I am in continual Danger, when in Company, of being led an ignis fatuus [will-o'-the-wisp] Chase by it, without the strictest Caution and watchfulness over my self." But he would continue to let it run barely checked all his life, eventually doing great damage to his presidency.

One issue that concerned Enlightenment thinkers was who was the greater man, Cicero or Cato? Montesquieu thought Cato was. As regards to Cicero, he concluded,

*His genius was superb, but his soul was often common. With Cicero,*
*virtue was the accessory, with Cato, glory. Cicero always thought of*
*himself first, Cato always forgot about himself. The latter wanted*
*to save the republic for its own sake, the former in order to boast*
*of it.*

If Adams was a Cicero, Washington was a Cato—a comparison
that would frustrate Adams later in life. For the Revolutionary
generation, silent virtue almost always would be valued more than
loud eloquence.

## The Preceptor

WHILE AT HARVARD, ADAMS ALSO REPEATEDLY DELVED INTO A POPULAR
eighteenth-century textbook, Robert Dodsley's *The Preceptor: Con-*
*taining a General Course of Education Wherein the First Principles of*
*Polite Learning Are Laid Down in a Way most suitable for trying the*
*Genius, and advancing the Instruction of Youth.* It is a book that more
than most fulfills the promise of its subtitle. "I read it over and
over," Adams remembered. "I recommended it to others, particularly to my Chum David Wyer, and I took the Pains to read a great
Part of it to him and with him."

*The Preceptor* was a touchstone for his generation. George Washington owned a copy, apparently purchased for his stepson's education. In its two thick volumes, Dodsley lays out what a boy must
learn to become a basically educated gentleman. Dodsley himself
was an extraordinary figure. He began his life as a footman to an
illegitimate son of Charles II and turned himself into a London
literary entrepreneur. He went on to become a printer, publisher,
and bookseller, as well as an occasional poet and playwright. He
counted among his friends Alexander Pope and Samuel Johnson.

To create his textbook, Dodsley drew up a twelve-part outline
and then farmed out the writing of most of each section to a variety of scholars. The first edition of this innovative work appeared

in April 1748, with several more in the following years. It became enormously influential both in Britain and in the colonies, where it was published by Benjamin Franklin. It was used widely in schools and also imitated unblushingly by other producers of textbooks.

Reading it helps us recover some of the perspectives the American Revolutionary generation had on world events. One major reason to study history, *The Preceptor* explains, is that too many people hold high opinions of figures such as Julius Caesar and Alexander the Great. "They never consider them as the Authors of Misery to thousands, as laying waste Countries out of Wantonness and Ambition, spreading Desolation where-ever they came, and depriving Multitudes of what they hold most dear and valuable." Here is how Dodsley captures the lesson of that most crucial of events, the fall of the Roman Republic:

> *Could Rome have been saved from Slavery, the Eloquence of Cicero, and the Virtue of Cato, those intrepid Defenders of Liberty and Law, seemed to offer fair for it. . . . Brutus and Cassius, animated by a Zeal for Liberty, endeavoured to rescue their Country from Slavery by killing the Usurper; and the Eloquence of Cicero seconding the glorious Design, gave at first some Hopes that Rome might yet see better Days.*

But it was not to be.

The history section of this huge tome ends with the beginning of the Christian era. Later, Dodsley teaches a bit of British history in explaining the nature of its monarchy. But the rest of European and world history, from Year 1 to the then-present, is ignored.

In a second volume, published in 1769, he turned to moral philosophy—which, as he presented it, was essentially the question of the public duties of the individual, what a person owes to his or her society. Here the phrasing in places feels like a blueprint for the Declaration of Independence, which would not appear for another seven years. Discussing the moral duties "Of the People," Dodsley states, in two ponderous sentences, that it is the duty of the people to resist tyranny. This passage, while long and wordy, should be read with the patience that people in the eighteenth century were accustomed to give to the printed word. If read slowly, considered clause by clause, it can convey great power:

> As the People are the Fountain of Power and Authority, the original Seat of Majesty, the Authors of Laws, and the Creators of Officers to execute them; if they shall find the Power they have conferred abused by their Trustees, their Majesty violated by Tyranny or by Usurpation, their Authority prostituted to support Violence or screen Corruption, the Laws grown pernicious through Accidents unforeseen or unavoidable, or rendered ineffectual through the Infidelity and Corruption of the Executors of them; then it is their Right, and what is their Right is their Duty, to resume that delegated Power, and call their Trustees to an Account; to resist the Usurpation, and extirpate the Tyranny; to restore their sullied Majesty and prostituted Authority; to suspend, alter, or abrogate those Laws, and punish their unfaithful and corrupt Officers. Nor is it the Duty only of the united Body; but every Member of it ought, according to his respective Rank, Power, and Weight in the Community, to concur in advancing and supporting those glorious Designs.

Here were the seeds of the Revolutionary sentiment that would become so potent in the colonies in the 1770s. Sovereignty flows from the people, who have the power to withdraw it, and the duty to do so if the delegated authority abuses it.

But a gentleman needed to know more than just philosophy and history. Dodsley also included a section on how to write a letter. In this, he relied in part on examples from Cicero and Pliny. That inclusion is hardly surprising. The name of Dodsley's bookstore and also of his publishing imprint was Tully's Head, a reference to Marcus Tullius Cicero, whose supposed image was painted on the store's sign. Other eighteenth-century London bookstores boasted similarly classical names: Homer's Head, Horace's Head, Virgil's Head, and Seneca's Head.

For all its inclusiveness, one subject that is absent from the book's twelve areas of learning is religion. Christianity simply did not loom as large in colonial America as it would a century later, or indeed does now in much of the United States. As the intellectual historian Darren Staloff puts it, part of understanding the Enlightenment is seeing that to its thinkers, there was a "fundamental irrelevance of religious revelation to the great issues of public life." A cultural historian, Howard Mumford Jones, concludes that from 1775 to 1815, religion had less influence in American life than it did in any later such forty-year period. This would change in the decades after the Revolution as elite control of American culture weakened.

## Adams and the Enlightenment

MOST OF ALL, AT HARVARD, JOHN ADAMS LEARNED TO BE A CHILD OF the Enlightenment. What does that mean?

It is probably a mistake in emphasis to focus on the "ideas of the Enlightenment," as Bernard Bailyn, one of the leading American specialists on the Revolutionary era, does repeatedly. The cultural historian Robert Darnton, in an aside about the philosophes of the French Enlightenment, comments that "only rarely did they develop ideas undreamed of in earlier generations." It is an error because what was distinctive about the Enlightenment was not a system of political thought or a set of new philosophical notions. Rather, the Enlightenment was more a process than a result. Its core was a cast of mind, or to revive a useful term from the mid-twentieth century, a frame of reference. Immanuel Kant, when asked in 1784 to define "enlightenment," called it a "true reform in ways of thinking." To be sure, there were commonalities in what was thought about. Enlightened types tended to place their faith in progress, freedom, and the improvability of mankind. As the intellectual historian Caroline Winterer put it, "To be enlightened was to be filled with hope." The opposite of enlightenment, states her predecessor Carl Becker, was "superstition, intolerance, tyranny."

In sum, to be enlightened was to have an energetic way of examining the world with skepticism and self-confidence. "What was most important and really new about the Age of Reason was the sublime confidence of the intellectuals and societal leaders in the power of man's reason," writes the scholar William Goetzmann. "Human nature, like all other nature, was a constant that yielded to rational inquiry." In other words, they thought it possible to use reason and observation to discern the eternal laws of nature and then to use that understanding to aid human progress. This sounds airy, but it could be quite practical. Indeed, the foundations of the Industrial Revolution were put in place by Enlightenment thinkers exploring new technologies such as steam power.

By having the self-confidence to apply the methods of scientific inquiry to human situations, they developed several new scholarly fields. In his magisterial study of the Enlightenment, Peter Gay states that Montesquieu invented sociology in *The Spirit of Laws*, that Edward Gibbon founded the modern writing of history with *The History of the Decline and Fall of the Roman Empire*, and that Adam Smith did the same for economics with *The Wealth of Nations*. (Xenophon's *Oeconomicus* might from its title appear to claim to be a foundational document, but it really is about how to manage a household, which is what the word means in Greek.) Gay does not mention it, but Hume's essay on "The Populousness of Ancient Nations" also was an early venture into creating the field of demography. Another Scot, James Hutton, came up with an astonishing new way to think about time, and so invented modern geology, a subject to which we will return. It is noteworthy that several of these innovative scholarly ventures—the ones by Montesquieu, Gibbon, and Hume—were rooted in the studies of the history of Rome.

## Mayhew, Political Power, and the People

THE ANCIENTS PROVIDED A GENERAL BACKGROUND FOR THIS NOVEL way of thinking, to which Adams was receptive even while in his teens. Such views were invigorated by revived attention to ancient republicanism. One of the leading proponents was a dynamic young preacher whom Adams often went to hear, Boston's Jonathan Mayhew. It was a small world—Mayhew was a cousin of Adams' tutor at Harvard. This Mayhew had graduated from Harvard in 1744 and then voyaged to the University of Aberdeen in Scotland, where he earned a divinity degree in 1749. A son of Experience and Thankful Mayhew, this Mayhew is remembered today as the man who devised the brilliant colonial rallying cry "No taxation without representation."

In one sermon, Mayhew discussed how his education politicized him. "Having been initiated in youth, in the doctrines of civil liberty, as they were taught by such men as Plato, Demosthenes, Cicero, and other renowned persons among the ancients; and such as Sydney and Milton, Locke and Hoadley, among the moderns, I liked them; they seemed rational."

There was a rich background to that powerful thought, reaching back two centuries. Scottish philosophers long had maintained that it is natural and right for there to be limits on the power of monarchs. In 1579, George Buchanan, a humanist Scottish philosopher who taught in Scotland, Portugal, and France (where the great essayist Michel de Montaigne was one of his students), stated emphatically that kings must earn and retain the consent of the governed: "It is right that the people confer the political authority upon whomsoever they will." John Locke took up the idea and explicated it about a century later in his *Two Treatises of Government.* An eighteenth-century Scottish poet summarized the thought,

> *Of pow'r THE PEOPLE are the source,*
> *The fountain-head of human force;*
> *Spurn'd by their Subjects, WHAT ARE KINGS,*
> *But useless, helpless, haughty things?*

The view that there are limits to the powers of rulers traveled with the colonists to New England, where the relationship between church, state, and the people became a subject of intense discussion.

As early as 1644, Roger Williams (Cambridge, 1627), the colonial Puritan dissident, had argued in a book that "the Soveraigne, orginal and foundation of civill power lies in the people." Hence, he added, governments were entitled to exercise power only as long as they held the trust of the people. So, he continued, if the government controls the established church, then the church ultimately must answer to the people. Thus, he concludes, the people "have the power to governe the Church, to see her do her duty, & to correct her, to redress, reform, establish, & c." Notably, the word "liberty" appears some fifteen times in his book.

The next step from there was to actively oppose their government as a matter of religious conscience. That is, if the people are ultimately responsible and if they are faithful Christians, they must oppose the government when they see its actions conflict with being a good Christian. In 1750, Mayhew, fresh from receiving his Scottish divinity degree, preached a sermon in Boston celebrating, somewhat shockingly, the hundredth anniversary of the execution of King Charles I. One of the lessons, the radical young man noted, was that "no civil rules are to be obeyed when they enjoin things that are inconsistent with the commands of God." Indeed, such resistance to authority was "a duty, not a crime."

Adams was paying attention to such thinking. He would later note that this was the sermon that made Mayhew's reputation. He studied it repeatedly before he went off to college. "I read it, till the Substance of it was incorporated into my Nature and indelibly engraved on my Memory," he told Thomas Jefferson decades later. "It was read by every Body, celebrated by Friends, and abused by Enemies."

## Adams the Schoolteacher

SOON AFTER HE FINISHED COLLEGE, ADAMS TRADED THE GLORIES OF studying Enlightenment thinking for the drudgery of teaching school in a small town. Three weeks after graduating from Harvard in the summer of 1755, he rode forty miles west to Worcester, where he became the teacher at the Center School. The town had just one church and no newspaper; it didn't even have a post office to enable him to easily stay in touch with friends. He would not be happy in this job, but he had little choice. Unlike the other early presidents, he had to live off his labor.

He was lonely in Worcester, then a town of about 1,500. From the beginning he seems to have sensed that the schoolmaster's life was not for him. "I have no Books, no Time, no Friends. I must therefore be contented to live and die an ignorant, obscure fellow," he wailed in his diary one rainy day in April 1756.

He does not seem to have been particularly interested in his work. He records almost nothing in his diaries about what he taught, or even what books he used. The day before that previous entry, he grumbled that "I never have any bright, refulgent ideas. Every Thing appears in my mind, dim and obscure like objects seen thro' a dirty glass or roiled water." That last sentence hints at persistent depression.

As a teacher, he may have assigned to his older students two of the most popular and influential textbooks of the time—Charles Rollin's *Ancient History*, as well as his old college favorite, Dodsley's *Preceptor*. Both were in his library. While at Harvard, he had noted in his diary that he had spent "a Clowdy morning" reading Charles Rollin's *Method of Teaching and Studying the Belles Lettres*, which is basically an introduction to education by the rector of the University of Paris.

Rollin was even better known for his *Ancient History*, which was published in French in sixteen volumes from 1730 to 1738, with the first translation into English appearing a year after that. It, along with his later work on Roman history, soon became what one historian terms "a principal medium through which they [colonial Americans] learned about classical heroes." Adams thought Washington had gotten most of his knowledge of the ancient world from that text, stating that, "Rollins ancient History you know is very generally diffused through this Country. . . . From Rollins I Suspect, Washington drew his Wisdom, in a great measure." Rollin was so popular that later in the century, Ezra Stiles (Yale, 1746), the president of Yale College, would write to Thomas Jefferson that he had grown weary of such predigested material: "I have heretofore gone over the greater part of the Latin and Greek Historians, in their Originals . . . for I am very sick of your Gibbons's, Robertsons, Rollins the best of them. They are at best but Manuductions [that is, guidance] and should be read with a Constant Recourse to the Original Authors."

Like many histories written in the eighteenth century, Rollin's works were not just records of events, but also instruction manuals about how to live, and especially how to acquire virtue. Adams found Rollin's books "worth their weight in gold.—for his excellent reflections on every remarkable event that occurs in history he informs his readers of the true source of every action and instructs them in the method of forming themselves upon the models of virtue to be met with in History." This was the first time Adams used the word "virtue" in the classical sense of public-spiritedness that would be so central to his generation.

But John Adams was not made for the classroom, and he knew it. In mid-1756, he decided to study under a Worcester lawyer, James Putnam. Later, when launched on a legal career, he allowed himself in his diary briefly to glance back at his teaching days, remembering only "the Mischievous Tricks . . . and the stupid Dulness of my scholars." In his new life, he was advised by one of his legal seniors to spend less time reading the ancient Greeks, whom the older man dismissed as a "meer Curiosity."

Adams criticized himself constantly in his diary. One reason for this may have been that throughout his life, he seems not to have acquired any genuine mentor or personal lodestar. Washington had his older half brother Lawrence, and later Christopher Gist on the frontier. Jefferson had George Wythe. Madison in turn had Jefferson. But Adams seems to have been too querulous to be taken on by such a moral sponsor. Putnam, who taught him law, did not even give him letters of recommendation when Adams rode off to Boston. "Now I feel the Disadvantages of Putnams Insociability, and neglect of me," he wrote as he began his law practice. "Had he given me now and then a few Hints concerning Practice, I should be able to judge better at this Hour than I can now."

This persistent absence in Adams' life of a mentor may explain why he was so self-admonishing. For example, one day in January 1759, he reminded himself: "Let no trifling Diversion or amuzement or Company decoy you from your Books, i.e. let no Girl, no Gun, no Cards, no flutes, no Violins, no Dress, no Tobacco, no Laziness, decoy you from your Books." The books on which he needed to concentrate, he continued, are, "Seneca, Cicero, and all other good moral Writers. . . . Montesque, Bolinbroke, . . . &c. and all other good, civil Writers, &c." Multiple similar passages suggest that Adams, lacking the guidance of an older friend, was trying to mentor himself.

## The American Cicero

AS ADAMS PURSUED A CAREER IN LAW, HE SET OUT TO MAKE HIMSELF A Cicero of the new world. He would look to the Roman for how to become respected both as an orator and as a public man. "Reputation ought to be the perpetual subject of my Thoughts, and Aim of my Behaviour," he told himself in March 1759. "How shall I gain a Reputation! How shall I Spread an Opinion of myself as a Lawyer of distinguished Genius, Learning, and Virtue." In his own time, this likely was seen more as a noble goal than as overweening ambition. In the same entry, Adams wrote that despite studying law, he didn't really know much about local Massachusetts laws: "I know much less than I do of the Roman law." He immersed himself in the works of Cicero and other ancient Romans—Horace, Ovid, Lucretius, Marcus Aurelius. His library eventually would amount to over three thousand books, with the ancients looming much larger than did modern writers, of whom he appears only to have dipped into Shakespeare, Milton, Pope, Addison, and Swift.

He set out on his way to become a great man—certainly a lawyer, perhaps a judge or other high official, perhaps a commentator on government—and may not have been shy about saying so. One of his closest friends, Jonathan Sewall (Harvard, 1748), wrote to Adams when he was twenty-five years old that "who knows but in future Ages, when New England shall have risen to its' intended Grandeur, it shall be as carefully recorded among the Registers of the Leterati, that *Adams* flourishd in the second Century after the Exode of its first Settlers from Great Brittain, as it is now, that *Cicero* was born in the Six-Hundred-&-Forty-Seventh Year after the Building of *Rome*?" Gordon Wood suspects this was gentle spoofing among friends, but Adams seems to have taken it to heart as a goal. One scholar puts it well when he comments that Adams "always wrote for the public as if he had a toga on."

On July 6, 1760, Adams noted in his diary that he had gone to listen to the sermon of Jonathan Mayhew. He offers no comment on what he had heard. But he was influenced by the radical views of Mayhew, who died young, in 1766. In an open letter to the people of Massachusetts written on the eve of the War for Independence, Adams referred to Mayhew as "a clergyman equalled by a very few of any denomination in piety, virtue, genius or learning."

He would later state that he had felt the first breezes of the Revolution stirring around then. There was, he wrote, "in 1760 and 1761, An Awakening and a Revival of American Principles and Feelings, with an Enthusiasm which went on increasing till in 1775 it burst out in open Violence, Hostility and Fury." He considered Mayhew to be among the five leading figures in this movement, the people who were "the most conspicuous, the most ardent and influential." It was during this time as well that Adams drafted an essay on power that restated ancient Greek views on government—that monarchy degenerates into despotism, aristocracy into oligarchy, and democracy into anarchy. He never published that piece, but other of his commentaries began appearing in Boston newspapers.

The most remarkable aspect of John Adams' early years is that he succeeded in the improbable goal he set then of becoming a great man. Twenty years later he would be among the most important participants in the Continental Congresses. He would nominate George Washington to lead the nation's new Army. And he eventually would become the second president of the United States.

Yet he remains an odd figure. If Washington is the most remote of the founders, Olympian in stature, Adams is his opposite, the most modern—quirky, striving, self-obsessed, vibrating with anxiety and vanity. An observation by the novelist Anthony Trollope also applies to Adams: "Cicero was a man thoroughly human in all his strength and all his weakness. . . . He was very great while he spoke of his country, which he did so often; but he was almost as little when he spoke of himself—which he did as often."

For Adams, education was always a means to an end. For a smart, driven young man from a modest background, books about government, politics, and law were the road to reputation, honor, and power.

◆━━━━▶

## Chapter 4

# Jefferson Blooms at
# William & Mary

T HOMAS JEFFERSON WAS THE MOST AESTHETICALLY MINDED OF
the first four American presidents. He read widely, conducted
scientific observations, played music, and created wonderful architecture, most notably his Roman-inspired home, Monticello.
Looking at this record, Darren Staloff, an insightful historian of
early American thinking, goes so far as to assert that Jefferson
was "America's first great Romantic artist." This Romantic label
indeed offers a useful frame for considering Jefferson, especially
when trying to comprehend his howling contradictions. Romanticism, by privileging the heart above the head, excuses illogical
thinking and exalts unreasonable passion. Jefferson captured this
outlook when in writing flirtatiously to a stunning young married
woman, he confessed that "I am but a son of nature, loving what I
see and feel, without being able to give a reason, nor caring much
whether there be one." Years later, he proudly told John Adams
that "I like the dreams of the future better than the history of
the past." Among other things, this Romanticism gave Jefferson
license to be self-indulgent in a manner that the stoical George
Washington never would permit himself.

What one person sees in Jefferson as Romantic might be seen
by another as the influence of the Greeks—who were also a major part of the inspiration for nineteenth-century Romanticism.
Either way, the point to take away here in the context of neoclassicism is that Jefferson was the only one of the first four presidents
to be arguably more Greek than Roman, more Epicurean than

Ciceronian. One of Jefferson's descendants told Henry Randall, a mid-nineteenth-century biographer of Jefferson, that generally speaking, Jefferson "was more partial to the Greek than the Roman literature; and among the Greeks, the Athenians were, in all respects, his chosen people." In his tastes and cast of mind, Jefferson was ahead of his time. Both these inclinations, toward ancient Greece and especially its Athenians, were a departure from the eighteenth-century norm, but would become fashionable in the nineteenth. This preference for the Greeks may have inoculated Jefferson against the stiff, Roman-like Federalism of Adams and Washington.

## The Tutors

IN COLONIAL TIMES, THE CHILDREN OF THE WEALTHY SOUTH USUALLY began their educations at the feet of a young man who recently had graduated from college. One of the most complete records of colonial tutoring was left by Philip Fithian, a 1772 product of Princeton who, before becoming a Presbyterian minister, contracted for a year to teach the seven children of Robert Carter, one of Virginia's wealthiest planters. The girls were to be given the basics of reading, writing, and numbers. The boys got all that and then went on to practical skills of mathematics, surveying, and a smattering of law. In addition, the boys were given at least a veneer of socially desirable knowledge in Latin, philosophy, and history. An entry in Fithian's diary underscores the social aspect of learning. One Monday in March 1774, Bob Carter, then aged sixteen, "begg'd me to learn him lattin; his Reason he tells me is that yesterday Mrs Taylor told him he must not have either of her Daughters unless he learn'd Latin."

The plantation schoolhouse met five days a week for a few hours both in the morning and the afternoon, but the schedule was often interrupted by visits from itinerant dancing and music teachers, as well as by parties being thrown at nearby plantations. The purpose of education among Virginian elites was not to produce intellectuals, or even doctors or lawyers, but to form young gentlemen, and dancing was treated as just as essential as reading books. The Carter family was not greatly academically inclined, nor was Fithian. The plantation had an impressive library, containing most of the ancient masters and many contemporary authors, but Fithian devotes more space in his diary to recording the family's multiple illnesses, languorous outings, and sumptuous meals of rockfish, crab, fruit, ham, and beef, accompanied by wine, grog, port, and porter.

Jefferson's study would have been more intense, given that he was not just another wealthy boy, but clearly a bright one who could go far in law or politics. He came to classicism early, if a bit uncertainly. At the age of five he was sent to a neighborhood school to begin learning his letters and numbers. Four years later he began to learn Latin from a "Mr Douglas a clergyman from Scotland [who] was but a superficial Latinist, less instructed in Greek, but with the rudiments of these languages he taught me French." In 1757, not long after his father died, the boy moved on to another tutor, James Maury, a man of French Huguenot background who had graduated from William & Mary around 1740. Jefferson wrote later that Maury, in contrast to his first teacher, was "a correct classical scholar, with whom I continued two years." But even Maury thought that the purpose of learning a bit of history, literature, and geography was essentially social, in that a smattering of such knowledge would enable "a Virginia gentleman" to converse with confidence and thus save him from the embarrassment of making "a ridiculous & awkward Figure in Life."

Indeed, judging by Jefferson's literary commonplace book, into which he copied passages from authors who had caught his attention, Maury immersed the young man in the classics. There are few better ways to study a literary passage than to write it out in one's own hand, feeling each word and following the flow of thought. Not surprisingly for an intelligent fourteen-year-old who had just lost his father, Jefferson was especially inclined toward commentaries on mortality. He began by copying several passages from Cicero's *Tusculum Disputations* about the inevitability of death. Jefferson liked Cicero's essays, considering him "the first master" of style, but in notable contrast to the taste of the time, held the Roman's speeches in low esteem. The best models of oratory, he wrote, were "Livy, Tacitus, Sallust, & most assuredly not in Cicero."

## A School for Scandal

COLLEGES IN THE COLONIAL ERA COULD BE UNRULY, AND THE TINY one at which sixteen-year-old Thomas Jefferson arrived late in the winter of 1759–60 was in tumult. The year before Jefferson enrolled at William & Mary, Jacob Rowe, a twenty-eight-year-old Cornish graduate of Trinity College, Cambridge, became professor of moral philosophy at the college, replacing a faculty member who had been dismissed. In the same year that he arrived, Rowe was arrested for making "scandalous and malicious" comments about the Virginia House of Burgesses at a private party, such as saying some members of that body should be hanged for passing a law that reduced the compensation of clergymen. He was forced to apologize and pay the court costs.

When Jefferson joined the student body, then numbering about sixty, Rowe was teaching ethics, and Jefferson became one of his students. But then another new faculty member arrived. Goronwy Owen, a young Welsh poet, was to be master of the college's grammar school. Owen, an Oxford dropout, was even rougher cut than Rowe. He was a "castoff, a misfit, a drunk and a brawler" who had arrived in the New World as "a last resort."

Rowe and Owen hit it off, smashingly. Just a few months later, in August 1760, the two clergymen were charged with leading students in a brawl with the townspeople. Rowe was ordered to "remove himself and his effects at once from the college." Later the same year, the school's president was hauled before the college's governing body, the Board of Visitors, on the charge of being habitually drunk. He did not deny it and solved the problem by dying that December. Conditions at the college at this time were, writes one historian, "pathetically absurd."

Amidst this turmoil, Jefferson was taught almost exclusively by William Small, a 1755 graduate of Marischal College in Aberdeen, Scotland. "Fortunately the philosophical chair became vacant soon after my arrival at college, and he [Small] was appointed to fill it per interim," Jefferson wrote in his autobiography. Jefferson appears to draw a subtle distinction between Small and some of the other faculty members. The Scotsman, the only non-cleric on the faculty, was "a man profound in most of the useful branches of science, with a happy talent of communication, correct and gentlemanly manners, & an enlarged and liberal mind." In that last phrase, Jefferson hints at the Scottish empiricism he likely learned from Small.

Not surprisingly, given Jefferson's years of being taught by Douglas and Small, two Scots, his views would come to reflect Scottish thinkers of the time. The historian Ralph Ketcham detects in Jefferson's thinking "the basic influence . . . of Hutcheson, Thomas Reid, Adam Smith, and other Scottish Enlightenment philosophers." This Scottish influence would remain with him throughout his life, most notably in its emphasis on testing ideas against observation through one's own senses.

## The Scots Come Alive

SCOTLAND'S INFLUENCE ON AMERICAN HISTORY WAS PROFOUND AND remains underappreciated. The story of this development is fascinating. In the early eighteenth century, Scotland was a poor country, isolated in the northwestern corner of Europe. Yet in the subsequent decades it achieved a high literacy rate and enjoyed an intellectual explosion, with, as noted above, Scots more or less inventing the fields of modern economics and geology, as well as eventually setting off the Industrial Revolution with the steam engine.

The Scottish divergence from English thinking had its roots in changes that began two hundred years earlier, when the Scottish church, long independent of the English one, underwent a Calvinist reformation from which the Presbyterian Church emerged. This new church placed a strong emphasis on literacy, because it believed the people should be able to read their Bibles. In 1661, it became church policy that every Scottish town should have a schoolmaster educated in Latin, while rural parishes should have a minister capable of giving basic instruction to country youth.

Within a few generations, the effect of this policy could be seen across Scotland. By 1750, according to some estimates, 75 percent of Scots could read, compared to 53 percent in England. Scotland's literacy rate may have been the highest in Europe. One of the literary results of the Scottish Enlightenment is still with us: the *Encyclopaedia Britannica*, which began appearing in Edinburgh in 1768.

The Enlightenment unfolded far differently in Scotland than in England. Uniquely, Scotland's Enlightenment was university-based, giving its academic institutions a dynamism that English universities in particular lacked. J.E.G. De Montmorency, a historian of education, states that English universities were bypassed altogether by the Enlightenment as they experienced "a century of educational sleep" in the 1700s. "I spent fourteen months" at Oxford, Edward Gibbon disapprovingly recalled. "They proved the fourteen most idle and unprofitable of my whole life." Adam Smith, who won a scholarship to Oxford for graduate work after taking a degree at Glasgow, complained in *The Wealth of Nations* that "in the university of Oxford, the greater part of the public professors have, for these many years, given up altogether even the pretence of teaching."

While the two English universities slumbered, having "degenerated to a large extent into a preserve for the idle and the rich," the Scottish ones at Edinburgh and Glasgow rapidly modernized. The Scottish institutions led the English-speaking world in having their faculty members specialize in one or two subjects, instead of making them responsible for teaching the university's entire curriculum. Edinburgh made this change in 1708; Glasgow followed in 1727. Both schools were open to new thinking. For example, the groundbreaking work by Isaac Newton of Cambridge in mathematics and physics was taught in the Scottish universities before it was in his own. "Edinburgh is a hot-bed of genius," confidently states a character in the 1771 novel *The Expedition of Humphry Clinker*, by the Scottish writer Tobias Smollett. "The university of Edinburgh is supplied with excellent professors in all the sciences; and the medical school, in particular, is famous all over Europe."

There also were major financial differences. Scottish universities were relatively inexpensive, charging tuition fees just a tenth that of the English ones. As one educational historian puts it, "Any boy who could do the work was welcome; the money necessary for the relatively small tuition fees and lodgings in town could usually be scraped together somehow." For example, early in the nineteenth century, the adolescent Thomas Carlyle, later a Scottish philosopher, mathematician, and historian, enrolled at Edinburgh just by walking eighty miles to the city and presenting himself.

Scottish universities were remarkably cosmopolitan for their time, far more integrated into the European intellectual world than were their English peers, which by law required oaths of religious allegiance. Their relative tolerance enabled the northern universities to attract visitors from as far as Russia and Portugal. One result of this multinationalism was that the Scottish approach to law was heavily influenced by the French. In fact, writes Arthur Herman, "many Scottish lawyers in the seventeenth century still went to France to complete their law training rather than to England." That's significant in the context of classicism because much more than English law, French jurisprudence had its roots in ancient Rome. The point of transmission from the ancient world to the modern one was the rediscovery of the *Codex* of Emperor Justinian I, a hefty summary of Roman civil law which that ruler had ordered compiled in the sixth century AD. In the Italian city of

Bologna in about 1115, a jurist named Irnerius began using the old book to teach Roman law. This revived knowledge soon spread to southern France and then to the law school at Orleans, where it was picked up by Scottish students and taken home by them.

As a consequence, Scottish legal thinking deferred less to precedent than the English did, and was more open to classical principles and judgments based on reason. Alexander Bayne, who taught Scots law at Edinburgh, stated in 1722 that "we consider the Roman laws which are not disconform to our own fixed Laws and Customs, to be our own law." Lord Kames went even further, stating that "our law is grafted on that of Old Rome." As a law student he kept on his desk a copy of Justinian's *Codex*. Jefferson would read extensively in Kames for his legal education, copying out some thirty thousand words of his.

## Tobacco, the Chesapeake, and Scotland

A CHANCE OF COMMERCE CREATED THE PATHWAY FOR SCOTTISH SCHOLars to travel to America. In 1707, the Act of Union, which combined Scotland with England and Wales, opened the American trade—most notably, tobacco—to Scottish merchants, who until then had officially been excluded. "As the Union opened the Door to the Scots into our American colonies, the Glasgow Merchants presently embraced the Opportunity," Daniel Defoe wrote in his travelogue of Scotland, compiled in the 1720s. So many Scots were eager to work in America, he added, that "if it holds on for many years more, Virginia may rather be called a Scots than an English plantation."

Entering the tobacco trade on a large scale would be a culture-altering experience for the Scots. It was, writes the historian T. M. Devine, "Scotland's first global enterprise," its debut role "on the world commercial stage." They first officially imported tobacco in 1715, and Glasgow soon became a major trader in the American tobacco crop. By about 1760, its merchants had supplanted their competitors to the south, bringing in more than all English ports combined. The Scottish merchants reexported almost all this tobacco, mainly to France (whose smokers preferred the sweet Virginia leaf) and Holland (which favored the more pungent Maryland product), with most of the remainder going to Scandinavia.

The Scots thrived in the tobacco business for several reasons. Partly because of North Atlantic winds and currents, shipping was faster to America by the route around northern Ireland to Scotland than it was going around the south of England, sometimes by as much as two weeks. Operating costs were lower in Glasgow than in London, partly because customs collectors may have been more pliable. The Scots also modernized the business itself, buying whole shiploads in Virginia, rather than using the slow and unwieldy English system of consignment. Finally, the Scots streamlined their banking system, offering innovations such as branch offices and new forms of credit. More than others, Scottish bankers seemed to grasp that time is money, both to producers and to buyers.

## A Vast New Sense of Time

NEW WAYS OF THINKING ABOUT TIME WERE IN FACT AN ESSENTIAL ELEment of the Scottish Enlightenment, which also took off during the eighteenth century. The most striking example of this came from the Scottish scientist James Hutton, who played a crucial role in creating the field of geology. His key concept was a geological scale of time—that is, the vast, non-human amount of time it takes for rock to break down into sediment on the seafloor and then to metamorphose through heat and pressure into new forms of rock. In 1788, he concluded that in examining our planet, "we find no vestige of a beginning,—no prospect of an end."

Hutton took this new approach at a time when the conventional wisdom was that the Earth was just six thousand years old. The notion that the Earth was older than the biblical account allowed had been floating around among Enlightenment thinkers, notes one historian of geology, but Hutton was the first "to perceive that the age of the Earth was so great as to be almost beyond human comprehension." Hutton proposed to think in huge ranges of years—millions upon hundreds of millions—to conceive of the great processes of rock formation, disintegration, and re-formation.

There was a parallel here to the neoclassicism that was at the core of the Enlightenment. Its thinkers understood that their politics and philosophies were built on the rubble of the ancient world. Hutton captured the inquisitive spirit of his time when he commented to a friend that given sufficient attention, "a bag of gravel is a history to me, and . . . will tell wondrous tales."

One measure of the significance of a new idea is the degree to which it spurs new thinking in other areas. Truly big ideas provoke paradigm shifts. Hutton's thinking about the age of the world appears to be related to Adam Smith's on economics and even more to James Watt's work on steam engines. The span of geological time—the current thinking is that the Earth is about 4.6 billion years old—also suggested that the Earth may not have been created only for the use of humans, who according to Hutton's scale are relative newcomers. Charles Darwin in turn may have arrived at his theory of natural selection in part by combining Hutton's conception of vast time with his friend Adam Smith's theories of the free market, applying both to the natural world. Darwin himself had attended the University of Edinburgh but dropped out after deciding he did not want to be a doctor. About five years later, at the end of 1831, he began his years-long voyage aboard the HMS *Beagle* by reading a copy of a geology textbook based on Hutton's theories.

There probably is a good book to be written about how the sense of time changed first in the Enlightenment and then in the Industrial Revolution. Clocks abounded in the houses of the founders, placed in corners, on mantelpieces, and atop entryways. "Probably more than any other of the notable American statesman, Jefferson had a special interest in timepieces," notes a curator at the Smithsonian Institution. On the ground floor of Monticello, every room but one has a clock. The control of time had moved from the church tower to inside the house, and in doing so had become more precise.

## The Scots Tutor America

THE SCOTTISH PRESENCE BECAME AN ESSENTIAL ASPECT OF THE COLOnial American economy.

During his handful of years of practicing law, Jefferson frequently represented Glasgow merchants seeking to recover loans on which Virginia planters reneged. Tobacco of course was also one of his major crops.

Young university graduates in Scotland looking for work—and there were more of them around, because the country's infant mortality rates dropped during the eighteenth century—found inexpensive passage to America aboard the tobacco ships, in a kind of reverse intellectual Gulf Stream. At the peak of the tobacco trade, in the 1760s, about twenty-six ships sailed every year from Glasgow to the Chesapeake—that is, about one every two weeks. Among the early Scotsmen to arrive was James Blair (Edinburgh, 1673), who helped found William & Mary in 1693 and then presided over it for some fifty years. All in all, it has been calculated that some 211 men who had college or university degrees from Scotland emigrated to America between 1680 and 1780, with many of them landing in tobacco country on the shores of the Chesapeake Bay. That region received more graduates from Scottish institutions than from Oxford and Cambridge. Likewise, more Americans enrolled at the University of Glasgow during the colonial period than went to either Oxford or Cambridge.

So it was hardly unusual that Jefferson had a young Scot as his first tutor. "It has been the custom heretofore to have all their Tutors, and Schoolmasters from Scotland," noted Philip Fithian

(Princeton, 1772), the Carter family tutor, who was an anomaly in that he was from New Jersey—albeit one dispatched from there to Virginia by the president of Princeton, who was himself a Scotsman. As a historian of early American education put it, "It is not much of an exaggeration to say that, outside of New England, the Scots were the educators of eighteenth-century America."

Intensifying the impact of the Scottish Enlightenment, the tobacco ships also transported boxloads of books. The Foulis brothers, at the time the leading publishers of classical literature in the English-speaking world, were located in Glasgow, making it convenient to get their books aboard America-bound vessels. The Foulises were known for taking great pains to make their books both beautiful and accurate. Their so-called immaculate 1744 edition of the works of the Roman poet Horace—a particular favorite of Enlightenment thinkers—was widely believed not to contain a single mistake. In fact, there actually were six errors eventually found in the entire work, but this was still exceptional, coming in an era when many books contained one or more mistranslations or typographical errors per page. Jefferson preferred Foulis editions all his life, praising "the perfection of accuracy . . . found in the folio edn of Homer by the Foulis of Glasgow. I have understood they offered 1000–Guineas for the discovery of any error in it, even of an accent, & that the reward was never claimed."

Because of the tobacco connection, the Caledonian influence was strongest in the mid-Atlantic colonies and the South. Far more than the French, German, or English versions of the Enlightenment, the Scottish approach influenced late colonial America. New England was the region least affected by the Scottish intellectual revolution, but even in Massachusetts, some Scottish influence seeped in, through divines who received their higher degrees in Scotland, and by the odd émigré, such as John Campbell, founder of the first colonial American newspaper, the weekly *Boston News-Letter.* Harvard's early commencements featured debates by graduating students. This was "a practice unknown at contemporary Cambridge and Oxford," notes one academic, but "duplicates contemporary commencement sheets from the University of Edinburgh."

In sum, as one historian puts it, "the Scottish Enlightenment, above all other versions of that western world intellectual phenomenon, took on a heightened significance in the fashioning of the early republic. The story of the rise of the Scottish Enlightenment and the transmission of its ideas to America is fundamental to the history of American thought."

Notably, the empiricism of the Scottish philosophers appears to have stuck with Jefferson all his life. He relied on the evidence of his senses, taking them to convey the basic facts of the world. As an old man he wrote a letter to John Adams summarizing his view of reality:

> *Rejecting all organs of information therefore but my senses, I rid myself of the Pyrrhonisms* [the ancient Greek philosopher Pyrrho's doctrine of complete uncertainty] *with which an indulgence in speculations hyperphysical and antiphysical so uselessly occupy and disquiet the mind. A single sense may indeed be sometimes decieved, but rarely; and never all our senses together, with their faculty of reasoning. They evidence realities; and there are enough of these for all the purposes of life, without plunging into the fathomless abyss of dreams & phantasms. I am satisfied, and sufficiently occupied with the things which are, without tormenting or troubling myself about those which may indeed be, but of which I have no evidence.*

## Jefferson Studies with Yet Another Cato

MEANWHILE, MATTERS DIDN'T IMPROVE AT THE SMALL, TROUBLED College of William & Mary. In 1762, Jefferson moved from there a few blocks to the east to study law in the offices of George Wythe, a man of what Jefferson called "exalted virtue." Becoming Wythe's student, he later wrote, was "one of the most fortunate events" of his life.

George Wythe, then about thirty-five years old, would become a lifelong friend and inspiration to Jefferson. Among his other legal work, he advised George Washington on land acquisitions. Perhaps even more than Jefferson, Wythe saw the new world through a classical lens. Unusually, he had studied the ancient texts with his widowed mother, who somehow had managed to learn Latin and Greek. Little is known about her background, but she must have been an excellent teacher, for Wythe became known, Jefferson wrote, as "the best Greek and Latin scholar in the state." Wythe, he added, "might truly be called the Cato of his country."

In keeping with the Scottish approach, Wythe as a judge tended to cite classical precedents far more than was usual in the English legal system. As chief of the Virginia Chancery Court in the 1790s, he reviewed twenty-one cases and cited classical literature some eighty-five times. "Classical allusions were exceedingly rare in English courts, since Roman precedents were irrelevant to the common law," observes one historian.

Wythe's knowledge of ancient literature "has been rarely equaled in this country," concurred William Wirt, a near-contemporary who would go on to be the United States' longest-serving attorney general. "He was perfectly familiar with the authors of Rome and Greece; read them with the same ease, and quoted them with the same promptitude that he could the authors in his native tongue." Indeed, Wirt found Wythe excessive in his classicism, which is saying something for an era in which elites were saturated in Greco-Roman allusions: "He carried his love of antiquity rather too far; for he frequently subjected himself to the charge of pedantry."

Indeed, Wythe was so prone to cite classical literature that his contemporaries seemed to treat it a bit sardonically. "He could hardly refrain from giving a line of Horace the force of an act of Assembly, not could forbear from quoting the authority of Aulus Gellius [a minor Latin grammarian]," sighed one Virginia chronicler.

## Jefferson's Readings

———

IT WAS UNDER WYTHE THAT JEFFERSON RECEIVED WHAT ONE SCHOLAR calls "his real education." He studied two subjects with Wythe—the law and ancient literature, especially Greek. Under his new teacher, he seems to have begun by diving into Euripides, followed by Herodotus and Homer.

Jefferson's literary commonplace book, a kind of diary of his reading with excerpts, shows what books held his attention at this time. The entries are undated, but experts on his handwriting say that it was probably in the early 1760s that he copied in Greek a quotation from Euripides, the fifth-century Athenian tragedian, that in translation reads: "The words of truth are simple, and justice needs no subtle interpretations, for it has a fitness in itself; but the words of injustice, being rotten in themselves, require clever treatment." Jefferson did not always follow this counsel to be simple in his writing, but he certainly seemed to remember it when he drafted the Declaration of Independence more than a decade later. There are some seventy quotations from Euripides in his commonplace book, more than from any other author.

The longest single set of extracts in the commonplace book is from *The Philosophical Works of the late Right Honorable Henry St. John, Lord Viscount Bolingbroke,* constituting some 40 percent of the entire collection. Jefferson wrote those down a year or two later, in about 1765. Now largely forgotten, Bolingbroke, a British politician and writer, was seen in the eighteenth century as a major figure in political and ethical philosophy. Jefferson copied into his book Bolingbroke's irreligious observation that while Christ did not offer a complete system of ethics, the ancient world did: "A system thus collected from the writings of ancient heathen moralists, of Tully [Cicero], of Seneca, of Epictetus, and others, would be more full, more entire, more coherent, and more clearly deduced from unquestionable principles of knowledge." Jefferson would come to own some thirteen volumes by Bolingbroke and hail Bolingbroke's style as of "the highest order." This may have been because the Englishman's prose style was strongly classical.

It wasn't just Virginians who were taken with Bolingbroke. John Adams also read him assiduously as a young man, and mentions the Englishman several times in his diaries. Typical is this entry from December 1, 1760: "I arose by the dawning of the day, and by sunrise had made my fire and read a number of pages in Bolingbroke." Adams agreed with Jefferson on Bolingbroke's high style but not on his attack on Christianity:

> *His Ideas of the English Constitution are correct and his Political Writings are worth something: but in a great part of them there is more of Faction than of Truth: His Religion is a pompous Folly: and his Abuse of the Christian Religion is as superficial as it is impious. His Style is original and inimitable: it resembles more the oratory of the Ancients, than any Writings or Speeches I ever read in English.*

At that point in American life, to say that someone matched the style of "the Ancients" was the highest possible praise.

Alexander Pope's *Essay on Man*, one of that poet's most famous works, is addressed to Bolingbroke, and in fact was deeply influenced by him. (Pope also was a friend of Joseph Addison, author of the play *Cato*, and wrote a poetic prologue for it, invoking "virtue" three times in its first seventeen lines.) In his *Essay*, Pope famously instructed the reader to

> *Know then thyself, presume not God to scan;*
> *The proper study of Mankind is Man.*

Jefferson seems to have read *Essay on Man* as an adolescent, and copied some of its lines into his commonplace book, as he did similar sentiments from Bolingbroke: "I say that the law of nature is the law of god. . . . [Of] this I have as certain, as intuitive, knowledge, as I have that two and two are equal to four, or that the whole is bigger than the part."

Jefferson's early religious skepticism is reflected in another passage from Bolingbroke that questions the notion that Christ died for man's sins:

*Let us suppose a great prince governing a wicked and rebellious people. He has it in his power to punish, he thinks fit to pardon them. But he orders his only and beloved son to be put to death to expiate their sins.*

Even Jefferson's reading of Shakespeare had a classical aspect. Of the sixteen passages of Shakespeare that he copied into his commonplace book, more than half are from two of the plays set in ancient Rome—*Julius Caesar* and *Coriolanus*. He also wrote out four lines from Ben Jonson's play *The Cataline Conspiracy*.

At some point—it isn't clear when—Jefferson also delved into the works of Xenophon. Today we remember that Greek soldier and philosopher primarily for his *Anabasis*, an account of the retreat of Greek mercenaries from what is now central Iraq to the Black Sea, after being hired to fight on the losing side in a Persian civil war in 401 BC. But the founders read quite widely in other works by Xenophon, especially the *Memorabilia*, his memoir of Socrates. Jefferson greatly preferred Xenophon's account of Socrates to Plato's. "Of Socrates we have nothing genuine but in the *Memorabilia* of Xenophon," he asserted. "For Plato makes him one of his Collocutors merely to cover his own whimsies under the mantle of his name."

The two accounts of Socrates indeed differ sharply. Plato's Socrates, writes the classical scholar Jeffrey Henderson, is "unworldly, aloof, and hyper-intellectual," while Xenophon's is "down-to-earth, handy, and practical as well as philosophical and comfortable in any society." In particular, Henderson adds, Plato's Socrates shows no interest in running a large farm, while Xenophon's goes on at some length about it and displays expertise in the subject. In his agrarian disposition, Xenophon's Socrates certainly seems closer to Jefferson's views. At one point, for example, the Greek philosopher persuades one of his interlocutors that "farming is the fairest, noblest, and most pleasant way to earn a living," a sentiment Jefferson held throughout his life.

## Jefferson and Montesquieu

IN 1767, JEFFERSON, WITHOUT ANY FANFARE, TRANSITIONED INTO PRACTICING law. Two years later he was elected to the House of Burgesses. Perhaps as a consequence of his new political position, his reading turned from philosophy to governance. He ordered a stack of books from T. Cadell, a London bookshop, among them John Locke's *On Government* and the works of Montesquieu.

He also began a legal commonplace book, to record passages that struck him in his studies of law. Most of it is just a basic study of English law of the day—definitions of property, marriage, and so on. "In cases of burglary, an actual breaking is necessary," he copied. "If the window of a house be open, and a thief with a hook draw out some good of the owner, it is not burglary."

He also wrote out twenty-seven excerpts from the writings of Charles-Louis de Secondat, Baron de La Brède et de Montesquieu. This seems to have been his first encounter with the French philosophe. Decades later he would cool to Montesquieu, but at this point, he seemed quite taken with him. Locke, by comparison, receives just one passage in the legal commonplace collection.

Jefferson also copied out a section of Temple Stanyan's *Grecian History*, the standard text of the eighteenth century, which may have helped shape his future views of American independence. The Sicilian city of Syracuse began as a colony of Corinth, notes Stanyan, but it grew "large and beautiful," and as it "increased in power," it came to renounce its "obedience" to Corinth. So, too, would come a time when it would become necessary for the American colonies to renounce the political bands that had connected them with their mother country, and to assume among the powers of the earth a separate and equal station.

## Jefferson the Epicurean

EPICURUS DOES NOT SEEM TO APPEAR IN EITHER OF THE COMMONPLACE books, literary or legal, which raises the question of when Jefferson first encountered the philosopher who would influence him so deeply. The available evidence indicates that it happened in March 1767. His "Memorandum Books" show that he then was reading Diogenes Laertius, a third-century AD biographer of Greek philosophers. Laertius' work concludes with a long and enthusiastic discussion of Epicurus that quotes this philosopher extensively. "Pleasure is the beginning and end of living happily," Epicurus states in a letter that Laertius quotes. But, he continues, "we are not speaking of the pleasures of a debauched man, . . . but we mean the freedom of the body from pain, and of the soul from confusion."

Oddly, for all his influence and extensive writings, few of Epicurus' actual words have survived, mainly in the form of a handful of letters and a short collection of his sayings. Most of what we know of his teaching comes from the commentaries of others—mainly Diogenes Laertius, the Roman poet Lucretius, and Cicero. Even the known facts of his life are few. Epicurus was born in 341 BC on Samos, an island just off the coast of today's western Turkey. His father probably was a schoolteacher, and he seems to have helped his father and then gone on to teach himself. While an adolescent, he began to think about philosophy, probably beginning with the nature of chaos. He developed a regional following. In 306 he moved to Athens and established "the Garden," a community where he taught his view that the best use of life was to seek tranquility and pleasure. His school achieved some notoriety for admitting women, who were perhaps prostitutes, as students, and also because he was suspected of disregarding the gods. He died in about 270 of a painful blockage caused by kidney stones.

Jefferson would remain devoted to Epicurean thought for the remainder of his life. He summarized that belief system thusly:

*Happiness the aim of life.*
*Virtue the foundation of happiness*
*Utility the test of virtue . . .*
*Virtue consists in*

>  1. *Prudence*
>  2. *Temperance*
>  3. *Fortitude*
>  4. *Justice*

A few years later he bought a six-volume set about Epicurus by the French astronomer, priest, and philosopher Pierre Gassendi.

Later in life, in a letter to William Short (William & Mary, 1779), his former private secretary, he would declare that "I too am an Epicurean." He considered the ancient Greek to have given us the "most rational system remaining of the philosophy of the ancients, as frugal of vicious indulgence, and fruitful of virtue as the hyperbolical extravagancies of his rival sects." When one seeks to understand Jefferson, it is almost always helpful to look to Epicurus.

## What Jefferson Did Not Know or Do

JEFFERSON IS IN MANY WAYS THE MOST COMPLEX OF THE FOUNDERS, someone with, as the historian Carl Becker puts it, a "sensitized mind [that] picked up and transmitted every novel vibration in the intellectual air." But it is also vital to remember what Jefferson did not know or do. He would not bear arms in the War for Independence. He criticized slavery repeatedly in his life but never did much to end it.

Nor did he ever personally experience the American frontier, which is odd. Washington had traveled deeply into it, and Jefferson's own father rode all over Virginia's frontier, but Jefferson would never go beyond Virginia's Shenandoah Valley, just a day's ride west of his home. This fact bears some contemplation. The frontier, and the huge, rich expanse beyond it, was a major factor in American life at the time of the Revolution, and would remain so for another 120 years—but Jefferson never ventured into it, although he would send others to explore it. It was an odd omission for such an inquisitive man. One can only wonder if Monticello's position facing eastward is symbolic of his perspective.

He would prove far more mobile in his travels in Europe. Peter Gay, the historian of the Enlightenment, may have been correct when he asserted that, "Thomas Jefferson was European to the bone." Or perhaps Jefferson was just too much of an Epicurean to want to endure the discomforts of frontier life. As he once wrote in a parting letter to a lover, the beautiful Italian-English artist Maria Cosway: "The art of life is the art of avoiding pain." That is a recipe for Epicureanism, but it also provides a pathway for emotional withdrawal. Indeed, that letter continued, "The most effectual means of being secure against pain is to retire within ourselves, and to suffice for our own happiness."

This approach might also have enabled him to justify his failure to examine his own contradictions, if by doing so he would suffer pain or confusion. It might have been too discomfiting for him to recognize that as a man, he was forward thinking but not forward acting. This tension may have been one reason he would be so ambivalent and uneven in his exercise of power.

◆━━━◆

## Chapter 5

# Madison Breaks
# Away to Princeton

O F THE FIRST FOUR PRESIDENTS, JAMES MADISON WAS THE ONE most influenced by Scottish thinking of the time, which led him to the Enlightenment and from there to Roman and Greek history and philosophy.

He was born into wealth, the great-great-grandson of an English ship's carpenter who in the mid-seventeenth century began accumulating land in Virginia. By the time of the birth of James Madison a century later, his family's plantation consisted of thousands of acres of beautiful, rich farmland and forest that looked west toward the Blue Ridge and Shenandoah Mountains. His first teachers probably were family members, who gave him the basics of reading and writing.

From the ages of eleven to sixteen, little "Jemmy" Madison, as his friends and parents called him, studied under Donald Robertson, about whom little is known except that he was born in Scotland in 1717, attended the University of Edinburgh, and emigrated to Virginia in the early 1750s. Madison thought him an excellent teacher, later describing him as "a man of great learning, and an eminent teacher." Not much more is known about this early instructor of the future president.

## Madison and Montesquieu

LUCKILY, THERE ARE RECORDS OF THE CONTENTS OF ROBERTSON'S LIbrary. So we can conclude that, like John Adams, Madison probably was educated partly by Dodsley's *Preceptor*, which stood on Robertson's shelves, alongside works by Horace, Justinian, Sallust, Montaigne, Locke, and Montesquieu.

The last of those authors bears pausing to consider, because the works of Montesquieu constituted a bridge between the Enlightenment and the classical world. In his study of the Enlightenment, Peter Gay finds that "Montesquieu was the most influential writer of the eighteenth century." The Frenchman's thinking had an impact from France to Russia to Italy, Gay adds, but most of all in Scotland. There, his *Spirit of Laws* became "the common coin of learned discussion," always in the background even when not explicitly acknowledged.

Montesquieu came from nobility. He was born in 1689 in a fourteenth-century castle with a moat about ten miles south of the southwestern French port of Bordeaux. He received the classical education then traditional in the aristocracy, and went on to study law. His first book, published in 1721, was *Persian Letters*, a wry look at French society through the eyes of two fictional Persian travelers. Next came his study of the Roman Republic, *Considerations on the Causes of the Greatness of the Romans and Their Decline.*

His masterpiece, *The Spirit of Laws*, appeared in 1748. Though politically controversial in France for its skepticism of monarchy, it was enormously successful and soon was translated into English and other languages. Sir Isaiah Berlin, the twentieth-century British philosopher, concluded that Montesquieu's impact remains all around us, pervasive yet often unseen, in the form of modern liberal democracy. Three hundred years ago, Berlin wrote, the French philosophe

> advocated constitutionalism, the preservation of civil liberties, the
> abolition of slavery; gradualism, moderation, peace, internation-
> alism, social and economic progress with due respect to national
> and local tradition. He believed in justice and the rule of law; de-
> fended freedom of opinion and association; detested all forms of

*extremism and fanaticism; put his faith in the balance of power
and the division of authority as a weapon against despotic rule by
individuals or groups or majorities; and approved of social equality, but not to the point at which it threatened individual liberty;
and of liberty, but not to the point where it threatened to disrupt
orderly government.*

It is probable that during his five years with Robertson, Madison read *The Spirit of Laws* and pondered its observations on law,
justice, and governance. Here the young man would have been
introduced to many of the questions that would occupy him for
decades, particularly during the drafting of the Constitution and
in his defense of it in the Federalist Papers. How can a republic
be made sustainable? And can a large and expanding nation even
be a genuine republic? How can smaller entities confederate into
something larger? Is there a way for a nation to wield the power of
a large state while retaining the flexibility of a smaller one?

In his writings, Montesquieu always looked first and foremost
to Rome and Greece. "It is impossible," he sighs happily at one
point, "to be tired of so agreeable a subject as ancient Rome." The
beginning of *The Spirit of Laws* is essentially a meditation on how
to inject ancient wisdom into modern governance. Of the twenty
chapters in Montesquieu's Book XI, for example, twelve are about
the Romans and Greeks. Hardly a page of its first volume goes by
without some look into the classical world—an invocation of the
details of the laws of Rome, Athens, and Sparta; or the observations of Plato, Tacitus, and Livy; or a denunciation of the licen-
tiousness of ancient Syracuse.

Montesquieu concluded that large nations could not be republics, flatly stating that "it is natural for a republic to have only a
small territory; otherwise it cannot long subsist." This observation would become a major issue when Americans two decades
later turned to drafting a Constitution.

In *Considerations on the Causes of the Greatness of the Romans and
Their Decline*, Montesquieu dwelled even more on the peculiar

vulnerabilities of republics. "What makes free states last a shorter time than others is that both the misfortunes and the successes they encounter almost always cause them to lose their freedom," the French thinker warned. "A wise republic should hazard nothing that exposes it to either good or bad fortune. The only good to which it should aspire is the perpetuation of its condition." Such observations are of historical interest to us, but to the colonial generation they must have carried the urgency of news bulletins. Could they design a republic that avoided the pitfalls the Frenchman described? If so, how?

Jefferson was notably ambivalent about the French philosopher. "In the science of government Montesquieu's spirit of laws is generally recommended. It contains indeed a great number of political truths; but almost an equal number of political heresies: so that the reader must be constantly on his guard." Jefferson did not detail his objections, but he likely was irked by Montesquieu's conclusion that a major cause of Rome's decline was Epicurean thought.

Madison finished off his secondary education by studying two years with Thomas Martin, a 1762 graduate of the College of New Jersey at Princeton.

That brought a significant decision: Where to go to college? There had been no question that if John Adams went to college, it would be to Harvard, and the same was true for Jefferson with William & Mary. But Madison was living in a new era. By 1769, when it came time for him to make his pick, resistance floated in the air of the colonies. The Stamp Act, meant to assert British authority over the colonies and to raise revenue to pay for the French and Indian War, had been fought, successfully, leading to its repeal in 1766. But it soon was followed by other punitive moves by Parliament, collectively known as the Townshend Acts.

One American college caught Madison's eye. It had led the way in engaging with the times: the College of New Jersey, now known as Princeton. It was to the America of the 1760s what the University of California at Berkeley would be two hundred years later, a hotbed of political activism, capturing public attention.

## Madison's Choice

———

INFLUENCED BY MARTIN, MADISON DECIDED AGAINST ATTENDING WILliam & Mary, which would have been the normal choice for a wealthy young Virginian. Irving Brant, Madison's most thorough biographer, calls Madison's decision to go to distant Princeton "an act of near-treason to Virginia." Madison said later that with his fragile health, he wanted to avoid the swampy, even pestilential climate of Williamsburg. He also may have been put off by the Virginia college's decaying reputation—it was, reports one historian, "in a dissolute and unenviable state." But Madison probably was being discreet. Times had changed from when one simply went to the nearest college.

Also, Madison was a son not of the old Virginia Tidewater, but of the newer settlements farther west in the foothills of the Blue Ridge. This area was home to several Presbyterian missionaries educated at Princeton, so he may have seen his choice of Princeton partly as an act of loyalty to the Piedmont.

At about the same time Madison was contemplating his future course, George Washington likewise decided against sending his dissolute stepson, Jacky Custis, to William & Mary. Having looked into the state of the college and its environment, Washington recorded that "from the best enquiries I could make whilst I was in, and about Williamsburg I cannot think William and Mary College a desirable place to send Jack Custis to—the Inattention of the Masters, added to the number of Hollidays, is the subject of general complaint; & affords no pleasing prospect to a youth who has a good deal to attain, & but a short while to do it in." Likewise, Robert Carter, an influential Virginia planter who had attended William & Mary before studying law in London, and who had hired Philip Fithian to tutor his children, decided that the college was "in such confusion at present, & so badly directed, that he cannot send his Children with propriety there for Improvement & useful Education—That he has known the Professors to play all

Night at Cards in publick houses in the City, and has often seen them drunken in the street!"

Washington's disinclination to send young Custis to William & Mary probably was not political in motivation, because he eventually decided to enroll him at King's College in New York, now Columbia University. King's was the most Tory of any college in the colonies, having been founded by Anglicans in conservative reaction to Princeton and Yale. After delivering the boy to New York, Washington managed to take in a performance of *Hamlet*—apparently the first time he ever saw Shakespeare staged. But his attention to his stepson's education proved otherwise fruitless, as the restless young man dropped out only a few months later.

James Madison was a far more diligent young man than Jacky Custis. Unlike much of Virginia's gentry, Madison was never seduced by the pastimes of gambling, boozing, and horseracing. In the summer of 1769, he set out northward for Princeton on horseback, accompanied by his tutor, his tutor's brother, and a favored enslaved person named Swaney. Young Madison was a good match for the young college, which led American higher education at the time in both educational progressivism and political activism. Its leaders expressly looked beyond educating ministers to preparing men to run their society. Samuel Davies, president of the college in 1761, proclaimed that it was "a Seminary of Loyalty, as well as Learning, and Piety; a Nursery for the State, as well as the Church."

Founded in 1746, the college was just five years older than young Madison. Like the Scottish universities, it was religiously tolerant. The college's founders had stated "that those of every religious Denomination may have free and equal Liberty and Advantage of Education in the said College any different Sentiments in Religion notwithstanding."

Just by choosing to go there, Madison may have been following an inclination toward political engagement. Here there is a contrast with his eventual mentor, the more sensual Thomas Jefferson, who loved many things—among them, books, ideas, music, wine, French cuisine, and married women. As the historian Mary

Sarah Bilder observes, the colder Madison, who did not marry until the age of forty-three, may have loved just one thing: politics. And also, perhaps, maps—in his library at Montpelier he had some two hundred maps and atlases. But not people. "Mr. Madison a gloomy, stiff creature, they say is clever in Congress, but out of it has nothing engaging or even bearable in his manners—the most unsociable creature in Existence," commented Martha Dangerfield Bland, wife of another Virginian politician.

Madison must have reveled in colonial Princeton. As one biographer phrases it, the college "smoked with rebellion." One visitor to the campus was perplexed to find that the young men, whom he had expected to be preparing for the ministry, plunged into "discussing . . . the most perplexing political topics." As another Madison biographer put it, "The College of New Jersey in Madison's day was the seedbed of sedition and nursery of rebels Tory critics charged it with being." The college could get away with such activism in part because it was not as financially dependent on a provincial legislature as were other colleges of the time. Early political and religious differences with New Jersey's government had forced it to become relatively self-sufficient. This environment must have been electrifying to a contemplative young man who had grown up somewhat isolated in rural Virginia.

Significantly for Madison's future thinking, Princeton was also the first national college, even before there was a nation. The college had been "conceived of as an integrative institution," "an intercolonial and cosmopolitan institution as Harvard, William and Mary, and Yale had never been," and it had quickly become so. At a time when 90 percent of Harvard's student body came from Massachusetts and 75 percent of Yale's from Connecticut, Princeton by design drew from the entire Eastern Seaboard. Of 301 young men who attended it in the two decades before Madison arrived, 59 percent were from New York, Pennsylvania, and New Jersey; 28 percent from New England; and 13 percent from Delaware, Maryland, Virginia, North Carolina, and South Carolina. There also were students from Canada and the West Indies.

It was a good place for Madison to develop an understanding of both the commonalities and sectional interests of the colonies.

Another sign of Madison's politicization was that he had been there only a few weeks when he mailed to Martin, his old tutor, two copies of a pamphlet on the English republican radical John Wilkes. Later that year, Madison attended a commencement exercise at which honorary degrees were awarded to two leaders of colonial American resistance to the British: John Hancock (Harvard, 1754) and John Dickinson. Hancock had been arrested the previous year and his sloop, *Liberty*, had been seized, supposedly for not paying duties on a shipment of madeira wine, in a case that appeared to be trumped up. Dickinson later acquired a reputation as a conservative revolutionary, but at this point was known for his series of public letters that "more than any other individual articulated the radical position of the 1760s."

## Madison Meets Witherspoon

IN ITS REACH, IN ITS ECUMENISM, AND IN ITS VERY STYLE, THIS LIVELY school was surprisingly Scottish. The College of New Jersey of 1769 was "a provincial carbon copy of Edinburgh," concludes Douglass Adair, a specialist in the intellectual history of the founders. The resemblance was in large part attributable to one dynamic man, John Witherspoon, the Scottish-born president of the college. Witherspoon in just a few years, states one of Madison's biographers, had "remade the college into a major outpost of the Scottish enlightenment." He also would develop into a significant political figure, ultimately becoming the only clergyman or college president to sign the Declaration of Independence or to serve in the Continental Congress.

President Witherspoon is a striking and unusual figure in early American history. He was the first person brought from overseas to lead an American college. A 1739 graduate of the University of Edinburgh, he had emigrated in 1768 to the colonies not as a young man looking for a start in life, as so many tutors did, but as a married man with five surviving children. Yet even in his middle age he had a rebellious streak. A heavyset but vigorous and charming man of medium height, he brought great energy to the college, updating the syllabus, expanding the library, and generally making the college more competitive. Remarkably, he managed simultaneously to upgrade admission standards, expand the enrollment, and put the college on a sound financial footing. Partly because of Witherspoon's contributions, the college library grew to 1,500 volumes, considered impressive at the time. Here is how one intellectual historian summarizes his achievement: "Witherspoon put the College of New Jersey at the head of higher education in America, where it remained at least until the revitalization of Yale under Timothy Dwight at the end of the eighteenth century and the renaissance of Harvard early in the nineteenth."

Like any good product of the Scottish Enlightenment, Witherspoon steered by classical reference points. When he built a country house outside Princeton in 1773, he named it Tusculum, for the town southeast of Rome where Cicero had his country villa. Not surprisingly, his favorite French writer was Montesquieu. For his journalism, he employed the pseudonym Epaminondas, a reference to the great Theban general who appears in Xenophon's *Hellenica*.

Preparing for a planned trip to promote the college and persuade the planters of Jamaica, Barbados, and other parts of the West Indies to send their sons to Princeton, Witherspoon wrote a speech describing the college's approach. The curriculum was the classical one of Greek and Latin languages, philosophy, history, and mathematics. But he also was making room for the teaching of science, as well as English and French literature, at the time considered daring moves. As it happened, he did not make the Caribbean voyage, but mailed to planters in the islands copies of the talk he had prepared.

He also was a progressive about discipline. He informed his audiences that he did not believe in flogging his students: "No correction by stripes is permitted." Rather, he said, the students are governed by "the principles of honor and shame." All the teaching, he said, was done by himself and three tutors, but he planned to add a professor of mathematics. The school was independent of government, led by those averse to "a fawning, cringing spirit," and aimed to imbue a "spirit of liberty and independence," he stated.

"All persons, young and old, love liberty: and as far as it does them no harm, it will certainly do them good," he wrote in an essay. "Let them romp and jump about as soon as they are able."

## Madison the Student

ARRIVING AT NASSAU HALL, WHICH HOUSED THE COLLEGE, MADISON would have seen the bust of Homer then overlooking its central doorway. Entering the college, he would find one drawback to his having studied with Scottish tutors. He learned, to his chagrin, that he spoke French with a Scottish brogue that made him quite incomprehensible to speakers of the language.

Aside from that embarrassment, he took to Princeton swimmingly, despite being pale, sickly, and small, standing a few inches above five feet and weighing less than 140 pounds. He was slight even by the standards of his own time. The writer Washington Irving, encountering him years later, would write, "Ah! poor Jemmy!—he is but a withered little apple-John." Madison was extremely discreet about his health, but many years later would allude to his seizures in autobiographical notes, stating that "causes preventing him from entering the Army, viz his feeble health, and a Constitutional liability, to sudden attacks, somewhat resembling Epilepsy, and suspending the intellectual functions."

It may be telling that the two students who became his closest friends at Princeton were not other sons of the Southern gentry, like him, but rather the offspring of successful urban merchants of the North. William Bradford was the son of a Philadelphia printer, publisher, and bookseller, while Philip Freneau's father was a wine importer in New York. Neither of the fathers owned enslaved people. Madison's fellows noticed almost immediately his intense studiousness. Despite his physical fragility, Madison studied far into the night, even though the students were awakened at five o'clock for morning prayers. They and the tutors took their meals together, occasionally joined by President Witherspoon. "The general table-drink is small-beer or cyder. For supper, milk only is the standing allowance."

Madison found an atmosphere of intellectual freedom. Samuel Blair, in his overview of the college from the previous decade, emphasized that students were free to disagree with their teachers: "In the instruction of the youth, care is taken to cherish a spirit of liberty, and free enquiry; and not only to permit, but even encourage their right of private judgment, without presuming to dictate with an air of infallibility, or demanding an implicit assent to the decisions of the preceptor."

The freshman course focused on Greek and Latin authors—Horace, Cicero's *Orations*, Lucian's *Dialogues*, Xenophon's *Cyropaedia*. In the last of these, they would read about an ancient constitution that mandated equal rights and freedom of speech for its citizens. It was a sign of the thoroughness of Madison's preparation that just about a month after arriving, he took and passed the freshman-year examinations, and so was allowed to skip that first year of studies. Thus he began with the sophomore course, which plunged deeper into Greek and Latin, and began classes on "the sciences, geography, rhetoric, logic, and the mathematics."

Politics swirled through the corridors of Nassau Hall. In the summer of 1770, the merchants of New York bowed to Parliament and began importing British merchandise, ending their observance of a general colonial agreement to shun imports. Madison reported to his father that the students of Princeton responded with a funereal protest march in mid-July and that a message from the New Yorkers "to the Merchants in Philadelphia requesting their concurrence was lately burnt by the Students of this place

in the college Yard, all of them appearing in their black Gowns &
the bell Tolling." That fall, at the end of Madison's first year, one
of the commencement speakers was Witherspoon's son James,
whose subject was the obligation to resist a king who acts cruelly
or unlawfully.

The junior year added logic and moral philosophy, the latter a
core subject for Witherspoon. In the first sentence of his 1748 *Enquiry Concerning Human Understanding*, Hume had defined "moral
philosophy" as "the science of human nature." Witherspoon, for
his part, divided the subject into "Ethics" and "Politics." The former
might be taken as being about governing the individual, while
the latter is about governing society. Today such a course might
be considered something like an overview of political and social
science. Back then it would have been seen as instruction on how
to be a virtuous person and how to cultivate a society of virtuous
individuals—with all the import that virtue carried in the eighteenth century.

Half of Witherspoon's lectures in the subject, records one educational historian, were on issues such as the "problems of rights
and obligations, government and society property and contracts,
and civil and international law." He placed a special emphasis on
the need for civil liberty, and so on the consequent obligation of
free men to resist tyranny. In one lecture he listed the legitimate
reasons for rebellion. "There was a high value in this to Madison,"
wrote one of his biographers, "for it introduced him to public law
as something alive and growing, and it helped him to see America
as a field for its growth."

Attending Witherspoon's fourth lecture on moral philosophy,
Madison first would have heard the professor examine various definitions of "virtue," and then consider how it operates in the world.
"True virtue certainly promotes the general good," Witherspoon
stated. "Private and public interest . . . are distinct views; they
should be made to assist, and not destroy each other."

In the next lecture, Witherspoon discussed how conflicts between the interests of different people or groups might be addressed in government:

*Hence it appears that every good form of government must be complex, so that the one principle may check the other. It is of consequence to have as much virtue among the particular members of a community as possible; but it is folly to expect that a state should be upheld by integrity in all who have a share in managing it. They must be so balanced, that when one draws to his own interest or inclination, there may be an over poise upon the whole.*

In this discussion of checks and balances, Witherspoon may have planted the seeds of the all-important tenth of Madison's Federalist Papers, written nearly two decades later, in which Madison explains how interests can balance each other in a government expressly designed to curb excessive power in any one person or branch. At the same time, Madison appears to have disregarded or discarded Witherspoon's view that "the Roman Empire fell of its own weight," a warning against nations growing too large.

In the senior year, all previous subjects were reviewed, with a new emphasis on writing and debating, or "disputation." These older students learned to speak before audiences, delivering both sermons and orations. The evidence is that the weak-voiced Madison was not very good at either form of public speaking and was excused from giving a speech at his graduation. He officially graduated in September 1771, but stayed on studying until the following spring, mainly, he said, because he felt too weak to travel home. But he also simply may not have wanted to leave Princeton.

## Washington Aroused, Jefferson Not So Much

BY APRIL 1769, EVEN STOLID GEORGE WASHINGTON WAS BEGINNING TO sound a bit revolutionary. It was typical of him that when he was pondering a problem, he tackled the issue as directly as possible. So, for example, he opened a letter to his neighbor, the pensive George Mason, with the thought that

> *At a time when our lordly Masters in Great Britain will be satisfied with nothing less than the deprivation of American freedom, it seems highly necessary that something shou'd be done to avert the stroke and maintain the liberty which we have derived from our Ancestors.*

But the question, he continued, was just how to keep hold of that "liberty"? Taking up arms ultimately may prove necessary, he ventured, but only as a last resort. Interim steps would be required. Hence, he was mulling the "non-importation agreement" being circulated among leaders of the colonies.

Mason responded the very same day. "Our All is at Stake," he agreed.

Thomas Jefferson was a bit distant from this talk of taking up arms. In 1769 he began work on his great architectural endeavor, the home atop a rural Virginia hill he dubbed Monticello. For materials, he shunned English wood in favor of the more Latinate brick. For design, he was inspired by Palladio, the great sixteenth-century Italian architect, who himself borrowed heavily from the buildings of ancient Rome. One can only wonder if Jefferson was influenced by Socrates' admonition, reported by Xenophon, that a dwelling should be designed so that "each room invited just what was suited to it." A dome, unknown to the Greeks but the characteristic form of Roman architecture, eventually would top the home he designed.

## The Rise of Revolutionary Classicism

OTHERS WERE MORE ENGAGED, ESPECIALLY IN BOSTON. AS COLONIAL politics became more unstable, American political activists would rely heavily on classicism, in part to signal their virtue, but also their intent. Beginning in 1768, Samuel Adams penned a series of articles attacking the British, using the pseudonym Vindex, a reference to the Gaulish leader of what is now central France who rebelled against the emperor Nero. Vindex was described by the Roman historian Cassius Deo as "powerful in body and of shrewd intelligence . . . skilled in warfare and full of daring for any great enterprise; and he had a passionate love of freedom and a vast ambition." Vindex died in the process, but set off a series of events that would topple Nero in 68 AD.

In March 1770, British soldiers shot and killed several people in the central part of Boston. On the second anniversary of that Boston Massacre, Joseph Warren (Harvard, 1759) delivered a speech to an overflow audience at the Old South Meeting House. By some accounts, he wore a toga while speaking. It was an attachment to freedom, he began,

> which raised ancient Rome from the smallest beginnings, to that bright summit of happiness and glory to which she arrived; and it was the loss of this which plunged her from that summit, into the black gulf of infamy and slavery. It was this attachment which inspired her senators with wisdom; it was this which glowed in the breasts of her heroes; it was this which guarded her liberties, and extended her dominions, gave peace at home, and commanded, respect abroad. . . .

But, he warned, when Rome's leaders forgot their dignity and were seduced by corruption, then its soldiers, "urged only by hopes of plunder and rapine, unfeelingly committed the most flagrant enormities; and hired to the trade of death, with relentless fury they perpetrated the most cruel murders, whereby the streets of imperial Rome were drenched with her noblest blood." The same, he implied, was happening on the cobblestoned streets of Boston.

Heed the Roman example, he urged his listeners: Oppose oppression, disdain luxury, and remain united and patriotic. Do so, he promised, and "you may have the fullest assurance that tyranny, with her accursed train, will hide their hideous heads in confusion, shame and despair." Then America may be "a land of liberty" and "the seat of virtue."

Even the more conservative older colleges began to heed the changing political climate. At William & Mary, the confusingly named James Madison, a cousin of the future president, would one day be president of the college. But in 1772, when he delivered a commemorative oration, he was still a student. In it, he offered the basic political recipe of colonial classicist politics, albeit a bit awkwardly: "The active Soul, kindling with public Virtue, communicated its searching Flame, refined natural Liberty into civil Society, Uncertainty into the secure Enjoyment of Property, and Danger into an Asylum against all Invasion. Thus from mutual Consent arose the Body politic." Nor was Harvard immune to the growing republicanism of the times. In 1773, it ceased the practice of listing members of a given class by their family's standing, and began to do so alphabetically.

## Madison Meets Jefferson

LIKE MANY NEW GRADUATES OUT IN THE WORLD, MADISON SOON longed for his bright college years and pals. "I want again to breathe your free Air," he wrote to his college friend William Bradford (Princeton, 1772), a future attorney general. He was particularly upset by the persecution of Baptists in his part of the state for preaching without a license from the government. In Culpepper, not far from his home in Virginia, there were "5 or 6 well meaning men in close Goal [jail] for publishing their religious Sentiments which in the main are very orthodox." This punishment, he wrote, "vexes me the most of any thing whatever." There also was a bit of a class aspect to this: The Baptists were critical of the luxurious indulgences—notably, dancing, drinking, horseracing, and gambling—around which many in the Virginia gentry built their lives.

Two years later, Madison first met Thomas Jefferson. Eventually Madison, eight years younger and at least eight inches shorter, would become the white son Jefferson never had. The older man gushed about him. In his abortive attempt at an autobiography, Jefferson saluted "the rich resources of his luminous and discriminating mind. . . . Never wandering from his subject into vain declamation, but pursuing it closely in language pure, classical, and copious." With those powers, he added, "were united a pure and spotless virtue."

There are several different Thomas Jeffersons—the Latinate lawyer, the flowery wooer of other men's wives, the slave owner looking to increase his profits, the direct and powerful stylist of the Declaration. He is often a bit pompous, maintaining his distance both socially and emotionally. With Abigail Adams and some other married women he found attractively intelligent, he is tenderly seductive. But with Madison, he is conversational and lucid. It is in his letters to Madison that we probably come as close as we ever can to glimpsing the real Jefferson, or at least the least guarded one. Those communications would become especially noteworthy in the late 1780s, when Jefferson was overseas while Madison was working on the Constitution, and then a decade later, when the two were plotting against the Federalists and building the first American opposition party to contend for power.

## Part II

# APPLICATION

⟛⟜

Over the second half of the eighteenth century, the Revolutionary generation would grapple again and again with questions of the most fundamental sort. They knew they were venturing into a new world, politically. What sort of society did they want? How would a modern republic work, and how could they try to ensure its survival? Could a republic on the geographical scale of the thirteen colonies even be governable, given the relatively small size of the ancient city-states? The republics of the Greeks, the Romans, and, in the mid-seventeenth century, the English, had all proven short-lived. Could the Americans do better? Could they devise a national republic that could last?

There were very few answers available, especially from recent history. Instead, they reached back to the classical world. They would apply the lessons they saw in the experience of the Roman Republic and, beyond that, the Greek cities. It would prove a distant and hazy guide, but it was the only one they had.

*Chapter 6*

◄─────►

# Adams and the
# Fuse of Rebellion

O F THE FIRST FOUR PRESIDENTS, JOHN ADAMS WAS FIRST OUT OF
the gate on revolution as the solution to the troubled colonial
American relationship with Britain. "Adams threw himself into
Resistance to the Crown from the very beginning of the imperial crisis," note the historians Stanley Elkins and Eric McKitrick.
While Washington still was seeking favor in that empire, while
Jefferson quietly was studying law, and while Madison was just a
boy, Adams raised the banner of rebellion. The people of Boston
led the way toward independence, and he was among those who
led that city in that direction. Many decades later, he would remi-
nisce to Jefferson about how it happened:

*What do We mean by the Revolution? The War? That was no part
of the Revolution. It was only an Effect and Consequence of it. The
Revolution was in the Minds of the People, and this was effected,
from 1760 to 1775, in the course of fifteen years before a drop of blood
was drawn at Lexington.*

That assertion of it being over by 1775 isn't completely true, because the Revolution could have failed in a variety of ways during
the fighting. But Adams is right that many of the changes in the
way of thinking happened before the first shot was fired. And he
was one of the first to light the fuse of the Revolution.

## Adams: "Let us dare"

———

UNSETTLED TIMES PROPEL PEOPLE TO PROMINENCE QUICKLY. A SINGLE pamphlet, or even one short essay, could put a person into the center of the public arena, especially if he or she could offer new ways to think about the emerging political order. John Adams was perfectly positioned to do just that. He began by making notes to himself about the situation in Massachusetts as tensions arose over the Stamp Act, passed by Parliament in March 1765 and aimed particularly at colonial lawyers and newspapers. His initial draft began with a visionary thought, one that would prove surprisingly prescient:

> Liberty, . . . which has never been enjoyd, in its full Perfection, by more than ten or twelve Millions of Men at any Time, since the Creation, will reign in America, over hundreds and Thousands of Millions at a Time.

It was a striking point at which to begin assessing the political situation, by looking deep into the future of the nation, when it would be vastly more populous than it was when he was writing. This is Adams at his best, taking the longest possible view as a way of organizing his strategic thinking, looking at American politics as the Scotsman Hutton had looked at the rocks of the Earth.

That summer, Adams began rallying Bostonians with a series of essays that appeared weekly in the *Boston Gazette*. He began by reminding them that their ancestors who crossed the Atlantic to settle in Massachusetts were not ignorant. "To many of them, the historians, orators, poets and philosophers of *Greece* and *Rome* were quite familiar." He depicted them as true sons of the Enlightenment, who in their modernism had no time for notions of divine right:

> They knew that government was a plain, simple, intelligible thing founded in nature and reason and quite comprehensible by common

*sense. They detested all the base services, and servile dependen-*
*cies of the feudal system. They knew that no such unworthy de-*
*pendences took place in the ancient seats of liberty, the republic of*
*Greece and Rome.*

So, he concluded, "Liberty must at all hazards be supported. We
have a right to it, derived from our Maker." This was about as succinct a summary of the radical American position as was possible:
The American people had no need for a king to stand between
them and God. Rather they had a God-given right to liberty.

It was time, he told his readers, for Americans to begin thinking and speaking in this revolutionary new way.

*Let us dare to read, think, speak and write. Let every order and*
*degree among the people rouse their attention and animate their*
*resolution. Let them all become attentive to the grounds and prin-*
*ciples of government, ecclesiastical and civil. Let us study the law*
*of nature; search into the spirit of the British constitution; read the*
*histories of ancient ages; contemplate the great examples of Greece*
*and Rome. . . .*

Given his mood swings and acute vanity, Adams is not always
a reliable narrator of his own life. Even so, his own assessment of
the extraordinary impact of his essay is worth noting:

*it had an Effect upon the People of New England beyond all Imag-*
*ination. . . . perhaps no one thing that ever was written or done*
*contributed more than that Publication, to unite the People of*
*New England, as one Man in the Resolution of opposing force, to*
*the stamp Act, and of having recourse to Arms rather than submit*
*to it.*

Six weeks after the Stamp Act went into effect, Adams concluded the year with a characteristic diary entry. First, he was politically attentive. "The Year 1765 has been the most remarkable
Year of my Life," he noted. "The People, even to the lowest Ranks,

have become more attentive to their Liberties, more inquisitive about them, and more determined to defend them, than they were ever before known or had occasion to be."

Then he wallowed in self-pity. He bewailed how the Stamp Act, by bringing the courts to a standstill, had stymied his rise as a lawyer:

> *Thirty Years of my Life are passed in Preparation for Business. I have had Poverty to struggle with—Envy and Jealousy and Malice of Enemies to encounter—no Friends, or but few to assist me, so that I have groped in dark Obscurity, till of late, and had but just become known, and gained a small degree of Reputation, when this execrable Project was set on foot for my Ruin as well as that of America in General, and of Great Britain.*

On January 1, he began the new year by predicting, correctly, that the British would have difficulty enforcing the act. "They will find it a more obstinate War, than the Conquest of Canada and Louisiana."

## "The ball of revolution"

OTHER COLONISTS WERE EXCITED BY THE REVOLUTIONARY FERVOR IN Boston and worried by the clumsy British reaction. The Stamp Act was passed in March 1765. Protests began that summer, even though the act would not take effect until November 1. Down in Virginia, on May 29 of that year, Patrick Henry, speaking out against the act, strode up to the very line of treason. It was his first full week as a member of Virginia's House of Burgesses, and he was delivering his maiden speech. He finished by citing two examples of tyrants who had been killed. "Caesar had his Brutus, Charles the First his Cromwell, and George III [at this point, the Speaker of the House, John Robinson, shouted, "Treason!" and the cry was taken up by others] may profit by their example."

According to some accounts, he then arched his back and cried at his interrupters: "If this be treason, make the most of it." It was a magnificent bellow.

There was no visitors' gallery at the time, so Thomas Jefferson, then a twenty-two-year-old law student in Williamsburg, and just seven years younger than Henry, stood by the open door of the chamber, watching this speech. Jefferson had known Henry for years, since Henry's days as a saloonkeeper in Hanover, Virginia. Even as an adolescent, Jefferson had found Henry a bit backwoodsy. "His manners had something of the coarseness of the society he had frequented: his passion was fiddling, dancing & pleasantry. He excelled in the last," Jefferson wrote. This observation was not just Jefferson being a haughty young colonial gentleman. Henry was notorious in the Hanover area as an idler, more fond of hunting, fishing, and dancing than of work.

Jefferson was more impressed by Henry's public speaking. He wrote later that he "heard the splendid display of mr Henry's talents as a popular orator. They were great indeed; such as I have never heard from any other man. He appeared to me to speak as Homer wrote."

There have been some questions about what Henry's exact words were in some of his speeches, but in 1814, Jefferson gave his eyewitness account of Henry's denunciation of the Stamp Act to Henry's biographer, William Wirt. "I well remember the cry of treason, the pause of Mr. Henry at the name of George III, and the presence of mind with which he closed the sentence, and baffled the charge vociferated," Jefferson told him.

With that speech, Jefferson said, "he was certainly the man who gave the first impulse to the ball of revolution," at least in Virginia. The colonial governor apparently agreed about the impact of Henry's speech. On June 1, he dissolved the House of Burgesses and did not call it again for a year.

Jefferson would never be an admirer of Henry's character. The two would become antagonists during Jefferson's term as governor of Virginia, and Jefferson after that developed what he called a "mixed aspect" about the rambunctious Henry. He explained:

*I think he was the best humored man in society I almost ever knew,
and the greatest orator that ever lived. He had a consummate kno-
lege of the human heart, which directing the efforts of his eloquence
enabled him to attain a degree of popularity with the people at
large never perhaps equalled. His judgment in other matters was
inaccurate in matters of law it was not worth a copper: He was avaritious & rotten hearted. His two great passions were the love of
money & of fame: but when these came into competition the former
predominated.*

## Jefferson Emerges

———

THE BRITISH GOVERNMENT RESPONDED TO THE AMERICAN DEMANDS
with a cascade of acts meant to intimidate them. Each one was
harsher, and each one provoked the colonialists more, antagoniz-
ing and uniting them. The Tea Act of 1773, for example, would
lead to the Boston Tea Party in December of that year. This in
turn provoked the Coercive Acts, meant to make an example of
Boston by closing its port, ruining its businesses, and replacing its
government with British military rule.

Virginians were also burdened by business problems. Ten London banking houses failed in mid-1772, leading to a credit crunch.
During that contraction, surviving London banks called in their
outstanding loans to American planters, among others. This
hit especially hard among Virginians, who were responsible for
some £1.4 million—that is, about half the total debt in the colonies
to British merchants. To raise the cash to pay their debts, they
flooded the market with tobacco, which in turn caused its price to
drop by about half, making their finances even worse.

Dissident Americans decided to meet in what they would call
the First Continental Congress. In preparing for that gathering,
Thomas Jefferson stepped on the national stage for the first time,
at the age of thirty-one. As happened with Adams and his essay,
Jefferson was able to offer a way of thinking about the changing

politics of the colonies, to capture the changing mood of many and distill it into words. For Jefferson, this came in the form of his written advice to Virginia's delegation heading to the Congress, which soon was issued as a pamphlet under the title *A Summary View of the Rights of British America*. It was an odd debut. As one modern analyst puts it, the essay is both tendentious and a mishmash. In essence it was an awkward rhetorical rehearsal for some of the subjects Jefferson would cover with greater clarity two years later in the Declaration of Independence, especially in cataloguing the abuses and usurpations of British officials against America.

Even so, timing is everything in politics. What young Jefferson had to say had not been said before, so his words made a splash with his peers, who sat in taverns and living rooms and listened to them read aloud. George Washington noted in his account book that he purchased a copy on August 6, 1774. Two years later, John Adams noted in his diary that Jefferson "had been chosen a Delegate in Virginia, in consequence of a very handsome public Paper which he had written for the House of Burgesses, which had given him the Character of a fine Writer." That reputation in turn would propel Jefferson to be included in the group drafting a Declaration of Independence.

One of Jefferson's favorite ancient authors was Tacitus, the Roman chronicler. "Tacitus I consider as the first writer in the world without a single exception," he once wrote. Jefferson did not cite Tacitus by name in his discussion of American rights, but he almost certainly has the Roman's *Germania*—a sentimental portrayal of the German tribes as free-spirited people of lusty, hard-drinking, two-fisted independence—in mind when he traces Americans back to their Saxon roots. He lauded the freedom of the Germanic tribes described by Tacitus, the bold Saxons who, Jefferson wrote, "left their native wilds and woods in the North of Europe [and] . . . possessed themselves of the island of Britain." This eventually led him into a lengthy and unhelpful discussion of the differences between Saxon laws of landholding (of which he approved) and Norman laws on the subject (of which he did not).

What is most significant about the pamphlet is its flatly militant tone. As Pauline Maier puts it, "Because Jefferson refused to be constrained by the conventions of British politics, including that which insisted 'the king can do no wrong,' *A Summary View* became the first sustained piece of American political writing that subjected the King's conduct to direct and pointed criticism."

We should leave behind our "expressions of servility," Jefferson contended, and show the king we are not seeking his favors but reminding him of our rights. He ended with an absolute statement: "the god who gave us life, gave us liberty at the same time." In other words, to reduce American freedom was to challenge God. Underscoring the new brasher attitude toward the British monarch, the forty-four-page pamphlet was printed with a quotation from Cicero on its title page about the duty of the "supreme magistrate" to respect the rights of the people.

Looking back on the document decades later, Jefferson opined that its "only merit was in being the first publication which carried the claim of our rights their whole length." But that in itself was quite an achievement, as he surely knew. When he traveled to Philadelphia for the Congress, he attracted attention. "Yesterday the famous Mr. Jefferson a Delegate from Virginia . . . arrived," Rhode Island's Samuel Ward wrote in a letter to his brother. "He looks like a very sensible spirited fine Fellow, and by the pamphlet which he wrote last summer he certainly is one."

## A Congress of the Continent

AT THE NORTHERN END OF THE AMERICAN COLONIES AT ABOUT THE same time, Jonathan Sewall (Harvard, 1748), a strong Tory who was a close friend of John Adams, met him at a court session in the town of Falmouth (now Portland), Maine, then a district of Massachusetts. Sewall asked Adams to go for a walk with him. They strolled out to Munjoy Hill, at the eastern end of the city, offering a fine vista of Casco Bay and beyond, to the cold blue waters of the North Atlantic. Sewall had an urgent request for Adams. Hearing that his old friend had been chosen as a delegate to the Continental Congress, he begged Adams not to go. The irresistible power of Britain will surely crush the American movement, Sewall argued. No, Adams replied, I must go. "The die was now cast; I had passed the Rubicon; swim or sink, live or die, survive or perish with my country, was my unalterable determination."

Adams left Boston in mid-August 1774 for that congressional meeting in Philadelphia, to be held in September and October. It was his first journey outside New England. En route, in Princeton, New Jersey, he attended a sermon by John Witherspoon on Sunday, August 28. "A clear, sensible, Preacher," he told his diary. The same day, he heard about some of the eloquent Virginians he would meet. One of the New York delegates told him that "the Virginians speak in Raptures about Richard Henry Lee and Patrick Henry—one the Cicero and the other the Demosthenes of the Age."

From his home in the Virginia Piedmont, James Madison was watching political developments at a distance. Writing to his friend William Bradford in Philadelphia, Madison warned that we should not "presume too much on the generosity & Justice of the crown." Rather he said, it was "advisable as soon as possible to begin our defence." He was right—a rupture was looming. In October, in a document known as the "Continental Association," the Congress agreed, "under the sacred ties of Virtue, Honour, and Love of our Country," once again to boycott British goods.

At that first Congress, Joseph Galloway of Pennsylvania, a political ally of Benjamin Franklin, proposed that the colonies remain part of the empire, with a colonial parliament and a leader appointed by the king. (Franklin had suggested something similar twenty years earlier, in response to the outbreak of the French and Indian War.) The proposal was rejected, and Galloway, opposed to independence, departed the Congress. A few years later he would become the Loyalist governor of British-occupied Philadelphia.

## Into War

---

EVENTS BEGAN TO ACCELERATE EARLY IN 1775. THE PRINCIPLES OF THE Revolution, Adams wrote in February of that year, were that all men are equal, and that power is delegated to leaders by the people. These, he continued, "are the principles of Aristotle and Plato, of Livy and Cicero, of Sydney, Harrington and Lock." Ancient precedent showed, Adams argued, that the British did not enjoy natural authority over the Americans. "The Greeks planted colonies, and neither demanded nor pretended any authority over them, but they became distinct independent commonwealths."

In March 1775, Patrick Henry rose to speak in Richmond. He concluded by shouting "Give me liberty—or give me death." To ensure his audience grasped the allusion to Cato, he thrust an ivory letter opener toward his chest, in imitation of a scene in Addison's play.

Many in Britain warned that King George and his allies were on the wrong course, that a confrontation with the Americans would not end well. In January, William Pitt the Elder, a former prime minister, rose in the House of Lords to support a motion to pull British troops out of Boston. "I have read Thucydides, . . . but I must declare and avow that for solidity of reasoning, force of sagacity, and wisdom of conclusion, . . . no nation or body of men can stand in preference to the general congress of Philadelphia."

Brushing aside such admonitions, the British Parliament weeks later declared the colony of Massachusetts to be in a state of rebellion. When one side in a conflict declares war, common sense would say that a state of war exists. By that reasoning, the American Revolution began then, in February 1775, rather than sixteen months later, when the Second Continental Congress announced to the world its recognition of the fact of war.

News of the battles of Concord and Lexington on April 19, 1775, struck the colonies like lightning. Washington saw his choice clearly and cast it in terms true to the central role that "virtue" played in his life. "Unhappy it is though to reflect, that a Brother's

Sword has been sheathed in a Brother's breast, and that, the once happy and peaceful plains of America are either to be drenched with Blood, or Inhabited by Slaves. Sad alternative! But can a virtuous Man hesitate in his choice?"

Washington had been a respected member of the House of Burgesses, but not a particularly active one. One reason for his quiescence was that military affairs had been more the province of London than of Williamsburg. But when the Second Continental Congress convened in May 1775, its members looked around and saw few men with martial experience. One, sitting among them, pointedly wearing his old militia uniform, was Colonel George Washington of Virginia. He soon was asked to sit on one committee to raise an army, and on another to finance it.

Boston needed defense. John Adams proposed Washington to lead it. Choosing a Virginian to lead the task would make it a national effort, rather than a regional one, Adams explained. His cousin, Samuel Adams, also of Massachusetts, seconded the idea. The vote was unanimous. Washington was to become, in his physical presence, the embodiment of the national defense, quite literally. He was, at first, the sole member of the United States Army.

In mid-June he rose in Philadelphia to accept the post. He spoke of his honor and reputation, the two most valuable things in his life:

> Mister President, Tho' I am truly sensible of the high Honour done me in this Appointment, yet I feel great distress, from a consciousness that my abilities & Military experience may not be equal to the extensive & important Trust: . . . But lest some unlucky event should happen unfavourable to my reputation, I beg it may be rememberd by every Gentleman in the room, that I this day declare with the utmost sincerity, I do not think my self equal to the Command I am honoured with.

He had just been given command of a nearly nonexistent army whose mission was to take on the world's greatest military power. There was no American navy. Yet he had a significant asset that was invisible. At forty-three years old, he was seasoned enough to command the new army, yet still young enough to learn and change as he did.

In Massachusetts the very next day, British redcoats charged up a slope against American militiamen who had dug quick fortifications on two elevations just to the north of Boston harbor. Bunker Hill and Breed's Hill were located on a peninsula, so the British could have easily used boats to maneuver their forces around them, cutting off the militiamen and letting them wither on the vine. Their ships' cannons then could pound the colonials at will. Instead, British commanders chose to order a frontal attack, apparently in the belief that their men could easily rout the untested Americans. It proved a far tougher fight. The British took the hills, but at a very high price. Their casualty rate of about 50 percent resembled those of Braddock's some twenty years earlier. General William Howe's entire staff was killed or wounded, and a total of nearly one hundred officers were lost.

## Slaves Can Revolt, Too

ON AUGUST 18, 1775, AN EVENT OCCURRED THAT MIGHT HAVE GIVEN SOME perceptive men pause. Thomas Jeremiah, a free man of color, a successful harbor pilot, and probably the wealthiest African American in the colonies, was hanged in South Carolina for allegedly working to support an insurrection of African Americans. "His whole life was a refutation of whites' basic justification for slavery, which was that Africans, by their nature, deserved to be slaves," concludes one modern historian.

Slave rebellion was the great fear of the South, and the British contemplated taking advantage of it. Rumors spread that Lord Dunmore, the British governor of Virginia, planned to offer freedom to enslaved people who would fight for his side. "It is imagined our Governor has been tampering with the Slaves & that he has it in contemplation to make great Use of them in case of a civil war in this province," a worried James Madison wrote to a friend. He saw this as the great weak point of the American position. "To say the truth, that is the only part in which this Colony is vulnerable; & if we should be subdued, we shall fall like Achilles by the hand of one that knows that secret."

Later that year Dunmore indeed issued a royal proclamation declaring martial law and promising freedom to slaves who joined the royal forces. This concern about freeing the slaves, concludes the historian Jill Lepore, was the factor that, more than the issues of taxation and representation, or the fighting in Massachusetts, "tipped the scales in favor of American independence." Washington, learning about the proclamation from his encampment outside Boston, was alarmed. "That Arch Traitor to the Rights of Humanity, Lord Dunmore, should be instantly crushd," he warned, without irony. "Otherwise, like a snow Ball in rolling, his army will get size."

Parliament declared the American colonies to be in a state of "open and avowed rebellion" and vowed "to bring the traitors to justice." King George followed that up with a speech in which he accused the American rebels of engaging in a "desperate conspiracy."

Adams, meditating on the turn of events, and spurred especially by an act of treason against the Americans, concluded that the outcome depended on whether the Americans were sufficiently virtuous. He wrote to a former law student of his that "Virtue, my young Friend, Virtue alone is or can be the Foundation of our new Governments, and it must be encouraged by Rewards, in every Department civil and military." He returned to the thought six months later, writing to his friend Mercy Otis Warren that

> Public Virtue cannot exist in a Nation without private, and public Virtue is the only Foundation of Republics. There must be a positive Passion for the public good, the public Interest, Honour, Power, and Glory, established in the Minds of the People, or there can be

*no Republican Government, nor any real Liberty. And this public
Passion must be Superiour to all private Passions.*

This was about as succinct an example as exists of the influence
of the classical model on the thinking of the Revolutionary generation. That model soon would be tested as the war intensified
and spread.

## Chapter 7

◆━━━◆

# Jefferson's Declaration
# of the "American Mind"

T HOMAS JEFFERSON HAD SEVERAL DIFFERENT STYLES AS A WRITER.
In his descriptions of nature he could be clear and spry. Here,
for example, is his deft account of the confluence of the Potomac
and Shenandoah Rivers at Harpers Ferry:

> The passage of the Patowmac through the Blue ridge is perhaps one
> of the most stupendous scenes in nature. On your right comes up
> the Shenandoah, having ranged along the foot of the mountain an
> hundred miles to seek a vent. On your left approaches the Patow-
> mac, in quest of a passage also. In the moment of their junction they
> rush together against the mountain, rend it asunder, and pass off
> to the sea.

But his pen was not always so lucid. His correspondence with
women, especially married ones, such as Maria Cosway, Abigail
Adams, and Angelica Church, could be breathily cloying. And in
his legal and governmental work, he tended, as did many others in
his time, to be long-winded and Latinate, prone to select the long
word when a short one would do. Consider these mind-numbing
sentences:

> Or the case may be likened to the ordinary one of a tenant for life,
> who may hypothecate the land for his debts during the continuance
> of his usufruct; but at his death the reversioner (who is also for life

*only) receives it exonerated from all burthen. The period of a gener-*
*ation, or the term of it's life is determined by the laws of mortality,*
*which, varying a little only in different climates, offer a general aver-*
*age, to be found by observation.*

He also tended toward the convoluted when in political difficulty, as in this wartime sentence: "I have too good an opinion
of their love of order to believe that a removal of these troops
would produce any irregular proofs of their disapprobation, but
I am well assured that it would be extremely odious to them." In
1792, for example, Jefferson wrote to George Washington to try to
explain away his feud with Alexander Hamilton; one can almost
see Jefferson nervously tugging at his collar as he wrote these tan-
gled sentences:

*I knew that, to such a mind as yours, persuasion was idle & im-*
*pertinent: that before forming your decision, you had weighed all*
*the reasons for & against the measure, had made up your mind on*
*full view of them, & that there could be little hope of changing the*
*result. Pursuing my reflections too I knew we were some day to try*
*to walk alone, and if the essay should be made while you should be*
*alive & looking on, we should derive confidence from that circum-*
*stance, & resource if it failed.*

Contrary to his image, Jefferson was not really a literary man.
He had prodigious talents and a boundless range of interests, yet
his tastes in literature were surprisingly pedestrian, as his prose
often was. His choices in poetry were mundane at best. In his
youth he was fond of Edward Young, putting these mawkish lines
from Young's *Night-Thoughts*, one of the most popular poems of
the eighteenth century, into his commonplace book:

*The knell, the shroud, the mattock, and the grave;*
*The deep damp vault, the darkness, and the worm;*
*These are the bugbears of a winter's eve.*

As one literary historian puts it, "Jefferson's literary tastes and preferences are, for their time, thoroughly conventional and unexceptional."

When he was older, his favorite poet was "Ossian." That name is in quotation marks because, though purportedly the work of a third-century Gaelic poet, such an author did not really exist. "I think this rude bard of the North the greatest Poet that has ever existed," Jefferson wrote in 1773. Ossian was later revealed to be an invention of the eighteenth-century Scottish poet James Macpherson, who had claimed he was translating material he had discovered. In Jefferson's defense, it should be noted that Goethe and Napoleon were also taken in by Macpherson's fabrications.

Jefferson also disdained most novels, which he termed "poison" that entertained but did not instruct. He seems to have overlooked that works of fiction often can deepen one's understanding of complex human behavior. The only work of prose fiction quoted in his literary commonplace book is Laurence Sterne's *Tristram Shandy*.

## Jefferson's Masterpiece

YET THERE IS, AMONG JEFFERSON'S DIVERSE WRITINGS, ONE GREAT, shining exception: The Declaration of Independence. The English writer and wit G. K. Chesterton lauded it, accurately, as "perhaps the only piece of practical politics that is also theoretical politics and also great literature."

The Declaration is remarkably un-Jeffersonian in its style. (For the convenience of the reader, the final version of it is included in an appendix at the end of this book.) It is a model of strong, plain political prose. In it, verbs push nouns, and words tend to be solid and short. The reason for this departure in his style, he explained years later, is that he tried to write in simple, clear terms because he considered the Declaration to be "an appeal to the tribunal of the world." As such, he wrote "in terms so plain and firm as to command their assent and to justify ourselves in the independent stand we are compelled to take."

In other words, he was writing not for his elite peers, but for the people. So here he became more like Thomas Paine, whose essay *Common Sense* had appeared six months before Jefferson drafted the Declaration and had quickly become a national sensation, appearing in some twenty-five editions within the year. In the pamphlet, Paine eschewed classical citations and allusions, relying more on references to the Bible and images from farm life. Unusually for the political commentary of the time, he offered no accusations of Caesarism, no denunciations of Catilines, no calls for a new Cato. Paine did not even denounce factionalism, also mandatory in eighteenth-century political writings. "Virtue" appears several times, but two of those references are to make the negative point that virtue is not a hereditary trait.

In short, Paine was emphatically not about the past. "We have it in our power to begin the world over again," he proclaimed in a postscript to *Common Sense* appended a month after its first appearance. "A situation, similar to the present, hath not happened since the days of Noah until now. The birth-day of a new world is at hand." This was indeed a new voice, bright and clear.

Jefferson heard that voice and appears to have sought to echo it. "This was the object of the Declaration of Independence," he wrote. "Not to find out new principles, or new arguments, never before thought of, not merely to say things which had never been said before; but to place before mankind the common sense of the subject." Jefferson's explicit use here of "common sense" was perhaps a nod toward the influence of Paine. Jefferson had received the pamphlet in the mail in February of 1776, not long after it was published.

It may have helped that Jefferson drafted the document not atop a hill in a remote Virginia plantation, but in the rooms he had rented in Philadelphia, the biggest city in America, from Jacob Graff, a German-born bricklayer. When he was overseeing Monticello, Jefferson was not required to persuade, only to order. But in Philadelphia he would hear coming through his window the voices of the people he now needed to address—the workingman, the European immigrant, the shopkeeper, the sailor.

He set out in the Declaration, he asserted, not just to present his own views but to give "expression of the American mind, and to give to that expression the proper tone and spirit called for by the occasion." But that was disingenuous. Jefferson really was attempting something far more difficult. He was employing a plain American idiom while attempting to move the American mind into the future. He was pushing them hard, and far beyond any existing consensus. One month before the Declaration was passed, only four colonies had instructed their delegates to support independence. But the Declaration's appearance would do much to change that.

## A Declaration of Epicureanism

JEFFERSON BEGINS BY STATING THAT "WHEN, IN THE COURSE OF HU- man events, it becomes necessary for one people to dissolve the political bands which have connected them with another. . . ." This is good prose, almost conversational, and a great way to start. It goes on to say that we owe everyone else an explanation of what we are doing.

This first paragraph also contains one of the few hints of religion in the document—a quick reference to "the Laws of Nature and of Nature's God." It is one of the few mentions Jefferson makes of God, while "Jesus Christ" and "Christianity" are entirely absent. (Congress, in editing the document, would insert more.) Jefferson emphatically wanted no establishment of religious authority or tests of belief. By contrast, the Delaware state constitution, writ- ten and adopted just thirty-five miles to the south in that same summer of 1776, required anyone holding office to "profess faith in God the Father, and in Jesus Christ His only Son, and in the Holy Ghost, one God, blessed for evermore; and . . . acknowledge the holy scriptures of the Old and New Testament to be given by divine inspiration."

The second paragraph is probably the key passage of writing in all of American history. In it, Jefferson sets forth the beliefs of these people who are declaring themselves a new nation upon the Earth. We can all recall how it begins: "We hold these truths to be self-evident, that all men are created equal." The last five words of that sentence sweep aside millennia of unequal births and preordained lives and define these new Americans as a people who subscribe to a revolutionary belief. In the context of the late 1700s, it is even a bit pugnacious: *Do you think you are better than us?* In this new nation, all people—or at least all white men—would have equal standing before the law. That was a Hutton-like leap of the imagination.

The Declaration's entire second paragraph is also a garden of Epicurean belief, though not explicitly. It bears repeating that Jefferson was writing for the American masses, not the classical classes. To that end, he would be influenced by the ancients—but he would not cite them.

At twenty-two lines, the second is the longest paragraph in the document. The first sentence of this paragraph ends with the assertion that among the "unalienable rights" of these equal men are "life, liberty and the pursuit of happiness." This is the essence of Epicureanism. In *Our Declaration*, a wonderful line-by-line and word-by-word explication of the Declaration of Independence, the political philosopher Danielle Allen comments that "the Declaration shimmers with a sublime optimism." This is nowhere more true than in that phrase.

The language here also makes explicit Jefferson's divergence from Locke, who in his "Second Treatise on Civil Government" had used the phrase, "life, liberty and estate" (that is, property). Jefferson here replaced that last word with "happiness"—and in the process encouraged a social revolution. This is how Jonathan Israel summarizes the alteration:

> *Where in Locke property is the basis of social division into classes, Jefferson's formulation marginalized the principle of social class.*

*The landless could no longer be regarded as either so marginal or so subordinate as in Locke. Where Locke nurtured a negative conception of liberty, centered on protection of property, for Jeffersonians liberty was a positive, developmental concept to be upheld and advanced by the state and its agencies.*

Having covered a lot of ground in the first sentence of that second paragraph, Jefferson moves on in the next sentence to demolish the notion of the divine origin of government. Governments are made by men, he states, and receive their powers from "the consent of the governed." Although he does not mention it, that idea originated with the Scottish philosopher George Buchanan almost two hundred years earlier, starting a train of thought that was carried by Scottish tutors to their American pupils.

It means that all power comes from the people—a notion that would be reinforced eleven years later by the opening phrase of the Constitution, "We the people."

Jefferson also may have had in the back of his mind another rather elaborate classical literary reference, albeit a secondhand one. In this paragraph, two of Jefferson's key phrases, about "inalienable rights" and "consent of the people," echo an exchange in Lord Lyttelton's *Dialogues of the Dead.* (Lyttelton's work, written during the 1760s, is itself expressly an imitation of a work by Lucian of Samosata, a first-century AD Syrian satirist who wrote in Greek—and was an Epicurean.) In his 32nd Dialogue, Lyttelton, himself a politician and friend of Alexander Pope, imagines an exchange in which Servius Tullius, the legendary sixth king of Rome, asks, "Is not Liberty an inherent, inalienable Right of Mankind?"

Lyttelton then has Marcus Aurelius, the Roman emperor-philosopher and a contemporary of Lucian's, respond, "Forms of Government may, and must, be occasionally changed, with the consent of the People." The emperor also is made to say, "Liberty, like Power, is only good for those who possess it, when it is under the constant Direction of Virtue."

Like Jefferson's first sentence in this paragraph, the second one ends with the word "happiness"—in this case, the people have the right to organize their government in the manner that seems to them "most likely to effect their safety and happiness."

The very next word in the Declaration, at the beginning of the second paragraph's third sentence, is another Epicurean buzz-word. "Prudence," Jefferson writes, dictates that governments are not changed lightly. This is the first of the four virtues listed by Jefferson as the essence of the Epicurean way of life, the other three being temperance, fortitude, and justice.

And yes, there also was some influence of Locke in the document. "When a long train of abuses and usurpations" are imposed upon a people, Jefferson says, "it is their right, it is their duty, to throw off such a government." The Englishman had written in his "Second Treatise" that the people should rouse themselves if oppressed by "a long train of Abuses, Prevarications, and Artifices."

## Indicting the King

"LET FACTS BE SUBMITTED TO A CANDID WORLD," JEFFERSON CONTIN-ues, and turns to his charges against the king, a list of some twenty sentences that constitutes about half the entire document.

But Jefferson engages in a rhetorical sleight of hand here. He gives no specifics. By not identifying "names, dates, or places," argues the rhetorician Stephen Lucas, Jefferson "magnified the seriousness of the grievances by making it seem as if each charge referred not to a particular piece of legislation or to an isolated act in a single colony, but to a violation of the constitution that had been repeated on many occasions throughout America. The ambiguity of the grievances also made them more difficult to refute."

Jefferson then delivers the sum of this indictment. The American people have weighed the character of the king and found him wanting. He just is not good enough for them. "A prince, whose character is thus marked by every act which may define a tyrant, is unfit to be the ruler of a free people." Reading this, one can almost hear the applause of the Scottish political philosophers.

The final two paragraphs deal with what the document has asserted have become two separate peoples, the British and the Americans. "We have warned them . . . We have reminded them . . . We have appealed to their native justice, . . . and we have conjured them" to stop their king. But, "they too have been deaf to the voice of justice." Remember here that "justice" is the last of Jefferson's four key Epicurean virtues.

So, he concludes, we are now "the representatives of the United States of America, in General Congress, Assembled, appealing to the Supreme Judge of the World." (That last phrase was inserted in the congressional editing process.) We are "and of right ought to be free and independent states." All bonds are cut. We are "absolved from all allegiance to the British Crown," and "all political connection . . . is and ought to be totally dissolved." As if not quite believing it, he repeats the phrase "free and independent states."

In the last sentence, the signers "pledge to each other our lives, our fortunes and our sacred honour." In other words: *We will not back down. Our virtue is at stake.*

## Signing the Declaration

MEMBERS OF CONGRESS TOOK THAT VOW SERIOUSLY. THE INITIAL SIGNing of the document, on July 4, 1776, was a moment of "Silence and Gloom," Benjamin Rush would recall to John Adams. Decades later, he asked Adams in a letter,

> *Do you recollect the pensive and awful silence which pervaded the house when we were called up, one after another, to the table of the President of Congress, to subscribe what was believed by many at that time to be our own death warrants?*

The only moment of relief came when the portly Benjamin Harrison (attended William & Mary), a Falstaffian figure, grimly joked to the smaller Elbridge Gerry (Harvard, 1762) that "I shall have a great advantage over you Mr: Gerry when we are all hung for what we are now doing. From the size and weight of my body I shall die in a few minutes, but from the lightness of your body you will dance in the air an hour or two before you are dead." They were conscious that they represented only part of the American population, faced many internal opponents, and possessed no army to speak of—and that they were publicly challenging the world's leading power. Jefferson's old tutors would have been proud: Nineteen of the fifty-six signers of the Declaration were of Scottish or Ulster Scot extraction.

John Adams, who had been thinking about the importance of virtue to the fledgling republic, now harbored some private doubts. "Yesterday the greatest Question was decided, which ever was debated in America," he wrote to his wife. But, he wondered, were the people good enough to carry it through?

> The new Government . . . will require a Purification from our Vices, and an Augmentation of our Virtues or they will be no Blessings. The People will have unbounded Power. And the People are extreamly addicted to Corruption and Venality, as well as the Great.—I am not without Apprehensions from this Quarter.

The Declaration shifted public opinion and especially rallied radicals. It was greeted at Princeton, for example, with great enthusiasm. As one contemporary account put it, "Nassau Hall was grandly illuminated, and *independency* proclaimed under a triple volley of musketry, and universal acclamation for the prosperity of the *United States*. The ceremony was conducted with the greatest decorum."

At about the same time, American soldiers in New York responded to a public reading of the Declaration by pulling down the gilded statue of King George III that dominated the southern end of Broadway in Manhattan. The statue, made of two tons of lead and painted with gold leaf, portrayed him as a Roman emperor astride a horse. It had been a present to the city from the king himself in 1770. Washington admonished that in the future, his soldiers should leave such actions to civilian authorities. By some accounts, portions of the monarch's statue were melted down and made into musket balls for the Revolutionary Army.

## A Continuing Challenge

ALL IN ALL, JEFFERSON HAD CARRIED OFF AN EXTRAORDINARY FEAT, relaying a lifetime of classical learning about liberty and rights but employing strong, straightforward prose that could be read aloud on street corners and in taverns and understood by all who listened. He had not just explained to the people the reasons for revolt, but created a document of lasting philosophical and literary merit that still resonates today as we try to understand and direct our country.

Whether or not Jefferson intended it, his phrase that everyone was created equal created a test for future generations, a standard against which to measure the nation again and again. That is why it figures significantly in several of the most memorable speeches and statements in American history. Two examples came from women in the 1840s. Elizabeth Cady Stanton, at the first American convention on women's rights, shocked some Americans in 1848 with the Seneca Falls Declaration, which stated in part that "We hold these truths to be self-evident: that all men and women are created equal." In the same decade, dissident female millworkers in Lowell, Massachusetts, demanded "EQUAL RIGHTS, or death to the corporations."

A third echo came, of course, in the Gettysburg Address. Midway through the nation's most severe test, President Abraham Lincoln, in Gettysburg, Pennsylvania, to commemorate the battle that had ended there on July 4, 1863, began by invoking Jefferson's words: "our fathers brought forth on this continent a new nation, conceived in liberty and dedicated to the proposition that all men are created equal." Lincoln owned a little leather-bound notebook in which he had pasted newspaper clippings as well as the second paragraph of the Declaration of Independence.

Then in August 1963, one hundred years after Lincoln, one of the most powerful moments in Martin Luther King Jr.'s best-remembered speech came when he quoted that same phrase. "I have a dream," he declared, "that one day this nation will rise up and live out the true meaning of its creed: 'We hold these truths to be self-evident, that *all* men are created equal.'"

Fifteen years later, Harvey Milk, an openly gay San Francisco politician, again invoked that phrase in a speech when he said that, "No matter how hard you try, you cannot erase those words from the Declaration of Independence."

As Pauline Maier observes, part of the power of this section of the Declaration is that it's more about "what we ought to be" rather than "what we are." As such, it continues to speak to us now, issuing a challenge across more than two centuries.

◆━━━◆

## Chapter 8

# Washington

*The Noblest Roman of Them All*

T HE PARADOX OF WASHINGTON IS THAT THIS LEAST CLASSICALLY educated of the first four presidents was also the most Roman of them in character, and was seen as such by his contemporaries. While Washington's peers threw themselves into ancient Rome, he had Rome thrown at him. It was his fate to become "the most thoroughly classicized figure of his generation," according to one specialist in American classicism. Indeed, there eventually would be not one but two biographies of Washington published in America that were written in Latin.

Washington would not have been able to read those accounts, because he never learned Latin. Nor is there a record of him reading many of the ancient works in translation. Even so, the history and characters of ancient Rome would shape Washington's life, partly through his own aspirations and partly through how his contemporaries viewed him. Because ancient history provided much of the political vocabulary of his times, he would use it even if he wasn't schooled in it.

In his youth, he had been interested in Caesar and had read a bit about him. Later, as an adult, he sought to model his public persona upon Cato—upright, honest, patriotic, self-sacrificing, and a bit remote. Then, fighting for American independence, Washington had a new Roman role thrust upon him, that of the celebrated general Fabius, who defeated an invader from overseas mainly by avoiding battle and wearing out his foe. Finally, after the war, he would play his greatest role, the commander who relinquished power and returned to his farm, an American Cincinnatus.

Of all those Roman roles, the one that had the greatest effect on American history was the one with which he was least comfortable—that is, becoming the American Fabius during the War for Independence. It was not an easy adjustment. In 1776, George Washington still had a lot to learn. As a general he would suffer a terrible series of military setbacks in the second half of that year—but to his credit, he reacted by reflecting and then adjusting. If the best measure of a general is the ability to grasp the nature of the war he or she faces and then to make changes, Washington was among the greatest the United States ever had. This is not perceived even today because he would score few victories during the entire war. But it was not a war that would be won by battles. It was a different sort of conflict, as he came to understand while he slowly, almost grudgingly, learned to fight as a modified Fabian.

As with almost all things classical, the Roman general Fabius was better known to Washington and his peers than he is now. He was celebrated by Rome for defeating the shocking invasion of Hannibal by refusing to give battle. Hannibal of Carthage began from his base in Spain. In 218 BC he marched through today's France and then crossed the Alps into northern Italy, where he scored two overwhelming victories against Roman armies. Panicking, the Romans finally turned to Fabius, declaring him dictator for the period of the emergency. Born in 280 BC, Fabius was known even as a youth for his firm, low-key manner, but also for supposedly being slow in thought.

Hannibal desperately needed more victories to encourage non-Roman cities on the Italian peninsula to join his side. Understanding this imperative, Fabius denied him a decisive battle, instead attacking Hannibal's supply lines and foraging parties. Taking advantage of local knowledge, he tended to keep his force in the hills, where Hannibal's cavalry would be less effective than on the plains. Shadowing Hannibal's soldiers but not attacking, Plutarch writes, Fabius "gave them no rest, but kept them in continual alarm." Hannibal ranged over Italy, even fighting to the walls of Rome, but never managed to win decisively. Hannibal finally left Italy in 203 BC, sailing back to Carthage empty-handed after nearly fifteen years of campaigning. Fabius died shortly afterward. Hannibal himself eventually went into exile from Carthage and died in around 180 in what is now Turkey, most likely committing suicide by poison to avoid being taken prisoner by a vengeful Rome.

We do not know how much Washington knew about Fabius. The three major sources of information on the Roman general are histories of Rome written by Livy and Polybius, plus a biography of him in *Plutarch's Lives*. There is no record of Washington's reading Livy or Polybius or of his even owning a copy of either. It is possible they were among those he catalogued vaguely as "Latin books—14 volumes."

All of the first four presidents possessed copies of *Plutarch's Lives*, as did most educated people of the time. Adams, Jefferson, and Madison cited him frequently. John Adams once mourned to a friend that "we are so bigoted to Thucidies Livy, Plutarch and Tacitus, Hume Robertson and Gibbon that we read little else." There is no equivalent book today with which familiarity would be assumed by all members of a political elite. Even Washington, not much of a reader except in a handful of topics that intrigued him—notably agricultural innovation and, late in his life, the abolition of slavery—owned a copy of *Plutarch's Lives*. However, there is no evidence that he ever read the book, as he never quotes Plutarch in his surviving writings—his diary, speeches, orders, and letters.

What his contemporaries read in Plutarch about Quintus Fabius Maximus was that he "set Forth to oppose Hannibal, not with intention to fight him, but with the purpose of wearing out and wasting the vigour of his arms by lapse of time." Plutarch concludes that, as best as he can determine, "Fabius never won any set battle but that against the Ligurians" (that is, the tribe in the area of today's Italian Riviera that Fabius drove northward into the Alps). Hannibal was certainly the more effective tactician—one of the greatest of all time—but Fabius must be counted the more successful strategist.

## Historians Fumble Fabianism

————

THE NATURE OF WASHINGTON'S STRATEGY HAS BEEN A MESSY SUBJECT for students of the Revolutionary War. This may have occurred because most of them come to the war as political or social historians, rather than from a military perspective. For example, one otherwise knowledgeable writer, assessing Washington's powerful political position after the war, derogates his military record thusly: "Washington had not achieved this kind of adulation as a result of battlefield brilliance, having lost more fights than he won, sometimes quite badly, most notably in his incompetent failure to hold New York, where he squandered thousands of troops needlessly." He adds that, "during the war, he simply acted as if every defeat really was a victory." Such conclusions miss the point that wars are more than just a string of battles, and that battles sometimes are not the decisive factor in conflict.

One persistent point of confusion in studies of the War for Independence dates back to the nineteenth century. This is the conflation of two distinctly different approaches: a war of posts and a Fabian strategy. In the former, one fights defensive battles from fortresses; in the latter, one avoids battle altogether and seeks to defeat an enemy by wearing him out. Washington's contemporaries understood the difference. "The idea, about this time, seems to have been taken up of making our resistance a war of posts," one American officer who was there in New York at the time wrote in a memoir. "This sort of war, however, . . . in a country without regular fortresses, appears to be scarcely practicable."

Yet some modern historians conflate these two distinct approaches into one. For example, Joseph Ellis writes that "Washington came to accept the fact that he must adapt a more defensive strategy and fight a 'War of Posts.' Also called a 'Fabian strategy' . . . it was a shift in thinking that did not come naturally to Washington." A second historian, Edward Lengel, states that "much has been made of Washington's supposedly 'Fabian' view of warfare. It has also been called a war of position, or posts." Lengel then argues emphatically that "Washington's reputation as a Fabian . . . is unjustified." But such an argument disregards Washington's own words, as well as the writings of those around him and the record of how he acted in response to events and opportunities. It is odd because Washington's contemporaries clearly saw him as taking a Fabian approach—though not all of them endorsed it.

To be sure, leading an indirect campaign was not an instinctive step for Washington. He was naturally aggressive and inclined to be impatient. But like everyone else, generals are altered by the extravagant pressures of war, and Washington, relatively young at the age of forty-three when he took top command, could observe, reflect, and adjust more than most senior commanders. The George Washington of 1777 would not be the same man he had been in 1775. At the war's outset, he did not understand three of its key elements: the role of the militia in the fight, the kind of war he needed to pursue, and the allied intervention that would eventually reshape the war.

There were three stages in Washington's evolution. First, in 1775 and much of the following year, he was inclined to take the offensive. Second, after a string of stinging setbacks around New York City in the summer of 1776, he shifted to a war of posts. This interim step was, again, not a Fabian approach, but was rather a retreat into fortresses from which he would invite the enemy to bring the fight to him. American troops may not be able to meet British regulars on the open battlefield, Washington was calculating, but perhaps they could fight from behind barriers. The stunning American victory at Bunker Hill a year earlier was the model for this.

But when Washington tried it in the New York area later in 1776, this approach of entrenching failed miserably. So by early 1777 he was reluctantly figuring out a third approach—that is, what an indirect, Fabian strategy might look like. He would pursue this for years, only occasionally offering battle when politics forced him to or when the British left an opening.

Winning battles does not necessarily win wars. Indeed, losing a battle can sometimes be an advantage, because a tactical setback can sometimes result in a strategic gain, if by engaging the enemy one slows his movement, distracts him from other targets, or just wears him down. For example, Benedict Arnold's confrontation of the British on Lake Champlain in October 1776 resulted in him being "defeated soundly, but the tactical defeat proved an immense strategic gain. The lengthy naval arms race prevented [Major General Sir Guy] Carleton [the British commander] from conquering upstate New York before the winter of 1776–77." That in turn gave the Americans time to rebuild their forces and go on to win the Battle of Saratoga in the same area a year later.

Astute chroniclers of military operations therefore focus not just on battles but on what actually wins wars. As Mark Kwasny describes it, the Revolutionary War began with a militia fight in Massachusetts. In the South, it mainly was a war of skirmishes. And even in the cockpit of the war, the middle colonies area surrounding New York City, more often than not it took the form of "partisan war"—that is, an irregular or guerrilla war waged in the shadows, often by part-time fighters operating in small, fluid units and then melting back into the civilian population. Part of Washington's education was recognizing that this was indeed the nature of the war in which he was engaged. The British persisted in perceiving the war as similar to the conventional eighteenth-century European dynastic fights they knew, writes R. Arthur Bowler. They were wrong, he finds: "It proved instead to be a popular war, a war in which the people were involved."

There is no question that Washington got off on the wrong foot at beginning of the war. Both his perceptions and instincts required modification. His aggressive nature did not serve him well, and neither did the urgings of Congress to attack. His military thinking early on was conventional, painfully so. He failed to see the big strategic picture; instead, his thinking was down in the weeds of tactics. Take, for example, his advice to a regimental commander he had known for decades:

*In all your marches, at times, at least, even when there is no possible danger, move with front, rear, and flank guards, that they may be familiarized to the use; and be regular in your encampments, appointing necessary guards for the security of your camp. In short, whether you expect an enemy or not, this should be practised; otherwise your attempts will be confused and awkward, when necessary. Be plain and precise in your orders, and keep copies of them to refer to, that no mistakes may happen.*

This was the sort of plodding tactical advice a major or lieutenant colonel might offer to an untried company commander, but it was not the stuff with which wars are won. Washington needed to elevate his gaze to a higher level of war. Effective tactics are helpful to have, but without a strategy, they can be useless, like a powerful car without a steering wheel.

When Washington wrote that letter, he had not yet developed a strategic understanding of the conflict. Lacking that, he in that note slipped back to tactical matters, as generals sometimes do when they are overwhelmed or new to the fight. Until he began to understand the war at the level of generalship, he would not know how to prosecute it and so would not grasp the effect the militias could have if used well. That understanding would come as he reflected on the nature of his war and began to adapt his operations to reflect those recognitions. He was better at this sort of observation and contemplation than were most of his contemporaries, and indeed than most generals are, both then and now. It was Washington's greatest military skill. It may not have been genius, but it was close.

But that was yet to come. In 1775, at the war's outset, he understood neither the war nor his militiamen, the part-time citizen-soldiers who would prove key to his eventual strategy. He was contemptuous of the men he saw encamped near the Harvard campus, especially their leaders. "Their Officers generally speaking are the most indifferent kind of People I ever saw," he wrote in August 1775. "I have already broke one Colo. and five Captain's for Cowardice, & for drawing more Pay & Provision's than they had Men in their Companies. there is two more Colos. now under arrest, & to be tried for the same Offences." He confided to his cousin that he thought the rank and file better, but still un-impressive. "I daresay the Men would fight very well (if properly Officered) although they are an exceeding dirty & nasty people." Washington may have been undergoing a bit of culture shock with those flinty, egalitarian New Englanders.

His first inclination in Boston, from the summer of 1775 into the following winter, was to throw his forces into a complex two-pronged attack, with some moving up the Roxbury Neck and others attacking by boat. "I was not only ready, but willing and de-sirous of making the Assault," he informed John Hancock, the pres-ident of the Second Continental Congress. For a variety of reasons, this plan never was implemented, which was fortunate, because it would have been difficult to execute even by disciplined troops led by seasoned commanders. Washington did not have either of those on hand, so it was foolhardy to concoct such an approach. Luck-ily for him and for the future of the United States, this attack was made unnecessary by the British withdrawal the following spring to Nova Scotia and their subsequent redeployment to New York.

In addition, the ill-considered American invasion of Canada, also launched in 1775, was initiated more at the behest of Congress than of Washington, but he supported it. During this time, Washington also faced down John Thomas, an unruly Massachusetts general who, disappointed over a relatively trivial issue of military prece-dence, had decided to resign. You cannot step down, Washington warned, "without relinquishing in some Degree" your "publick Virtue & Honour." In this case, deploying those classical values worked. When the American commander of the invasion of Can-ada died, Washington dispatched the sensitive General Thomas to replace him. Thomas also expired (of smallpox), and the entire mis-begotten Canadian foray wound up costing the new Continental Army some five thousand troops, a loss it could barely afford.

Washington knew things were not going well and that his approach to the war was lacking. Indeed, at one point early in 1776 he allowed himself some private musings about what would happen if he lost the war, which many people thought would be decided in a year or two at most. In a letter to his brother-in-law

Burwell Bassett, he hinted at his plan for that. "Thank you heartily for the attention you have kindly paid to my landed affairs on the Ohio, my interest in which I shall be more Careful of as in the worst event, they will serve for an Asylum."

In August he plunged into direct combat against the British in and around New York City. He commanded 23,000 soldiers, not all of them seasoned; the British in turn had 32,000, plus 10,000 sailors who in a pinch could be thrown into a fight. The British flotilla was huge, amounting to some 430 vessels, enabling British commanders to move troops at will among Staten Island, Long Island, Manhattan, and the mainland. John Adams was eager for the confrontation: "We live in daily Expectation of hearing of some great Event. May God almighty grant it may be prosperous for America."

Adams' wish was not granted. The Americans first were driven off Long Island and then northward across Manhattan. Washington committed a series of blunders and was lucky to escape the two battles with as many men as he did. He wrote of the fight in Manhattan that he was stunned to see his men "running away in the most disgraceful and shamefull manner, nor could my utmost efforts rally them or prevent their flight." This is a general at odds with his troops, blaming them too much in order to avoid the hard fact that he had not led them well.

Others found it painful to watch Washington flailing, especially those under his command. John Haslet, commander of the 1st Delaware, one of the best regiments in the Army, privately was losing faith in Washington, and confided to a friend in Congress that his troops were as well. Washington could not seem to make up his mind, a situation always demoralizing for subordinate commanders. "The Genl I revere, his Character for Disinterestedness Patience & fortitude will be had in Everlasting Remembrances; but the Vast Burthen appears much too much his own," Haslet wrote to Caesar Rodney. "We have alarm upon alarm—Orders now issued, & the next moment reversed. Wd to heaven Genl [Charles] Lee were here is the Language of Officers and men."

The day after Haslet wrote that dejected letter, another smart officer, Nathanael Greene, took the bold step of writing a harsh but realistic message to Washington. "Part of the Army already has met with a defeat, the Country is struck with a pannick, any Cappital loss at this time may ruin the cause," the Rhode Islander warned his commander. So, he advised, rather than attack British positions, the Americans should "avoid any considerable misfortune. And to take post where the Enemy will be Obligd to fight us and not we them." Writing this letter was an act of courage on the part of Greene. He was speaking truth to power, telling his far more seasoned commander that he was fighting the war the wrong way. Greene, who would go on to become Washington's most effective general, conducting his own Fabian campaign in the South, also was offering an imaginative military judgment and pointing the way toward an alternative approach.

Washington was impressed. Soon afterward, he notified Congress that he was changing his strategy and now would aim to fight a defensive "war of posts," though was still figuring out just what that would be: "On our side the War should be defensive, It has been even called a War of posts, that we should on all occasions avoid a general Action or put anything to the risque unless compelled by a necessity into which we ought never to be drawn."

He remained unsure of the way forward. "In confidence I tell you that I never was in such an unhappy, divided state since I was born," Washington confessed to his cousin Lund Washington, who was overseeing Mount Vernon, and with whom he shared some of his darkest thoughts. He was in a moment of transition. People like to talk about how change is good, but they often forget how awkward, even exhausting and painful, it can be.

He would try this fortress approach in the following months, making the enemy come to him. Yet again he would fail, with the losses in November of Fort Washington, at the northern tip of Manhattan, and Fort Lee, directly west across the Hudson River. This time his unseasoned troops did not run away when they were in forts. Instead, they quickly surrendered. These were expensive setbacks, with more than 3,000 troops lost or captured at Fort Washington alone. "This is a most unfortunate affair and has given me great Mortification as we have lost not only two thousand Men that were there, but a good deal of Artillery, & some of the best Arms we had," Washington wrote in a private letter that understated his losses. "I am wearied almost to death with the retrograde Motions of things."

Following this dual reverse, he retreated with his surviving troops across the Hudson and into New Jersey. Washington's perceptions were changing. So was his vocabulary. At this point, the word "assault" disappears for months from Washington's orders to his subordinates and his reports to Congress. By contrast, he used the word "misfortune" a lot that year, including three times in one three-paragraph report to John Hancock. In late 1776 he also leaned heavily on the word "mortification" to describe his feelings, using it some seven times in his official correspondence of that period.

Still unsure of how to fight and whether to stick with this new defensive "posts" approach, Washington appeared to some around him as painfully indecisive. This was natural—he was in an intermediate stage—but it further undercut confidence in him. This is how Douglas Southall Freeman, a sympathetic biographer of Washington, summarizes this period: "The defence of Long Island had been worse than futile; Kip's Bay had been a disgrace, and October 28 at White Plains a humiliation; the surrender of Fort Washington had been a major disaster; the retreat through Jersey had involved a threat to Philadelphia and, indeed, to the very life of the United States."

What Washington's critics did not see then, and sometimes not even now, was that being indecisive was decidedly preferable to being decisively wrong.

## Joseph Reed's Unfaithful Letter

———

ONE OF THE MOST PAINFUL MOMENTS IN WASHINGTON'S MILITARY CAreer came at this anguished time. On November 30, 1776, he was

handed a note written by General Charles Lee, who was commanding a separate force and who had seemed wary of moving
it to support Washington's. The letter was addressed to Washington's military secretary, Colonel Joseph Reed (Princeton, 1757),
but Reed was absent, and Washington, eager to learn Lee's military plans and assuming it was an official dispatch, opened it.

As he read it, he must have been horrified. What he held in his
hand was a personal note from General Lee to Reed, and a highly
indiscreet one. Reed, it would develop, nine days earlier had dispatched a letter to Lee that detailed the British amusement over
Washington's inept handling of Forts Lee and Washington. They
"hold us very cheap in Consequence of the late Affair at Mount
Washington where both the Plan of Defence & Execution were
contemptible," he wrote. And Reed knew exactly whom to blame:
"An indecisive Mind is one of the greatest Misfortunes that can be-
fall an Army—how often have I lamented it this Campaign." You,
General Lee, would not have left those troops to be captured at Fort
Washington, Reed had added: "I have no Doubt had you been here
the Garrison at Mount Washington would now have composed
a Part of this Army"—rather than being held as prisoners of war.

Reed's note was the opposite of the candid letter Greene had
written to Washington three months earlier. Here, one of Washington's closest aides seemed to have concluded that Washington
had failed and was telling that to the man he hoped would replace
Washington, effectively offering to transfer his loyalty. And he
was quick to inform Lee that he was hardly alone in this view.
"Nor am I singular in my Opinion—every Gentleman of the Family the Officers & soldiers generally have a Confidence in you."
It was deeply unprofessional: As a matter of military discipline,
Reed owed it to express such disturbing thoughts to Washington
first, before taking them elsewhere.

Washington did not have Reed's letter in front of him, but he
could guess at it well enough, from Lee's brief response. He was
mortified, he later would recall. Lee's own note began with a hearty
endorsement of Reed's negative view of Washington's recent performance as a commander. "I receiv'd your most obliging flatter-

ing letter—lament with you that fatal indecision of mind which in war is a much greater disqualification than stupidity or even want of personal courage— . . . but eternal defeat and miscarriage must attend the man of the best parts if curs'd with indecision."

"Fatal indecision of mind"—what a slam. Washington showed his most tightly wound sense of honor in forwarding Lee's letter to Reed. "The inclosed was put into my hands by an Express from the White Plains," he explained in a three-paragraph cover note. "Having no Idea of its being a Private Letter, much less Suspecting the tendency of the Correspondence, I opened it, as I had done all other Letters to you, from the Same place and Peekskill, upon the business of your office." In this Olympian response, Washington was saying, You have been found out. I thought you a better man than this. But rather than take you to task, I am explaining to you why I, as a man of honor, happened to open your mail. Washington would distance himself emotionally from Reed, yet continued to work with him—a sign of his understanding that, given the stakes in the war, he could not let personal feelings, no matter how well founded, interfere with the task at hand. This was Washington the stoic.

Several months later, Reed, perhaps thinking enough time had elapsed for Washington to cool down, wrote to ask for a private conversation with Washington about the matter. Washington ignored that request, but months after that, in June, took a moment in a letter to respond. "True it is, I felt myself hurt by a certain Letter. . . . I was hurt, not because I thought my judgment wrong'd by the expressions contain in it, but because the same Sentiments were not communicated immediately to my self." In other words, it wasn't my emotions that mattered as much as your lack of military virtue. You failed in your duty to me and to the Army. He said he had always been open with Reed and welcomed his views, which

*entitled me, I thought, to your advice upon any point in which I appeared to be wanting—to meet with any thing then, that carried with it a complexion of witholding that advice from me, and*

*censuring my Conduct to another was such an argument of disen-*
*genuity that I was not a little mortified at it.*

He was absolutely right in these words. The good of the country came before his own personal feelings, but Reed had helped
neither with his underhanded letter to Lee.

## Washington's Low Point

LIFE GREW STEADILY GLOOMIER FOR WASHINGTON. ON THE SAME DAY
that he learned of Reed's lack of faith in him, the British issued an
amnesty offer to the people of New Jersey. Some 3,000 would accept, signing oaths of loyalty to the king. Among them was Richard Stockton (Princeton, 1748), who thus became the only signer
of the Declaration of Independence to abjure it. (To make matters
worse, the malleable Stockton, who was in poor health, later would
reverse his reversal and sign an oath supporting the rebels.) "Many
a disguised tory has lately shewn his head," noted Thomas Paine.

Northern New Jersey was the population center of the thirteen
rebellious colonies, which was significant in a war that was fought
not to take land but to win the allegiance of the people. The wa-
vering spirit of the public was reflected in the lack of support that
Washington was receiving from the local militias. He was becoming both dismayed and worried. On December 14, he noted in a
letter that "the spirits of the People . . . are quite sunk by our late
misfortunes."

Four days later he seemed almost in despair as he wrote to his
brother Samuel. He had roughly 3,000 men fit for duty, according
to a careful count made by Lieutenant James Monroe, the future
president. "If every nerve is not straind to recruit the New Army
with all possible Expedition I think the game is pretty near up,"
he wrote. "You can form no Idea of the perplexity of my Situation.
No Man, I believe, ever had a greater choice of difficulties & less
means to extricate himself from them."

Washington had tried to fight the British in two different ways, and both had failed. His army was melting way. His senior subordinates doubted him. The people were losing heart.

He needed a win, something to rally his men and deter fence-sitters from joining the Loyalists. Truth be told, he also needed it to shore up his own position. Reed's faithless letter to General Lee highlighted Washington's need for something to show he was the right general to lead the American army. It was at this time that the conspiratorial General Lee confided to another general, Horatio Gates, that "entre nous, a certain great man is most damnably deficient. . . . In short unless something which I do not expect turns up we are lost."

And so the war came to Princeton. On November 29, 1776, Witherspoon suspended operations at the college. He acted just in time. On December 7, British troops occupied the campus. The basement of Nassau Hall, the college's building, was made a jail for locals suspected of rebel leanings. Even worse, the female camp followers of the British army had learned in New York City that books could be traded for gin or fine clothes, so they descended upon the college's collection. Between them and some of the Hessians (German soldiers hired by the British), "they soon gutted the library, the museum, and the lecture-rooms; carried off or destroyed every volume upon the shelves; and broke up all the philosophical and mathematical instruments for the sake of the brass fittings." They then pillaged Witherspoon's house. A friend reported to Thomas Jefferson that "Old Weatherspoon has not escap'd their fury. They have burnt his library. It grieves him much that he has lost his controversial Tracts. He would lay aside the Cloth to take revenge of them."

## A Much-Needed Victory

IN MID-DECEMBER, WASHINGTON STEPPED UP HIS USE OF THE NEW Jersey militias, dispatching a veteran officer, the hard-drinking, hard-fighting Brigadier General "Scotch Willie" Maxwell, to stiffen them with a forward force of Continental soldiers. Washington's orders to Maxwell are instructive, revealing his growing understanding of the militias and how to use them effectively. He tasked them to gather intelligence and to nibble at the foe's extremities, tiring and distracting the British:

> *You are to be extreamely vigilant & watchful to guard against surprizes, & to use every means in your power to obtain a knowledge of the Enemys Numbers—Situation—and designs. If at any time you should discover that they are moving from Brunswick and that Quarter towards Trenton, or the Delaware in other parts, endeavour, if it can be attempted with a probability of success, to fall upon their Rear, & if nothing more can be done, annoy them in their March.*
>
> *Every piece of Intelligence wch you may think of Importance for me to know, communicate it without loss of time.*

This is a commander who is learning. Washington was not just consuming intelligence, but also generating it with how he used forces in the field.

Washington finally got the victory he so badly needed at the end of December 1776, when he crossed the Delaware River, surprised the isolated Hessian garrison at Trenton, and took some 948 prisoners. Congress was so relieved by his report of the victory that it printed his letter about it. In early January, after a second fight on the south side of Trenton, Washington attacked the British forces at Princeton. At that battle on the campus, Alexander Hamilton by many accounts directed his battery of cannon to fire at the college chapel, with one six-pound shot hitting a portrait hanging there of King George II. Hamilton might have happily blasted any part of the college, given that it had rejected his application to matriculate there as an advanced student.

The shock waves of these victories crossed the Atlantic to hit tobacco merchants in London. "The unhappy capture of the Hessian detachment at Trent Town and the subsequent skirmishes in the Jersey . . . blasted the agreeable prospect of a speedy settlement," one tobacco agent reported to his home office. What's more, he added, Washington's successes had boosted recruitment of soldiers by the Americans and also bolstered the credit of American-issued paper money. All politics being local, he fretted that this series of events would drive up the price of American tobacco.

## Washington vs. Adams on Strategy

IT IS A CLICHÉ, AND A BAD ONE, THAT GENERALS TRY TO "FIGHT THE last war"—that is, do what worked the last time out. That does not give them enough credit. Rather, they tend to fight the war they would like to fight or the one that they expected to fight. But neither of those responses is usually sufficient. The foremost task of a general is to understand the nature of the war he or she faces—which often turns out to be a third way, neither the one preferred nor the one expected. This sort of discernment is especially difficult at the foggy, uncertain, unpredictable opening phase of a conflict.

Once a commander feels he or she grasps the nature of the war, the next job is to assess the tools at hand to fight it:

⊙ What resources are available, and how might they be employed to address the task at hand?
⊙ What can I ask my troops to do, and what should I recognize as exceeding their capabilities?
⊙ Which of my subordinate commanders are true wartime leaders, and which of them just looks good?

Answering these questions is the hard work at the core of generalship. It is a sign of the difficulty of top command that most people in it fail, especially because the answers change—what was effective last week may not be effective next week, because an adept enemy also learns and changes. Sometimes victory goes simply to the commander who fails least.

Addressing the third of these questions, sorting out subordinate commanders, was a particularly onerous task for Washington. He would be horribly disappointed in different ways by three of the generals who early in the war appeared most promising: Horatio Gates and Charles Lee, who undercut him, and Benedict Arnold, who betrayed the entire cause.

Washington, to his everlasting credit, did not fail. By early in 1777, writes Kwasny, in one of the best studies of Washington's generalship, "he clearly had abandoned the strategy of a war of posts." Rather, he became a modified Fabian, pursuing "a more fluid war of maneuver, skirmish, and occasionally full-scale battle. As long as the British kept coming out of their camps and fighting, he could use the militia and detached regulars to inflict damage while protecting the main army."

Most important, he had learned how to use the soldiers he had. Yes, militiamen were not regulars. They tended to scatter and run in set-piece battles, especially when hit in the open by volleys from well-drilled British troops, sometimes followed by a terrifying bayonet charge. Yet condemning such troops was like criticizing a saw for not being a hammer. At first Washington seemed exasperated by the nature of the militias, writing in January 1777 that "if the Militia cannot be prevaild upon to restrain the Foraging parties & to annoy and Harrass the Enemy in their excursions & upon a March they will be of very little use to us, as I am sure they can never be brought fairly up to an attack in any serious matter." Adding to his annoyance at the time, he had been told that militia commanders had absconded with a good deal of the British supplies captured at Princeton.

But with time, he learned better how to use them for what they were, and to avoid misusing them. "It is of the greatest importance we should learn to estimate them rightly," Washington later instructed. "We may expect every thing from ours, that Militia is capable of; but we must not expect from any, services for which Regulars alone are fit."

In other words, these men could be militarily effective when used in a manner that played to their strengths. Let them fight near their own towns, amid familiar fields, forests, and hills, and they would prove more resilient. Encourage them to take on isolated British patrols. And when the situation was quiet, let them slip home to tend to their farms. It was not a recipe for conventional military glory, but it did point the way toward a strategy for possibly defeating the British.

Attacking British foraging parties and supply convoys had more military impact than one might think. While battles happen only occasionally, an army must eat every day. For much of the time, on any given day, the real war was these small skirmishes with isolated British units. "We have had a pretty amusement known by the name of foraging or fighting for our daily bread," a Scottish redcoat named James Murray reported in a letter. "As the rascals are skulking about the whole country, it is impossible to move with any degree of safety without a pretty large escort." One militia tactic was to leave cattle out in the open and then ambush the British as they tried to capture the herd.

There also were side benefits: The more the British foraging parties were harassed, the less they were able to scavenge food and supplies from the local Americans. Also, the British forces, rather than resting and recovering during the winter, were fatigued by the need for constant patrols, usually in large numbers. Most eighteenth-century armies tried to avoid fighting in winter, when it was difficult to keep animals fed. But the American militias were unusually effective in the cold season, for two reasons: Farmers serving in the militias were not as busy tending their crops, and supplies were harder for the British to come by, forcing enemy foraging parties to march further afield even as the days grew short. The American irregulars were so successful in New Jersey that eventually the British had most of their supplies shipped in from New York City. There was an additional political side benefit in that the militias could regulate the people, keeping an eye on Tories and fence-sitters in their midst. If a man did not show up for his local militia muster, he knew he might face hard questions, formal or not, from friends and neighbors.

The longer such skirmishing lasted, the more the British would falter. They might lose two men one day, ten the next, and then see forty taken prisoner in an ambush on the third. When the British ejected the American army from New York City in August and September of 1776, they had fielded 31,600 soldiers. By February of 1777 they had just 14,000, with the rest simply gone—killed, badly wounded, seriously ill, captured, or deserted.

The British became painfully conscious of this new American approach. "Though it was once the fashion of this army to treat them in the most contemptible light, they are now become a formidable enemy," a British colonel in New Jersey reported to his father in England. The key for the Americans was finding ways to ensure that such small-scale fighting *did* continue.

By March of 1777, Washington's revised mode of fighting was becoming clearer to all. "General How has invareably pursued the Maxims of an invader this Campaign, by indeavoring to bring us to a General Action, and avoid skirmishing," Nathanael Greene, who would go on to become Washington's best general, tried to explain to John Adams. "General Washington as every defender ought has followed directly the contrary conduct, by indeavoring to Skirmish with the Enemy at all times, and avoid a general engagement."

This emerging shape of the war was even recognized thousands of miles away in England. Horace Walpole, the son of a former prime minister and himself a politician, wrote to a friend that "the provincials . . . seem to have been apprised that protraction of the war would be more advantageous to them than heroism. Washington, the dictator, has shown himself both a Fabius and a Camillus [an early Roman general]. His march through our lines is allowed to have been a prodigy of generalship."

Adams, who for unknown reasons seemed to believe he was an expert on military affairs, was having none of it. He responded to all this Fabianism with a blast:

> It is high Time for Us to abandon this execrable defensive Plan. It
> will be our Ruin if We do not. Long Lines, and defensive Systems
> have very near, undone Us. . . . Our Army has ever been such an
> hugh enormous Mass of Deadness and Torpor, that I dont wonder
> their Inactivity has bred the Plague among them. We must have a
> fighting enterprizing Spirit conjured up in our Army. The Army
> that Attacks has an infinite Advantage, and ever has had from the
> Plains of Pharsalia to the Plains of Abraham, the Plains of Trenton
> and Princeton.

(Pharsalia, the field in Greece where Caesar defeated Pompey, is
mentioned in the first speech given by Cato in Joseph Addison's
play.) This letter was drafted but not sent, as even Adams realized that it was too insulting and, as he put it, "unpolite" in its
tone.

But he was hardly finished. Later that spring, Adams wrote and
sent to Greene an 800-word missive relating at great length the
wiles of Sulla during the Roman Civil Wars, and warning that the
Americans not be similarly hoodwinked into deserting by British
commander Howe. "Howe is no Sylla, but he is manifestly aping
two of Syllas Tricks, holding out Proposals of Truces and bribing
Soldiers to desert," he admonished. But even as Adams griped,
Washington's third approach was becoming more distinct and
better understood. He was becoming a Fabian.

## Hamilton Explains Washington's Strategy

ALEXANDER HAMILTON, AS ARTICULATE AS HE WAS BRASH, JOINED
Washington's staff in March 1777. As part of his new post, he often was sent on missions to elucidate war plans to Washington's
subordinate commanders and others. In one letter that year, he
explained why rolling the dice on a major battle was an unwise
gamble. In doing so he laid out the logic of waging indirect war:

*I know the comments that some people will make on our Fabian
conduct. It will be imputed either to cowardice or to weakness: But
the more discerning, I trust, will not find it difficult to conceive that
it proceeds from the truest policy, and is an argument neither of the
one nor the other. The liberties of America are an infinite stake.
We should not play a desperate game for it or put it upon the issue
of a single cast of the die. The loss of one general engagement may
effectually ruin us, and it would certainly be folly to hazard it, unless our resources for keeping up an army were at an end, and some
decisive blow was absolutely necessary; or unless our strength was
so great as to give certainty of success. Neither is the case. America
can in all probability maintain its army for years, and our numbers
though such as would give a reasonable hope of success are not such
as should make us intirely sanguine.*

Hamilton concluded with a marvelously succinct summary of
American strategy: "Our business then is to avoid a General engagement and waste the enemy away by constantly goading their
sides, in a desultory teazing way."

Hamilton wrote that at the age of just twenty, if he was indeed
born in 1757, as he told people. (The evidence nowadays indicates
that he probably was born in 1755, so he may have been writing
at the slightly riper age of twenty-two.) His letter certainly reflects
the thinking of Washington, Greene, and others, but nonetheless
it is noteworthy because of the clarity and energy of its prose.

Hamilton had an odd kind of genius about waging war. In this,
as in so many other ways, good and bad, he was the opposite of
John Adams. Two years earlier, when the war was barely underway, he had foreseen how the Americans should fight. Hamilton
wrote in an essay that

*The circumstances of our country put it in our power, to evade a
pitched battle. It will be better policy, to harass and exhaust the soldiery, by frequent skirmishes and incursions, than to take the open
field with them, by which means, they would have the full benefit
of their superior regularity and skill.*

This was a fair prediction of the strategy Washington eventually would pursue. The surprise is that such a young man should have had such depth of understanding. Some experts think that despite his relative lack of education, Hamilton had been influenced by the skeptical new thinking coming out of Edinburgh and Glasgow. "Perhaps the most pervasive feature of Hamilton's *Farmer Refuted* . . . is the way in which those habits of mind most characteristic of the Enlightenment—especially the Scottish—are reflected throughout most of its pages," write Stanley Elkins and Eric McKitrick. "There is a conviction, at once hard and utopian, that both one's learning and one's experience may be used instrumentally, to lay hold of the future and shape it."

By mid-1777 Washington had settled into this new "desultory teazing" way of war, in the process developing—and expressing—a new appreciation of his militiamen. In June 1777 he wrote: "I must observe, and with peculiar satisfaction I do it, that on the first notice of the Enemy's movements, the Militia assembled in the most spirited manner, firmly determined to give them every Annoyance in their power and to afford us every possible aid."

Washington now would attack at times of opportunity, but not seek to decide the war through big battles. When some of his generals counseled him to consolidate all American troops—regulars and militias—in one spot, he reacted with horror. "If this is really the intention I should think it a very ineligible Plan," he admonished one of his generals. Rather, he said, the militias being raised in New Hampshire and Massachusetts might best aid his main force by harassing British lines of communication and supply, and also cutting off possible lines of retreat: "A tolerable Body of Men once collected there would make Mr Bourgoigne anxious for his Rear—oblige him to advance circumspectly and to leave such strong Posts behind, as must make his main body very weak, and extremely capable of being repulsed by the force we shall have in front." This more subtle use of militias had the added advantage of helping them to compensate for their lack of military skills and discipline.

Professor Ellis summarizes Washington's next step well:

*The strategic key was the Continental Army. If it remained intact as an effective fighting force, the American Revolution remained alive. The British army could occupy Boston, New York, and Philadelphia, and it did. The British navy could blockade and bombard American seaports with impunity, and it did. The Continental Congress could be driven from one location to another like a covey of pigeons, and it was. But as long as Washington held the Continental Army together, the British could not win the war, which in turn meant that they would eventually lose it.*

Even now, not all historians understand this. One recent work offered a summary that ignores the approach laid out explicitly by Hamilton, stating that "most of the campaigning season of 1777 had been consumed in fruitless maneuverings, marches and countermarches." Had Hamilton been able to read that, he might well have responded, *Precisely so! And the point is that at the end of that year, we still had an army.*

In fact, Washington was implementing a smart variation on the Fabian strategy. With hindsight it is clear that there existed a strong strategic parallel between the circumstances of the ancient Roman situation and the American Revolution. In both cases, the defender was facing an invader from overseas who had to cross land and sea barriers in order to bring in additional supplies and troops. Those hurdles made attacking the invader's supply lines and exhausting his troops an especially productive approach. Supplies were harder for him to find, and replacements had to come from afar. That point was made repeatedly in the small bookshelf of the military instruction manuals that became part of Washington's traveling headquarters.

But John Adams did not understand this. The more seriously Adams was in error, the more emphatically he raged against the Fabian approach, telling his wife that "I am sick of Fabian Systems in all Quarters. The Officers drink a long and moderate War. My Toast is a short and violent War. They would call me mad and rash &c. but I know better." Alas, he did not.

Adams was no more reliable in his assessment of the British military leadership. "Howe is a wild General," he wrote, a view not shared by many, then or now. Washington more accurately assessed Howe as "a Man of no enterprize"—that is, someone who would not show initiative.

Adams also was 180 degrees off in judging the benefits of foreign military assistance. He advocated that the United States have "no military Connection" with France and "receive no Troops from her." Had his advice been followed, the decisive Battle of Yorktown—at which French ships proved essential and French troops helpful—might have turned out differently or never happened at all.

## The Political Risk of the Fabian Strategy

AS ADAMS' ATTACKS SHOW, A CONSTANT RISK OF THE FABIAN STRATEGY was how it was perceived. Others could depict Washington as slow or indecisive. Indeed, Thomas Paine, who should have known better, having traveled as an embedded writer with the Americans during their 1776 retreat across New Jersey, would never forgive Washington for pursuing this strategy of "doing nothing." "You slept away your time in the field," he charged years later in an open letter denouncing Washington. "Nothing was done in the campaigns of 1778, 1779, 1780, in the part where General Washington commanded, except the taking of Stony Point by Anthony Wayne. . . . The Fabian system of war, followed by him, began now to unfold itself with all its evils; but what is Fabian war without Fabian means to support it?" It isn't clear what Paine meant by that question, except that he seemed to doubt Washington that had the skills to execute such a strategy.

Washington certainly was aware of such sentiments, and may have shared some of them himself. A naturally aggressive commander, he would always be a reluctant Fabian. "He was a fighter," states the British scholar Marcus Cunliffe. "He erred not through timidity, which would have proved fatal in the long run, but through pugnacity."

As a modified Fabian, he knew there were also times when he would be compelled to give battle. Sometimes the reason was to build up morale or to rally the militias. Sometimes it was political. For example, in mid-September 1777, Washington had to show the American people that he would not give up their capital of Philadelphia without a fight, so he engaged in a pitched battle at Brandywine Creek, a few miles west of the city. "It was incumbent upon him to risk a battle, to preserve that capital," General Howe later observed. It was the single largest engagement of the war, and one of the worst for the Americans, who seemed not to have scouted the ground on which they fought, an inexplicable military blunder. Washington was badly defeated. Among the dead lay James Witherspoon, the son of the president of Princeton who at his graduation seven years earlier had given an eloquent address on the need to resist bad kings. Later that month the British marched into Philadelphia.

Three weeks after Brandywine, Washington attacked the British again, this time on the northern outskirts of Philadelphia, at Germantown. Again, he was tactically unsuccessful. Benjamin Rush sourly wrote to John Adams that Washington has been "outgenerald and twice beated."

Yet again: Battles won are not wars won. In the Germantown fight Washington suffered a tactical setback but maintained his strategic advantage by steadily wearing down his foe. General Howe, more conscious of the trend of the war than either Rush or Adams, said later in his testimony to the House of Commons that "the most essential duty I had was, not wantonly to commit his Majesty's troops, where the object was inadequate. I knew well that any considerable loss sustained by the army could not speedily, or easily be repaired."

And sometimes battles can be very important indeed. In the fall of 1777, Generals Gates and Arnold (the latter had not yet defected) scored a major victory far to the north, in Saratoga, New

York. This proved to be the most significant fight of the war, because it led a few months later to the formal American alliance with France. Thereafter, the British would not just be facing American rebels, but also a major European power, not just in America, but also at sea and around the world. British commanders contemplating troop movements would always be looking over their shoulders for French warships. After Saratoga, writes Piers Mackesy, in the most insightful analysis of British strategy in the war, "the centre of gravity was no longer in Philadelphia, but in Paris."

Some of those around Washington feared that after Brandywine and Germantown, and perhaps with the contrast of Saratoga in mind, Washington might abandon the Fabian approach and seek that elusive rousing victory. "A General Action is by all means to be avoided by us at present," cautioned Major General John Sullivan of New Hampshire, who had commanded the American right wing, hard against the bank of the Delaware, during the first battle of Trenton, and then, a week later, the same wing at the battle of Princeton. He also counseled Washington to ignore the recommendations of the naysayers: "Had Fabius attended to the Advice given him by the Roman youth[,] Hannibal would have found Little Difficulty in possessing himself of Italy."

The Marquis de Lafayette, the young Frenchman who advised Washington and rose to high position in the American Army, also grew concerned by the critics. He wrote to Washington later that year denouncing, in a palpably French accent, those "Stupid men who without knowing a Single word about war undertake to judge You, to make Ridiculous Comparisons; they are infatuated with [General Horatio] Gates without thinking of the different Circumstances, and Believe that attaking is the only thing Necessary to Conquer. . . . who want to push You in a moment of ill Humour to Some Rash enterprise Upon the lines or Against a much stronger army." A week later, Major General Arthur St. Clair (attended University of Edinburgh) offered similar counsel, telling him to stick to the path of "the less Shewy but regulated Conduct of Fabius."

Stringing the British along was, in fact, precisely the right strategy. It took advantage of the abilities of American forces and minimized their weaknesses. Moreover, the British could not figure out an effective way to counter the Fabian approach. Washington faced down four British commanders during the war. As Nathaniel Philbrick puts it, "As one after the other of his British opponents, from Thomas Gage to William Howe (with Clinton and Cornwallis soon to follow), returned to England in disgrace, he had found a way, despite having lost more battles than he had won, to keep his army, and by extension his country, together." Time was on Washington's side, if he could hold the army together and not lose it in the field.

Americans generally endorsed the approach. In the popular view, Washington had done the right thing the right way. One American composed a poem to Washington thus commending him: "I Saw great Fabius Come in state/ I Saw the british Lions fate." To the French, Washington became "Le Fabius de l'amérique." John Adams may have never gotten on board, but his son John Quincy Adams (Harvard, 1787) eventually did, concluding decades later that the Fabian strategy had "succeeded in our Revolutionary War."

Long after the war, Washington, in a note to a subordinate, seemed to summarize the change his personality had undergone during those difficult years. "In all important matters," he advised, "deliberate maturely, but. . . . execute promptly & vigorously." Through the crucible of war he had proven himself to be the noblest Roman of them all.

## Chapter 9

# The War Strains the
# Classical Model

O NE WINTER'S DAY AT VALLEY FORGE, COLONEL JOHN BROOKS OF Massachusetts, who had fought at Concord, White Plains, and Saratoga, confided to a friend that the Army was in worrisome shape: "In my opinion nothing but virtue has kept our army together through this campaign." That sentence is comprehensible only if "virtue" is read in the eighteenth-century sense of the word, meaning public-spiritedness, or putting the common good above one's own interest.

Yet that same winter in that same camp, Washington began to sense that relying too heavily on the public-mindedness of Americans was becoming a dangerous course. "A small knowledge of human nature will convince us," Washington wrote in a report to a visiting committee of Congress, that

> with far the greatest part of mankind, interest is the governing
> principle; and that, almost, every man is more or less, under its
> influence. Motives of public virtue may for a time, or in particular
> instances, actuate men to the observance of a conduct purely dis-
> interested; but they are not of themselves sufficient to produce
> a persevering conformity to the refined dictates and obligations of
> social duty. Few men are capable of making a continual sacri-
> fice of all views of private interest, or advantage, to the common
> good.

Washington seems to be warning here that what got the rebels to this point would not be enough to carry them through to victory. They were expecting too much of people.

In a nutshell, Washington was sensing the limits of virtue as a driver of the new country. He is not often seen as a political philosopher, but in his own quiet way he was ahead of most of his peers. That spring, he unburdened himself to a Virginian member of Congress about the way forward. It is worth quoting at length, in part because Washington here begins to anticipate some of the arguments that would emerge a decade later during the Constitutional Convention's debates about the need to account for the role of self-interest in public life:

> *Men may speculate as they will—they may talk of patriotism— they may draw a few examples from ancient story of great atchievements performed by it's influence; but, whoever builds upon it, as a sufficient basis, for conducting a long and bloody War, will find themselves deceived in the end. . . . I do not mean to exclude altogether the idea of patriotism. I know it exists, and I know it has done much in the present contest. But I will venture to assert, that a great and lasting War can never be supported on this principle alone—It must be aided by a prospect of interest or some reward. For a time it may, of itself, push men to action—to bear much—to encounter difficulties; but it will not endure unassisted by interest.*

In modern terms, Washington was sensing that there was something wrong with the model. To cast Washington as an astute social and political analyst may seem a stretch, until we remember that he was a master at observing and learning from experience, at the difficult task of simply perceiving what was really going on around him. Remember also that his thoughts and senses would have been tuned intensely that winter to the question of what would hold together his army and what might weaken or even dissolve it. As the historian Glenn Phelps puts it, "The War for Independence was a great influence on the development of George

Washington's public philosophy." Washington would emerge from the war, Phelps adds, persuaded that "in republican government, virtue must always be tied to interest."

Washington also may have had some discussions with others about this emerging perception. He would have known that some members of Congress were themselves pondering the danger of relying overmuch on public virtue. Elbridge Gerry of Massachusetts, for example, had written in November 1776, that, "The Want of public Virtue . . . is too apparent to admit of a Doubt." Washington, Gerry, and others were sensing that the times were changing, and that this new America might require a new approach.

Washington's insight would be articulated and then refined into political theory by James Madison ten years later. The two men would work closely together for a time in the 1780s, when Jefferson was off in France. One wonders if they found common ground in realizing that the neoclassical dependence on virtue was insufficient to deal with the new realities of the United States.

Washington's doubts would deepen as the war dragged on, but he still clung to the notion that virtue somehow might revive. "Unless we can return a little more to first principles, & act a little more upon patriotic ground, I do not know when it will [end]—or—what may be the issue of the contest," he fretted in March 1779. He was dismayed by seeing "too many melancholy proofs of the decay of public virtue." In another anguished letter later that spring, he confessed that, "I have said more than enough; & shall add no more on this head—but lament, which I do most pathetically that decay of public virtue with which people were inspired at the beginning of this contest."

## Washington's Forgotten Victory

ONE OF WASHINGTON'S GREATEST FABIAN VICTORIES WAS BLOODLESS, and so tends to be overlooked in most histories of the war. That quiet triumph came at dawn on June 17, 1778, when the British began evacuating Philadelphia. They had benefited little from the eight months of occupation there, most notably in failing to force Washington to face them in a decisive confrontation.

The entry of the French into the war changed the British strategic view of it, and especially the ability of British forces to maneuver by sea. Where the British had once been able to float their troops from port to port at will, they now had to contend with the prospect of the French fleet catching them—or bottling them up in one of those ports. General Sir Henry Clinton, taking command in Philadelphia from Howe, who had resigned, was ordered by London to deliver more than a third of his 15,000 troops to the West Indies and Florida to help counter the French there, and then move the remainder to New York City, where many of the remaining British forces would consolidate.

Joseph Galloway, who was overseeing Philadelphia's Loyalist government, was appalled by the British decision to leave the city. He had helped the British find food and horses, as well as run a spy network for them. He even had conducted a census of the political affiliations of the adult male population. He and the British knew that the departure would frighten Loyalists up and down the seaboard, as well as erstwhile rebels who had come in to seek British pardons. "The rebels were inspired with fresh hopes; the friends of government were dismayed," General Howe would recall in his testimony before Parliament on the conduct of the war.

That was putting it mildly. Howe's secretary, Ambrose Serle, recorded in his diary that Philadelphia's Loyalists were "filled . . . with melancholy on the Apprehension of being speedily deserted, now a Rope was (as it were) around their necks & all their Property subject to Confiscation." Galloway, in particular, looked upon the situation "with Horror & melancholy," as he would be "exposed to the Rage of his bitter enemies, deprived of a Fortune of about £70,000, and now left to wander like Cain upon the Earth."

He was right to be distraught. Loyalists were left in a bind. The only thing worse than not being protected at all was to first be protected and thus encouraged to shed one's neutral or ambiguous stance, and then to lose that protection and so be exposed to retaliation by the rebels. In a war for the allegiance of the people, the British could hardly have made a worse move. Loyalists were shocked: If the British were unwilling to expend resources to hold onto the rebel capital, then how much more vulnerable were Tories in other lower-profile areas? John Shy, one of the most insightful analysts of the war, concludes that after this point Loyalists could be "fairly sure of one thing: the British government no longer could or would maintain its presence, and sooner or later the rebels would return. Under these circumstances, civilian attitudes could no longer be manipulated by British policies or actions."

In sum, the British withdrawal from Philadelphia was a major defeat, if a nearly silent one. Yes, Washington had not brought about this outcome by himself. The British retreat began with the American victory the previous year at Saratoga, which encouraged the French to ally with America, which in turn forced the British to recalculate their vulnerabilities and their allocation of resources, which ultimately led to the abandonment of Philadelphia. But if Washington is to be held responsible for losses not entirely of his own making, so too should he be credited for similarly wrought victories.

Galloway, unfortunately for him, had accurately assessed his future prospects. He sailed to England, where he proceeded to pen a blistering series of neoclassical denunciations of British supporters of the American Revolution, which he titled *Letters from Cicero to Catiline the Second*. He accused Charles Fox, leader of the Whig opposition, of treachery resembling that of the infamous Roman conspirator. He predicted that "all your secret intrigues shall be exposed to the full view of your fellow-citizens, that they may guard against your seduction, and save themselves from that ruin, which like another Catiline, you have long meditated against your country." He also would criticize "the notorious indolence" of Admiral Lord Howe's naval operations in the war. He would die in exile.

Watching from outside Philadelphia that summer, Washington now knew exactly what to do and how to do it. He first ordered his militia commander in New Jersey to harass British units, slowing and fatiguing them, and to report back to him constantly. He wrote to his commander there, Philemon Dickinson (named for an old Greek myth that Ovid had written about), that "I rely on your activity to give the enemy all possible obstruction, in their march; and that you will give me instant and regular intelligence of every thing, that passes."

The enemy had developed a grim appreciation of the ability of militiamen to attack, fall back, hide, and attack again. Johann Ewald, a discerning Hessian officer, recorded that he had never "seen these maneuvers carried out better than by the American militia, especially by that of the province of Jersey. If you were forced to retreat through these people you could be certain of having them constantly around you." Ewald likened the British retreat from Philadelphia to New York during those muggy days to Xenophon's ten thousand Greeks fighting their way home after their defeat in Babylon. "Bygone heroes could not have had more hardships on their marches than we endured," he wrote.

As the British entered New Jersey, their baggage train stretched out a full twelve miles, making a long and enticing target for American militiamen. Meanwhile, Washington's regulars caught up with the departing British forces in the middle of New Jersey, in a messy encounter now remembered as the Battle of Monmouth. In a kind of combined arms operation of the eighteenth century, the regulars charged the British while the militias hung on their fringes, especially denying them safe access to watering holes. This would be Washington's last battle until Yorktown, more than three years later. Much of the subsequent fighting in the war occurred in the south, as the British searched for more sympathetic Americans on whom to base their operations. But even in the middle colonies there would be constant nipping by irregulars at British forces, who slowly pulled back into the Atlantic ports.

## Meanwhile, Back in Virginia

———

THOMAS JEFFERSON DID NOT HAVE A GOOD REVOLUTIONARY WAR. AS governor of Virginia, from 1779 to 1781, he was a bust. All state leaders faced trouble in supporting the war, but Jefferson was particularly listless even in responding to the three British incursions into his state late in the war. In the last one, in 1781, the notorious British cavalry commander, Colonel Banastre Tarleton, nearly nabbed him at Monticello. Jefferson escaped astride his horse Caractacus—named for the British chieftain who led resistance to the Roman invasion in the first century AD—riding southwest up the steep green slope of Carter Mountain, avoiding the main roads. As Tarleton smugly phrased it, "he provided for his personal liberty by a precipitate retreat." Decades later, embittered Federalists would mock Jefferson as "the Carter-Mountain hero" who had proved somewhat ". . . skittish / When menac'd by the bullying British."

Jefferson later would feebly explain that as governor, he was "unprepared by his line of life and education for the command of armies." It was a dismaying defense to mount, and especially for someone with ambitions to lead the nation. To be charitable, Jefferson may have learned from the experience, as Washington did from his defeats in the French and Indian War. Even so, if Washington had behaved as slowly and ineffectively during the Revolution as Jefferson did, the war could have ended with a British victory by December of 1776.

## The British
## (and William & Mary)
## Take a Beating

———

IN SEPTEMBER 1781, AFTER FOUR LONG YEARS OF FOLLOWING AN INDI-rect approach, Washington finally was able to cast off the Fabian strategy and operate in the conventional offensive posture he found more natural. When he saw the opportunity presented by the presence of French ships and troops to trap the British on the Virginia coast, he moved resolutely. "The instant he had assurance of naval superiority on the allied side, he used it to effect the swift concentration that proved decisive," observes Douglas Southall Freeman.

Washington took his forces south to execute a move with the French fleet against the British. With the French cruising offshore, he besieged the army of General Cornwallis at Yorktown, just to the east of Williamsburg. In large part because of effective French aid, both at sea and on land, this campaign culminated five weeks later with the surrender of Cornwallis' force. The British army continued to hold New York City, but the war effectively was over. It would take another twenty-two months to arrive at a signed peace treaty, and many months more for both sides to ratify it.

The nearby College of William & Mary was a casualty of this last major fight. The college buildings had been occupied by French troops, who converted them into a hospital for their ill and injured. They erected a huge three-story latrine on one side of the building, with a pit underneath it, thus enabling the patients to defecate without having to go up or down the stairs. The resulting stench was astonishing, reported James Tilton, a Delaware regiment surgeon assigned to tend to the American wounded sent there. He remembered that "this sink of nastiness perfumed the whole house very sensibly and, without doubt, vitiated all the air within the wards."

## Washington Rejects Caesarism

AS THE WAR FADED AWAY, WASHINGTON REJECTED YET ANOTHER ROMAN model: He would not become a Julius Caesar, the general who takes over the nation. He probably could easily have done so, had he wanted to.

In the spring of 1783, Washington's officer corps, encamped outside Newburgh, New York, a few miles north of West Point, was on edge. They felt unsupported by the American people, some of whom had grown rich on the war while they had fought and bled. They were especially unhappy with the failure of Congress to send them the pay they had been promised.

In his scheming way, young Alexander Hamilton may have brought the matter to a head. He had left the Army and been appointed to the Continental Congress, arriving in November 1782. He quickly began looking for ways to pressure that body to become more serious about raising revenue. In mid-February, Hamilton wrote to Washington for the first time in over a year. He wanted, as he put it, "to suggest to you my ideas on some matters of delicacy and importance." Hamilton's impudent notion was that "the claims of the army" could be made "useful" to Congress. But, he added, perhaps too clever by half, "the difficulty will be to keep a *complaining* and *suffering army* within the bounds of moderation" [Hamilton's italics].

So, he suggested, perhaps Washington should not interfere if the Army's officers made public protests about their pay and pensions. And maybe Washington should even quietly encourage such protests. If so, he counseled, conspiratorially, Washington should keep his role quiet: "This however must not appear: it is of moment to the public tranquillity that Your Excellency should preserve the confidence of the army without losing that of the people."

Hamilton was treading here on dangerous ground. He was inviting Washington to conspire with him to manipulate the Army into intimidating Congress. He concluded this extraordinary letter by giving Washington a rude nudge. Washington, he warned, was seen by some officers as so heedful of respecting Congress that he had failed to adequately support the soldiers' interests. "I will not conceal from Your Excellency a truth which it is necessary you should know. An idea is propagated in the army that delicacy carried to an extreme prevents your espousing its interests with sufficient warmth." Was Hamilton insinuating that Washington was putting his own image and feelings before the needs of his soldiers? In other words, did Washington lack the virtue to do what was required? Coming from the twenty-six-year-old Hamilton to the commanding general of the U.S. Army, this veered very close to insult.

Meanwhile, according to notes taken by James Madison, Hamilton was telling fellow members of Congress that Washington's volatile temper was intensifying even as his popularity in the Army was diminishing. Hamilton, a bit recklessly, was stirring up trouble at both ends of the situation.

Pressure on Washington was increasing. Joseph Jones, a Virginia friend of Washington's who was serving in Congress, wrote to warn the general that he was hearing rumors of insubordination in the Army. "Reports are freely circulated here that there are dangerous combinations in the Army, and within a few days past it has been said, they are about to declare, they will not disband untill their demands are complied with."

Tellingly, Washington did not respond to Hamilton for three weeks, causing the young man some unease. On March 5, Hamilton apprehensively queried the general: "I had the honor of writing to your Excellency lately on a very confidential subject and shall be anxious to know as soon as convenient whether the letter got safe to hand." This is how conspirators write: Did you get my extremely sensitive letter or was it intercepted?

In fact, Washington had finally responded to Hamilton's spidery plan just the previous day. He would not join in any schemes. Rather, he wrote, "I shall pursue the same steady line of conduct which has governed me hitherto; fully convinced that the sensible, and discerning part of the army, cannot be unacquainted (although I never took pains to inform them) of the services I have rendered it, on more occasions than one." He was saying that rather than act out a charade, he instead would stand on his record of service to respond to any internal grumbling.

But even as Washington was writing, events were getting ahead of him. On Monday, March 10, an unsigned letter circulated in the camp stating that it was time for officers to stop asking Congress for their back pay and to start demanding it. If they did not get satisfaction, it advised, they should consider rebelling. The nation, it claimed, "tramples upon your rights, disdains your Cries—& insults your distresses." It called on the officers of the camp to "Awake—attend to your Situation & redress yourselves." We know now that the letter was written by an aide to Horatio Gates, a general who was a continual torment to Washington. A parallel letter called for a meeting of officers the next day, a Tuesday.

Washington may have had a general sense of what was brewing, but when he read the actual words, he was outraged. He immediately apprehended that he faced a profound discipline problem among his officers. This must have mortified such a proud, restrained man. His personal example—that is, his virtue—had proven insufficient. What's more, he was being manipulated by civilians in Congress.

The following day he issued a general order, carrying the weight of his command, in which he denounced the "ananominous paper" and expressed his disapproval of "such disorderly proceedings" as holding a meeting of officers in response to an anonymous letter. He ordered all senior officers, from major to general, plus one from each company (that is, captains or lieutenants), to assemble not that day, but four days later, at noon. This may have been intended to give them a few days to cool off. The officers would assemble at the camp's "Newbuilding," a structure also known by the troops as "the Temple of Virtue." What better place for Washington to speak at a crucial moment, having dedicated his life to the pursuit of eighteenth-century public virtue?

Washington wondered about the origins of the officers' conspiracy. "There is something very misterious in this business," he wrote to Hamilton. He explained that he had issued his order for the meeting "to rescue them from plunging themselves into a gulph of Civil horror from which there might be no receding"— that is, to head them off from taking "hasty and fatal steps." Just as he finished writing to Hamilton, he was informed that a second anonymous letter was circulating. Given that he already had responded with a general order, this amounted to a clear challenge to Washington's authority.

Washington responded by donning his most Roman persona. On March 15, the general appeared at the planned meeting, at which Gates was presiding, and asked if he might address the group—which of course as the commander, he could do without asking. When he spoke, he did not question their rights to express their views or order them to desist. Rather, in what is now known as "The Newburgh Address," he invoked his personal honor. I was here first, he told them, I was with you throughout, and I have been your example. "I have never left your side one moment. . . . I have ever considered my own Military reputation as inseperably connected with that of the Army." Has my personal virtue and honor not been enough for you? Seeing it challenged in anonymous letters, he continued, "my indignation has arisen." "Indignation" is a loaded word that carried a powerful meaning for Washington. For example, he had described Benedict Arnold's treason as causing in him "astonishment and indignation."

It was about as much anger as Washington ever allowed himself to show in public, except in two moments of surprised rage in battle. Here at Newburgh, as at Kips Bay and Monmouth, he felt bitterly disappointed by some of his officers. The difference was that those outbursts were spontaneous, while here he had been stewing for days. By some accounts, he finished by putting on his glasses to read aloud a letter, apologizing in an aside that he had gone nearly blind in the service of his country. With that quiet explanation, he quelled the officers' insurrection.

"The Storm . . . is dispersed," he reported to Joseph Jones, his friend in Congress, on March 18. "The Virtue, & patient forbearance of the Army, on this, as upon every other trying occasion which has happened to call them into action, has again triumphed." He had put down "a most insiduous attempt to disturb the repose of the Army, & sow the seeds of discord between the Civil & military powers of the continent." Washington's quashing of military dissent would resonate down through the decades, underscoring that the American armed forces are subordinate to civilian authority, most especially when the officer corps disagrees with Congress.

## "A dangerous instrument"

HAMILTON THEN HALF APOLOGIZED TO WASHINGTON FOR HIS ROLE. "I often feel a mortification, which it would be impolitic to express, that sets my passions at variance with my reason." Still, he confessed, he was not really very sorry:

> But supposing the Country ungrateful what can the army do? It must submit to its hard fate. To seek redress by its arms would end in its ruin. . . . I confess could force avail I should almost wish to see it employed. I have an indifferent opinion of the honesty of this country, and ill-forebodings as to its future system.

This provoked Washington to respond in personal terms. "I read your private letter of the 25th. with pain," Washington replied. When Washington used that word "pain," invoking deep personal feeling, he was showing that he was deadly serious. He admonished the young man to knock off such talk about the Army's using threats of violence against Americans to get its way: "The idea of redress by force is too chimerical to have had a place in the imagination of any serious mind in this Army."

Washington then reproached Hamilton for trying to pull the Army into domestic politics. "I will now, in strict confidence, mention a matter which may be useful for you to be informed of," he began. Some "leading" members of the Army, he wrote, suspect that some members of Congress have tried to use the Army as "mere Puppets to establish Continental funds." He chided Hamilton for toying with the national defense simply to raise revenue. "The Army (considering the irritable state it is in, its sufferings & composition) is a dangerous instrument to play with," he warned.

Surprisingly, despite this incident, Hamilton retained Washington's confidence. Many years after the war, the general would defend Hamilton to John Adams, stating that the young man had served as his "principal & most confidential aid" and that he had found him "enterprising, quick in his perceptions, and his judgment intuitively great: qualities essential to a great military character."

A few months after the Newburgh showdown, as he prepared to step down from his command, Washington issued a warning to his countrymen. We have won the war, he told them in a message issued from his headquarters, but now you must secure the peace:

> it is in their choice and depends upon their conduct, whether they will be respectable and prosperous or contemptible and Miserable as a Nation. . . . it is yet to be decided whether the Revolution must ultimately be considered as a blessing or a curse: a blessing or a curse, not to the present Age alone, for with our fate will the destiny of unborn Millions be involved.

In this same letter to the states, he also gave a surprisingly long and explicit bow to the Enlightenment, seeing it as a kind of philosophical nest for the fledgling republic:

> the foundation of our Empire was not laid in the gloomy Age of ignorance and superstition, but at an Epocha when the rights of Mankind were better understood and more clearly defined, than at any former period—The researches of the human Mind after social happiness have been carried to a great extent, the treasures of knowledge acquired by the labours of Philosophers, Sages and Legislators, through a long succession of years, are laid open for our use and their collected wisdom may be happily applied in the establishment of our forms of Government.

Finally, he came to a conclusion about the militias that was very different from the view with which he had begun the war. "The Militia of this Country must be considerd as the Palladium of our security and the first effectual resort," he told the states. He was at war's end a very different man from the one he had been in 1775.

## Washington's Last Roman Role

WASHINGTON'S LAST ROMAN ROLE WOULD BECOME HIS FINEST. HE HAD rejected becoming a Caesar. Instead, he would become another Cincinnatus—that is, the Roman soldier who, according to legend, saved his country in 458 BC. Roman tradition states that he was plowing his fields when he was called to lead the rescue of a Roman army that was besieged southeast of the city by an army of Aequians. He was given the temporary title of dictator. He triumphed in just sixteen days, then resigned his office and returned to his waiting plow.

The story of Cincinnatus was a reassuring one, because the Revolutionary generation had an abiding fear of the power of generals. There were few historical examples of military leaders willingly giving up power. And to the contrary, they were conscious of the relatively recent example of Oliver Cromwell, who a century earlier had led the way in establishing an English republic, only to become a dictator who passed power to his inept son. Washington owned a biography of Cromwell; Madison put in his copybook some damning lines about the man by Alexander Pope; and Adams referred to him frequently, writing once that "there never was a greater self deceiver than Oliver Cromwell."

On December 22, 1783, the Confederation Congress, then meeting at the statehouse in Annapolis, Maryland, threw a formal dinner and ball for Washington, with the guests numbering in the hundreds. The next day at noon he appeared before Congress and formally resigned his position as commander of the Army. When he rose to speak, the members of Congress remained seated, denoting the subservient role of the military to civilian leadership. "Having now finished the work assigned me, I retire from the great theatre of Action," he stated. He bowed to Congress, then walked to his carriage with his wife and headed home to Mount Vernon, arriving in time to celebrate Christmas there.

It is possible that too much is made of Washington's decision to step down—but probably not. It was a magnificent deed of renunciation and was recognized as such at the time. He, like the rest of his class, approached it from the perspective of classical republicanism. For him, it was always about virtue—seeking it and being esteemed by those who had it. "To merit the approbation of good & virtuous Men is the height of my ambition," Washington had told Jefferson as peace approached.

One early instance of someone labeling Washington a modern Cincinnatus appears in a letter from François-Jean de Beauvoir, Marquis de Chastellux, who as a French liaison officer to Washington had become friendly with the American general. It is worth pausing a moment to consider Chastellux, because he was a wonderful exemplar of his time. He was not just a soldier, but also a proud exponent of the French Enlightenment who before the war had composed a lengthy work titled *De la félicité publique*—that is, an essay "On Public Happiness." Typical of the time, this book was about a bit of everything, running the gamut from ancient Greek and Roman history to the nature of government debt in the eighteenth century. To top off his credentials, in 1775 Chastellux had been elected to Seat 2 in the Académie Française, the chair held twenty years earlier by none other than Montesquieu. As the war ended, Chastellux wrote to Washington to express a wish that he could "proceed to Virginy, where I am told, your excellency is retired like an other Cincinnatus."

Washington responded that in fact he was dreaming of exploring the American frontier. "I shall not rest contented 'till I have explored the Western Country," he wrote. In a letter written the same day to a Frenchman with whom he was even closer, he invited the Marquis de Lafayette to accompany him on just such a grand ramble around the new nation:

> I have it in contemplation . . . to make a tour thro' all the Eastern States—thence into Canada—thence up the St Lawrence, & thro'

*the Lakes to Detroit—thence to lake Michigan by Land or water— thence thro' the western Country, by the river Illinois, to the river Mississippi, & down the same to New Orleans—thence thro' the two Carolina's home—A great tour this, you will say—probably it may take place no where but in imagination, tho' it is my wish to begin it in the latter end of April of next year; if it should be realized, there would be nothing wanting to make it perfectly agreeable, but your Company.*

In other words, when the war ended, his thoughts turned back to the place where he had been educated in war and diplomacy— the American frontier. But instead of fighting the French there, as he had a quarter of a century earlier, he wanted a Frenchman to accompany him.

John Adams, often both accurate and ungenerous, thought that Washington was, as usual, putting on a big act:

*If he was not the greatest President he was the best Actor of Presidency We have ever had. His Address to The States when he left the Army; His solemn Leave taken of Congress when he resigned his Commission; his Farewell Address to the People when he resigned his Presidency.*

But the fault here lay not in Washington but in Adams. It would be to Adams' detriment as president that he would not be able to lead so well in public as his predecessor did. Washington understood, as Adams did not, that especially in a new republic, these large gestures would resonate with the people. In this nation, the people were not the governed, they were sovereign, which meant their needs must be addressed. Adams never liked that fact or even really understood it, and that failure would haunt his presidency.

It was at about this point, just as the war was ending, that Benjamin Franklin grew exasperated with Adams, who was with him in France for peace talks with the British. In a letter to Robert Livingston, secretary of foreign affairs under the Articles of Confederation, Franklin summarized Adams memorably: "He means well for his Country, is always an honest Man, often a Wise One, but sometimes and in some things, absolutely out of his Senses." This pithy sentence may be the single most illuminating thing ever written about John Adams.

In November 1783, with the treaty concluded, the British military finally withdrew from New York City. In a kind of echo of his forgotten victory of retaking Philadelphia, Washington entered Manhattan on their heels.

◇━━◇

## Chapter 10

# From a Difficult War
# to an Uneasy Peace

THE ARTICLES OF CONFEDERATION, WHICH GOVERNED THE UNITED States from 1781 to 1789, are regarded nowadays as an oddity, a misfired contraption. One single-house legislature, the U.S. Congress, was responsible for running the federal government, but it lacked the power to raise money, except by requesting the states to send it. It was not really a national government, but rather more like the European Union is today, a weak body unable to compel member states.

But from the point of view of the time, the Articles might be regarded as an extraordinary success in that when they were in effect, the infant nation survived and grew. Indeed, one modern view is that the Articles really deserve a bit more credit. Under them, the new United States became an alliance of republics. As such, the new confederation was "as strong as any similar republican confederation in history," concludes Gordon Wood.

As a permanent structure, the Articles of Confederation did not work. But as a means of transition, a bridge into the future, it served a purpose and, arguably, succeeded brilliantly. Edmund Morgan, another giant in the field, writes: "If the American Revolution was in any sense a civil war"—which in part it was—"the Confederation did a much faster and better job of reconstruction than the United States did after Appomattox." That is, the American Revolution did not turn on itself, with the victors shattering into warring factions and a government that maintains power only by the exercise of violence against citizens, as has happened so often after other successful rebellions, as in France in the eighteenth century and Russia in the twentieth.

A peaceful outcome was not a given. The Revolutionary generation would have had in mind Montesquieu's warning that the great first hurdle of nationhood was surviving the shift from war to peace. In his analysis of what ruined Rome, he stressed the difficulties victorious soldiers had in becoming compromise-oriented politicians: "Warriors who were so proud, so audacious, so terrible abroad could not be very moderate at home. To ask for men in a free state who are bold in war and timid in peace is to wish the impossible."

In the same work, Montesquieu made a striking observation: "At the birth of societies, the leaders of republics create the institutions; thereafter, it is the institutions that form the leaders of republics." So the real issue facing the victors of the American Revolution was to create a structure solid enough to survive and begin to develop institutions that would sustain it in the long term. The question was, how to get to the point where American institutions could develop leaders?

## Paine's Impatience with Classicism . . .

IN APRIL 1783, AS THE WAR WAS ENDING, THOMAS PAINE QUESTIONED whether Americans needed to abandon the classical approach to public life. As usual, he was ahead of the wave.

Paine himself is an interesting problem. He is probably the most unfairly neglected of the founders. He played a huge role in the Revolution but is seen, both then and now, as an outsider. Unlike the first four presidents, Paine was not building a society he planned to run. Rather, he was offering a running critique of events, from a point of view skeptical of power and authority.

His stance made him a natural critic of classical republicanism. "I cannot help being sometimes surprised at the complimentary references which I have seen and heard made to ancient histories and transactions," he wrote in *The American Crisis*. "The wisdom of civil governments, and the sense of honour of the states of Greece and Rome, are frequently held up as objects of excellence and imitation." But, he continued, we "do dishonorary injustice to ourselves" if we must "go two or three thousand years back for lessons and examples." At any rate, he said, Rome's founders were thugs when compared to those leading the American Revolution. "Rome . . . was originally a band of ruffians. Plunder and rapine made her rich, and her oppression of millions made her great. But America needs never be ashamed to tell her birth." (Paine does not address here what is to us the obvious issue that the people running America also oppressed hundreds of thousands of enslaved people.) His book mentions neither Cato nor Cicero, which makes it unusual among American political books published around the time of the Revolution.

Paine's impatience with "the mist of antiquity" was not shared by the people who ran the early United States. But he was articulating a feeling that was out there, among other people, especially those not privileged to attend college. It was a feeling that would only grow.

## . . . And Hamilton's

AT THE OTHER END OF THE POLITICAL SPECTRUM, ALEXANDER HAMILton also was sensing the limits of both the Confederation and the classical republican model. "The confederation itself is defective and requires to be altered; it is neither fit for war, nor peace," he had written in a letter in September 1780. "The fundamental defect is a want of power in Congress." The states were too powerful, and the central government lacked authority to maintain the union. "The leagues among the old Grecian republics are a proof of this. They were continually at war with each other, and for want of union fell a prey to their neighbours."

Given a chance, he insisted, people would pursue their own

self-interest, and that impulse was what would dominate the new nation. "It is as ridiculous to seek for models in the simple ages of Greece and Rome, as it would be to go in quest of them among the Hottentots and Laplanders." Were we, Hamilton asked, to share goods and wives and eat black broth, as the Spartans did? No, he said, "We may preach till we are tired of the theme, the necessity of disinterestedness in republics, without making a single proselyte."

A few years later, Hamilton again argued for distance from the classical world:

> Neither the manners nor the genius of Rome are suited to the republic or age we live in. All her maxims and habits were military, her government was constituted for war. Ours is unfit for it, and our situation still less than our constitution, invites us to emulate the conduct of Rome, or to attempt a display of unprofitable heroism.

George Washington also emerged from the war frustrated by the Articles of Confederation. "No man in the United States is, or can be more deeply impressed with the necessity of a reform in our present Confederation than myself," he wrote to Hamilton as the conflict ended. "No man perhaps has felt the bad efects of it more sensibly; for to the defects thereof, & want of Powers in Congress may justly be ascribed the prolongation of the War, & consequently the Expences occasioned by it. More than half the perplexities I have experienced in the course of my command, and almost the whole of the difficulties & distress of the Army, have there origin here."

## Madison Studies and Prepares

JAMES MADISON, TOO, WAS MEDITATING ON THE FUNDAMENTAL TENsion between the high aspirations and the harsh realities of the new country. He began to consider how to reconcile them.

In 1780, he had left Virginia for Philadelphia to take his seat in Congress, bringing along with him as a servant an enslaved man named Billey. Madison did not go home for three full years—perhaps a sign of his emotional and intellectual distance from Virginia or his family or both. For nearly three years in the north, Billey breathed the spirit of liberty.

In 1783, Madison, then thirty-two years old, wrote to his father about Billey's future with a mixture of personal anxiety and political understanding. "I have judged it most prudent not to force Billey back to Va. even if could be done. . . . I am persuaded his mind is too thoroughly tainted to be a fit companion for fellow slaves in Virga." The nature of that "taint" was that Billey had seen freedom, Madison noted. "I . . . cannot think of punishing him by transportation merely for coveting that liberty for which we have paid the price of so much blood, and have proclaimed so often to be the right, & worthy the pursuit, of every human being." Of course it also would be dangerous to have Billey back on the plantation, spreading the word to his family, friends, and coworkers about the free black people he had seen in Philadelphia.

That recognition of the gap between American reality and American aspirations may have been on Madison's mind a few years later when he began working on the Constitution. Billey must have been both talented and trusted. Once freed, he would become Madison's business agent in Philadelphia, under the name William Gardner. A decade later, Madison had him deliver a plow for Thomas Jefferson's farm. After Gardner died, reportedly falling overboard from a ship while ill, his widow, Henrietta, became Jefferson's laundress in Philadelphia.

In 1784, believing that the Articles of Confederation system was doomed, Madison began to contemplate the problems of ancient Greek confederacies. He had several questions on his mind, all relating to the fragile condition of the United States. What had brought down ancient republics? What made them so fragile? Were there gaps between their theory and practice? Did they have inherent flaws that caused them to fail? Were these avoidable? Was Montesquieu correct in thinking that republics had to be small? If so, could American government be structured in a different way that would make it more sustainable? Here he could begin by revisiting his college readings of Thucydides and Xenophon, but he soon would need more. He embarked upon a multiyear study of these issues.

It was an extraordinary effort, requiring not just persistence but a large leap of the imagination. In this way, Madison resembled the Scottish Enlightenment thinkers such as Hutton, the geologist who had looked at familiar old things in radical new ways. Noah Feldman's biography observes that Madison was doing something novel:

> Aristotle in his Politics *had already engaged in comparisons between different sorts of constitutional arrangements, and Montesquieu had tried to offer a general theory of the relationship between the "spirits" of different polities and the way they were organized. But as a systematic effort to identify the core working elements of all the confederacies known to have existed, Madison's document was unprecedented.*

In March 1784, Madison asked Jefferson, then preparing to sail to Europe to help in trade negotiations (and later to succeed Benjamin Franklin as the American envoy to France), to ship to him books on the history of ancient systems of government, especially confederations. "I must leave to your discretion the occasional purchase of rare & valuable books, disregarding the risk of duplicates. You know tolerably well the objects of my curiosity. I will only particularise my wish of whatever may throw light on the general Constitution & droit public of the several confederacies which have existed."

A year later, he added to that request, asking for "treatises on the antient or modern fœderal republics—on the law of Nations—and the history natural & political of the New World; to which I will add such of the Greek & Roman authors where they can be got very cheap, as are worth having and are not on the Common list of School classics." There also was a new book about travels in

China that he wanted to see. He also desired a good compass and a telescope, perhaps built into a cane, explaining that "in my walks for exercise or amusements, objects frequently present themselves, which it might be matter of curiosity to inspect, but which it is difficult or impossible to approach." In a sign of the wide range of interests of the two men, he concluded with a freestanding post-script question: "What has become of the subterraneous City discovered in Siberia?"

Jefferson responded with trunks full of books for Madison's "course of reading," shipping a total of about two hundred volumes to his younger friend and also inviting Madison to "make free use" of the extensive library he had left behind in Monticello.

Madison reported happily plunging into this "literary cargo." In the same letter, he worried about "the danger of having the same game played on our confederacy" that Philip of Macedon used against the Greeks to undermine their alliance. In his notes on confederacies, he concluded that "Greece was the victim of Philip. If her confederation had been stricter, & been persevered in, she would never have yielded to Macedon."

Madison sat in the library at his father's house near Orange, Virginia, its three tall windows looking west across a long descending pasture toward a beautiful vista of the Blue Ridge. And he stayed in that room and read for months and months. It may be just an accident that Jefferson's Monticello and Madison's Montpelier, for all their similarities, such as Doric columns, bricks, and fine views, have a fundamental difference in orientation: Jefferson's creation faces east, toward the flatter part of Virginia, while Madison's inherited house looks westward, toward the mountains and, beyond them, the future of the nation. After all, buildings can convey messages their designers may not have intended. Most famously, Jefferson in creating Monticello sought to conceal the face of slavery as much as possible, placing it underground. His house sat atop a tunnel that held the kitchen, the smokehouse, and other areas where his enslaved people worked. A dumbwaiter and a revolving shelved door further minimized their presence around his dining table.

## Adams' Own Effort

---

IN LONDON, MEANWHILE, JOHN ADAMS COMPOSED HIS BEST-KNOWN work, *A Defence of the Constitutions of Government of the United States of America*, the sole piece of writing he finished that is longer than an essay. This was not for lack of trying—in his post-presidential years, he would take up an autobiographical manuscript and put it down several times, finally leaving it a fragmentary tangle of resentment, bitterness, and frustration.

In this rambling constitutional study, Adams surveyed all sorts of governments in the ancient and modern worlds, and concluded, as others did, that the most effective and sustainable form is one that is "a mixture of monarchy, aristocracy, and democracy, extolled by Polybius." That ancient Greek historian had tried in his work to explain the rapid rise of the Roman Republic. Polybius wrote that he intended to analyze how "it came about that nearly the whole world fell under the power of Rome in somewhat less than fifty-three years."

Polybius was a Peloponnesian Greek aristocrat born in about 208 BC who witnessed Roman ways firsthand as a semi-hostage living for seventeen years in a noble family's house in Rome. When he was at last told he was free to go home to Greece, he had grown so close to them that he chose instead to accompany one of them, Scipio Aemilianus, on a military expedition against Carthage.

In his history of the rise of Rome, Polybius attributes the power of the city in part to its culture of loyalty and virtue, but also to the mixture of powers within the Republic. He saw the consuls bringing an element of monarchy and the Senate an aspect of aristocracy, but the people also holding power in the form of tribunes who could veto acts of the consuls and Senate. "The best constitution," he wrote, is "that which partakes of all these three elements." This view deeply influenced Adams and many other Americans of the Revolutionary generation.

Adams in turn wrote that "there can be no government of laws, without a balance, and there can be no balance without the three orders." He further recommended an independent judiciary and legislature, with no mixture of the executive and legislature (as, for example, is the case in Britain, with members of Parliament becoming cabinet members). Moreover, he applauded having more than one legislative body, in order to hamper the passage of laws in the heat of the moment. As he put it in a letter at about the same time, "Human Passions are all unlimited and insatiable." He also advocated having a strong executive with the power to constrain the other two branches of government.

Why is the form of government so crucial? Because, Adams reminds us, "Pythagoras, as well as Socrates, Plato, and Xenophon, were persuaded that the happiness of nations depended chiefly on the form of their government."

At about the same time, a pamphlet appeared in London that challenged Montesquieu's notion that republics must stand on a foundation of virtue. "The truth is, Montesquieu had never study'd a free Democracy," argued William Vans Murray, a London-educated Maryland lawyer and later a member of Congress and a diplomat, in explaining what he saw as the Frenchman's error. No such foundation was needed in a truly free system, he thought. But the young man himself was no great predictor of the trends of American political life. "Faction, which in Rome was ever written in bloody inscriptions, is unknown" in the United States, he asserted. "It is unknown, because the American democracies are governments of laws and not of parties." Just how wrong Vans Murray was about the state of American politics would soon became evident. Violence and faction lurked around the corner.

## Shays' Rebellion Shakes Americans

EVEN AS VANS MURRAY WAS WRITING, THE FARMERS OF WESTERN MAS-sachusetts were gathering to challenge the postwar distribution of power in the United States. Daniel Shays, the leader of the insurgents, was a veteran who had fought at Lexington, Bunker

Hill, and Saratoga. He was, wrote another veteran of Lexington, "A Man without Education—But not without Abilities." When he came home from the war, he remained unpaid for his service and so was unable to pay his debts. Many of his neighbors were in similar straits: By one count, nearly a third of the adult males in Hampshire County, in western Massachusetts, carried debts they could not repay.

The insurrection expanded steadily through the summer and fall of 1786. In December, it prevented the holding of courts, stopping seizures of forfeit land and freezing the collection of debts. The following month, three columns of men, one of them led by Shays, marched on the federal arsenal at Springfield, Massachusetts, which held more than a thousand barrels of gunpowder, as well as thousands of muskets with bayonets.

The Confederation government proved unable to respond to the crisis. In October the Confederation Congress authorized recruiting soldiers to counter the insurgents, but provided no money with which to do so, instead asking the states to provide the funds, which they did not.

The government of Massachusetts itself did even worse. When it first mustered units of the militia in the western part of the state, hundreds of its members sided with the insurgents. In response, Governor James Bowdoin (Harvard, 1745), bypassed his legislature and created a new militia force, funded largely by wealthy Boston merchants. This temporary state force, numbering some four thousand men, occupied the federal arsenal, where it took possession of some artillery pieces.

The new state militia purposely fired its first cannon shots over the heads of the besieging insurgents. But when the rebels failed to turn back, the militia commander ordered the barrels lowered. A volley of grapeshot left four men dead and many more wounded. The rebels dispersed, and some of their leaders fled the state. The crisis was over, but the entire affair had made the federal government look like an inept bystander.

Shays' Rebellion would provide the backdrop for the great event of the next two years—the convening of a meeting that, exceeding its mandate, would write a new fundamental law for the nation. That would be followed by an intense nationwide debate over approving that law. In one such discussion, Pennsylvania's James Wilson would argue that people did not really grasp how fragile the political situation was at the time of the Shays uprising and how many people in other states were inclined to follow suit. "The flames of internal insurrection were ready to burst out in every quarter, . . . and from one end to the other of the continent, we walked on ashes, concealing fire beneath our feet." Many of those listening to Wilson could have caught, in his last phrase, the allusion to the lines of Horace lamenting civil war and warning of the dangers of "stepping over fires smouldering/ under the treacherous ash."

In a letter to his father, James Madison summarized his view of the situation:

> We learn that great commotions are prevailing in Massts. An appeal to the Sword is exceedingly dreaded. The discontented it is said are as numerous as the friends of Govt. and more decided in their measures. Should they get uppermost, it is uncertain what may be the effect. They profess to aim only at a reform of their Constition and of certain abuses in the public administration, but an abolition of debts public & private, and a new division of property are strongly suspected to be in contemplation.

One can almost see Madison rubbing his hands in quiet glee. Given his quick political instincts, he may have sensed that the insurrection would strengthen those who, with him, backed a stronger national government.

The Shays affair effectively set the table for the Constitutional Convention by highlighting the ineffectiveness and fragility of the existing system. "It may, in fact, be difficult to overemphasize the degree to which this rebellion jolted American political reflections," writes the historian John Agresto. Shays and his comrades ultimately would be given a silent memorial in the Constitution's Article IV, Section 4, which among other things guarantees the states protection against both foreign invasion and "domestic Violence."

At Mount Vernon, George Washington also was watching the situation with deepening concern. Responding to a letter from John Jay, then secretary for foreign affairs in the Articles of Confederation government, he concluded that "we have probably had too good an opinion of human nature in forming our confederation. . . . We must take human nature as we find it. Perfection falls not to the share of mortals." He later would write of this period that "it was for a long time doubtful whether we were to survive as an independent Republic, or decline from our fœderal dignity into insignificant & wretched fragments of Empire."

John Adams, as usual, was even more pessimistic. "Our Country men have never merited the Character of very exalted Virtue," he wrote from London at about the same time. "If it is indeed true, that there is a general Degeneracy, it is an allarming Consideration."

Even those running the government were growing impatient with the inept functioning of the American system. Early in 1787, Jay reported to Jefferson in Paris that "our Governments want Energy, and there is Reason to fear that too much has been expected from the Virtue and good Sense of the People." He told John Adams that "our Government is unequal to the Task assigned it, and the People begin also to perceive its Inefficiency."

Internal divisions only invited foreign intervention, Jefferson worried. He later wrote that, under the Articles of Confederation, "it could not but occur to every one that these separate independancies, like the petty states of Greece, would be eternally at war with each other, & would become at length the mere partisans & satellites of the leading powers of Europe."

As the historian Daniel Howe puts it, the founding generation was "fed up with the Articles of Confederation and their reliance on uncoerced public virtue." The moment had come, he continues, to consider whether "the vices could, through wise contrivance, be made to do the work of virtues." Thinking through this apparent paradox would become the specialty of James Madison. He began pulling the strings that might lead to change.

In September 1786, several states had dispatched representatives to Annapolis, Maryland, to discuss commercial relations between the states. Hamilton and Madison had different ideas. As Richard Brookhiser puts it, they "hijacked it [the meeting] to write a report calling for a national convention a year later" at which a new blueprint for American government would be drafted. The Confederation Congress—following a bill introduced by Madison—agreed to call such a meeting. "Political foes who underrated James Madison did so at their peril," observes the biographer Ron Chernow.

## Madison Emerges

THE TIME WAS RIPE. IN FEBRUARY 1787, MADISON WORRIED THAT THE Confederation government was nearing collapse:

> the present System neither has nor deserves advocates; and if some very strong props are not applied will quickly tumble to the ground. No money is paid into the public Treasury; no respect is paid to the federal authority. Not a single State complies with the requisitions, several pass them over in silence, and some positively reject them. The payments ever since the peace have been decreasing, and of late fall short even of the pittance necessary for the Civil list of the Confederacy. It is not possible that a Government can last long under these circumstances.

In April, he wrote notes to himself that questioned the intellectual underpinning of the system. He never seems to have finished or published it, but his draft began to circulate. The system shaped by classical republicanism was not working, he asserted. "Republican Theory" was one thing, he wrote, but "fact and experience" have proven another.

Not only was the structure of the United States flawed, but so was the classical conception behind it, he argued. The time had come to accept that "all civilized societies are divided into different interests and factions, as they happen to be creditors or debtors—Rich or poor—husbandmen, merchants or manufacturers—members of different religious sects—followers of different political leaders—inhabitants of different districts—owners of different kinds of property &c &c." But if "different interests and factions" were inevitable, then faction would have to be accepted and interest would have to be seen not as sinful but as natural. What would a government designed to accommodate them look like?

Madison had some ideas, and began to shape the discussion. "My ideas of a reform strike . . . deeply at the old Confederation, and lead to . . . systematic change," he informed Edmund Randolph, the governor of Virginia, who would become a key ally at the Constitutional Convention. Madison also told George Washington that "to give a new System its proper validity and energy, a ratification must be obtained from the people, and not merely from the ordinary authority of the Legislatures." In these letters he laid out the basic elements of what would become known as the Virginia plan, which in turn would be the core of the eventual Constitution. In the following year he would perform a series of tasks that would earn what Gordon Wood calls "the now widely accepted view that Madison was the most astute, profound, and original political theorist among the founding fathers."

## Chapter 11

# Madison and
# the Constitution

*Balancing Vice with Vice*

T HE HIGHER THE STAKES, THE MORE THE REVOLUTIONARY GENERA-
tion tended to turn for wisdom to the Romans and Greeks.
American classicism crested during the 1780s, as Americans pondered the future shape of their government. Yet by the end of the
Constitutional Convention, the tide had begun to turn against
such faith in ancient wisdom. And by the time of the state meetings to decide whether to ratify the proposed Constitution, the
current was running out hard.

For the framers of the Constitution, Enlightenment thinkers—
who again were intensely focused on the problems of ancient
Greek and Roman government—stood just behind the classical
authors. Foremost among that group was Montesquieu, who accounted for some 60 percent of references made to Enlightenment
writers by American political commentators of the 1780s. One
reason for the Frenchman's ubiquity is that both sides, Federalists
and anti-Federalists, would find in his works passages to support
their positions.

But the outcome of all this would be surprisingly unclassical: a
Constitutional Convention that would devise what one historian
calls "a new basis of republican government, a way of achieving
a viable self-government that did not require virtue as its base."
There would be no mention of "virtue" in the new foundational

document that emerged. In a way, the drafters used classical thought to escape its influence.

## Designing Men

THEY BEGAN GATHERING IN PHILADELPHIA IN MAY 1787. MADISON WAS the first to arrive. Even now, we tend to see the Constitution through his eyes and words. He was aware that he was present at the creation of a new government. In his research, he had been struck by the lack of records of how the governments of ancient states were established, and thus seized the opportunity to leave behind a thorough accounting. He decided, he wrote,

> to preserve as far as I could an exact account of what might pass in the Convention whilst executing its trust, with the magnitude of which I was duly impressed, as I was with the gratification promised to future curiosity by an authentic exhibition of the objects, the opinions & the reasonings from which the new System of Govt. was to receive its peculiar structure & organization. Nor was I unaware of the value of such a contribution to the fund of materials for the History of a Constitution on which would be Staked the happiness of a people great even in its infancy, and possibly the cause of liberty throughout the world.

But there was a bit more to it. As Richard Brookhiser, one of Madison's more perceptive biographers, observes, "Madison was not only serving the muse of history." Madison also was a consummate politician, which means he was adept at wielding power and so understood that "information is power."

In addition, Madison's account is not entirely reliable. The historian Mary Sarah Bilder demonstrated in an intricate 2015 study that Madison fiddled with his notes on the Constitution all his life, combining some speeches, revising others, and omitting some of his comments that would be politically embarrassing if revealed, such as his desire in 1787 to constrain the powers of the states.

The conventioneers settled in and began their deliberations by considering an extraordinary series of fundamental questions: Should the presidency be one person or several? Should each state have one vote in the Senate? Should state governments be abolished? Perhaps most of all, how could a representative system be devised that did not allow the large states too much power, yet still embodied the will of all the people?

Early on, on May 29, 1787, the Virginia delegation offered a plan that addressed many of these questions. Madison had played a large role in conceiving and drafting it. Instead of the existing one-house Congress making up the entire federal government, they proposed a two-house national legislature, with the lower elected "by the people." The new central government would have a separate "National Executive" and a "National Judiciary," the latter consisting of "one or more supreme tribunals." Less successfully, the plan also proposed giving Congress the power to veto state laws (a pet proposal of Madison's) and creating a "Council of revision" peopled by officials from the executive and judiciary that would review all new laws before they were enacted.

In their deliberations, the delegates had three basic points of reference: how the existing states worked; how the British system worked; and what precedents other republics offered—some recently in Europe, such as the Dutch, and some from the ancient world, with some of those examples from Rome but most from ancient Greece. And so the classical allusions soon began to fly. Pierce Butler of South Carolina worried about excessive executive power, asking, "Why might not a Cataline or a Cromwell arise in this Country as well as in others?" The next day he reminded his colleagues to keep in mind that their product had to be acceptable to the people: "We must follow the example of Solon who gave the Athenians not the best Government he could devise; but the best they would receive." Butler was alluding to a comment reported by Plutarch in his *Life of Solon*, an Athenian lawgiver of the sixth century BC.

James Wilson, a Scottish-born lawyer from Philadelphia, warned against having a multi-headed presidency: "Three will contend among themselves till one becomes the master of his colleagues. In the triumvirates of Rome first Caesar, then Augustus, are witnesses to this truth. The Kings of Sparta, & the Consuls of Rome prove also the factious consequences of dividing the Executive Magistracy." But it was James Madison who would delve deepest into the classical world—and also would begin to explore how to move beyond its limitations.

## Madison's Central Role

AT THIRTY-SIX YEARS OLD, MADISON WAS RELATIVELY YOUNG. HE WAS not an impressive speaker. Short and frail, standing not much higher than five feet and weighing not much more than a hundred pounds, he was not physically imposing. He was not even a notable writer—there are few memorable phrases from his pen that we remember today. But he was knowledgeable. Through his studies he arrived in Philadelphia as what one biographer calls "the best-informed man in America on the principles of government."

Madison offered several comments in the first days of the convention and then, on June 6, delivered a major speech. The purpose of a national government, he began, was not just to deal with foreign powers and settle interstate disputes, but also to ensure "the security of private rights, and the steady dispensation of Justice." And that led directly to the question of how to balance competing interests. "In Greece & Rome the rich & poor, the creditors & debtors, as well as the patricians & plebeians alternately oppressed each other with equal unmercifulness." The solution, he concluded, was to go against the views of Montesquieu and create a large national republic: "The only remedy is to enlarge the sphere, & thereby divide the community into so great a number of interests & parties." He did not quite say so here, but he was portraying faction not as a problem but as a solution—or as the software industry phrase puts it nowadays, not a bug but a feature. The next day, in arguing for a relatively small Senate, he cited the example of the Roman tribunes, who "lost their influence and power, in proportion as their number was augmented."

Madison led the charge for a much stronger national system of government. On June 19, he argued that weakness at the core had been the fatal flaw of the Amphictyonic League, opening the way for intervention first by the rulers of Persia, and then, fatally, by Philip of Macedon. He returned to the point two days later, stating that "all the examples of other confederacies prove the greater tendency in such systems to anarchy than to tyranny."

The big states would not conspire together to gang up on the smaller ones, he maintained, because it is the nature of power to compete. "Carthage & Rome tore one another to pieces instead of uniting their forces to devour the weaker nations of the Earth. . . . Among the principal members of antient and Modern confederacies, we find the same effect from the same cause. The contintions, not the Coalitions of Sparta, Athens & Thebes, proved fatal to the small members of the Amphyctionic Confederacy."

Madison had the ear of the conventioneers. "Every Person seems to acknowledge his greatness," recalled one delegate, Georgia's William Pierce (attended William & Mary). He continued:

> He blends together the profound politician, with the Scholar. In the management of every great question he evidently took the lead in the Convention, and tho' he cannot be called an Orator, he is a most agreeable, eloquent, and convincing Speaker. From a spirit of industry and application which he possesses in a most eminent degree, he always comes forward the best informed Man on any point in debate. . . . He is easy and unreserved among his acquaintance, and has a most agreeable style of conversation.

Madison especially impressed them with his research, Pierce noted: "Mr. Maddison in a very able and ingenious Speech ran through the whole Scheme of the Government,—point out all the beauties and defects of ancient Republics; compared their situation with ours." The young Virginian was steering the convention toward a new government that would be very different from the diffuse state of the nation under the Articles of Confederation. It was an extraordinary achievement for Madison.

## Getting Amphictyonic

THE HISTORY OF THE AMPHICTYONIC LEAGUE, OR COUNCIL, THAT MADison referenced is obscure stuff to us, but it was not in early America, so it has continued relevance today. One reason that in the United States of the twenty-first century the 580,000 people of Wyoming are represented by two senators, the same number as the 40 million citizens of California, is because of the example of this league, which was a series of confederations of cities formed early in Greek history. The league's member states had equal voting rights without regard to size or power.

Modern scholars in fact describe the league as several organizations developed over the course of time for the purpose of enabling several cities to worship a god or place. But the Revolutionary generation tended to refer to it as one specific entity, as it were an ancient version of, say, NATO. The Amphictyonic League was a familiar subject to them, cited often as a possible model for restructuring the government of the colonies. One historian, reviewing the early American record, moaned that the Amphictyonic Council was "a parallel used almost *ad nauseam* during the colonial period, . . . commended as a force for interstate good will." For example, Samuel Johnson (Yale, 1714), the Tory president of King's College (later Columbia) in New York, had worried in 1760 that the colonists were drifting toward republicanism, which was seen by some as akin to mob rule. He suggested that the trend could be curtailed by reorganizing the colonies as a league or association under the direct control of a viceroy appointed by the king. This new configuration would resemble the Amphictyonic Council, he explained.

At the convention, delegates from smaller states repeatedly emphasized that the Amphictyonic structure gave equal numbers of votes to all members, big or small. "In the Amphictyonic confederation of the Grecian cities, each city, however different in wealth, strength and other circumstances, sent the same number of deputies, and had an equal voice in every thing," admonished Luther Martin (Princeton, 1766), the attorney general of Maryland. At the convention he delivered a three-hour address on this subject that exhausted some of his listeners, as well as Martin himself, who had to wait until the next day to deliver his conclusion. He cited that old warhorse of a textbook, Rollin's *Ancient History*.

When Oliver Ellsworth (Princeton, 1766) of Connecticut advocated giving smaller states equal representation, at least in the Senate, Madison fired back with a double-barreled historical citation: "He reminded Mr. E. of the Lycian confederacy, in which the component members had votes proportioned to their importance, and which Montesquieu recommends as the fittest model for that form of Government."

Madison also argued presciently that the conventioneers were focusing on the wrong question. More than anything, he wanted a strong central government to hold the nation together. Having such a government, he said, "is the great pervading principle that must controul the centrifugal tendency of the States; which, without it, will continually fly out of their proper orbits and destroy the order & harmony of the political System."

He believed that it was regionalism, not differing sizes of states, that most threatened the future of the Union. "The great division of interests in the U. States," he said, according to his notes, "did not lie between the large & small states; It lay between the Northern & Southern." In the long term he was right, unfortunately. But the solutions the conventioneers devised to placate the South and keep it part of the country, especially giving constitutional protections to the institution of slavery, would seven decades later lead the nation to civil war.

## Madison and Princeton at the Convention

MADISON'S TIME AT PRINCETON MAY HAVE INFLUENCED HIS BELIEFS. Remember here that the other colleges of Madison's time— Harvard, Yale, and William & Mary—had been regional or even local in their draw of students, while Princeton was administered consciously as a pan-colonial college, with students traveling to it from all the colonies of the American seaboard. At his college, notable also for its encouragement of political discussion, Madison moved among young men of diverse backgrounds, views, and accents, and watched them mix, and perhaps even check and balance one another in their own small, undergraduate ways.

Just as Madison had chosen a nationally minded college, so, too, in his political career he looked to national issues, note historians Stanley Elkins and Eric McKitrick. While a member of the Virginia Governor's Council during the Revolution, he had worked on supplying the Continental Army. When elected to Congress, he served on the committee overseeing the military operations of General Nathanael Greene in the South. "From the day he entered politics," they conclude, "the energies of James Madison were involved in continental rather than state problems. . . . His nationalism was hardly accidental." This continental perspective may have resonated with the eight other delegates at the convention who were Princeton graduates—more than from any other college. This reflected the geographical reach of the college.

For all that, Madison's influence at the convention peaked early, in June. The Virginia delegation's draft proposal dominated the early sessions, and as one of its authors, he engaged in defending it. Also, the early sessions were about broad structure and other fundamental questions, while later ones descended into the lesser issues such as the role of the vice president, and whether it should be the Congress or the Supreme Court that held the authority to impeach the president.

But Madison's classicism, at first so impressive, also may have started to grate on his listeners. In late June, Charles Pinckney of

South Carolina rejected all the analogies being made to ancient history. "The people of this country are not only very different from the inhabitants of any State we are acquainted with in the modern world; but I assert that their situation is distinct from either the people of Greece or Rome, or of any State we are acquainted with among the antients," he griped. For example, he asked, "Can the orders introduced by the institution of Solon, can they be found in the United States? Can the military habits & manners of Sparta be resembled to our habits & manners? Are the distinctions of Patrician & Plebeian known among us?"

Benjamin Franklin a few days later would make a similar remark. "We indeed seem to feel our own want of political wisdom, since we have been running around in search of it. We have gone back to ancient history for models of Government, and examined the different forms of those Republics which having been formed with the seeds of their own dissolution no longer exist."

For whatever reason, Madison would lose on a point he considered key, that of giving Congress the power to veto state laws. "The want of some provision seems to have been mortal to the antient Confederacies, and to be the disease of the modern," he would fret later that year to Thomas Jefferson. He got some of this authority in Article 1, Section 10, of the Constitution, which limits the powers of the individual states, forbidding them to make treaties or issue inflationary paper money, but he would worry after the convention that this was still not enough.

But no one got everything they wanted from the Constitution. When considering the document, it is useful to see it as a kind of peace treaty between the states.

## The Blot on the Constitution

CLASSICISM WOULD RECEDE LATER IN THE CONVENTION, BUT IT still would surface on occasion, most notably in the Southern defense of slavery. The delegates spent much time at the convention discussing that institution, but with no hope of ending it. The delegations from Georgia and South Carolina were emphatic: They would not sign any document that carried a whiff of emancipation.

Oddly, it was the same Charles Pinckney who had deplored ancient analogies who a month later invoked them to defend human bondage. "If slavery be wrong, it is justified by the example of all the world. He cited the case of Greece, Rome, & other antient States; . . . In all ages one half mankind had been slaves." Here the founders' reliance on the ancients was at odds with their other great influence, the thinkers of the Enlightenment. Montesquieu and Locke had both questioned slavery, but more in puzzlement than in flat-out denunciation, though Montesquieu came close when he wrote sarcastically that "It is impossible for us to suppose these creatures to be men, because allowing them to be men, a suspicion would follow, that we ourselves are not Christians." In recent years, the historian Holly Brewer has argued that Locke was not as enthusiastic about slavery as had been depicted, and that "as an old man he helped undo some of the wrongs he had helped to create."

They lived with this contradiction, both in the Constitution and in their daily lives. Princeton's John Witherspoon, who had signed the Declaration of Independence and would sit in the New Jersey meeting that gave that state's assent to the Constitution, was a leading advocate of liberty, yet he owned two slaves who labored in the hundreds of acres around his country house, Tusculum. At the same time, he admitted two free blacks to Princeton in the 1770s.

So the convention, which concluded in September 1787, would wind up passing the moral debt of slavery to later generations, who would have to pay in blood.

That said, there was one very powerful part of the Constitution that would resonate through the ages. Its three most essential words stand at the very beginning of the document: "We the people." It is the people, not the states or the federal government, that hold ultimate power. As James Madison would later write, "If we advert to the nature of republican government, we shall find that the censorial power is in the people over the government, and not in the government over the people." In the following decades, the American people would take this powerful idea that they were in charge and run with it in ways that the convention-eers could hardly have imagined.

## A Free Man in Paris

WHILE ALL THIS WAS GOING ON, THOMAS JEFFERSON WAS IN FRANCE, A freer man in Paris than he was in Virginia. His most famous con-demnation of slavery was first published privately there: "I trem-ble for my country when I reflect that God is just: that his justice cannot sleep forever." Jefferson seemed to have a different sense of the world when he was in Paris with the philosophes than he did when he was in rural Virginia, where he expressed views that tended to closely mirror "those of his planter brethren," as one historian phrases it.

Jefferson was surprised to find that the classical authors were not as popular in France as they were in the New World. "No body here reads them," he reported to Madison, with some exag-geration.

Despite that, in Paris he became more steeped in classicism than ever. Having studied the books of the ancients for decades, he now could follow the roads they had built to the ruins they had left. Touring southern France in the spring of 1787, he was entranced by its Roman arches, amphitheaters, and other remains. He was especially taken with the noble lines of a rectangular Roman tem-ple in Nîmes, locally called the Maison Carrée, or "square house," which he had read about in the writings of Palladio, the influential Italian architect. "Here I am, Madam, gazing whole hours at the Maison quarrée, like a lover at his mistress," he wrote to Madame Adrienne Tessé, to whom Jefferson had been introduced by her nephew, the Marquis de Lafayette. "From Lyons to Nismes I have been nourished with the remains of Roman grandeur. They have always brought you to my mind, because I know your affection for whatever is Roman and noble."

Underneath the light flirtatiousness, this letter contains significant thought that would affect how we think of our official buildings today. Jefferson would base his design of the capitol of Virginia on that shrine in Nîmes. While secretary of state, he would become deeply involved in the neoclassical design of the new capital of Washington, DC. Those acts alone would have earned him a place in history. As Gordon Wood puts it, "Almost single-handedly he became responsible for making America's public buildings resemble Roman temples."

It was at about this time that Jefferson, writing to Madison, drew a sharp and ambivalent portrait of John Adams. Jefferson had watched Adams closely in both Paris and London for months, he noted.

> *He is vain, irritable and a bad calculator of the force and probable effect of the motives which govern men. This is all the ill which can possibly be said of him. He is as disinterested as the being which made him: he is profound in his views: and accurate in his judgment except where knowledge of the world is necessary to form a judgment. He is so amiable, that I pronounce you will love him if ever you become acquainted with him. He would be, as he was, a great man in Congress.*

This clear-eyed assessment may have helped Jefferson maneuver a decade later when Adams became his political foe.

When he first laid eyes on the proposed Constitution, Jefferson was not enthusiastic. "There are very good articles in it: and very bad," he wrote. "I do not know which preponderate." He worried that the new system would suppress the spirit of rebellion. In the same letter, he made his famous assertion: "The tree of liberty must be refreshed from time to time with the blood of patriots and tyrants. It is it's natural manure."

He disliked that the Constitution allowed the president to be reelected to multiple terms, and so possibly could become chief executive for life. His other great objection, he told Madison, was the lack of a section explicitly providing and preserving the rights of the people. But, he added, the proposed Constitution could be amended as needed. So, he said, if the people approved it, "I shall concur in it chearfully." However, he later confessed that he did not at first believe that it would become the law of the land, because, he thought, not enough states would ratify it. He was, in his heart, not an advocate of a strong central government, telling one of his former law clerks that "I would rather be exposed to the inconveniencies attending too much liberty than those attending too small a degree of it." This preference would become the fundamental difference between him and Adams, and so between the Jeffersonians and the Federalists.

Jefferson's pessimism underscored the task that James Madison and other proponents of the proposed Constitution faced in seeking ratification by the states.

## The Federalist Papers Illuminate the New System

EVEN MADISON HIMSELF EMERGED FROM THE CONSTITUTIONAL CONvention somewhat disappointed. He still worried about the lack of a national veto over state laws. Likewise, Alexander Hamilton had wanted a far more aristocratic or monarchical system, with presidents and senators selected for life terms.

Yet unlike Jefferson, both Madison and Hamilton believed that ratifying the proposed Constitution, with all its flaws and compromises, was far more desirable than continuing the government under the Articles of Confederation. And so in the months after the convention, in the fall of 1787, the two threw themselves into campaigning for its passage by state conventions. They talked with each other, they persuaded others, and they wrote dozens of letters in their pro-ratification campaign. During the run-up to the convention, the youngest of our four subjects, Madison, had reported regularly to the oldest, George Washington, on the preparations for the meeting. Now, in the fall of 1787 and the following spring, the young politician faithfully kept the old general posted on the state of play of ratification in various states, writing to him ten times in the last part of that year and another twenty-one times in the first seven months of 1788.

Most remarkable of all, in just a few months between late October and late March, Madison and Hamilton, with a few contributions from John Jay, produced three dozen persuasive essays, now remembered as the Federalist Papers. (Another several dozen were produced later, for a grand total of eighty-five by August of 1788.) Peter Gay writes of this collection that "it is this document rather than the Declaration of Independence that strikes me as the most characteristic product of the American Enlightenment."

They brought to their task a new postcolonial perspective. Hamilton and Madison, the younger founders, differed from their elders in their relationship to classicism. They knew the ancient texts, but had less faith in the classical values propounded there. Some twenty-three of the eighty-five Federalist Papers quote or reflect classical authorities, and all of them were published under the pen name Publius. There are twice as many references to Greeks as to Romans, mainly because of Madison's interest in the governance of ancient Greek republics.

As early as 1775, Hamilton had mused in a letter that "it is not safe to trust to the virtue of any people." At the Constitutional Convention, he had elaborated on that thought: "We must take man as we find him," he had argued. "A reliance on pure patriotism has been the source of many of our errors." Reading that phrase raises an image of Hamilton and Washington conversing in a military tent on a dark night during the war on the thorny topic of the limits of virtue and patriotism.

In the world of the Federalist Papers, the pillar of "virtue" has fallen. When Madison does write about virtue, it often is not to invoke it but to emphasize that it is a finite resource in humans. For example, in an aside in Federalist 53 he refers to "the period within which human virtue can bear the temptations of power."

He is not saying that humans are wicked and have no virtue, just that virtue alone is insufficient. In other words, "a nation of philosophers is as little to be expected as the philosophical race of kings wished for by Plato."

## Making Faction Fix Itself

MADISON PASSED THE WINTER OF 1787—1788 IN NEW YORK CITY, WRITing essays and letters. One can only wonder if he had any social life while there. None such is reflected in his letters, which track the state of the ratification debate in various states and contain almost no small talk, even when engaging in it might have been politically helpful. He appears, as usual, to have been single-minded. Such introversion is especially unusual in someone who was so politically astute.

Madison's most extraordinary contribution would be his debut, Federalist 10, published on November 22, 1787. In it, he attacked the conventional classical republican view that to pursue one's own interest was to violate public spirit. For example, Abigail Adams, in a letter to her friend Mercy Otis Warren, had worried about men in whom "self Interest is more powerfull than publick virtue." "Sordid self-Interest" was "the natural Produce of base Minds," wrote Benjamin Franklin, who by the time of the Constitutional Convention was eighty-two years old, far more than the ages of Hamilton and Madison combined.

No, Madison responded. Do not waste your energies fighting party and faction. They will always be there. "The *causes* of faction cannot be removed," he stated, which means that "relief is only to be sought in the means of controlling its effects." The way to do that is to harness its energies by involving "the spirit of party and faction in the necessary and ordinary operations of government."

In other words, use one man's interest against another's. The more interests that are in play in the political arena, the smaller the chance that one intense passion will prevail. "Extend the sphere, and you take in a greater variety of parties and interests; you make it less probable that a majority of the whole will have a common motive to invade the rights of other citizens; or if such a common motive exists, it will be more difficult for all who feel it to discover their own strength, and to act in unison with each other."

So, he argues, counter to Montesquieu, big is good. The larger the republic, the more such checks will exist. "The extent of the union gives it the most palpable advantage. The influence of factious leaders may kindle a flame within their particular states, but will be unable to spread a general conflagration through the other states." In such "a well constructed union," he argued, there will be a "tendency to break and control the violence of faction."

Madison is saying the problem contains its own solution. In the essay's last paragraph, he concludes that "in the extent and proper structure of the union, therefore, we behold a republican remedy for the diseases most incident to republican government."

There is a lot of Hume here and a little Montesquieu, even though one of the purposes of this essay is to attack the Frenchman's notion that large republics were unsustainable. Madison was the most "Scottish" of the first four presidents in his thinking. Indeed, one scholar, Roy Branson, traces Madison's most innovative thinking, about how to accept and use party politics as a form of checks and balances, back to Hume and other Scottish thinkers. In making checks and balances the heart of the American system, Madison also was borrowing a bit from Montesquieu, who wrote that, "Constant experience shows us, that every man invested with power is apt to abuse it. . . . To prevent this abuse, it is necessary from the very nature of things, power should be a check to power."

In his next Federalist contribution, just eight days later, Madison again edged away from classicism. It is time to put aside "a blind veneration for antiquity," he stated, and try something new. What's more, he said, the Americans are ready to do so. They would know how to not let custom and tradition "overrule the suggestions of their own good sense, the knowledge of their own situation, and the lessons of their own experience."

The decline of classicism hung in the Manhattan air that winter. At about the same time, in the same city, Noah Webster (Yale, 1778) wrote an essay calling for Americans to move on from an educational system in which "the minds of youth are perpetually led to the history of Greece or Rome or to Great Britain; boys are constantly repeating the declamations of Demosthenes and Cicero, or debates upon some political question in the British Parliament." Generally, he said, Americans should pay less "attention to the dead languages." He asked, "What advantage does a merchant, a mechanic, a farmer, derive from an acquaintance with the Greek and Roman tongues?" In the new nation, knowledge would be seen not as a good in itself, but as a tool, to be judged by its usefulness, which would become the new American measure of things.

## Clams vs. Classicism

MADISON WAS NOT ENTIRELY DONE WITH THE ANCIENT WORLD, however. In Federalist 18, he returned to the subject of the Amphictyonic Council, arguing that its structure exacerbated tensions between member cities. "It happened but too often, according to Plutarch, that the deputies of the strongest cities, awed and corrupted those of the weaker, and that judgment went in favor of the most powerful party." Among other things, this was a reason for giving smaller cities the ability to resist coercion. Athens and Sparta "inflated with the victories and the glory they had acquired, became first rivals, and then enemies." That led to the eventual destruction of Athens, he noted. "Their mutual jealousies, fears, hatreds and injuries, ended in the celebrated Peloponnesian war; which itself ended in the ruin and slavery of the Athenians who had begun it." He warned again of foreign subversion, citing the intervention of Philip of Macedon. "By his intrigues and bribes he won over to his interests the popular leaders of several cities; by their influence and votes, gained admission into the Amphyctionic council; and by his arts and his arms, made himself master of the confederacy."

The lesson of this history, he concluded, is that "it emphatically illustrates the tendency of federal bodies, rather to anarchy among the members than to tyranny in the head."

Anarchy was on Madison's mind that winter as the individual states were in the process of debating whether to ratify the proposed Constitution. In late January, a member of the Massachusetts convention reported to him that eighteen to twenty members of the ratification meeting there were in fact veterans of Shays' Rebellion against that state's government. In other words, some of the people whom the Constitution was meant to restrain would be sitting in judgment of it. Madison gloomily passed the word to George Washington.

On top of that, one of Madison's sources of political intelligence in Virginia, John Dawson, wrote to warn him that their state would be swayed by the outcome in Massachusetts. "Never perhaps was a state more divided than Virginia is on the new Constitution. Its fate appears to hang in a great measure on the decision of Massachusetts bay. Shoud the convention of that state adjourn without doing any thing decisive, or shoud amendments be proposd, I think, Virginia will go hand in hand with her."

The Massachusetts meeting was the largest of the state conventions, with some 364 delegates jammed into the ground floor of a Boston church and hundreds of spectators crowding the galleries above them. Dozens of newspapers across the United States ran detailed accounts of the debates. Fisher Ames (Harvard, 1774), who would later become a prominent Federalist, delivered his first major speech, warning that, "Faction and enthusiasm are the instruments by which popular governments are destroyed. . . . A democracy is a volcano, which conceals the fiery materials of its own destruction. These will produce an eruption, and carry desolation in their way."

The high-flying oratory of the pro-Constitution side again rubbed the anti-Federalists wrong. Amos Singletary, himself an informally educated miller, worried biblically that:

*These lawyers, and men of learning, and moneyed men, that talk*
*so finely, and gloss over matters so smoothly, to make us poor il-*
*literate people swallow down the pill, expect to get into Congress*
*themselves; they expect to be the managers of this Constitution,*
*and get all the power and all the money into their own hands, and*
*then they will swallow up all us little folks . . . just as the whale*
*swallowed up Jonah. This is what I am afraid of.*

Jonathan Smith, a farmer from Berkshire County, in the western part of Massachusetts, which had been the center of Shays'
Rebellion, mocked Singletary's qualms. He was resolutely pro-
ratification, he said, in part because he had witnessed that insurrection. "I have lived in a part of the country where I have known
the worth of a good government by the want of it," he noted pointedly. "It brought on a state of anarchy, and that led to tyranny."
Calling himself "a plain man" who got his "living by the plough,"
Smith pointed across the room at Singletary. "My honorable old
daddy there won't think that I expect to be a Congress-man, and
swallow up the liberties of the people. I never had any such post,
nor do I want one."

One theme of the ratification debates is a sense that the classical
context was outmoded, like a suit of clothes a teenager has out-
grown. The nation was ready to move on. This impatience is reflected in an exchange between two anti-Federalists. Dr. Samuel
Willard launched on a disquisition about "the field of ancient history," discussing "Sparta, Athens and Rome," and especially the
Amphictyonic League's ability to resist Xerxes. Benjamin Randall
impatiently responded that, "The quoting of ancient history was
no more to the purpose than to tell how our forefathers dug clams
at Plymouth."

It looked like Massachusetts would vote against the Constitution. In late January, one "anti" delegate predicted that his side
would win decisively, with 192 against and only 144 in support.
Yet when the Massachusetts convention voted in early February,
it narrowly approved the new government, by a vote of 187 to 168.

During this time, in January and February of 1788, Madison

poured out a total of twenty-three essays, an extraordinary rate of production for someone who also was managing the pro-ratification campaign. He began Federalist 38 with a sweeping review of how governments were reformed in ancient Greece and Rome. He derived two lessons from this survey: First, the proposed Constitution improved on those ancient plans of government. Second, that it would be imprudent to turn down the proposed plan unnecessarily.

In Federalist 41, Madison mulled the existence of a standing army, saying it might be necessary but also should be watched most carefully. The lesson in the back of his mind was the ancient one: "the liberties of Rome proved the final victim to her military triumphs."

In Federalist 51, he emphasized again how checks and balances were necessary to offset self-interest. "Ambition must be made to counteract ambition. . . . It may be a reflection on human nature, that such devices should be necessary to controul the abuses of government. But what is government itself but the greatest of all reflections on human nature?" He concluded the thought with one of his more memorable observations: "If men were angels, no government would be necessary."

His last contribution, written at the end of February, has a vale-dictory air. In arguing that Senates help preserve republics, he re-turned to his ancient studies, invoking several classical examples. "History informs us of no long lived republic which had not a senate." Then he left for his home in Virginia, where he had been told there was opposition brewing against sending him as a del-egate to that state's ratification convention. He had experienced a remarkable twelve months, helping pull together the Consti-tutional Convention, then participating in it and painstakingly recording its progress, and finally campaigning unceasingly for its ratification.

Hamilton's contributions to the Federalist Papers were less en-amored of classicism. This may be in part due to his relative lack of learning—he had started at King's College (Columbia) in 1773, only to see it shuttered when the British occupied New York City in 1776. Jefferson considered him "half-lettered"—that is, only partially educated. But Hamilton was the fastest of learners and could have made a flashy show of knowledge had he wanted to. It is more likely that he did not share Madison's lingering veneration for antiquity. Hamilton long had been growing impatient with classical analogies and models. In Federalist 6, for example, Daniel Shays was as much on Hamilton's mind as the Greco-Roman world was. He was dismissive of both. Of the latter, he wrote, "Sparta was little better than a well regulated camp; and Rome was never sated of carnage and conquest."

Yet one aspect of classicism still held an appeal to his conspiratorial ways. He would use classical aliases to signal his frame of mind. Tellingly, notes Meyer Reinhold, the pseudonyms that he would employ in the remainder of his life—among them, Phocion, Cicero, Camillus, Pericles—"Were men of heroic virtue" who "were misjudged and persecuted by their people."

Ratification still hung in the balance. The Virginia vote would be crucial. Madison again would carry a big part of the load. "We think here that the situation of your state is critical," Hamilton, in New York, worriedly wrote in late May to Madison in Virginia. He then made it clear that he would pay dearly to have dispatches sent to him with as much speed as possible.

## Virginia Finally Meets

———

THOMAS JEFFERSON HAD LONG SEEN PATRICK HENRY AS A PROBLEM, confiding to Madison in a letter in 1784 partly written in code, that, "While Mr. Henry lives another bad [state] constitution would be formed, and saddled for ever on us. What we have to do I think is devoutly to pray for his death."

When Virginians met to consider the proposed national Constitution, former Governor Henry was indeed on the warpath. "I have the highest veneration for these people," he stated, referring to the framers of the Constitution. "But, sir, give me leave to demand what right they had to say, *We, the people* . . . instead of We, the states?"

Henry went on to portray the proposed Constitution as dangerous. "I see great jeopardy in this new Government. I see none from our present one." The Articles of Confederation had worked admirably, he maintained:

> *Something must be done to preserve your liberty and mine: The Confederation; this same despised Government, merits, in my opinion, the highest encomium: It carried us through a long and dangerous war: It rendered us victorious in that bloody conflict with a powerful nation: It has secured us a territory greater than any European monarch possesses: And shall a Government which has been thus strong and vigorous, be accused of imbecility and abandoned for want of energy? Consider what you are about to do before you part with this Government.*

He then added vaguely that "similar examples are to be found in ancient Greece and ancient Rome: Instances of the people losing their liberty by their carelessness and the ambition of a few."

The next day, Madison fired back. It was not the actions of the few, he contended, but of the many that most threatened the stability of the republic. "On a candid examination of history, we shall find that turbulence, violence and abuse of power, by the majority trampling on the rights of the minority, have produced factions and commotions, which, in republics, have more frequently than any other cause, produced despotism." Madison sparred with Henry for weeks. But it took a toll on him. After one debate, Madison took to his bed for three days, perhaps with one of his epileptic-like seizures. Jefferson would salute Madison's skill in responding to "the fervid declamation of Mr. Henry."

It eventually became clear that Henry, for all his oratorical power, was pushing a losing argument. Zachariah Johnston, a Revolutionary War veteran from the Shenandoah Valley, said on June 25, just before the Virginia convention voted, that "the great and wise State of Massachusetts has taken this step. The great and wise State of Virginia might safely do the same." The Shenandoah Valley group at the convention was respected, being "mainly composed of men who had seen hard military service, and were devoted to Washington." They would follow their general's lead.

Another venerated figure, George Wythe, Jefferson's old law mentor, had offered a motion to ratify. Virginia finally did so that afternoon, by a very small majority of 89 to 79. It became the tenth state to do so.

The only major question remaining was what New York would do. The Constitution was a fait accompli, and New York would be isolated if it declined. Still, the vote there remained uncertain. On July 4, in Albany, New York, anti-Federalists burned a copy of the Constitution and clashed with a pro-ratification crowd, leaving eighteen wounded and perhaps one dead—the body counts differ. Hamilton reported to Madison that "there has been a disturbance in the City of Albany on the 4th of July which has occasioned bloodshed." The question hung there for Hamilton and Madison: How widespread would violent opposition to the new Constitution be? Could it be undone by mobs?

Ultimately the New York vote was narrowest of all, a very grudging 30 to 27. It became the eleventh state to approve. At this point only North Carolina and Rhode Island remained outside the reconstituted nation. On September 15, 1788, Congress announced that the Constitution had been ratified and set dates for the election of a president. ("Rogue Island" finally would join on May 29, 1790, by a vote of 34 to 32, more than a year after George Washington had become president of the other twelve states.) Ratification had been a near-run thing.

The process was, to a surprising degree, James Madison's achievement. He arguably had done more than Jefferson (or John Adams, for that matter) to create the United States of America. Jefferson had drafted the more affecting Declaration, but Madison played a central role in the more practical Constitution.

It was an extraordinary record for a frail, introverted man without much of a public-speaking voice. That he overcame those obstacles indicates the strength of both his will and his intellect, as well as his dedication to discerning the lessons of the ancient world for the new United States.

## A Slender Reed

———

TIMES AND GOVERNMENT BOTH HAD CHANGED, BUT NOT ALL THE NA-tion's leaders had moved on. George Washington still clung to the concept of having a legislature peopled solely by good men who abhorred partisanship. He still steered by the light of virtue. For him, as for so many in his generation, states one scholar, "Faction was virtue's opposite."

At the end of 1788, Washington wrote from Mount Vernon to a Revolutionary War comrade that "it is my most earnest wish that none but the most disinterested, able and virtuous men may be appointed to either house of Congress: because, I think, the tranquility and happiness of this Country will depend essentially upon that circumstance." This was old think. To George Washington, "party" may still have carried some of the bloody conno-tations it had when he wrote, thirty-one years earlier, about a war action: "Our party killed one Indian (whose scalp they obtained) and wounded several others."

Washington seems not to have been paying attention, or at least not understanding, how American life had changed since he was a young man. The question for Madison and Hamilton in the coming years would become how to run the government while the old man was still in charge.

*Part III*

# AMERICANIZATION

⟨⟨⟩⟩

Historians usually depict the 1790s as the period that saw the awkward, painful emergence of divisive partisanship in America, and also as the last attempt by conservatives to contain the revolutionary spirit, or at least channel its direction. It was indeed all those things. But in the context of this book, it was the decade when the classical model ran out of steam. This would result, surprisingly quickly, in what one scholar terms "a radical shift in discourse" that demoted or diminished "all things classical."

Partisanship emerged stealthily. No one wanted to admit to it, and so no formal political organizations emerged as such. There were no conventions or primaries. Rather, early in the decade, loose groups began to form, mainly in opposition to the growing power within the Washington administration of Alexander Hamilton, secretary of the treasury from 1789 to 1795. Political parrying took the form of slashing personal attacks on the morals and ethics of emerging opponents, often describing them as disloyal conspirators. Some of this surfaced in squabbles between cabinet members. But it became public in the pages of the fiercely partisan newspapers of the day, as they battled over the defining issues of the decade——Hamilton's plans for the federal government, the proper response to the Whiskey Rebellion, the meaning of the French Revolution, and finally, the Federal counterattack on the newspapers themselves, in the form of the Alien and Sedition Acts.

## Chapter 12

# The
# Classical Vision
# Smashes into American
# Reality

*M*ODERN CHIVALRY, A SATIRICAL NOVEL BY HUGH HENRY BRACKEN-ridge, a Scottish-born comrade of James Madison in the Princeton class of 1771, conveys a sense of how hard Americans turned against the classical outlook in the 1790s and early 1800s. Brackenridge and Madison had been friendly at the college, and indeed may have been roommates for a spell. In the rambling novel's first volume, which appeared in 1792, Brackenridge relates the adventures on the American frontier of a Captain Farrago. The captain, a kind of American version of Don Quixote, is portrayed at the outset as a product of "an academic education" of the sort that the author and his friends received at Princeton, pointedly described as resulting in a "greater knowledge of books than of the world."

Farrago was, in fact, a man not quite keeping up with his times: "His ideas were drawn chiefly from what may be called the old school; the Greek and Roman notions of things." It may be illuminating to know that the word "farrago" is Latin for the kind of hodgepodge of low-grade grains used as cattle fodder.

The captain and his servant, the "bogtrotter" Teague O'Reagan, a wily Irishman who though illiterate eventually becomes a judge, enjoy a variety of adventures as they voyage across the new United States. Early on, in an alehouse, the captain finds some villagers discussing politics. Politicians merely flatter the people, who charge around like a herd of wild buffalo, argues one local. "Is there no such thing as public spirit?" the captain responds. "Is there not a spice of virtue to be found in a republic? Who would not devote himself for the public good?"

He seems to find agreement about the value of the old ways from one of his interlocutors. "The great mischief in democracy is party, said one orator, who had taken his pipe from his teeth, at the same time spitting on the floor." The point here seems to be that even the would-be Federalists were acting like vulgar democrats. Or perhaps simply that everyone now had political opinions and shared them freely.

The captain's adventures conclude in a sequel volume written in the early nineteenth century, with Farrago having been elected governor of a new state, where he promptly represses dissent with Napoleonic vigor. By the end of the tale, classical republicanism has become an object of ridicule. A lawyer turned poet sings a ballad that includes this verse:

> *The case has ever been the fact*
> *Since Brutus did exclaim,*
> *Virtue I have followed thee,*
> *But found an empty name.*

By this point classical learning is not just outmoded, it is an object of suspicion, even derision. At one point the narrator pauses to examine a question: "It naturally will be asked, considering the current of prejudice against learning, why . . . the school-master, was not lynched for publicly talking Latin." The answer, of course, is that "the people did not know it was Latin." Sometimes the ignorance of the mob is an advantage.

Entering a strange new settlement with his followers, Captain Farrago assures them that "there are no scholars amongst us, save a Latin schoolmaster, who has left off the business, and is going to become an honest man." Meanwhile, Teague O'Reagan, now a judge, decides to write his memoirs, but being unlettered cannot, so he engages the former schoolteacher to ghostwrite them.

As Brackenridge's hero found, in late-eighteenth-century America, the classical frame of mind had become an impediment for understanding the nature of the place. It especially inhibited traditionalists such as John Adams as they wrestled with the dynamic nature of what one historian calls a "unique, revolutionary, pluralistic, changing, progressive nation."

## Loyalty and Opposition

IN HIS FIRST INAUGURAL ADDRESS, DELIVERED IN NEW YORK CITY ON April 30, 1789, Washington promised to be a good steward of "the experiment entrusted to the hands of the American people." Washington uttered the words, but they almost certainly were drafted by James Madison, America's first great political insider. As Richard Brookhiser writes, "After Washington gave the speech in Federal Hall, Madison wrote the House's response, and Washington's answer to the House's response." In the same vein, the political philosopher Danielle Allen once remarked that a good part of early American history consists of such instances of Madison talking to himself, as he also did by encouraging a Constitutional Convention, then recording its proceedings, then writing papers commenting on the product, and then leading the introduction of the first ten amendments, the Bill of Rights.

Washington, Madison, and the other people leading the young nation were always conscious that there was nothing certain about the United States of America. Every crisis threatened to be an existential test of a new way of living, of how a society had been arranged. They could point to few, if any, instances in history of a democratic republic lasting more than a century or so. With that knowledge in mind, the 1790s would prove to be an alarming decade.

Another stumbling block was conceptual. The notion of a "loyal opposition" is that part of the process of good governance is organized questioning and criticism by those out of power, who in turn maintain deference to the larger state. But that concept had not yet developed in the Anglo-American world. Indeed, the phrase "His Majesty's Opposition" was not used in Parliament until decades later, in 1826. A search of *Founders Online*, the U.S. National Archives' compilation of the letters, speeches, diaries, and other writings of the founders, unearths not a single use of the phrase "loyal opposition." During the 1790s, there was not yet a vocabulary, or psychological space, for political competition. The emerging factions simply lacked the means to describe or accommodate what was happening.

As a result, the founders regarded oppositional activity as suspicious, the result of pernicious plotting. In the 1790s, as political pressures built, this stream of conspiracy thinking grew into a flood. Those in power viewed those who opposed them as enemies of the state. "The Federalists never saw themselves as a party but as the beleaguered legitimate government beset by people allied with revolutionary France out to destroy the Union," states Gordon Wood.

Here, the educations of the Revolutionary generation did not serve them well. The classical mindset would prove a poor framework in which to view the emerging politics of the 1790s, only making the situation worse. To describe their political foes, they reached back once again to Roman history, all too often to the Catilinarian conspiracy. Remember here that to be a "Catiline" was not just to grab for power, but to attack the soul of the nation, to threaten its way of life.

Moreover, the Revolutionary generation had been taught that this most vile sort of activity was a disturbing symptom of a diseased political environment in which, as English political theorist Edward Wortley Montagu had written, "Publick virtue, and the love of their country, . . . were extinct." (This writer, who died in 1761, should not be confused with the Edward Montagu who was the London agent for Virginia in the 1760s.)

They would have remembered with chagrin that Montagu also wrote that Catilinism was a signal not just of political opposition but of impending national catastrophe. "The conspiracies of Catiline and Caesar against the liberty of their country, were . . . the immediate cause of the destruction of the Republick," Montagu concluded in his *Reflections on the Rise and Fall of the Antient Republicks*—that is, Sparta, Athens, Thebes, Carthage, and Rome. The larger cause, he wrote, was love of luxury, which leads to corruption and thus to competing parties. Montagu employed the word "faction" some fifty times in his book. The symptoms of it were "luxury, effeminacy and corruption." In other words, the label "Catiline" implicitly means the beginning of the end of the nation. From this perspective, the growing schism in American politics appeared to lead straight to disaster.

Another of the popular eighteenth-century political writers, the Scot James Burgh, warned in addition that Hannibal had been undone by factionalism in Carthage. "Hannibal probably would have overset Rome, and saved his country . . . if he had not himself been overset by faction. Thus faction was the ruin of Carthage, and riches probably were the cause of faction."

Reinforcing such concerns, some of the founders likely also were familiar with Lord Bolingbroke's warning that the emergence of faction was a sign not just of evil on one side, but of corruption of the entire system:

> We must not imagine that the freedom of the Romans was lost, because one party fought for the maintenance of liberty; another for the establishment of tyranny; and that the latter prevailed. No. The spirit of liberty was dead, and the spirit of faction had taken its place on both sides.

Just to be politically aligned was, at least in the eyes of some Federalists, immoral and perhaps treasonous.

Even Jefferson at this point remained reluctant to embrace factionalism, at least in public. It meant giving up a conception of governance that he and his peers had held all their lives. "If I could not go to heaven but with a party, I would not go there at all," he avowed from Paris in March 1789. But he would soon sing a different hymn.

## Jefferson's Roman Response to Manhattan

IT WAS JEFFERSON, RETURNING TO AMERICA AFTER A FEW YEARS AWAY, who sensed the shift in the political climate most vividly. He departed revolutionary Paris in October 1789, and six months later was in New York City, the initial capital during the new era of the Constitution, where he was installed as the first secretary of state. He was startled by the reactionary politics he found there. "I found a state of things which, of all I had ever contemplated, I the least expected," he recalled years later in a document that admittedly might have been written partly to justify his later partisanship. As he made the round of welcoming dinners, he found that "politics were the chief topic, and a preference of kingly, over republican, government, was evidently the favorite sentiment." He felt isolated, noting that he was, "for the most part, the only advocate on the republican side of the question." Where had the revolution gone?

On the other side of the emerging political divide, John Adams, the new vice president, was also having a difficult time adjusting to the new realities of post-ratification America. He may have thought he was being conciliatory when he wrote to his cousin Sam Adams that "whenever I Use the Word Republick, with approbation I mean a Government, in which the People have, collectively or by Representation, an essential share in the Sovereignty."

His cousin responded with a polite but clear correction. "A Republic, you tell me, is a Government in which 'the People have an essential share in the Sovereignty.'" No, Sam Adams informed him: "Is not the *whole* sovereignty, my friend, essentially in the People?" Look at our new fundamental law, he admonished: "We the People is the stile of the federal Constitution." Sam Adams was correct, dramatically so. John Adams had yet to apprehend how much power had shifted to the people, both politically and culturally. He would spend much of his time in power in the 1790s resisting that trend, eventually going so far as to imprison newspaper editors who criticized him.

Jefferson especially disliked New York and Philadelphia, the first two national capitals, because they were homes to the merchants and financiers who so antagonized him. The monarchical minded, pro-English people in the United States have "some important associates from New York," he wrote in a letter to Lafayette. "Too many of these stock jobbers and King-jobbers have come into our legislature, or rather too many of our legislature have become stock jobbers and king-jobbers."

Eventually, as part of a deal Jefferson cut with Madison and Hamilton, the capital of the United States would not be among the moneymen. Rather, a new city would be built from scratch to the South, between Virginia and Maryland. Jefferson did not say so, but he must also have understood that moving the federal headquarters to the banks of the Potomac also placed it in an environment more inclined to support the perpetuation of slavery.

True to their natures, in building the new capital, President Washington would dwell on questions of land while Jefferson dedicated himself to architectural design. Washington personally selected the site of the White House. Under Jefferson's influence, the major buildings of the new capital would display Roman stylings, shimmering white under the southern sun. "The Federal City on the Potomac . . . was one of Thomas Jefferson's dearest undertakings," write Stanley Elkins and Eric McKitrick. "He subsequently gave more of his time, energy, and thought to that problem than did any other officer of the state." As secretary of state, he conceived of a competition to design a building for the Congress. He decided that it would be called not "The Congress House," as originally listed, but the Capitol, a nod to ancient history. This building, home to both houses of the federal legislature, would dominate Washington, DC, just as the Temple of Jupiter on the Capitoline Hill had been the most prominent religious building in ancient Rome. The upper house was already called the Senate, after the Roman example. The winning design—classical, as might be expected—was submitted by William Thornton, who had trained as a physician at the University of Edinburgh and later received a degree from the University of Aberdeen.

Jefferson prescribed that the bricks used in construction should follow ancient Roman proportions—a flattish eleven inches wide, twice that in length, and about two inches high, with "grain . . . as fine as that of our best earthen ware." As he described it, this new building would be "the first temple dedicated to the sovereignty of the people." Thus was set the neoclassical style of American official buildings, especially courts and state capitol buildings. Jefferson's design was in addition perhaps a bit of a monument to his own efforts to create a republic that was for, of, and by the people. Charles Dickens, visiting the city decades later, when it still had a raw feel, would label it "the City of Magnificent Intentions," a phrase that also summarizes Jefferson well.

Happily for Jefferson, the new capital was safely hundreds of miles away from "the speculators and Tories," to employ the expression Madison used in a 1791 letter to Jefferson.

## Madison Rides to the Rescue

AS THAT PUNGENT PHRASE INDICATES, MADISON WAS BECOMING avowedly partisan. Once again he was leading the way in American public life, this time by unabashedly embracing party politics. "In every political society, parties are unavoidable. A difference of interests, real or supposed, is the most natural and fruitful source of them," he wrote in the *National Gazette*, which was established in Philadelphia in October 1791 with assistance from him and Jefferson. Madison went on in that short essay to claim that natural law supported the existence of parties. "In all political societies, different interests and parties arise out of the nature of things, and the great art of politicians lies in making them checks and balances to each other." The answer to one party was the "check" of another. Indeed, in three short paragraphs totaling 321 words, he used that word "check" five times.

The purpose of the new newspaper, edited by Philip Freneau (Princeton, 1772), a college friend of Madison's, was to be an outlet for anti-Hamilton views, which made it the first nakedly partisan punch thrown in American history. Another old Princetonian, the sometime novelist Hugh Henry Brackenridge, also would write several columns for the newspaper.

Madison's own contributions to the *Gazette* hammered home a new insight. Faction in all its manifestations—partisanship, political competition, contention, compromises, rivalry, and the cutting of deals—was not part of the problem, it was part of the solution. Young Madison was more attuned to his time than were his Revolutionary elders and was decades ahead of them. Arguably, Madison in the early 1790s was playing the role that Washington did during the War for Independence, being the person who grasped the nature of the struggle in which the nation was engaged and then developed an effective strategic response to it.

Most other public men were not yet in step with this new world. "What caused the fall of Athens?" William Wyche, a New York lawyer, asked rhetorically in a 1794 speech in Manhattan. His answer: Faction. "Party is a monster who devours the common good," he warned.

Alexander Hamilton, one of the president's closest advisors during that time, was at this point somewhere between Madison and Wyche in understanding how politics were changing. Like Madison, he accepted that political parties existed, but like Wyche, he saw his opponents not as a necessary part of the system, but rather as mortal foes. He wrote to a new political ally that "Mr. Madison cooperating with Mr. Jefferson is at the head of a faction decidedly hostile to me and my administration, and actuated by views in my judgment subversive of the principles of good government and dangerous to the union, peace and happiness of the Country." In other words, he considered their disagreeing with him to be attacking the state.

John Adams, more than anyone, was clinging to the old ways. He griped to a friend that "I own I did not expect that truth, honor and virtue would so soon have been trampled under foot in America, as much aware as I was of the turpitude usually produced by ambitious rivalries." George Washington held similar views, though not so fervently expressed. As he contemplated standing for a second term as president, he considered the stakes to be huge—indeed, the very existence of the United States. "The abuses of public Officers—and of those attacks upon almost every measure of government with which some of the Gazettes are so strongly impregnated; & which cannot fail, if persevered in with the malignancy they now team, of rending the Union asunder," he wrote in a private letter.

A month after Washington sent that letter, Hamilton wrote privately about the nakedly ambitious Aaron Burr (Princeton, 1772), then a senator from New York, that "if we have an embryo-Cæsar in the United States 'tis Burr." There were few worse insults in eighteenth-century America.

Three days later Hamilton, who never seemed to have enough enemies to satisfy himself, lit into his main target, Jefferson. Every republic, he wrote in phrases laden with condemnation, has "the Catilines and the Cæsars of the community . . . who leading the dance to the tune of liberty without law, endeavor to intoxicate the people with delicious but poisonous draughts to render them the easier victims of their rapacious ambition; the vicious and the fanatical of every class who are ever found the willing or the deluded followers of those seducing and treacherous leaders." Jefferson was a sly one, he warned, a "Cæsar *coyley refusing* the proffered diadem" who in fact is "tenaciously grasping the substance of imperial domination." Hamilton ended the diatribe with a final reference: It was Caesar, the liberal, "who *overturned* the republic," he noted, while it was Cato, the conservative, "who died for it."

In a series of pseudonymous essays published around this time, from August through December of 1792, Hamilton blasted away at Jefferson, Madison, and their sponsorship of the *National Gazette*. Hamilton also reportedly told Jefferson he considered Julius Caesar "the greatest man that ever lived." Historians suspect that Hamilton was just baiting Jefferson with that remark. Even so, it was, when seen in the context of American classicism, a provocative crack.

Hamilton finally went to President Washington to protest about Jefferson, saying that the secretary of state had opposed him "from the first moment of his coming to the City of New York to enter upon his present office" and also had supported "a formed party" in Congress "bent upon my subversion." He also told the president that Jefferson was backing the nettlesome opposition newspaper, writing that, "I cannot doubt, from the evidence I possess, that the National Gazette was instituted by him for political purposes and that one leading object of it has been to render me and all the measures connected with my department as odious as possible."

Washington, exasperated, sought to repair the breach between his two key cabinet members. Jefferson, in a conversation with the president at Mount Vernon, countered that he had heard Hamilton say that "this constitution was a shillyshally thing of mere milk & water, which could not last, & was only good as a step to something better." Jefferson was telling Washington that it was Hamilton who was having a destabilizing effect.

Jefferson indeed was becoming an unabashed party man. He grumbled to Madison that he thought Hamilton was "daring to call the republican party a faction." Adams, sensing this shift, decried Jefferson's new direction in a letter to Abigail Adams. "I am really astonished at the blind Spirit of Party which has Seized on the whole soul of this Jefferson: There is not a Jacobin in France more devoted to Faction."

The initial tentative seedlings of organized political parties began to emerge at this time, in the form of Democratic Societies. They were inspired in part by revolutionary organizations in France, and indeed adopted the term "Citizen" to address each other, in the style of the French Jacobins. The first appeared in

Philadelphia in May 1793. Eventually there were about thirty-five spread across the states. These seem to have been rather inchoate in their activities, perhaps half fraternal clubs, half political discussion groups. They shared copies of anti-Federalist newspapers and encouraged people to vote. Some of the societies contemplated going further, with the one in Portland (now in Maine) requesting its members in 1794 to arm themselves in order to "be prepared to defend the Rights of Man."

## Jefferson on the Farm

---

JEFFERSON GREW INCREASINGLY UNHAPPY IN GOVERNMENT. HE COMplained, in one of his candid letters to Madison, that he labored all day and then found his "rare hours of relaxation sacrificed to the society of persons . . . of whose hatred I am conscious even in those moments of conviviality when the heart wishes most to open itself to the effusions of friendship and confidence, cut off from my family and friends, my affairs abandoned to chaos and derangement, in short giving every thing I love, in exchange for every thing I hate."

In the next paragraph, he shared an even more shocking observation, about the declining condition of George Washington. "The President is not well. Little lingering fevers have been hanging about him for a week or ten days, and have affected his looks most remarkeably. He is also extremely affected by the attacks made and kept up on him in the public papers. I think he feels those things more than any person I ever yet met with. I am sincerely sorry to see them."

A few weeks later, Washington finally erupted, losing his temper in a cabinet meeting about the French at which some of the newspaper attacks on him were mentioned. Washington did not express anger often, having spent decades working to contain his passions and emotions. But when he did let go, the detonation was memorable. Jefferson recorded it like a political seismograph:

*The Presidt. was much inflamed, got into one of those passions when he cannot command himself. Run on much on the personal abuse which had been bestowed on him. Defied any man on earth to produce one single act of his since he had been in the government which was not done on the purest motives. That he had never repented but once the having slipped the moment of resigning his office, and that was every moment since. That by god he had rather be in his grave than in his present situation. That he had rather be on his farm than to be made emperor of the world and yet that they were charging him with wanting to be a king.*

Jefferson's account rings true, especially that "*by god he had rather be in his grave,*" which feels like a verbatim transcription. One can only wonder at the emotional cost to Washington of this outburst. He truly must have been at the end of his rope.

Jefferson resigned as secretary of state at the end of 1793. John Adams confided to Abigail that he was happy to see him go. "His soul is poisoned with Ambition," Adams told his wife after he heard of Jefferson's intention to leave. A few days later he reported,

*Jefferson went off Yesterday, and a good riddance of bad ware. I hope his Temper will be more cool and his Principles more reasonable in Retirement than they have been in office. . . . He has Talents I know, and Integrity I believe: but his mind is now poisond with Passion Prejudice and Faction.*

Never does Adams seem to appreciate that Jefferson was trying to understand and adjust to the political realities of the new nation. Adams, failing to do so, would be blindsided by them a few years later.

Jefferson seems to have been genuinely happy at home, away from government. Responding to a note from his old legal tutor, George Wythe, about getting copies of Virginia laws that had been passed while Jefferson was governor, he affected nonchalance about government work:

*I may be able to engage some young man in Charlottesville to copy acts for those who need them, for hire. I have no body living with me who could do it, and I am become too lazy, with the pen, and too much attached to the plough to do it myself. I live on my horse from an early breakfast to a late dinner, and very often after that till dark. This occasions me to be in great arrears in my pen-work.*

This talk of putting hand to plow is a bit rich, given that it is implausible that Jefferson ever worked the fields, as indeed John Adams did. Nevertheless, he was accurate in insisting that his primary attention was on the state of his farm. He observed at one point that it was producing sufficient potatoes and clover "to feed every animal on my farm except my negroes." On the negative side, this is perhaps for us today the most stomach-turning sentence he ever wrote.

But he knew that out beyond his fields, the hold on the president of Hamilton and other Federalists—that is, advocates of a strong central government—was growing. This worried him, especially given his belief that Washington was declining in mental capacity. Without Jefferson around to remind Washington of republican principles, of giving as much power as possible to the people, "the federalists got unchecked hold of Genl. Washington," he complained. Jefferson becomes quite damning at this point: "His memory was already sensibly impaired by age, the firm tone of mind for which he had been remarkable, was beginning to relax, it's energy was abated; a listlessness of labor, a desire for tranquillity had crept on him, and a willingness to let others act and even think for him." Jefferson's dismal assessment might be doubted, but not the depth of his disappointment. He concluded somberly that Washington "had become alienated from myself personally."

He almost pleaded with Madison to come to Monticello. "I long to see you," he wrote in April 1795. "May we hope for a visit from you?" It was time to begin planning the presidential campaign of 1796. Jefferson and Madison were about to invent American presidential politics, and the older man's visionary thinking would need to be anchored by his younger friend's practical mind.

## The Whiskey Rebels

———

THE FEDERAL GOVERNMENT, SEEKING TO REDUCE ITS WAR DEBT, IM-
posed a tax on whiskey and other distilled spirits. The farmers of
western Pennsylvania felt unfairly burdened by the tax, especially
because its structure favored the larger year-round distillers of
the East. They responded with threats of violence to intimidate the
officials sent to collect it. Many of the rebels were veterans of the
Revolution, and local militias seemed to side with them. Their
efforts climaxed in 1794, stoking Federalist fears that factionalism and extreme democracy would indeed rip apart the country. Improbably enough, it was outside Pittsburgh at Braddock's
Field—the site of the shocking defeat suffered by the British general thirty-nine years earlier—that several thousand anti-taxers
gathered. Members of the three Democratic Societies in western
Pennsylvania appear to have been especially active in organizing
the tax resistance movement.

Using the Ciceronian pseudonym Tully, Hamilton published a
series of essays in Philadelphia newspapers denouncing the anti-
tax insurgents. The question, he wrote, is "Shall the general will
prevail, or the will of a faction? shall there be government, or no
government?" The only proper response, he added in the next essay, two days later, was to quote Cicero: "How long, ye Catilines,
will you abuse our patience." Summarizing the situation in a letter to President Washington, Hamilton wrote that "these acts of
violence were preceded by certain Meetings of Malcontent persons, who entered into resolutions calculated at once to confirm,
inflame and Systematize the Spirit of opposition."

A few months later, the signing of a new American agreement
with England, the Jay Treaty, provoked another round of violence
in Pennsylvania, New York, and Massachusetts. "It was very hard
for Federalists to believe that these outbursts, these lawless proceedings so uncomfortably reminiscent of the French Revolution,
were spontaneous," writes historian Marshall Smelser. "There
simply had to be a plot."

Jefferson and his followers saw the treaty as anti-French and unnecessarily pro-British. When Washington threw his enormous prestige behind the treaty, Jefferson bitterly quoted Addison's *Cato*: "a curse on his virtues, they've undone his country." Even worse, in the play, this is actually Cato's condemnation of Caesar. Deploying Cato against Washington indicates just how contentious Jefferson was feeling. Consciously or not, Jefferson was moving to a new level of ferocity in American politics. He quietly coached Madison in how to organize congressional opposition to the treaty.

## Washington's Warnings

WASHINGTON WAS INDEED CONCERNED THAT THE AMERICAN EXPERIment seemed to be falling apart. Would his life's work end in failure? Jefferson in his notes states that Washington had told Edmund Randolph, Jefferson's successor as secretary of state, that if the nation broke up, he would go with the North. It makes sense, given that Washington's sympathies were with the Federalists, who were more the party of the commercial North.

In 1796, Washington prepared to make another of his memorable exits, voluntarily stepping down after two terms as president. His countrymen saw him once again as assuming the role of Cincinnatus, the soldier who rescued his country and then relinquished power. In his farewell address—really a letter to the people, as it was not delivered as a speech but rather published in newspapers—Washington felt that Americans needed some clear directives. First, he told them that "it is of infinite moment, that you should properly estimate the immense value of your national Union." He warned them "in the most solemn manner against the baneful effects of the spirit of party."

He also urged them to be vigilant of "the insidious wiles of foreign influence," because "history and experience prove that foreign influence is one of the most baneful foes of Republican Government." Such a warning resonates even today, more than two centuries later.

The farewell address may have been the last major instance of classical republicanism being offered by a top official as the model for public behavior in America. "Tis substantially true, that virtue or morality is a necessary spring of popular government," he asserted in one of the letter's three invocations of "virtue."

## President Adams?

WITH WASHINGTON GONE, AMERICAN PARTISANSHIP WAS UNCORKED. Washington was succeeded in 1797 as president by John Adams, one of the stranger figures in American history. Adams' classical orientation would not serve him well when he was president. He would become a man out of time, proving unable to comprehend the rising surge of populism. He reacted to it eccentrically. There is a reason that in the center of today's Washington, DC, there are grand monuments to his predecessor and his successor, but none for him. Washington is on the one-dollar bill, Jefferson on the two, and even Hamilton on the ten, but Adams appears on none. At Mount Rushmore, Washington and Jefferson gaze out shoulder to shoulder, and again, Adams is nowhere to be seen. In one of his more discerning comments, he would reflect late in life that "Mausoleums, Statues, Monuments will never be erected to me."

Adams was not completely mistaken in assessing the precarious state of American politics. Populism tends to look good from a distance, but close up it can be frightening. Gordon Wood has observed that John Adams, coming from New England, had seen more of democracy in practice than had Thomas Jefferson of aristocratic Virginia. Adams never would have casually commented, as Jefferson once did to Adams' wife, that, "I like a little rebellion now and then. It is like a storm in the Atmosphere." Jefferson wrote that sentence a few weeks after receiving the pamphlet in which Adams condemned the brutality of the people.

## French Terror, French Virtue

IN THE 1790s, TWO MORE FEARS STIRRED THE CALDRON OF AMERICAN politics. The founders always had been acutely aware of the destruction of the Roman Republic and the short duration of the Athenian democracy. But now there was a new, contemporary example of a republic going sour, in France.

That was significant because in the late eighteenth century, the world had just two leading examples of "democratic republican" government—that is, nations ruled by the majority of the people. One was the United States. The other was France, and that became a problem for Jefferson. He had been in Paris to witness the revolution's first, exhilarating phase, but departed before it descended into terror. Jefferson had been optimistic at the outset of the upheaval in France, telling Washington at the end of 1788 that "the nation has been awaked by our revolution, they feel their strength, they are enlightened, their lights are spreading, and they will not retrograde." Like the Americans, he might have added, the French revolutionaries were dazzled by classicism. They often invoked Cicero and accused their political enemies of Catilinism.

For several years after he left Paris in October 1789, Jefferson maintained that the fates of the United States and France were intertwined. "I look with great anxiety for the firm establishment of the new government in France," he wrote to George Mason in February 1791. "I consider the establishment and success of their government as necessary to stay up our own."

But by mid-1793 it became clear that the French experiment had gone off track—first into a reign of terror, followed eventually by a "first consul," Napoleon Bonaparte, who would consolidate his power into a dictatorship. The unjustly neglected Gouverneur Morris, one of the livelier founders, became American ambassador to France in 1792. His reports to the president were far more pessimistic than Jefferson's had been. "The present Government is evidently a Despotism both in Principle and Practice," he wrote. "Terror is the order of the Day. . . . The Queen was executed the Day before Yesterday."

Even worse, Maximilien Robespierre, the leader of the French radicals, claimed that his group was motivated by virtue:

> If the basis of popular government in peacetime is virtue, the basis of popular government during a revolution is both virtue and terror; virtue, without which terror is baneful; terror, without which virtue is powerless. Terror is nothing more than speedy, severe and inflexible justice; it is thus an emanation of virtue.

This is a striking equation, insisting that terror and virtue go hand in hand. The thought builds an intellectual bridge between the ancient world and modern totalitarianism. It is itself a terrifying assertion to make.

Hamilton captured the Federalist repugnance for events in Paris. "In reviewing the disgusting spectacle of the French revolution, it is difficult to avert the eye entirely from those features of it which betray a plan to disorganize the human mind itself, as well as to undermine the venerable pillars that support the edifice of civilized society," he wrote.

By 1800, as he prepared to run for president, Jefferson was back-paddling as fast as he could. In a letter to a political ally, he emphasized that voters should be told that the fates of the American and French experiments were not linked, and that "whatever may be the fate of republicanism there, we are able to preserve it inviolate here." Make it clear, he added, that, "Our vessel is moored at such a distance, that should theirs blow up, ours is still safe." To that end, he added, we need to respect the will of the majority, even when we think it wrong, in the hope and belief that it eventually will come right.

There was another scare, far closer to American shores. In August 1791, only two years after the start of the French Revolution, slaves in France's colony of Haiti began their revolt, which ulti-mately proved successful, with the establishment of an independent republic led by black men. American slaveholders watched this unfold with fear. This was their worst nightmare.

## Conspiracies Abound

ON TOP OF THE FRENCH HORRORS, THERE WERE GENUINE CONSPIRA-cies at home. William Blount, a senator from Tennessee, conspired with the British to have them seize Louisiana, which he hoped would boost the values of his own vast landholdings by opening the Mississippi River to navigation through to New Orleans. In 1797, a letter by Blount about the arrangement wound up on John Adams' desk. He gave it to Jefferson, who had it read aloud in the Senate. Blount became the first federal official to be impeached and was expelled from the Senate.

Scandals grew out of conspiracies. An emigrant Scot journalist named James Callender became a leading propagandist for the Jeffersonians. In 1797 he published the sordid details of an affair Hamilton had conducted with a young woman named Maria Reynolds, who with her roguish husband had proceeded to blackmail him. Hamilton, defending himself, claimed he was a victim of "a conspiracy of vice against virtue."

Sometimes it seems as if Jefferson, Hamilton, and Adams, not knowing what to do in this increasingly bitter environment, simply attacked one another instead. Adams, always emphatic if not always accurate, held Hamilton in surprisingly low estimation. He was late to the Revolution, Adams claimed, and at one point quit the fight over "a miff with Washington." Adams did not even credit Hamilton with being Washington's best ghostwriter, as others did. "Great Art has been used to propagate an Opinion that Hamilton was the Writer of Washingtons best Letters and most popular Addresses: especially that to the Governors of the States on his resignation of his Command of the Army. This I know to be false. It was the joint production of Col. Humphries and another Gentleman a better Writer and more judicious Politician, whom I will not name at present."

Even Abigail Adams, usually more sober-minded than her mercurial husband, was looking for enemies under the bed. She attributed the growth of party feeling to an insidious French-led conspiracy to undermine the United States. "Their Emissaries are scatterd through all parts of this extensive union, sowing the seeds of vice, irreligion, corruption, and sedition," she wrote privately to an old friend in the spring of 1798. "Hence has grown up that spirit of Party, and of faction."

On the other side of the growing divide, Jefferson, though apprehensive, retained his core optimism. He assured a Virginia political ally that "a little patience and we shall see the reign of witches pass over, their spells dissolve, and the people recovering their true sight, restore their government to it's true principles." That was a provocative choice of words. One can only wonder if he was alluding to the witch trials a century earlier in Massachusetts, the home of leading Federalists such as John Adams, Theodore Sedgwick (attended Yale), Fisher Ames, and Rufus King (Harvard, 1777). One leading Federalist, Timothy Pickering, the secretary of state, actually was from the town of Salem, which had been the center of the seventeenth-century hysteria over witchcraft.

## The Alien and Sedition Acts

WHEN WE SEEK TO UNDERSTAND JOHN ADAMS, IT ALWAYS HELPS TO look to Cicero. And in considering Cicero, notes the classicist Moses Hadas, it is vital to remember that to him, "nothing was more important than the maintenance of the established order." Cicero, writes one of his biographers, was "a temperamental conservative caught in the nets of revolution." So, too, was Adams. He long had worried that the new nation would drift toward factionalism followed by separation or civil war.

Viewed in this Roman light, the Sedition Law of 1798 was "the capstone of the new Federalist system," writes legal historian Leonard Levy. But seen in the context of American history, it was the last gasp effort of classical republicanism to stave off surging populism. Adams and the Federalists were trying to rely on the values and preserve the approach that had brought them to independence. But in the process, they would only underscore how times had changed, and how elites could no longer shape how the broad mass of Americans would think and speak. Public opinion was exploding. During the 1790s, the number of newspapers published in the United States more than doubled from 100 to more than 250. Adams was appalled by this noisy babel of new American voices. It mattered little to him that the majority of newspapers were Federalist, or leaning that way, with some 103 in his camp and just 64 that were anti-Federalist. Nonetheless, the very existence of opposition journals was an affront. They were the seedbed of the new partisan vocabulary that was developing to allow Americans to discuss the emerging politics of the time.

Adams' defenders, then and now, argue that the Sedition Law rested firmly on existing English common law, and so was not a great departure. But this confuses theory with practice. In fact, in the new United States, as Levy writes, the law was rarely applied, and so American newspapers "operated as if the law of seditious libel did not exist."

By changing the enforcement of the common law and passing a new federal law on top of it, Adams was lashing out at the new political system that was emerging, with political parties as its machinery. As historian Jill Lepore puts it,

> The American two-party system, the nation's enduring source of political stability, was forged in—and, fair to say, created by— the nation's newspapers. Newspapers had shaped the ratification debate between Federalists and Anti-Federalists, and by 1791 newspapers were already beginning to shape the first party system, a contest between Federalists and those who aligned themselves with a newly emerging opposition.

Seen in the context of the American reality of the 1790s, rather than through the classical lens of an aging Revolutionary generation, Adams actually was acting in a reactionary and destabilizing manner.

Partly because of Adams' blunders, the final two years of his administration brought the politics of the new republic to a white heat. Political participation was increasing rapidly, often to the point of illegality, with voter turnout sometimes exceeding 100 percent of the eligible (white male adult taxpaying) population.

The fight culminated with the party in power cracking down on the opposition press. In the two years after the Sedition Law was enacted, twenty-five journalists were arrested and ten convicted. There were five major anti-administration newspapers at the time; the editors of four of them were indicted. One of the more notable cases involved Thomas Cooper, a Pennsylvania newspaper editor who in November 1799 published a handbill stating that President Adams was incompetent and had meddled with federal judges. For this he was found guilty of malicious libel, fined $400, and sentenced to six months in jail. Benjamin Bache, grandson of Benjamin Franklin, was indicted, but died of yellow fever before his trial. Thomas Greenleaf, the leading anti-Federalist editor in New York, also was charged but died in the same epidemic. The federal government then indicted Greenleaf's widow, Anna, for "being a wicked and malicious person seeking to stir up sedition." When she in turn fell ill, her printing foreman was charged with libel, fined, and sentenced to four months in prison.

Vermont's rowdy Republican representative, Matthew Lyon, was jailed for printing a letter to the editor that referred to "the bullying speech of your president and the stupid answer of your senate." "Ragged Matt, the democrat," as the Federalists liked to call him, was found guilty of sedition, sentenced to four months of imprisonment, and fined $1,000, quite a sum in the days when the median price of an American house was $614. While behind bars he was reelected to Congress with 4,576 votes, almost twice those of the runner-up. The government then imprisoned a Vermont newspaper editor who had sought to raise money to pay Lyon's fine.

This was pure political power poured into the judiciary. Enforcement of the law was selective and uneven, to the extreme. "Every defendant was a Republican, every judge and practically all the jurors were Federalists," records Smelser. It was not clear how far the judges would take this crackdown. In November 1798, William Cushing (Harvard, 1751), a justice of the Supreme Court, urged a Richmond grand jury to look into "combinations or conspiracies to raise insurrections against government, or to obstruct the operation of the laws made by proper authority."

Nor were judges of different views immune to prosecution. Jedediah Peck, a county court judge in upstate New York, was a Federalist yet had some qualms about the Alien and Sedition Acts. After he made them public, he was arrested and shipped in irons to New York City for a planned trial.

Hamilton smelled treason in the burgeoning opposition to the acts. He urged Theodore Sedgwick of Massachusetts, a Federalist leader in the Senate, to conduct a congressional investigation of "the tendency of the doctrines advanced by Virginia and Kentucke to destroy the Constitution of the U[nited] States." Turning over a few rocks, he added, would lead to discovery of "the full evidence which they afford of a regular conspiracy to overturn the government." Always plotting, Hamilton a few months later advised Timothy Pickering, who just had been fired by Adams as secretary of state, to "take with you copies and extracts of all such documents as will enable you to explain both Jefferson & Adams." In other words, bring with you any dirt you may have on those two. One historian terms this Hamilton letter an act of "political espionage."

## The Country Loses Its Father

WASHINGTON WAS DISGUSTED WITH THE STATE OF POLITICS. PEOPLE were "attacking every character, without respect to persons— public or Private, who happen to differ from themselves in Politics," he complained to Connecticut governor Jonathan Trumbull Jr.

(Harvard, 1759), who had been one of his aides during the war. Party loyalty was everything, while the quality of men was disregarded: "Let that party set up a broomstick, and call it a true son of Liberty, a Democrat, or give it any other epithet that will suit their purpose, and it will command their votes in toto!"

In November 1799, he wrote confidentially that "I have, for sometime past, viewed the political concerns of the United States with an anxious, and painful eye. They appear to me, to be moving by hasty strides to some awful crisis."

He would die a worried man. On Thursday, December 12, 1799, and the following day, Friday the 13th, he did farm oversight work on horseback, even though the weather was an atrocious mix of rain, snow, and sleet. That evening he was hoarse. Between two and three on the morning of Saturday, December 14, he awoke Martha to tell her he felt ill, and that his throat was painfully sore. Doctors came and during the course of the day bled him four times, which probably sped him toward his demise that evening. His secretary, Tobias Lear (Harvard, 1783), reported to President Adams that Washington went out like a Roman: "His last scene corresponded with the whole tenor of his life.—Not a groan, nor a Complaint escaped him in extreme distress.—With perfect resignation, and in full possession of his reason, he closed his well spent life."

In his will Washington tried to free as many of the enslaved people on his plantation as legally possible. Some were the property of Martha and her heirs. Others were married to those owned by Martha. He was the only founder involved in human bondage who tried to emancipate so many enslaved people. One can only wonder if this is because, as a man who learned mainly by observation and experience, he had come to see the practice of race-based slavery differently than his peers did. Jefferson was far better at avoiding reality than was Washington.

The death of Washington was a major psychological moment for the early republic, now fatherless in a real sense. In Philadelphia, Abigail Adams wrote the day the papers there carried the news of his passing that "every countanance is coverd with Gloom." John

Adams had said in his inaugural address of Washington that, "His Name may be still a rampart, and the Knowledge that he lives a Bulwark, against all open or Secret Ennemies of his Countries Peace." Now that great safeguard of the republic was gone. People knew it really was the end of an era. The death was "commemorated all through the country by the tolling of bells, funeral ceremonies, orations, sermons, hymns and dirges, attended by a mournful sense of loss, seeming to cast a pall over the entire heavens," wrote Samuel Griswold Goodrich, then a youth and later an immensely popular nineteenth-century writer under the pen name Peter Parley. He recalled a doleful hymn composed for the occasion that ended with the couplet,

> *With grief proclaim from shore to shore,*
> *Our guide, our Washington's no more.*

Adams' son-in-law, William Stephens Smith (Princeton, 1774), took the news ominously. The last great restraint on partisanship was gone. "Now the President will be fretted, perplexed, and tormented; now the full force of party will be brought forward," he worried. "He will now find himself, like the Roman Cato, sustaining a painful prëeminence."

But President Adams did not just attack his ideological adversaries. Considering himself above petty party politics, he also lashed out at Hamilton, a fellow Federalist, who was rumored to have ambitions to lead a military takeover of the government. In one note, he tartly observed that "General Washington never assumed the Character of perpetual Dictator—. That Pretension was reserved for one of his Aids."

## Resisting "a new order of things"

DAVID DAGGETT [YALE, 1783], A PROMINENT CONNECTICUT FEDERAList, used an oration on July 4, 1799, to attack the Jeffersonians:

"The object of this party is to destroy ancient systems—ancient habits—ancient customs—to introduce a new liberty, new equality, new rights of man, new modes of education, and a new order of things." Daggett might not have chosen the best occasion on which to give a divisive speech, but his description of the new party was fairly accurate. In Europe, Daggett would not have been considered as speaking for the aristocratic class. He had paid for his way through law school partly by working as a butler. But different battle lines were being drawn in the new United States, one reason the politics of the time were so tempestuous. There was indeed "a new order of things" emerging, as Daggett stated. Especially, the workingman expected to be heard, and would no longer reflexively defer to the wealthy and well-educated.

On the other side of the political divide, William Manning, a farmer in Billerica, Massachusetts, composed a stirring call for the new order. "I am not a Man of Larning my selfe for I neaver had the advantage of six months schooling in my life," he began. "I am not grate reader of antiant history for I always followed hard labour for a living." What he did know of those "antiant" events was that the "long & bloody history about the fudes & animoityes, contentions & blood sheds that hapned in the antiant Republicks of Athens, Greesh & Roome & many other nations" all boiled down to a struggle between "the few & the Many." He was firmly on the side of the latter, believing that the greed and ambitions of the few formed the core of the problem:

> The higher a Man is raised in stations of honour power and trust the greater are his temtations to do rong & gratify those selfeish prinsaples. Give a man honour & he wants more. Give him power & he wants more. Give him money & he wants more. In short he is neaver easy, but the more he has the more he wants.

So, he argued, government by aristocrats was not the solution, as Daggett thought, but the problem. "The Reasons why a free government has always failed is from the unreasonable demands & desires of the few. They cant bare to be on a leavel with their fellow creatures." Manning was unable to get his manifesto published, partly because the two editors to whom he sent it already had been arraigned for seditious libel. Yet it is noteworthy for illuminating how some Republicans were thinking at the time—and perhaps why, a few years later, they would displace the Federalists so rapidly and completely.

When Washington was alive, he was all the Federalists needed to make their case. But with him gone, they had almost nothing else to offer the American people. It is striking that as a political movement they left behind them no essential speech or essay that stated who they were and why the American people should support them. One of the few memorable Federalist documents, to be put alongside the government reports of Hamilton, is Noah Webster's dictionary of the American language, which he compiled during the first quarter of the nineteenth century. Webster's work seems to represent a fallback position for moderate Federalists: If you cannot control the people, perhaps you can control their language, and thus how they think and speak. As one scholar states, "Webster's main motivation for writing and publishing it was not to celebrate American life or to expand independence. Instead, he sought to counteract social disruption and reestablish the deferential world order that he believed was disintegrating."

Not only was Washington gone, but Adams was often absent from his job, spending seven months of 1799 not at the capital but "angrily secluded" at his home in Massachusetts. Thomas Jefferson wrote later that at about this time, in 1798 and 1799, he worried that "a final dissolution of all bonds, civil & social, appeared imminent." Jefferson drafted the Kentucky Resolutions, a series of statements opposing the Alien and Sedition Acts and toying with secession. Madison did much the same in Virginia, saying the acts were unconstitutional, though he did so more moderately. Both sets of resolutions were adopted by their state legislatures.

The question was on the table: Could the United States survive without Washington as its unifying symbol?

## The Conspiracy Most Feared

———

SLAVE UPRISINGS WERE ANOTHER DREADED FORM OF CONSPIRACY, AND sometimes the fears were grounded in reality. In Virginia, Governor James Monroe called out the militia to put down a rumored revolt in the Richmond area. This effort, now known as Gabriel's Rebellion, "is unquestionably the most serious and formidable conspiracy we have ever known of the kind," Monroe informed his old legal mentor, Thomas Jefferson. These black insurrectionists received none of the leniency shown the white men who had participated in Shays' Rebellion and the Whiskey Rebellion. Some twenty-six enslaved men were executed in Virginia. "Nothing is talked of here but the recent conspiracy of negroes," James Callender wrote to Jefferson from the Richmond jail, where he had been imprisoned for his journalism. This insurrection and a subsequent one eventually would induce the state of Virginia to pass a law requiring freed blacks to leave the state, meaning that being set free required a person to leave forever one's family and friends, and everything else one had known while in captivity.

As psychiatrists know, sometimes what people don't talk about is as important as what they do. All of the founders almost certainly were aware of Spartacus, the gladiator who famously led a slave revolt in ancient Rome. But *Founders Online*, which is compiling the works of the founders in searchable form, shows that in all their letters, speeches, pamphlets, and other writings, only John Adams, the only one who never owned an enslaved person, ever refers to him. To everyone else, slavery was treated as much as possible with a conspiracy of silence. It was the greatest failing of the founders, hardly explainable even today.

◆━━━◆

## Chapter 13

# The Revolution of 1800

*The People, Not the Plebes*

THREE YEARS OF LIVING WITH JOHN ADAMS AS PRESIDENT LEFT Thomas Jefferson in a radical mood. He sounded almost like Thomas Paine when in 1800 he wrote to an old friend that "I have sworn upon the altar of god, eternal hostility against every form of tyranny over the mind of man." Like many people at the time, he did not trust the post office to safely convey his correspondence, telling a political ally in Kentucky that he had been advised "it is better to get a friend to forward it by some of the boats."

Such unruly sentiments were one reason Hamilton despised Jefferson. But Hamilton hated Aaron Burr more, writing to a friend, "He is as unprincipled & dangerous a man as any country can boast; as true a *Cataline* as ever met in midnight conclave." He repeated the charge in another letter later that year, when it had become clear that either Burr or Jefferson would be the next president. "He is truly the *Cataline* of America," Hamilton wrote.

Burr had an odd way of bringing together people to oppose him. Hamilton was so appalled by Burr that he found himself in the startling position of supporting Jefferson, albeit privately. "It is too late for me to become his apologist," he wrote about Jefferson, perhaps with a wry smile. He continued:

> *Nor can I have any disposition to do it. I admit that his politics are tinctured with fanaticism, that he is too much in earnest in his democracy, that he has been a mischevous enemy to the principle measures of our past administration, that he is crafty*

*& persevering in his objects, that he is not scrupulous about the means of success, nor very mindful of truth, and that he is a contemptible hypocrite.*

But, he added, Jefferson would not act merely to benefit himself. Burr, by contrast, Hamilton wrote, was "a man of extreme & irregular ambition—that he is selfish to a degree which excludes all social affections & that he is decidedly profligate. . . . a man who on all hands is acknowledged to be a complete Cataline in his practice & principles."

Hamilton also considered John Adams to be incompetent and unequipped for the tasks of the presidency, though presumably Adams' reluctance to give Hamilton a top position in the Army played some role. "Not denying to Mr. Adams patriotism and integrity, and even talents of a certain kind, I should be deficient in candor, were I to conceal the conviction, that he does not possess the talents adapted to the Administration of Government, and that there are great and intrinsic defects in his character, which unfit him for the office of Chief Magistrate." Oddly, no one seemed to consider that Hamilton's attack on the president might have violated the Sedition Act. Adams, for his part, would later write of Hamilton that he possessed "all the Vanity and Timidity of Cicero, all the Debauchery of Marc Anthony and All the Ambition of Julius Caesar."

Typically vituperative, Adams twice referred to Hamilton as the "bastard brat of a Scotch Pedler." Yet for all their differences, Hamilton and Adams agreed that Burr was a danger to the nation. "Burr was a Catiline, a Bankrupt, an unprincipled Scoundrell, a damn'd Rascall and a Devil," Adams concluded.

One of the more popular texts of the eighteenth century was a history of the ancient world by a philosophical French priest, the Abbe Millot. His epitaph for Catiline also summarizes Burr well: "He was one of those men who are born to perform great actions, but by being slaves to their passions, seem to be only capable of, enormous wickedness." Jefferson, Adams, and Hamilton likely knew those words—Jefferson recommended Millot to others frequently, Hamilton and Madison cited him in the Federalist Papers, and Adams had eight volumes of Millot in his library.

Jefferson and Burr emerged from the election of 1800 tied in the vote of the Electoral College. The result, writes Yale law professor Bruce Ackerman, was that "for a week in February 1801, America teetered on the brink of disaster." The House of Representatives voted some thirty-five times, with a tie each time. It was possible, Ackerman writes, that the constitutional system devised in 1787, which itself had replaced the Articles of Confederation of 1781, would collapse, and would have to be replaced by a new Constitution of 1802. The core problem, he continues, was that the authors of the Constitution had adhered to "the teachings of classical republican thought [which] . . . equated parties with factions and considered them unmitigated evils."

Finally, on the thirty-sixth ballot, James Bayard (Princeton, 1784), the representative from Delaware, perhaps having received some reassurances from the Jeffersonians that they would act moderately while in power, withdrew his support from Burr. That broke the deadlock, and Jefferson won.

## Jefferson's First Inaugural Address

THE TRUEST TEST OF A NEW DEMOCRACY IS NOT WHETHER A NEW leader is elected, but whether that new leader holds a second election and eventually turns over power. In that sense, the election of 1800, and the peaceful transition from Adams to Jefferson in 1801, is as historically significant as was Washington's stepping down four years earlier. "The revolution of 1800," Jefferson thought,

> was as real a revolution in the principles of our government as that of 76 was in it's form;. . . . The nation declared it's will by dismissing functionaries of one principle, and electing those of another, in the two branches, executive and legislative, submitted to their election.

John Adams, for all his disagreements with Jefferson, had a similar perspective on the degree of turmoil, writing that Hamilton's actions undermining his presidency laid the "foundation of the overthrow of the federal party, and of the revolution that followed."

Jefferson's first inaugural address, delivered on March 4, 1801, is a statement of an opposition party taking over. It was also the first inaugural address delivered in Washington, DC. In it, Jefferson made clear that he and his party had won, and that the Federalists had lost. But he vowed that he would not be vindictive. The will of the majority would prevail, but "the minority possess their equal rights, which equal law must protect, and to violate would be oppression." He promised "equal and exact justice to all men, of whatever state or persuasion, religious or political." Indeed, anti-Republicanism views would be left to "stand undisturbed as monuments of the safety with which error of opinion may be tolerated."

He also called for people to tone down their rhetoric, emphasizing that "every difference of opinion is not a difference of principle." He then listed his own principles, pointedly including freedom of the press. His argument at least in part was that this was a revolution of principle, not of opportunism.

"Virtue," that old warhorse, hardly made an appearance in this historically significant speech, one of Jefferson's best pieces of writing. Jefferson said he was sure that others in government would help provide the required "resources of wisdom, of virtue, of zeal." The notion of virtue, once so central to how people guided their lives, had shrunk to something nice to have. Jefferson concluded by stating that he saw his job as working for "the happiness and freedom of all."

Jefferson was indeed focused on the freedom of the press, quite literally. Just five days into office, one of his first actions as president was to reverse the fortunes of Thomas Cooper, the Pennsylvania newspaper editor who had been jailed the previous year for criticizing President Adams. Cooper soon was named to a post investigating a continuing land dispute between Pennsylvania and Connecticut. Jefferson pardoned Callender, the muckraking Scottish journalist who had been jailed under the Sedition Act. But Callender wanted much more, something like a nice, well-paid government job. He hoped to be rewarded for his efforts and imprisonment by being named postmaster of Richmond, Virginia. When the president did not do that, Callender turned on Jefferson, darkly warning that "he was in possession of things which he could & would make use of in a certain case." When Jefferson shunned him, Callender published those "things," which were the rumors—confirmed by DNA tests centuries later—that Jefferson kept an enslaved woman, Sally Hemings, as his mistress, and had fathered children with her. Callender wrote that Hemings' oldest son bore "a striking though sable resemblance to those of the President himself." Two years later, in July 1803, Callender's corpse would be found floating in shallow water in the James River.

At about the same time, Thomas Jefferson, that most unmilitary of presidents, did something that is often forgotten: He introduced and signed into law a bill to establish the U.S. Military Academy at West Point, New York. The new school soon would illuminate one path toward nonclassical higher education in America, with a curriculum that, by the 1820s, featured civil and military engineering, mathematics, French, chemistry, and geography. Henry Adams, a great-grandson of John Adams, would write in one of his histories that "the West Point engineers doubled the capacity of the little American army for resistance, and introduced a new and scientific character into American life."

## Adams Trades "virtues for manure"

JOHN ADAMS DID NOT ATTEND JEFFERSON'S INAUGURAL. HE FELT HUmiliated by losing the election, being the first president so rejected. "I was turned out of Office, degraded and disgraced by my Country," he would state, his feelings as usual on his sleeve. He

left the capital at four A.M. on the morning of Jefferson's inaugura-
tion, catching the early coach to Baltimore. Adams' defeat came
atop a personal tragedy, the premature death of his son Charles, a
severe alcoholic.

In a letter to a party loyalist written weeks after the inaugu-
ration, Adams sounded crushed. Back at his farm, he wrote, "I
thought I had made a good exchange . . . of honors & virtues,
for manure." Given his deeply held classical perspective and his
equally intense self-esteem, Adams could conclude only that the
American people, having rejected him, lacked sufficient virtue.
"The Virtue and good Sense of Americans, which I own I once
had some dependence on, and which have been trumpetted with
more extravagance by others, are become a byword," he mourned.
"It behoves all men to consider whether that intelligence & piety
and virtue in the great body of the people, upon which we have
all acknowledged our whole security to depend, has not failed our
expectations & disappointed all our hopes."

Back in private life, Adams' next step was typical of his brilliant but sour personality. He began to write a memoir to settle
old scores. George Washington would have seen writing an ex-
planatory autobiography as stooping to respond to critics. Instead,
Washington got the word out more discreetly, by having his biography written by an old friend—and then taking pains to go over
it thoroughly, making extensive notes.

Adams, by contrast, could hardly wait to take on his many critics personally. In October 1802, he began his memoir by stating in
the first paragraph that

> My Excuse is, that having been the Object of much Misrepresen-
> tation, some of my Posterity may probably wish to see in my own
> hand Writing a proof of the falsehood of that Mass of odious Abuse
> of my Character, with which News Papers, private Letters and pub-
> lic Pamphlets and Histories have been disgraced for thirty Years.

Later in the same document he would bewail "the torment of a
perpetual Vulcano of Slander, pouring on my flesh all my life time."

This is a man who seemingly retained every barbed word ever aimed at him.

He watched the Jefferson administration with horror, but reassured himself that at least the president lacked the strength of nerve to seek dictatorship. "Jefferson is not a Roman," he said jovially in a letter to Benjamin Rush. He seemed to understand, correctly, that the man in the White House was more Greek than Roman, and was in fact a follower of what he disparaged as "the poisonous pestilential & most fatal doctrine of Epicurus."

In another letter to his friend Rush, one that is quite extraordinary, he listed all his foes who came to ill fortune, reveling in their downfalls. Most notably, Adams here celebrated the fact that one pamphleteer "could not long refrain from abusing me, till his House was burnt and his Wife and Children in it, and himself Scortched to Such a degree that he died in a few days." This likely is the ugliest thing ever to emerge from Adams' pen.

Adams would never finish writing his memoirs, perhaps because he found it so difficult to counter what he considered "a Secret and deliberate design" to destroy his reputation. Putting that project aside, he retreated into rereading a biography of Cicero. There he found eerie parallels between the decline of the Roman Republic and the condition of the United States. "I Seem to read . . . the History of our own Country for forty years past. Change the Names and every Anecdote will be applicable to Us." Viewing himself through the prism of ancient history seems to have assuaged his embittered mind. His heart bled for Cicero—and so, inseparably, for himself. "Poor Cicero, watched, dreaded, envied, by all: no doubt Slandered by innumerable Emissaries, despised, insulted, belied." He utterly rejected the notion that Adams or Cicero wallowed in self-regard. "Do you call this Vanity? It was Self Defence, Independence, Intrepidity."

But there was more. With Adams, there was always more:

Cicero was libelled, Slandered insulted by all Parties; by Caesars Party, by Catilines Crew, by Clodius's Mermidons, Aye and by Pompey the Patricians and the Senate too—He was persecuted and

*tormented by turns and by all Parties and all Factions, and some-*
*times by combinations of all of them together, and that for his most*
*virtuous and glorious Councils and Conduct. . . . Injured, insulted*
*and provoked as I am, I blush not to imitate the Roman. . . .*

As the historian Linda Kerber notes in an aside, Adams had an image of himself as "The Last Roman." He was stuck in time. It is probably fortunate for him that he never produced a finished memoir. It would only have diminished his reputation further, had he written it in the tone he used years later in a letter to Jefferson: "How many Martyrdoms must I Suffer?"

## A Jeffersonian Plum on Federalist Turf

JEFFERSON TOOK OFFICE ANGERED BY THE RASH OF LAST-MINUTE AP-
pointments Adams had made just before leaving the federal government. Of everything Adams ever did, Jefferson later told Abigail Adams, this was the sole act that truly antagonized him:

*I did consider his last appointments to office as personally unkind.*
*They were from among my most ardent political enemies, from*
*whom no faithful cooperation could ever be expected, and laid me*
*under the embarrasment of acting thro' men whose views were to*
*defeat mine; or to encounter the odium of putting others in their*
*places. It seemed but common justice to leave a successor free to act*
*by instruments of his own choice.*

After some brooding, Jefferson devised his response to Adams' "scenes of midnight appointment." It seemed at times that everybody in the country wanted a job from Jefferson. Early in his first term a contentious episode arose in Connecticut, that most determinedly Federalist of states—even more than Massachusetts, because it was more politically stable.

Celebrating Jefferson's election, Abraham Bishop (Yale, 1778), a prominent Republican in Connecticut, and so a notable figure in the political minority there, claimed in a celebratory speech that Jefferson had prevented a Federalist monarchy from being established. Rather, he stated, the Democratic Republican victory amounted to a bloodless revolution. Bishop concluded by assuring his happy audience that "the reign of terror is no more: The alien and sedition acts have expired: Aristocratic federalism is suffering its last pangs."

Jefferson's administration rewarded Bishop indirectly, by making his aged and milder father the collector of customs for the port of New Haven, a position so desirable and lucrative that the new vice president, Aaron Burr, wrote to Jefferson about who should get it. The post brought with it an income of $5,000 a year, equaling that of the treasury secretary and surpassing that of the chief justice. It was, writes one biographer of Jefferson, "the best political plum in Connecticut."

The appointment outraged Connecticut's Federalists. One, Theodore Dwight, brother of the president of Yale College, penned a satire denouncing "Ye tribes of faction" made up of "Drunkards and Whores/ And rogues in scores." Some eighty leading merchants of New Haven wrote to Jefferson to object to what they saw as the politicization of the customs office.

Jefferson replied forcefully. Dumas Malone, his encyclopedic biographer, says that Jefferson's defense of the appointment was the first statement written by a president expressly as a leader of a political party. The new president declared that he was just doing openly what Adams had done without admitting it. Did you Federalists think you held a monopoly on government jobs? he asked. He did not attempt to invoke "virtue" in his response. That measure was gone. Open patronage had become the coin of American politics.

Privately, Jefferson was more disparaging of the Federalist claim on offices. Just a handful were ousted, he wrote, but "the whole herd have squealed out, as if all their throats were cut."

## Throwing Classicism Out with Federalism

THE ELECTORAL WINNERS, IN ASSERTING THEMSELVES, WENT AFTER not just elites, but the classicism that elites had so long used as their political vocabulary. They saw classicism as a symbol of elitism—and they were right in doing so. But in the course of that, classical learning became something of a political punching bag for the new men. An essay in the newspaper *Argus* asserted that Federalists despised workingmen who "have not snored through four years at Princeton."

The cultural climate was changing even among some younger Federalists. Edmund Trowbridge Dana (Harvard, 1800) charged in an essay in a Boston magazine that American poetry of the time was mired in the ancient world. "One is hagridden . . . with nothing but the classicks, the classicks, the classicks!" He continued:

> . . . our posies are all senseless; forced exoticks nourished by foreign fire, painted leaves of tiffany wound on formal wire. When, oh when, shall the winter of criticism be passed and the springtime of passion return! when shall the library be deserted for the fields. . . . when, oh when, shall the idolatry of learning be superseded by the worship of truth!

He was tired of sitting "primly with Addison," of reading Pope. It was time for a new "vigour," for more "passion." Less rhetoric and thinking, more nature and feeling was the call of the day. "We have striven to be faultless, and neglected to be natural," he wrote. In this sweeping dismissal of library learning, of the ancient world, of musty metaphors, and the emphasis instead on the need for personally discovered truth, one can sense the advent of American Romanticism. Appropriately, this was written during the presidency of Thomas Jefferson, who as discussed earlier had his own tendencies toward Romanticism in his preference for the possible over the real, as well as for the Greeks over the Romans.

But cultures generally do not change overnight, and reformers remained in a minority among Federalists. Strikingly, the same issue of *The Monthly Anthology and Boston Review* that began with Dana's sharp rejection of classicism concluded with an old school poem that compared George Washington to—who else?—old Cato:

> *The grateful incense Heaven's high favour won,*
> *And CATO liv'd again——in WASHINGTON.*

Perhaps inevitably, the anonymous poet hoped that

> *No sordid passions e'er possess the soul,*
> *But publick Spirit animate the whole——*

But the Federalist shelf was bare. The party's intellectuals had little to offer except to insist that the old ways were the best ways, which was an increasingly tough sell in a dynamic new nation. "The best ages of Rome afford the purest models of virtue that any where are to be met with," advised an essayist in the short-lived *New England Quarterly Magazine.* "The Roman historians are the best that ever existed. The dramatic merit and eloquence of Livy; the profound philosophy of Sallust; the rich and solemn pencil of Tacitus, all ages of the world will admire." The argument mounted here assumes that the issue at hand was about the best model of virtue to pursue. That was, at best, a doubtful proposition in early nineteenth-century America.

Likewise, an anti-Jefferson satire of the time by Thomas Green Fessenden (Dartmouth, 1796) charged that the Jeffersonians were "wretches [who] announce hostility/ To talents, virtue, and civility." Fessenden mourned the decline of public-spiritedness and advised "the scum" who had risen to power to heed their "betters." His solution to the tensions of the time was for every man in the nation to "be contented in his station." Know your "rank," he admonished, and remember that,

> *Blest is the man with wooden head*
> *Who labours for his daily bread.*

He also railed against permitting propertyless men to vote. Such raw condescension was no way to win popular support in the new America. What we have here is someone challenging against almost every cultural and societal trend he sees around him—most especially the very notion of seeking popular support.

The world the Federalists had known and briefly ruled was going away. Theodore Sedgwick of Massachusetts, by then the speaker of the house, mourned that "the aristocracy of virtue is destroyed." He was right, even if he did not like the fact of the matter.

Eventually the Federalists, realizing that to survive they would have to act like a party, formed more than two hundred chapters of a new Washington Benevolent Society. These were, writes Gordon Wood, "ostensibly charitable organizations but in reality arms of the party." Yet even this effort was halfhearted, he adds, because "they saw themselves as the wise, natural rulers of society, and thus found it virtually impossible to conceive of themselves as an opposition party."

But it was too late to save the Federalists. A new social order, stripped of classical republicanism, and even opposed to it, was emerging in America. The Federalists rejected it, and it in turn rejected them. In the following decades the party slowly would evaporate, absent from the ballot box, but still present for a while in the judiciary. In 1807, for example, Theophilus Parsons (Harvard, 1769), the Federalist chief justice of Massachusetts, ruled that not all citizens were equal before the law in the case at hand, a slander charge, because "rank and condition" affected the degree of injury caused by act. The judge seems not to have understood that America was rapidly becoming a nation where the notion of social rank no longer existed.

## "This American world was not made for me"

———

AARON BURR SPITEFULLY REVELED IN HAMILTON'S PLIGHT, CHUCKling to Jefferson that "Hamilton seems to be literally Mad with spleen and envy and disappointment—as far as I can yet judge, his efforts are perfectly impotent."

Hamilton was indeed at sea. The following year, he confessed his dismay in striking terms in a letter to Gouverneur Morris:

> Mine is an odd destiny. Perhaps no man in the UStates has sacrificed or done more for the present Constitution than myself—and contrary to all my anticipations of its fate, as you know from the very begginning I am still labouring to prop the frail and worthless fabric. Yet I have the murmurs of its friends no less than the curses of its foes for my rewards. What can I do better than withdraw from the Scene? Every day proves to me more and more that this American world was not made for me.

This was a painful conclusion for him to reach, that the new nation that he had worked so hard to build seemed to have no place for him. One can only wonder about the psychological strain this brilliant, ambitious man must have felt. He had voluntarily moved to America, only to see the country move away from him. It clearly was not becoming the nation he had envisioned.

Two years later, after Hamilton was shot and killed in a duel with Aaron Burr, Morris would deliver Hamilton's eulogy. He noted in his diary the difficulties of preparing his remarks:

> The first Point of his Biography is that he was a Stranger of illegitimate Birth. Some Mode must be contrived to pass over this handsomely. He was indiscreet, vain and opinionated. These things must be told or the Character will be incomplete—and yet they must be told in such Manner as not to destroy the Interest. He was on Principle opposed to republican and attached to monarchical Government—And then his Opinions were generally known and have been long and loudly proclaimed. . . . I must not either dwell on his domestic Life—He has long since foolishly published the Avowal of conjugal Infidelity.

Morris nicely elided the issue of Hamilton's illegitimacy by assigning him a divine origin: "It seemed as if God had called him suddenly into existence, that he might assist to save a world!" As for Hamilton's many indiscretions, well, Morris declared, "He disdained concealment."

Another prominent Federalist, Fisher Ames, eulogized Hamilton more conventionally: "No man, not the Roman Cato himself, was more inflexible, on every point that touched, or only seemed to touch, integrity and honor." He was akin to a "Hercules, treacherously slain in the midst of his unfinished labors, leaving the world overrun with monsters." He was "fervid as Demosthenes, like Cicero full of resource." He had "virtue so rare, so bold." And so on, in the vocabulary of a political era that, fittingly, already had passed even before Burr's bullet struck Hamilton's abdomen.

Privately, Ames also was giving up on the United States. "Our country is too big for union, too sordid for patriotism, too democratick for liberty," he confided to a friend at about this time.

## Burr's Conspiracy

DESPITE BURR'S ACTIONS, JEFFERSON'S POPULARITY GREW STEADILY. In the election of 1804 he overwhelmed the Federalist opposition, taking fifteen of seventeen states, including even Massachusetts, for 162 electoral votes to just 14 for the Federalist candidate, Charles Pinckney.

But Aaron Burr had more trouble up his sleeve. From early on, Burr's conduct "inspired me with distrust," Jefferson wrote. The Virginian did not know the New Yorker well when the two became president and vice president. "There has never been an intimacy between us, and but little association." In the spring of 1806, Burr—having killed Hamilton and been dropped as vice president—protested to Jefferson that he had been little rewarded for his support and to warn "that he could do me much harm."

Jefferson responded to this threat by saying that, "as to any harm he could do Me, I knew no cause why he should desire it."

Burr went west and fell into some kind of murky plot. In 1807, Jefferson reported to Congress on Burr's efforts to somehow establish an independent nation in the Ohio River Valley, or perhaps attack into Mexican territory, or maybe both. This was the greatest conspiracy of them all. During the winter of 1800–1801, Aaron Burr had nearly become president of the United States. Six years later, he was put on trial for treason against it. "His conspiracy has been one of the most flagitious of which history will ever furnish an example," Jefferson reported to the Marquis de Lafayette. "He meant to separate the Western states from us, to add Mexico to them, place himself at their head."

Burr was, Gordon Wood concludes, a man of secrets and lies. The biggest difference between him and the founders was not ideological. Rather, it was that he just did not care about the things they cared about. "One searches Burr's papers in vain for a single thoughtful letter about political philosophy or government," Wood wrote. He was "immune to the ideology and values of the Revolution," especially its "classical conception of leadership." Jefferson took to calling him "our Cataline."

## Madison Succeeds Jefferson

MADISON SERVED UNDER JEFFERSON FOR EIGHT YEARS AS HIS SECRE-tary of state, but—given Jefferson's rich overseas experience—his job really was more to be the president's closest friend and political advisor, helping him solidify the Jeffersonian victory over the Federalists.

When Madison succeeded Jefferson as president in 1809, he trotted out some of the old classical rhetoric. In his first inaugural address, he said he was grateful for the confidence expressed in him by "a free and virtuous nation" and said he planned to rely on "the well tried intelligence and virtue of my fellow Citizens." But the phrases feel tired and obligatory. Indeed, he would almost repeat himself in his second inaugural, describing the United States as "composed of a brave, a free, a virtuous, and an intelligent people." This was inaugural mush.

Madison nowadays is regarded as having been an uncertain president who led the country into the largely unnecessary War of 1812. Yet his contemporaries seem to have valued him more highly. More than fifty-seven American towns and counties are named for him, the most for any president. Even John Adams, in his own backhanded way, rated Madison above himself, Jefferson, and even Washington. He would later tell Jefferson that, "I pitty our good Brother Madison. . . . I pitty him the more, because, notwithstand a thousand Faults and blunders, his Administration has acquired more glory, and established more Union, than all his three Predecessors Washington Adams and Jefferson put together."

Meanwhile, the aging Jefferson, after presiding over the national political shift away from classical values, began himself to recede into the classical world. He may have helped unleash American culture, but did not necessarily like the direction the people were taking it. Rather than change with the times, he reverted to the ways of his youth, to his classical pursuits, especially the Greeks, favoring Homer over Virgil, for example. His granddaughter reported that in his last years, "He went over to the works of Eschylus, Sophocles and Euripides."

In a letter to President Madison mainly about his sheep Jefferson concluded with a quotation from Horace's very Epicurean sixth epistle:

Vive, vale, et siquid novisti rectius istis
Candidus imperti sinon, his ulere mecum.


That is, in the translation of the eighteenth-century English poet Christopher Smart, "Live: be happy. If you know of any thing preferable to these maxims, candidly communicate it: if not, with me make use of these."

Jefferson told Adams that he was turning away from attending to current events and going back to his books. This may have been in part because his cohort in life had died off—he noted to Adams that he was the sole surviving signer of the Declaration of Independence living south of the Potomac. At the age of sixty-nine, he was still on horseback every day, he noted, but walked little, "a single mile being too much for me." As for politics, he said, "I think little of them, and say less. I have given up newspapers in exchange for Tacitus and Thucydides, for Newton and Euclid; and I find myself much the happier."

## Chapter 14

# The End of
# American Classicism

A FTER JEFFERSON'S "REVOLUTION," THE UNITED STATES FACED TWO great stumbling blocks in the early decades of the nineteenth century. First, there was built into the system a tension between elitism, with an aging aristocracy still trying to tell the rest of the country how to live, and a growing egalitarianism, under which the majority rejected such guidance. That was resolvable.

But there also was a more insidious problem. The republic had built into it a fatal contradiction: It was founded on a faith in freedom yet on the fact of slavery. The founders had made a deal with the devil, and some suspected as much. In a satirical essay published when Jefferson was president, Josiah Quincy, who had deplored what he saw as Republican attacks on classical learning, contended that "democrat" was not actually a Greek word at all. Rather, he joked in a Federalist magazine, it had been discovered to be a word used by a First Peoples tribe in Virginia that meant "a great tobacco planter, who had herds of black slaves." The essential principle of being a democrat, he added rather baldly, was "sexual connection with all women—matrimonial alliances with none." This was an allusion to Jefferson's vow in his first inaugural address to seek "friendship with all nations, entangling alliances with none"—and to rumors of Jefferson's sexual liaisons with women both free and enslaved.

Because of slavery, fears of a civil war bubbled constantly under the surface. In his second inaugural, Jefferson had conceded that some feared that by expanding the country, his Louisiana

Purchase "would endanger our union." He countered, Madison-like, that "the larger our association, the less it will be shaken by local passions." As would become evident some fifty-six years later, Jefferson and Madison were wrong. Continuing and irresolvable conflict over whether slavery would be permitted in the nation's new lands, the area acquired during Jefferson's presidency, would spark the bloodiest event in American history, the Civil War.

John Adams said if it came to a choice, he would favor war. "Civil War is preferable to Slavery and I add that foreign War and civil War together at the Same time are preferable to Slavery." And in a characteristic lament, he claimed that he had been warning the country for some "fifty years" about the pitfalls it faced, only to be disregarded. "If the Nation will not read them or will not understand them, or are determined to misinterpret or misrepresent them, that is not my fault." When it came to avoiding blame and dodging responsibility, Adams was nearly as adept as Jefferson.

## Jefferson vs. Plato

———

JEFFERSON LOVED THE IDEA OF A "REPUBLIC," WHICH HE SAW AS A SYS-tem in which power was held and exercised by the people. So it is a bit surprising to learn that he despised the most famous book with that word as its title, Plato's *Republic*. He considered the great Greek philosopher an obscure mystic. Early in the summer of 1814, while at his summer home in isolated southwestern Virginia, "I amused myself with reading Plato's republic," he reported to John Adams. But in the next sentence he corrected that thought. "I am wrong however in calling it amusement, for it was the heaviest task-work I ever went through." He was, he explained, repelled by what he called "the whimsies, the puerilities, and unintelligible jargon of this work," and put it down wondering why the world so respected "such nonsense as this." He had concluded, he said, that Plato's reputation had been kept alive "chiefly by the adoption & incorporation of his whimsies into the body of artificial Christianity."

But he was still high on the classics in general. To a young man starting at Columbia College, he urged studying the sciences—astronomy, mathematics, chemistry—but told him not to disregard the ancient texts:

> *I would advise you to undertake a regular course of history & poetry in both languages, in Greek, go first thro' the Cyropaedia, and then read Herodotus, Thucydides, Xenophon's Hellenies & Anabasis, Arrian's Alexander, & Plutarch's lives, for prose reading: Homer's Iliad & Odyssey, Euripides, Sophocles in poetry, & Demosthenes in Oratory; alternating prose & verse as most agreeable to yourself. In Latin read Livy, Caesar, Sallust Tacitus, Cicero's Philosophies, and some of his Orations, in prose; and Virgil, Ovid's Metamorphoses, Horace, Terence & Juvenal for poetry.*

It was no secret to his contemporaries that Jefferson had been influenced far more by the philosophers of the ancient world and of the Enlightenment than he had been by Christian beliefs. Indeed, when the ex-president sought to sell his impressive personal library to rebuild the Library of Congress, which had been burned by British forces during the War of 1812, Cyrus King, a Federalist congressman from Massachusetts, questioned whether the nation really would benefit from such an injection of "infidel philosophy." A New Hampshire newspaper complained that many of Jefferson's books were in foreign languages and so "wholly unintelligible to 9/10ths of the members of Congress." It was a sign of how the composition of American leadership had changed.

## An "act of suicide": The Missouri Compromise

———

AS THE QUESTION OF SLAVERY IN NEW STATES GREW MORE URGENT, JEFferson emerged a bit from his classical cocoon and began to read newspapers again. He was horrified by what he read about the deal to allow Missouri in as a slave state, balanced with making Maine a state separate from Massachusetts, along with a line extending westward from the northern border of Tennessee, above which slavery would not be permitted. In this he saw the possible ruin of the nation. "This mementous question, like a fire bell in the night, awakened and filled me with terror," he wrote after the congressional vote on this Missouri Compromise. "A geographical line, coinciding with a marked principle, moral and political, once concieved and held up to the angry passions of men, will never be obliterated; and every new irritation will mark it deeper and deeper." Such a division, he added, amounted to an "act of suicide on themselves and of treason against the hopes of the world."

Indeed, it made him question the actions of his entire life. "I regret that I am now to die in the belief that the useless sacrifice of themselves, by the generation of '76. to acquire self government and happiness to their country, is to be thrown away by the unwise and unworthy passions of their sons, and that my only consolation is to be that I live not to weep over it."

If he and the other founders had found a way to end slavery, that "fire bell in the night" probably would not have been ringing. Unsympathetically but accurately, Darren Staloff, the intellectual historian, comments that "the paradox he had elided by rhetorical sleights of hand had come home to roost."

In 1821, Jefferson, fearful that imposing federal decisions about slavery on the Southern states would lead to war, cast the issue in classical terms: "if Congress has a power to regulate the conditions of the inhabitants of the states, within the states, it will be but another exercise of that power to declare that all shall be free. are we then to see again Athenian and Lacedemonian confederacies? to wage another Peloponnesian war to settle the ascendancy between them?" That was indeed exactly what would happen four decades later, when a new Confederacy, priding itself on its warrior skills, emerged to challenge the more urban North.

Others were thinking along the same lines. Debating the Missouri Compromise, Senator James Barbour of Virginia, a friend of Jefferson, warned the North to beware of treading on the potent sensitivities of the South. "Our people are as brave as they are loyal," he averred. "They can endure anything but insult. The moment you pass the Rubicon, . . . they will throw back upon you your insolence and aggression." In the same debate, Senator Richard Johnson of Kentucky seconded the thought, explicitly invoking the prospect of internecine conflict:

> You will jeopardize the harmony of the Union, which may possibly ultimate in a civil war. Recollect, Greece was destroyed by division, and Rome by consolidation. Then let us be content with our inheritance, and profit by their example. . . . The examples of Greece, of Carthage, and of Rome show us the danger of being moved by a momentary excitement of popular passion.

South Carolina's William Smith chimed in with another Southern theme, that the Romans, when a republic, had endorsed slavery, but lost their freedoms when they incited slave rebellions. "No human efforts can ever abolish slavery," he assured the Senate. Southerners in Congress were quick to threaten violence against anyone who tried to do so, and sometimes followed through. One chronicler counts some seventy violent incidents between members of Congress in the three decades after 1830.

## Jefferson, Adams, and Madison Move On

ON JULY 4, 1826, THE FIFTIETH ANNIVERSARY OF THE DECLARATION, Adams and Jefferson both died. On Jefferson's bedside table were some French political pamphlets, a volume of Seneca's works, and Aristotle's *Politics*.

Sometime in the early 1830s, James Madison, preparing for his own death, penned his final advice to the nation he had done so much to build. "The advice nearest to my heart and deepest in my convictions is that the Union of the States be cherished & perpetuated," he wrote. He then invoked a figure from the works of the

ancient Greek poet Hesiod, not much quoted by the Revolutionary generation. "Let the open enemy to it be regarded as a Pan-
dora with her box opened; and the disguised one, as the Serpent
creeping with his deadly wills into Paradise."

A traveler in Virginia in May 1833 went out of his way to visit
Madison because, he wrote, he wished to visit "almost the last
of the Romans." He found the former president lying in his bed
in a thick silk robe, reading a book, and observed that Madison
had realized the "happy old age that Cicero has so touchingly and
beautifully described." Madison died three years later.

## America Moves West

AT THE SAME TIME AS MADISON WAS FRETTING OVER THE FUTURE OF
the country, Alexis de Tocqueville, an observant young Frenchman sympathetic to the American experiment, traveled widely
in the United States. The American people, he noted, had moved
on from classical models. "Democratic peoples hold erudition in
very low esteem and care little about what happened in Rome
and Athens," he wrote in his celebrated study, *Democracy in America*. "What they want to hear about is themselves, and what they
ask to be shown is a picture of the present." But then Tocqueville
himself may have been unsympathetic to Greco-Roman studies,
having failed in classics as a schoolboy.

The Enlightenment also was falling into disrepute. In Europe,
the disappointments of the Age of Reason—most notably, the
butchery of the French Revolution—led to less adulation of ratio-
nality and more of feeling. The smoke, slums, and labor abuses
of the Industrial Revolution also led some people to question the
centrality of reason and to a new appreciation of nature. From
these feelings emerged nineteenth-century Romanticism.

The classical world was not abandoned altogether, but there was
a distinct shift in how it was regarded. Following Jefferson's lead,

Rome especially receded in the public imagination, and the older world of the Greeks moved up, leading to the Greek Revival, especially in architecture. In the first quarter of the nineteenth century, travelogues about Greece boomed. Every literate Englishmen who traveled seems to have left a rapturous record of his first view of Athens, "the sacred city," as one of them called it. The great English Romantic poets—Shelley, Keats, Byron, and Coleridge—all went Greek, each in his own way. "We are all Greeks," Shelley mandated. "Our laws, our literature, our religion, our arts, have their root in Greece." Shelley was not correct in this, but accuracy was not the point of such passionate enthusiasm.

Most Americans were not so romantic, and no longer feeling a need to defer to it or to the values and mores of elites, they left the ancient world behind them. And as America changed, with social reformers seeking to discipline behaviors, some of the ways of the Greek and Roman worlds fell into further disrepute. The anti-alcohol "teetotaler" movement, which took off in the 1830s, disapproved of all consumption of alcohol, including the wine of which the Greeks and Romans were fond.

Other Americans expressed horror at the ancients' acceptance of homosexuality, defining it as a "crime against nature," involving acts "not fit to be named among Christians." The legal scholar Edward Livingston (Princeton, 1781), in a set of proposed laws for the state of Louisiana that he compiled in the 1820s, could not bring himself to use the word, let alone define it. "Although it certainly prevailed among most of the ancient nations," he conceded, homosexuality "cannot operate here; . . . the repugnance, disgust, and even horror, which the very idea inspires, will be a sufficient security that it can never become a prevalent one in our country." Simply offering a legal definition of homosexual acts, he worried, "would inflict a lasting wound on the morals of the people." Livingston, who had been mayor of New York City and a member of Congress, would in the following decade be named secretary of state under Andrew Jackson.

The last president to feel thoroughly at home in the classics was the crotchety John Quincy Adams, a former professor of rhetoric and oratory at Harvard who, before taking his seat in Congress, had spent months reading Cicero for two hours a day.

Political power moved west. In 1828, America ousted John Quincy Adams and elected its first president from the trans-Appalachian states, Andrew Jackson of Tennessee. Jackson was an anti-intellectual who knew what he didn't like, which included secessionists. In 1830, at a Washington dinner celebrating the birthday of Jefferson, a parade of states' rights men criticized the federal government and supported the notion that states could "nullify," or reject, federal rulings. The governor of Georgia stood to denounce the United States government for ruling "with the absoluteness of Tiberius, with less wisdom than Augustus, and less justice than Trajan or the Antonines."

Jackson, though a slaveholder and cotton planter, responded with a powerful rejection of such sentiments, shocking the Southerners present by flatly toasting, "Our Federal Union. It must be preserved." Later, in a formal rejection of nullification, Jackson stated that, "The Constitution of the United States . . . forms a government, not a league." That last word would resonate with anyone familiar with the debates around the time of the writing of the Constitution that examined the leagues and confederacies of the ancient Greek republics.

After being reelected, Jackson was invited to visit Harvard to receive an honorary doctorate of laws. John Quincy Adams, appalled, asked the president of Harvard if the offer could be withdrawn. "Why, no," came the democratic reply. "As the people have twice decided this man knows enough to be their ruler, it is not for Harvard College to maintain that they are mistaken." Adams did not attend the ceremony for Jackson, recording in his diary that he did not desire to witness Harvard's "disgrace in conferring her highest literary honors upon a barbarian who could not write a sentence of grammar and hardly could spell his own name."

The ways of American politics continued to develop along the partisan lines foreseen by James Madison. Jackson's vice president, Martin Van Buren, himself later the president, would lead the way in developing a mature system of political parties in the 1820s and 1830s, with conventions, platforms, and party discipline. In his autobiography he explained his thinking on the subject, stating that he knew:

> . . . *as all men of sense know, that political parties are inseparable from free government, and that in many and material respects they are very useful to the country.* . . . *The disposition to abuse power, so deeply planted in the human heart, can by no other means be more effectually checked.*

So, he said, wise heads, when considering parties, should "recognize their necessity" and "give them the credit they deserve." This was a long way from the views of the first two presidents.

The people were quite willing to obey Jefferson's edict to pursue happiness, but they intended to do it on their own terms. Hamilton had been correct back in 1782 when he insisted that the disinterestedness prescribed by classical republicanism would not survive as the model in the United States. And there had always existed a strain of anti-classicism in American politics, especially among the anti-Federalists.

## A Free Market in Commerce, Politics—and Religion

AMERICANS IN THE EARLY NINETEENTH CENTURY——AT LEAST WHITE ones—began to enjoy a competitive free market in three crucial areas: commerce, politics, and religion. In sharp contrast to the ways of Europe, all three of those realms were unregulated, non-hierarchical, and driven by individual decisions. As an inhabitant of a Mississippi River town happily shouts out in the *Adventures of Huckleberry Finn*, "You pays your money and you takes your choice!" That may be the most American sentence ever written.

A bit surprisingly, competition became the rule even in religious affairs. With the state no longer involved in churches, licensing their leaders, supporting them financially, and overseeing appointments, sects proliferated. Samuel Stanhope Smith had graduated from Princeton about the time James Madison first appeared on the campus, and had married John Witherspoon's eldest daughter and would succeed him as president of the college. On the eve of the new century, Smith applauded a nation in which people could pick and choose among faiths as they saw fit:

> *In America, a diligent and faithful clergy . . . can secure their favour only in proportion to their useful services. A fair and generous competition among the different denominations of christians, while it does not extinguish their mutual charity, promotes an emulation that will have a beneficial influence on the public morals.*

The few Federalists still around turned up their noses at the new men of religion, often self-selected and relatively uneducated, and more moved by the inner spirit than by the written word. Thomas Green Fessenden wrote a satire that ridiculed these "bawling, itinerant, field and barn preachers." He continued:

> *A stupid wretch, who cannot read,*
> *(A very likely thing indeed)*
> *Receives from Heaven a calling;*
> *He leaves his plough, he drops his hoe,*
> *Gets on his meeting clothes, and lo,*
> *Sets up the trade of bawling.*

This may be awkward poetry, but it is persuasive evidence that the Federalists remained out of step with the new America that was emerging. Yet Fessenden was correct to perceive a destabilizing tendency in evangelism. As the historian Charles Sellers summarizes the new religious approach, "Direct access to divine grace and revelation, subordinating clerical learning to everyperson's reborn heart, vindicated the lowly reborn soul against hierarchy and authority."

In both politics and religion, adds Gordon Wood, roused Americans could invoke fundamental documents—the Constitution and the Scriptures. And, in a departure, he notes, American evangelism and commercialism would go hand in hand. Thus Tocqueville observed that in America, preachers seemed equally concerned with "eternal felicity in the next world" and "prosperity in this."

There was little room for classicism in this new configuration. These new Americans would turn not to the ancient world but to themselves for guidance through belief systems, leading to a plethora of cults and movements in nineteenth-century America—Shaker communities, Mormonism, Millerite millennialism, utopian socialism, temperance, and most significantly for the nation's future, abolitionism. "By the early nineteenth century, America had already emerged as the most egalitarian, most materialistic, most individualistic—and most evangelical Christian—society in Western history," writes Wood. "In many respects this new democratic society was the very opposite of the one the revolutionary leaders had envisaged." The Revolution, he concludes, had not failed—rather, it had exceeded the expectations of those who led it.

Given the option to do so, Americans in the nineteenth century abandoned the rationalist secularism of the Revolutionary generation. In 1775, there was one minister for every 1,500 Americans. In 1845, there was one for every 500—a tripling of the ratio. Likewise, by that point in the nineteenth century, about a third of Americans were members of churches, twice the fraction at the beginning of the War for Independence. This new religiosity led some to question the morality of heeding examples from pagan Rome. The phrase "In God We Trust" would appear, not in Latin but in English, on American coins in the middle of the nineteenth century.

Those who were not religious were even less bound by the old ways. Lewis Gaylord Clark, editor of the influential magazine *The Knickerbocker*, declared that, "The present age is emphatically the Age of Fun. Everybody deals in jokes, and all wisdom is inculcated in a paraphrase of humor." An "Age of Fun." One can only imagine the apoplexy such an assertion would have provoked in John Adams, or the cold contempt it would elicit from George Washington.

In 1836, Washington Irving, well attuned to changes in American culture, coined the phrase "the almighty dollar," using it in his short story "The Creole Village." In the same year, Ralph Waldo Emerson, who made his mark by explaining to Americans how to think about themselves and their times, predicted in his journal that "this age will be characterized as the era of Trade, for everything is made subservient to that agency." He delved into that idea: "Superstition gives way; Patriotism; Martial ardor; Romance in the people; but Avarice does not." He also perceived a new similarity between commerce and politics. "Striking likeness in the mode of government and of trade. The fever of speculation in Maine and the prairies is matched by the ardor and restlessness of politicians—reckless experiment."

"Virtue" most of all declined as a cultural marker. In 1828, Noah Webster, a former editor of a Federalist newspaper, published the first edition of his famous *American Dictionary*, a project that had taken decades. Among his 70,000 handwritten entries, along with American novelties such as "skunk" and "squash," was "virtue." His first definition of the word was "strength." His second was "Bravery; valor." This was, he noted, "the predominant signification of *virtus* among the Romans." But then he buried that meaning, stating that "this sense is nearly or quite obsolete." Andrew Jackson would emphasize "virtue" in his farewell address of 1837, but mainly in the course of justifying his ferocious attacks on his political enemies.

By the mid-nineteenth century, Gordon Wood observes, the very meaning of "virtue" had changed, and "at times seemed to mean little more than female chastity."

## Classicism Mocked

———

BY 1839, AMERICAN IMPATIENCE WITH CLASSICAL MODELS WAS ROU-tine, even expected. Peter Parley, a widely popular author, in his children's history of Rome dismisses Cato with barely a sentence. "Had I the time, I could say much about Cato and Brutus; by many their characters are highly esteemed, but we must go on with our history." Must go on, indeed.

The following year, a statue by Horatio Greenough (Harvard, 1825) depicting George Washington as a bare-chested Roman was unveiled for display in the U.S. Capitol, only to be greeted with widespread ridicule. It eventually was moved out of the building. Davy Crockett, not generally known for his art criticism, censured another, similar depiction of Washington, commenting that "they have a Roman gown on him, and he was an American; this ain't right."

Seen in this context, Emerson was probably playing to the crowd when, in a lecture in 1844, he sniped at collegiate study of Latin and Greek as "warfare against common sense." In an earlier lecture, he rejected the foremost writers of the English Enlightenment in favor of more recent authors such as William Wordsworth and Thomas Carlyle: "In contrast with their writing, the style of Pope, of Johnson, of Gibbon, looks cold and pedantic."

One aspect these Romantic new thinkers appeared not to see was that classicism, and especially the common bond of a classical education, had helped the new nation coalesce. It may have been outmoded, old-fashioned, a bit unfeeling, even unrealistic. Yet for all that, it had provided some of the cords that connected elites in diverse regions. Now common vocabulary and shared vision had waned, and so there was one less thing to hold together a growing, divided, and disputatious nation.

In 1854, during the contentious debates over the Kansas-Nebraska Act—that is, over the future of slavery in new states—Michael Walsh, an Irish-born congressman from New York City, stood on the floor of the House of Representatives to discuss what had helped him make his way in America. It was most certainly not, he said, a classical education:

> A man can be a man of education without being drilled through college. It is far better to know the men among whom one lives, than to know men who have been dead three thousand years. If I am deficient in classical lore, I am pretty well booked up in the rascality of the age in which we live. . . . I would not barter away all the practical knowledge I have received in lumber and ship-yards for all the Latin that was ever spoken in ancient Rome. I had rather speak sense in one plain and expressive language, than speak nonsense in fifty.

## Deploying Aristotle to Defend Slavery

SOMEHOW THE PROBLEM OF SLAVERY, THE MOST FUNDAMENTAL ISSUE facing mid-nineteenth-century America, seemed to stir up old memories of classicism. Charles Sumner of Massachusetts, in his most famous speech, "The Crime Against Kansas," delivered in May 1856, began by noting that the population of Kansas exceeded that of

> Athens . . . when her sons, under Miltiades, won liberty for mankind on the field of Marathon; more than Sparta contained, when she ruled Greece, . . . more than Rome gathered on her seven hills, when, under her kings, she commenced that sovereign sway, which afterwards embraced the whole earth.

He accused one pro-slavery senator, David Rice Atchison of Missouri, of stalking into the Senate chamber, "reeking with conspiracy . . . and then like Catiline he skulked away." He likened the Southerners' approach to Kansas to the plundering of Sicily by Gaius Verres, the Roman provincial governor famously prosecuted by Cicero. But he ended by invoking the Bible and God. Two days later, a South Carolina congressman walked onto the floor of the Senate and nearly beat Sumner to death with a thick walking cane that bore a heavy gold head.

In opposing the spirit of the times, the South clung to the ancient world to defend the institution of slavery. The origins of this lay early in Aristotle's *Politics*, where there is a short passage, almost an aside, that, as one historian put it, had "a far greater influence on nineteenth century America than it ever did on ancient thought." Discussing the basic elements of the structure of society, such as family and village, Aristotle stated that "barbarians . . . have never yet risen to the rank of men, that is, of men fit to govern; wherefore the poets say, 'Tis right the Greeks should govern the barbarians.'" A bit later, he added that the master holds his place not because he is more skilled at the tasks at hand. Rather, he explained, "This authority is founded on the general superiority of his character." These passages, comments one historian, made Aristotle "virtually a sectional American hero. . . . Whenever a writer wished to stress the natural hierarchy of races and the ineradicable differences between types of men, he rushed straightaway to Aristotle's *Politics*."

Pro-slavery Southern academics wrapped themselves in Aristotle's cloak. "It has been contended that slavery is unfavorable to a republican spirit," argued Thomas Dew, president of William & Mary from 1836 to 1846. "But," he continued,

> the whole history of the world proves that this is far from being the case. In the ancient republics of Greece and Rome, where the spirit of liberty glowed with the most intensity, the slaves were more numerous than the freemen. Aristotle, and the great men of antiquity, believed slavery necessary to keep alive the spirit of freedom.

Yet even in this unhappy matter, classicism began to take a back seat to resurgent Christianity. The final line of defense for slavery was not ancient philosophy but the Bible. As Dew wrote, "When we turn to the New Testament, we find not one single passage at

all calculated to disturb the conscience of an honest slaveholder."
Slavery was doomed to end sooner than any of them thought possible. But its underlying ideology of white supremacy lives on, and
in fact in recent years has seen a resurgence, its proponents no
longer afraid to appear in public.

## The Coming of Industry

THE REMAINING FRAGMENTS OF AMERICAN CLASSICISM WOULD BE
steamrollered by the Industrial Revolution.

James Watt's steam engine was devised in Glasgow in 1781. In
the course of a few decades in the nineteenth century, human and
animal muscle were outstripped by this new power. Placing the
power of steam in boats had a liberating effect on the states between the Appalachians and the Mississippi, dramatically cutting
the time and money it cost to move grain, cotton, and other farm
products to market. It also reduced the prices of the cloth, clocks,
plows, and other manufactured goods those riverboats carried
back up the Ohio, Tennessee, Cumberland, Wabash, Monongahela, and Yazoo Rivers. In 1817, there were 17 steamboats operating on "western" rivers. By 1855, there were 727, most of them far
larger than their predecessors. Rising standards of living alerted
people to the causes of such changes.

What the steamboat began, the railroad and telegraph finished.
They often were built along the same line. Together they moved
people, goods, and information at speeds that were unprecedented
and somewhat mind-boggling. The pace of life quickened dramatically. Rarely has a transition between historic periods been embodied as well as it was on July 4, 1828, when Charles Carroll, the
last surviving signer of the Declaration of Independence, laid the
first stone of the Baltimore & Ohio Railroad, which would grow
to be one of the earliest great rail systems of the United States.

American colleges began to adjust to the times. The changes
they made did not by themselves kill American classicism, which

had been declining for decades, but they certainly underscored that the times were different. "There simply was so much more to know than ever before—in science, politics, economics, philosophy, and in almost any area of knowledge one might name—that the traditional curriculum could not possibly contain it," concludes Russel Blaine Nye in his study of the cultural life of the young United States. The classics lived on in Great Books programs, and in a general belief that earning a college degree in the liberal arts was a ticket to a respectable middle-class life.

In 1831, a speaker at a Yale commencement deemed the steam engine to be equal in its powers to the orations of Cicero. In 1847, Daniel Webster conceded in speech that New Hampshire boasted "no Virgil and no Eclogues." But, he continued, his native state possessed something better: a wave of extraordinary new technologies. "The world had seen nothing like it before. . . . The ancients saw nothing like it." In 1850, Thomas Ewbank, the U.S. commissioner of patents, went even further, exulting that, "A steamer is a mightier epic than the *Iliad*."

Twenty-four years after President Jackson stepped down, another frontiersman, the very different Abraham Lincoln, moved into the White House. Like Jackson, he lacked a classical education, but he had immersed himself in two great reservoirs of the English language—the King James Bible and the works of Shakespeare. He would preside over the biggest and bloodiest split in the nation's history. The Revolutionary generation had worried for decades that catastrophe would be brought by a loss of virtue, corruption, or perhaps foreign intervention. But in fact it was caused by something right in front of their eyes: slavery. Lincoln vowed to prevail in that war, even if, he said in his second inaugural address—one of the most powerful speeches in American history—it meant that "every drop of blood drawn with the lash shall be paid by another drawn with the sword."

In the years after that Civil War, the skeptical Scottish approach to education, made so crucial to American colleges by Witherspoon and others, also began to disappear. "It is a curious fact," observed the intellectual historian Perry Miller, "that one of the most radical revolutions in the history of the American mind took place . . . without exciting appreciable comment: the philosophy and the philosophers of Scottish Realism vanished from American colleges. . . . and were swiftly replaced by some form of idealism."

By the early twentieth century, a study of American colleges would express surprise at the "peculiar dominance" the classical curriculum had held in the early decades of American higher education. The author seemed to find it both exotic and inexplicable. "The whole career of Latin and Greek, their rise into unexampled prominence, and the strength with which they resisted encroachments on their prerogative, . . . forms an interesting chapter in our college annals," wrote Louis Franklin Snow.

Well into the twentieth century, Yale College maintained a requirement that all students pass a basic Latin examination. Former president William Howard Taft, a member of the Yale Corporation, had stood in the way of dropping it. But he died in 1930, and the requirement followed him to the grave a year later. Finally, in 1961, Harvard stopped issuing diplomas inscribed in Latin. A large part of the American past was not only forgotten, but even when glimpsed in a reference to, say, Cato or Catiline remained unrecognizable to most. The past had been buried.

# Epilogue

*What We Can Do*

WHAT WOULD THE FOUNDERS SAY ABOUT THE AMERICA OF TODAY? Is our nation what it was supposed to be, or what they hoped it would be? As Cicero asked in his first speech against Catiline: What kind of country have we become?

The picture is mixed.

Over the last 150 years there has been progress in expanding the franchise, so that women and nonwhites now exercise far more political power than the founders envisioned. I think they would be pleased to see that the machine they designed has proven both durable and flexible. More than anything else, I have learned in researching this book that America is a moving target, a goal that must always be pursued but never quite reached. As it has moved, it has expanded rights—for blacks, for other minority groups, for women, for the LGBTQ community, for others who have been oppressed—and revisited the question of what it means to provide equality before the law. This is not just the right thing to do but the smart thing. America works best when it gives people the freedom to tap their own energies and exploit their talents.

On the other hand, I think the founders would be appalled by how money has come to dominate American politics, particularly in the last forty years. They did not design the United States to be an oligarchy, governed by the rich few. Most would have deemed such an outcome inconsistent with being a republic. Money has always influenced our politics, but it now wields more clout than it has for most of our history. This is unhealthy, and undermines the representative democracy the framers labored to produce. As John Adams wrote, "Property monopolized or in the Possession of a few is a Curse to Mankind. We should preserve not an Absolute Equality.—this is unnecessary, but preserve all from extreme Poverty, and all others from extravagant Riches."

Here are ten steps that I think might help put us more on the course intended by the Revolutionary generation, to help us move beyond where we are stuck and instead toward what we ought to be:

## 1. Don't panic

Did the founders anticipate a Donald Trump? I would say yes. As James Madison wrote in the most prominent of his contributions to the Federalist Papers, "Enlightened statesmen will not always be at the helm." Just after Aaron Burr nearly became president, Jefferson wrote that "bad men will sometimes get in, & with such an immense patronage, may make great progress in corrupting the public mind & principles. This is a subject with which wisdom & patriotism should be occupied."

Fortunately the founders built a durable system, one that often in recent years has stymied Trump. He has tried to introduce a retrogressive personal form of rule, but repeatedly has run into a Constitution built instead to foster the rule of law. Over the last several years we have seen Madison's checks and balances operate robustly. Madison designed a structure that could accommodate people acting unethically and venally. Again, our national political gridlock sometimes is not a bug but feature. It shows our system is working. The key task is to do our best to make sure the machinery of the system works. This begins with ensuring that eligible citizens are able to vote. This ballot box is the basic building block of our system.

We should appreciate how strong and flexible our Constitution is. It is all too easy, as one watches the follies and failings of humanity, to conclude that we live in a particularly wicked time. In a poll taken just as I was writing the first part of this book, the majority of Americans surveyed said they think they are living at the lowest point in American history. So it is instructive to be reminded that Jefferson held similar beliefs about his own era. He wrote that there were "three epochs in history signalized by the total extinction of national morality." The first two were in ancient times, following the deaths of Alexander the Great and Julius Caesar, he thought, and the third was his own age.

As an aside, Trump's attacks on immigrants might raise a few eyebrows among the founders. Seven of the thirty-nine people who signed the Constitution were themselves born abroad, most notably Hamilton and James Wilson.

## 2. Curtail campaign finance

We should drop the bizarre American legal fiction that corporations are people, enjoying all the rights of citizens, including unfettered campaign donations as a form of free speech. Indeed, corporations possess greater rights than do people, as they cannot be jailed or executed, while citizens can and do suffer those fates. As the legal historian Zephyr Teachout has observed, the founders would have considered corporate campaign spending the essence of political corruption.

## 3. Re-focus on the public good

The coronavirus pandemic of 2020 reminded America of a lesson it had forgotten about *the public good*—a phrase that occurs over 1,300 times in *Founders Online*. Health is a public good—which is one reason everyone should have access to health care. In the longer term, so are education, transportation infrastructure, the environment, and public safety. These are the things that come under "the general welfare" of the people that is mentioned twice in the Constitution—the preamble and Article I, Section 8. The idea has its roots in an assertion by Cicero that "*salus populi suprema lex esto*"—that is, "Welfare of the public is the supreme law." Salus was the Roman goddess of "health, prosperity, and the public welfare." John Adams wrote in 1766, "The public Good, the salus Populi is the professed End of all Government." With that in mind, Americans need to put less emphasis on the property rights of the individual and more on the rights of the people as a whole. The market should not always be the ultimate determinant of how we live, or always allowed to shape our society. As the social philosopher Michael Sandel puts it, "to be free is more than a matter of pursuing my interests unimpeded, or satisfying my desires, whatever they happen to be. It is to share in self-government, to deliberate about the common good, to have a meaningful voice in shaping the forces that govern our lives." It may take a long time—a generation or two—to restore this balance to our system. We should follow Sandel's lead and start changing the discourse.

## 4. Promote, cultivate, and reward virtue in public life— but don't count on it

The next step is to treat people who think differently from you with courtesy. Hear them out. Try to understand their points of view. Ask yourself how they came to those views. Even better, ask them—not to score debating points, but to learn. At the very least, you might come away with a better understanding of where your own side has erred or overlooked aspects of the problem. As part of that dialogue, when members of your own side violate America's fundamental principles, speak out against them. This can be hard to do. It won't make you popular, but in the long run, it will be better for your side

As part of this, promote civic duty, seeing it as something good citizens do. "Virtue" has lost its weight and meaning, but it is still possible to honor the founders' intention by participating in the life of one's neighborhood, town, region, state, and country. Living in a small town in Maine, I was impressed to see how much its officials did voluntarily—such as a selectman driving to a town park to collect the trash and take it to the dump, or maintaining a confidential list of elderly townspeople who could not afford to have their driveways plowed and making sure that a town plow swung by to help. Along the same lines, we should assign more moral value to the donation of time, such as volunteering for a rural ambulance squad, than to the donation of money.

## 5. Respect our core institutions—and push them

Even at their most bitter moments, the founders all believed that government had a central role to play in American life, even if they disagreed how that should be manifested. By 1800, almost all had rallied to a set of common notions about the country. They generally held a respect for inquiry, for the establishment of facts, and for intense debate about their meaning. These attitudes were at the heart of the Enlightenment, and they still have a place in the United States today, even as we live under a president who is anti-Enlightenment, even though he would not know what that means.

We should question the view that the government is almost always the problem. Sometimes it is the solution, especially when it serves the common good.

In this context, it is worth remembering that in the early nineteenth century, much of the original opposition to "big government" in America—in this case, federal action in support of building roads and canals—came from slaveholders who feared what might follow. "If Congress can make canals, they can with more propriety emancipate," Nathaniel Macon, a senator from North Carolina (attended Princeton), privately warned a friend in 1818. John C. Calhoun (Yale, 1804), the leading ideologist of white supremacy, warned that if emancipation of slaves were permitted, "the next step would be to raise the negroes to a social and political equality with the whites." These were men who, one modern historian notes, were "willing to block the modernization of the whole country's economy in order to preserve their section's system of racial exploitation."

## 6. Wake up Congress

The branch of the federal government that has failed most in recent years has been Congress. Two of its major functions are to be the voice of the popular will and a check on the executive. The Senate especially seems chary of performing its constitutional duties.

The framers of the Constitution probably would be surprised and chagrined by the passivity of Congress in recent decades, and especially its failure to assert firmly its role as a co-equal branch of government with the executive. They intended Congress to be active, expecting it to be the most energetic branch of federal government.

One of the hallmarks of oligarchy is a legislature that is elected but tame, just active enough to divide and weaken the democratic spirit. To that end, having outspoken and controversial members of Congress is almost always beneficial. The House of Representatives especially should reflect the rowdy, demanding, contentious ways of the American people. We need more new, loud, and unpolished voices.

One thing to consider is whether we need to reinvigorate our checks and balances. The Constitution was designed to be amended—that is, improved. How can we better ensure that voting rights are respected? The gerrymandering of congressional districts in particular has had the effect of depriving the people who are not in power of a meaningful vote.

## 7. Enrich the political vocabulary

The Revolutionary generation had a mixed record in discussing political issues, and we can learn from both their successes and their shortfalls. They devised ways to speak about independence and equality, but struggled to develop a political vocabulary that addressed the persistence of partisanship. Do we have an adequate vocabulary for the issues of our own era—political decency, global warming, dealing with terrorism, the growing inequality in income and wealth? There is a role here especially for political commentators to try to imitate Madison in developing the concepts to deal with new situations. Do we need to "make America great again," or rather do we need to make America more American? And if the answer is the latter, how would that manifest itself?

## 8. Reclaim the definition of "un-American"

We actually can look up what it is to be American. The Declaration of Independence and the Constitution tell us, especially the Bill of Rights. Someone who became an American citizen yesterday enjoys all the rights of a person whose family landed here three centuries ago.

Political freedom begins with the freedoms of conscience, assembly, and speech. A congressional candidate slugging a reporter is un-American. So is preventing a controversial speaker from appearing at a university. So speak out on behalf of our rights, and remember that doing so begins by protecting the rights of others, even when we disagree with them. Especially protect repugnant speech, no matter how ugly. When in doubt, remember that someone might one day try to label your own views as too offensive to be allowed public expression.

## 9. Rehabilitate "happiness"

Today many Americans tend to think of "happiness" mainly in terms of pleasure-seeking, usually in physical form—sex, food, alcohol, sports, and video games that excite the senses. But by focusing on feeding the flesh we risk starving the mind and spirit. We need to appreciate the Enlightenment's broader, richer notion of happiness and make it again about finding one's place in the world, enjoying what we have and what we see in it, and appreciating the beauty of the Earth during our short time on it. None of that prescription would be a surprise to Jefferson. We should remember that as he laid out his path to happiness, the fourth of the Epicurean ideals he listed was "justice."

## 10. Know your history

Remember the founders made huge errors and decisions, most notably by writing slavery into the basic law of the land, with catastrophic consequences. As my friend Karin Chenoweth points out, slavery was not a stain on the country, it was woven into the original fabric. The nation was founded in part on the acceptance of slavery. American slavery in turn was constructed on racial lines—that is, a belief that black people were inferior to white people, which is the core of white supremacism. Slavery no longer exists in this country, but that belief system remains alive. As the nation moves forward, we need to be clear-eyed about where it came from.

In studying the founders' struggles and then thinking of where the country is today, we should recognize that the American experiment is still underway—and can be lost if we are not careful. In moments of doubt, we should focus on finding ways to continue and improve this experiment. Despite its flaws, it is worth it.

# Acknowledgments

HAVING SPENT THE LAST FOUR YEARS MENTALLY IN THE EIGH-teenth century, I now reluctantly return to our own time. Writing this book mainly in rural Maine made my mental time travel easier. Our house was built in 1812, when Madison was president. The nearest big town is named for Oliver Ellsworth, the forgotten third chief justice of the United States. The streets in that town carry better-remembered names such as Hancock, Franklin, and Washington. Farther up the road is Addison, named for the author of *Cato*. Closer by stands the small town of Brooks-ville, honoring an obscure Revolutionary War veteran who by chance was quoted at the beginning of my chapter 9.

I carried out much of my research farther south in Maine at Bowdoin College, named for Massachusetts politician James Bow-doin (Harvard, 1745), where most of the time I worked in and through the Hawthorne-Longfellow Library. I am grateful to the college for giving this book the research facilities it required. I ap-preciate Elizabeth McCormack, the dean for academic affairs, for extending the invitation to affiliate with the college as a visiting fellow. Robert Tyrer provided essential help in making the ini-tial connection, which Scott Hood then took over in completing. Clayton Rose, the president of the college, gave me a warm wel-come. Carmen Greenlee, Barbara Levergood, and Joan Campbell were openhearted at the library, and taught this old writer some new research tricks. David Gordon, chair of the history depart-ment, and Robert Sobak, chair of the classics department, put up with having a civilian wandering through their disciplines and hallways, and taught me a lot, in different ways. Barbara Elias introduced me to the college. Meghan Roberts schooled me on how the Enlightenment unfolded differently in France, England, and Scotland, and did me the special favor of being willing to tell me when I was wrong. Jean Yarbrough gave me a helpful Straussian perspective on Madison and Jefferson. Matthew Stuart guided me through some of the thickets of David Hume.

As will be clear to anyone looking at the source notes, this book relies on the research of well over one hundred esteemed historians. In particular I have tried to list in the source notes works that introduced me to ideas or citations I had not seen before. But I must repeat the names of a few of those scholars here.

In particular, three leading historians were generous with their time and knowledge.

Brown University's Gordon Wood got me off to a strong start and saved me several months of work by reviewing my basic plan and pointing out one major pitfall. He also graciously read the manuscript. Peter Onuf of the University of Virginia gave the first draft a generous and thoughtful reading. He also caught two errors, suggested how to sharpen some major themes, and persuaded me to broaden my approach to George Washington. I now understand why he is thanked in the acknowledgments sections of so many of the best books I have read on the Revolutionary era. Richard Kohn of the University of North Carolina helped me better understand Washington's position during the Newburgh controversy, and also was generous in explaining the nuances of civil-military relations in the 1790s.

There were more. John Mulhern of the University of Pennsylvania helpfully shared with me his thoughts and syllabus on Madison and the classics. Vanderbilt's Susan Ford Wiltshire provided help and encouragement in a lively exchange of emails. The Citadel's David Preston was generous in sharing with me obscure information and sources about the French and Indian War. The University of Virginia's Alan Taylor pointed me in the right direction in considering the Constitution as a peace treaty between the states.

I also am indebted to the illuminating work of several scholars whom I know only by their books, notably Meyer Reinhold, Joyce Appleby, Carl Richard, and Caroline Winterer.

I also appreciate being given access to the Perry-Castañeda Library at the University of Texas at Austin. Digitization is a wonderful thing, but for me, nothing compares to open stacks. I learned a lot sitting on the floors of the Perry-Castañeda in Texas, as well as the Hawthorne-Longfellow in Maine.

Officials of the historic sites of the first four presidents also provided valuable aid. Mount Vernon's Douglas Bradburn helped me through the avalanche of books about George Washington. At James Madison's estate at Montpelier, Elizabeth Chew and Christian Cotz were helpful, both in their own knowledge and in connecting me to Michael Dickens, an expert on Madison's time at Princeton. Dr. Dickens in turn was especially generous in allowing me to read and quote from his manuscript on Madison and Princeton, a work loaded with historical nuggets. Patrick Campbell did a fine job of showing me around Montpelier. At Monticello, Jennifer Lyon, John Ragosta, and Jim Heilman were helpful and informative.

At William & Mary College, Susan Kern, executive director of the Historic Campus and an expert on Thomas Jefferson's youth and his time at the college, gave me an eloquent tour that made the old bricks talk. At Colonial Williamsburg, both Kurt Smith and Bill Barker illuminated the character of Thomas Jefferson for me, and Smith did me the favor of showing me George Wythe's house through the eyes of Jefferson.

Critical readers have played an unseen but essential role in the production of my books. These are people I trust to take the first look and to tell me when they think I am off course. Karin Chenoweth, Richard Wiebe, and Ellen Heffelfinger helped me on the ground floor, in thinking about a proposal for this book, and then in looking at the first draft. Karin also wrote a critique of the first draft that is a model of thoughtful criticism. Her fingerprints are all over this book, but especially the introduction, which she conceived and showed me how to go about writing. Richard Wiebe went an extra mile and helped focus the epilogue. Sharp-eyed Ellen

Heffelfinger saved me from many solecisms. Richard Brookhiser pointed out a mistake that would have been embarrassing. He and Michael Lind both brought helpful perspectives in viewing the book as a whole. Vernon Loeb, a veteran critical reader of mine, posed good questions. Thomas Remington and Nancy Roth Remington both brought gimlet eyes to the manuscript, and also encouraged me to read the work of Michael Sandel. Tim Noah provided a thoughtful critique and pointed out how to improve part of the prologue. Colonel Robert Killebrew, U.S. Army (Ret.), combined editing and coaching in needed doses. Cullen Murphy provided a reassuring overview of the manuscript.

And a hug and thanks to my historian daughter, Molly Ricks, for help throughout, and to my friend Seamus Osborne for agreeing emphatically with her. Molly was an insightful and discerning reviewer of the manuscript. She has a hawk's eye for lazy writing. It was an unexpected joy to work with her critique of the first draft. My son, Chris Ricks, provided inquisitive support throughout the project.

Scott Moyers deserves a special mention. Working with him for a quarter of a century was one of the great pleasures of my life. My literary agent, Andrew Wylie, smoothed the process of getting this book afloat and then stepped in and led the way when we hit a rough patch. Jonathan Jao brought a sharp eye and a deft hand to the manuscript and carried it over the finish line.

I also wish to thank the unnamed people who over the last fifteen or so years have placed online so many of the books and other documents of our past. Contemporary databases are astonishing. Almost every book published in America in the eighteenth century is online, as far as I can tell—and what's more, is often searchable. I used the *Founders Online* site almost every day, and on occasion twenty or thirty times in one day. It is a gem. I also think I ventured into the archives of the *William and Mary Quarterly* several times a week for several years.

While I remain wary of the large information companies that now dominate the American economy, I must express my gratitude to Google, despite the damage it has done to the American newspaper business. During my research, again and again I would find that rare, even unfindable books from eighteenth century were available on Google Books—and searchable, too. The ability to search the entire works of an author enabled me to write with a certitude unavailable to previous generations.

And, as always, I wish to thank my wife, Mary Catherine, who inspired me every day with her thoughts and suggestions. The more I listen to her, the more I appreciate her knowledge and wisdom. Tapping her vast knowledge of American history has been a daily pleasure.

The errors—and there inevitably always are some, no matter how hard I try—are my own.

# Appendix:
# The Declaration of Independence

## In Congress, July 4, 1776.

———

THE UNANIMOUS DECLARATION OF THE THIRTEEN UNITED STATES OF America, When in the Course of human events, it becomes necessary for one people to dissolve the political bands which have connected them with another, and to assume among the powers of the earth, the separate and equal station to which the Laws of Nature and of Nature's God entitle them, a decent respect to the opinions of mankind requires that they should declare the causes which impel them to the separation.

We hold these truths to be self-evident, that all men are created equal, that they are endowed by their Creator with certain unalienable Rights, that among these are Life, Liberty and the pursuit of Happiness.—That to secure these rights, Governments are instituted among Men, deriving their just powers from the consent of the governed,—That whenever any Form of Government becomes destructive of these ends, it is the Right of the People to alter or to abolish it, and to institute new Government, laying its foundation on such principles and organizing its powers in such form, as to them shall seem most likely to effect their Safety and Happiness. Prudence, indeed, will dictate that Governments long established should not be changed for light and transient causes; and accordingly all experience hath shewn, that mankind are more disposed to suffer, while evils are sufferable, than to right themselves by abolishing the forms to which they are accustomed. But when a long train of abuses and usurpations, pursuing invariably the same Object evinces a design to reduce them under absolute Despotism, it is their right, it is their duty, to throw off such Government, and to provide new Guards for their future security.—Such has been the patient sufferance of these Colonies; and such is now the necessity which constrains them to alter their former Systems of Government. The history of the present King of Great Britain is a history of repeated injuries and usurpations, all having in direct object the establishment of an absolute Tyranny over these States. To prove this, let Facts be submitted to a candid world.

He has refused his Assent to Laws, the most wholesome and necessary for the public good.

He has forbidden his Governors to pass Laws of immediate and pressing importance, unless suspended in their operation till his Assent should be obtained; and when so suspended, he has utterly neglected to attend to them.

He has refused to pass other Laws for the accommodation of large districts of people, unless those people would relinquish the right of Representation in the Legislature, a right inestimable to them and formidable to tyrants only.

He has called together legislative bodies at places unusual, uncomfortable, and distant from the depository of their public Records, for the sole purpose of fatiguing them into compliance with his measures.

He has dissolved Representative Houses repeatedly, for opposing with manly firmness his invasions on the rights of the people.

He has refused for a long time, after such dissolutions, to cause others to be elected; whereby the Legislative powers, incapable of Annihilation, have returned to the People at large for their exercise; the State remaining in the mean time exposed to all the dangers of invasion from without, and convulsions within.

He has endeavoured to prevent the population of these States; for that purpose obstructing the Laws for Naturalization of Foreigners; refusing to pass others to encourage their migrations hither, and raising the conditions of new Appropriations of Lands.

He has obstructed the Administration of Justice, by refusing his Assent to Laws for establishing Judiciary powers.

He has made Judges dependent on his Will alone, for the tenure of their offices, and the amount and payment of their salaries.

He has erected a multitude of New Offices, and sent hither swarms of Officers to harrass our people, and eat out their substance.

He has kept among us, in times of peace, Standing Armies without the Consent of our legislatures.

He has affected to render the Military independent of and superior to the Civil power.

He has combined with others to subject us to a jurisdiction foreign to our constitution, and unacknowledged by our laws; giving his Assent to their Acts of pretended Legislation:

For Quartering large bodies of armed troops among us:

For protecting them, by a mock Trial, from punishment for any Murders which they should commit on the Inhabitants of these States:

For cutting off our Trade with all parts of the world:

For imposing Taxes on us without our Consent:

For depriving us in many cases, of the benefits of Trial by Jury:

For transporting us beyond Seas to be tried for pretended offences

For abolishing the free System of English Laws in a neighbouring Province, establishing therein an Arbitrary government, and enlarging its Boundaries so as to render it at once an example and fit instrument for introducing the same absolute rule into these Colonies:

For taking away our Charters, abolishing our most valuable Laws, and altering fundamentally the Forms of our Governments:

For suspending our own Legislatures, and declaring themselves invested with power to legislate for us in all cases whatsoever.

He has abdicated Government here, by declaring us out of his Protection and waging War against us.

He has plundered our seas, ravaged our Coasts, burnt our towns, and destroyed the lives of our people.

He is at this time transporting large Armies of foreign Mercenaries to compleat the works of death, desolation and tyranny, already begun with circumstances of Cruelty & perfidy scarcely paralleled in the most barbarous ages, and totally unworthy the Head of a civilized nation.

He has constrained our fellow Citizens taken Captive on the high Seas to bear Arms against their Country, to become the executioners of their friends and Brethren, or to fall themselves by their Hands.

He has excited domestic insurrections amongst us, and has endeavoured to bring on the inhabitants of our frontiers, the merciless Indian Savages, whose known rule of warfare, is an undistinguished destruction of all ages, sexes and conditions.

In every stage of these Oppressions We have Petitioned for Redress in the most humble terms: Our repeated Petitions have been answered only by repeated injury. A Prince whose character is thus marked by every act which may define a Tyrant, is unfit to be the ruler of a free people.

Nor have We been wanting in attentions to our Brittish brethren. We have warned them from time to time of attempts by their legislature to extend an unwarrantable jurisdiction over us. We have reminded them of the circumstances of our emigration and settlement here. We have appealed to their native justice and magnanimity, and we have conjured them by the ties of our common kindred to disavow these usurpations, which, would inevitably interrupt our connections and correspondence. They too have been deaf to the voice of justice and of consanguinity. We must, therefore, acquiesce in the necessity, which denounces our Separation, and hold them, as we hold the rest of mankind, Enemies in War, in Peace Friends.

We, therefore, the Representatives of the united States of America, in General Congress, Assembled, appealing to the Supreme Judge of the world for the rectitude of our intentions, do, in the Name, and by Authority of the good People of these Colonies, solemnly publish and declare, That these United Colonies are, and of Right ought to be Free and Independent States; that they are

Absolved from all Allegiance to the British Crown, and that all political connection between them and the State of Great Britain, is and ought to be totally dissolved; and that as Free and Independent States, they have full Power to levy War, conclude Peace, contract Alliances, establish Commerce, and to do all other Acts and Things which Independent States may of right do. And for the support of this Declaration, with a firm reliance on the protection of divine Providence, we mutually pledge to each other our Lives, our Fortunes and our sacred Honor.

# Notes

*A Note on Language*

xi   "We do not call ourselves 'Native American'": Richard Cullen Rath, *How Early America Sounded* (Cornell University Press, 2005), 145.

*Prologue:* What Is America?

xvii   "Whenever we as Americans have faced serious crises": Ralph Ellison, *Shadow and Act* (Random House, 1964), 106.

xviii   the influence of Enlightenment thinking on the founders: Daniel Walker Howe, "European Sources of Political Ideas in Jeffersonian America," *Reviews in American History* 10, no. 4 (December 1982), 29.

xxii   "Synthesis demands regard for complexity": Peter Gay, *The Enlightenment: An Interpretation: The Rise of Modern Paganism* (Alfred A. Knopf, 1966), x.

xxii   "How is it that we hear the loudest *yelps*": James Boswell, *The Life of Samuel Johnson* (Jones & Company, 1829), 352. Italics in original.

xxiv   "Their reading in the classics": Meyer Reinhold, *Classica Americana: The Greek and Roman Heritage in the United States* (Wayne State University Press, 1984), 20, 25.

*Part I:* Acquisition

1   a play about Cato: Thomas Fleming, "George Washington's Favorite Play," *Journal of the American Revolution* (11 December 2013), accessed online, as are almost all subsequent references to academic journals.

1   Joseph Addison's *Cato*: Paul Leicester Ford, *Washington and the Theatre* (The Dunlap Society, 1899), 1. See also Jared Brown, *The Theatre in American During the Revolution* (Cambridge University Press, 1995), 54; as well as Randall Fuller, "Theaters of the American Revolution: The Valley Forge 'Cato' and the Meschianza in Their Transcultural Contexts," *Early American Literature* 34, no. 2 (1999), 128.

*Chapter 1:* The Power of Colonial Classicism

3   James Madison kept a bust of Athena: Elizabeth Chew, vice president for museum programs, James Madison's Montpelier, email message to author.

4   a stable housed Caractacus: Henry Randall, *The Life of Thomas Jefferson*, Vol. 1 (Derby & Jackson, 1858), 69.

4    "Cleopatra ought not to be fed too high": "John Adams to Abigail Adams, 9 April 1796," *Founders Online*.

4    Among the enslaved: Elizabeth Dowling Taylor, *A Slave in the White House: Paul Jennings and the Madisons* (Palgrave Macmillan, 2012), 38; "Thomas Jefferson's List of Slaves at Poplar Forest (ca. 2–13 November 1814)," *Founders Online*; Henry Wiencek, *An Imperfect God: George Washington, His Slaves, and the Creation of America* (Farrar, Straus and Giroux, 2003), 99.

4    Our "Senate" meets in "The Capitol": I owe this observation of the names of our political parties to Howard Mumford Jones, *O Strange New World: American Culture: The Formative Years* (Viking, 1964), 229.

4    Our Supreme Court convenes: For the observation about the Supreme Court building as a Roman temple, I am indebted to Paul MacKendrick, "'This Rich Source of Delight': The Classics and the Founding Fathers," *The Classical Journal* 72, no. 2 (December 1976–January 1977), 104. The weight of the doors is from the website of the Office of the Curator, Supreme Court of the United States.

5    "He does not possess Wealth, it possesses him": Richard Gummere, *The American Colonial Mind and the Classical Tradition* (Harvard University Press, 1963), 127.

5    "A rolling stone gathers no moss": "From Benjamin Franklin to Samuel Cooper Johonnot, 25 January 1782," Franklin papers, *Founders Online*, 1; *The Moral Sayings of Publius Syrus*, trans. D. Lyman (L. E. Barnard, 1856), 48.

5    nodded to the ancient world in naming their settlements: Meyer Reinhold, *Classica Americana: The Greek and Roman Heritage in the United States* (Wayne State University Press, 1984), 257.

5    the "lynchpin" of public life: Joyce Appleby, *Liberalism and Republicanism in the Historical Imagination* (Harvard University Press, 1992), 21.

6    "virtue" appears about six thousand times: Based on a search of "virtue" on *Founders Online*, hereafter *FO*. There is some repetition as letters from one founder to another appear twice, in the papers both of the sender and the recipient.

6    "It is impossible to read in Thucydides": John Adams, "Preface" in *A Defence of the Constitutions of Government of the United States of America*, in *The Works of John Adams, Vol. IV*, ed. Charles Francis Adams (Charles C. Little and James Brown, 1851), 285.

6    look with admiration on the Greeks: Reinhold, *Classica Americana*, 97.

7    Polybius had criticized the people of Athens: Polybius, *Histories*, Book 6:44 in Richard Gummere, "The Classical Ancestry of the United States Constitution," *American Quarterly* 14, no. 1 (Spring 1962), 8.

7    "The history of Athens abounds": Edward Wortley Montagu, *Reflections on the Rise and Fall of the Antient Republicks* (A. Millar, 1759), 84.

7    "as brave and as free a people": John Dickinson, *Letters from a Farmer in Pennsylvania* (J. Almon, 1774), 29.

7    John Adams reported: "From John Adams to Benjamin Rush, 28 July 1789," *FO*.

7    a "Christian Sparta": Samuel Adams, *The Writings of Samuel Adams, Vol. IV, 1778–1802*, ed. Harry Alonzo Cushing (G.P. Putnam's Sons, 1908), 238.

7    "Cicero in Latin, and Xenophon in Greek": Edward Gibbon, *Memoirs of Edward Gibbon, Esq.* (Houghton, Mifflin, & Co., 1882), 107.

7    "The fame of Cicero flourishes at present": David Hume, *Philosophical Essays Concerning Human Understanding* (M. Cooper, 1751), 4.

7    These preferences extended across national and cultural boundaries: Harold Parker, *The Cult of Antiquity and the French Revolutionaries: A Study in the Development of the Revolutionary Spirit* (University of Chicago Press, 1937), 18–20.

7    Greek tragedians stood far in the background: Reinhold, *Classica Americana*, 332; For the German enthusiasm for ancient Greek literature during the nineteenth century, see Michael Lind, "The Second Fall of Rome," *The Wilson Quarterly* (Winter 2000), 50; see also W. H. Auden, "The Greeks and Us," in *Foreword and Afterwords* (Vintage Books, 1974), 4.

8    it was Terence: Meyer Reinhold, "The Classics and the Quest for Virtue in Eighteenth-Century America," in *The Usefulness of Classical Learning in the Eighteenth Century*, ed. Susan Ford Wiltshire (American Philological Society, 1976), 11.

8    "my favourite author": John Adams, "VI. 'U' to the *Boston Gazette*, 29 August 1763," *FO*.

8    Their attention to Rome was itself uneven: See, for example, David Bederman, *The Classical Foundations of the American Constitution: Prevailing Wisdom* (Cambridge University Press, 2008), 14.

8    "What gripped their minds": Bernard Bailyn, *The Ideological Origins of the American Revolution* (Belknap Press, 2017), 25.

8    "the Roman Republic attained to the utmost height of human greatness": Alexander Hamilton, "The Federalist No. 34 [5 January 1788]," *FO*.

8    "made himself perpetual dictator": John Adams, "1771. Thursday June 13th, [from the Diary of John Adams]," Adams Papers, *FO*.

9    Their articles became central to the political debate: Bernard Bailyn, "Political Experience and Enlightenment Ideas in Eighteenth-Century America," in *The American Historical Review* 67 (1962), 344; see also Alan Taylor, *American Revolutions: A Continental History, 1750–1804* (W. W. Norton, 2016), 92.

9    "gave unreserved endorsement to free speech": Forrest McDonald, *Novus Ordo Seclorum: The Intellectual Origins of the Constitution* (University Press of Kansas, 1985), 47. The comment on free speech appears in "Discourse on Libels," October 27, 1722, by John Trenchard [and Thomas Gordon], *Cato's Letters, Volume III* (J. Walthoe, T. and T. Longman, C. Hitch and L. Hawes, J. Hodges, A. Millar, J. and J. Rivington, J. Ward and M. Cooper, 1755), 292–99.

9  Who were these colonial men: Gordon Wood, *Revolutionary Characters: What Made the Founders Different* (Penguin Press, 2006), 25.

10  "rude, mis-shapen piles": Thomas Jefferson, "Notes on the State of Virginia," in *Thomas Jefferson: Writings* (Library of America, 1984), 276, 278.

10  Their academic diet: Gummere, *The American Colonial Mind and the Classical Tradition*, 55.

11  "a society built on and sustained by violence": Annette Gordon-Reed, *The Hemingses of Monticello: An American Family* (W. W. Norton, 2008), 54.

11  cutting off that person's toes: Edmund Morgan, *American Slavery, American Freedom: The Ordeal of Colonial Virginia* (W. W. Norton, 1975), 313.

11  "I have cured many a Negro": Wiencek, *An Imperfect God*, 26.

11  those who were flogged sometimes then "pickled": Wiencek, *An Imperfect God*, 47; see also "Testimony of Mr. Lemeul Sapington, A Native of Maryland," in *American Slavery As It Is: Testimony of a Thousand Witnesses* (Philadelphia: American Anti-Slavery Society, 1839), 49.

11  burned a woman at the stake: Irving Brant, *James Madison: The Virginia Revolutionist* (Bobbs-Merrill Company, 1941), 27, 49.

11  murdered in 1732 with poison: Douglas Chambers, *Murder at Montpelier: Igbo Africans in Virginia* (University Press of Mississippi, 2005), 8.

11  "famous false teeth": Wiencek, *An Imperfect God*, 112.

11  "A small boy being horsewhipped by a visitor": Henry Wiencek, *Master of the Mountain: Thomas Jefferson and His Slaves* (Farrar, Straus and Giroux, 2012), 108, 119. Wiencek has detailed how this letter was deliberately misrepresented and even suppressed by historians until 2005, in "The Dark Side of Thomas Jefferson," *Smithsonian*, October 2012. For the letter, see "To Thomas Jefferson from Martha Jefferson Randolph and Thomas Mann Randolph, 31 January 1801" (especially the postscript), *FO*.

12  "Roman slavery was a nonracist and fluid system": Stefan Goodwin, *Africa in Europe: Volume One, Antiquity into the Age of Global Expansion* (Lexington Books, 2009), 41. See also David Wiesen, "The Contribution of Antiquity to American Racial Thought," in *Classical Traditions in Early America*, ed. John Eadie (Center for the Coordination of Ancient and Modern Studies, University of Michigan, 1976), 195; see also Gordon-Reed, *The Hemingses of Monticello*, 45.

12  it was "not as harsh and exploitative as its modern analogues": Bederman, *The Classical Foundations of the American Constitution*, 103.

12  slaves had the right to petition the emperor for help: Susan Ford Wiltshire, *Greece, Rome, and the Bill of Rights* (University of Oklahoma Press, 1992), 125, 129.

12  "beings of an inferior order": *Dred Scott v. John F.A. Sandford*, 60 U.S. 393 (1857), Legal Information Institute, Cornell Law School.

*Chapter 2:* Washington Studies How to Rise in Colonial Society

13  The best example of this is George Washington: This paraphrases a comment made by Peter Onuf in a conversation with the author on 10 June 2019, Winter Harbor, Maine.

13  "I am conscious of a defective education": "From George Washington to David Humphreys, 25 July 1785," *FO*.

13  Washington "was So ignorant, that he had never read any Thing": "From John Adams to Benjamin Rush, 22 April 1812," *FO*.

14  that "Washington was not a Schollar is certain": "From John Adams to Benjamin Rush, September 1807," *FO*.

14  "His mind was great and powerful": "Thomas Jefferson to Walter Jones, 2 January 1814," *FO*.

14  Washington had a "propensity for rashness": Adrienne Harrison, *A Powerful Mind: The Self-Education of George Washington* (Potomac Books, 2015), 44.

15  "Perhaps the strongest feature in his character was prudence": These two quotations are also from the document cited above: "Thomas Jefferson to Walter Jones, 2 January 1814," *FO*.

16  "If the present work succeeds in humanizing Washington": Paul Leicester Ford, *The True George Washington* (J. B. Lippincott Company, 1897), 6.

16  "George Washington as a Human Being": Howard Swiggett, *The Great Man: George Washington as a Human Being* (Doubleday & Co., 1953).

16  "a fallible human being": James Thomas Flexner, *Washington: The Indispensable Man* (Little, Brown and Company, 1974), xvi.

16  "The goal of the present biography": Ron Chernow, *Washington: A Life* (Penguin Press, 2010), xx.

17  "born with his clothes on": Nathaniel Hawthorne, *The French and Italian Notebooks, Vol. 1* (Houghton Mifflin, 1888), 293.

17  he "allowed no one to be familiar with him": James Parton, *Life of Thomas Jefferson* (James R. Osgood, 1874), 369. To be precise about the origin of this anecdote, Parton states that "the story was related by Hamilton to Mr. John Fine of Ogdensburgh, who gave it [his written account] to Mr. Van Buren."

17  In the America of 1775: Katherine Harper, "Cato, Roman Stoicism, and the American 'Revolution'" (PhD dissertation, University of Sydney, Australia, 2014), 28–29.

17  the typical young white boy got at best a year or two of schooling: Harry Good and James Teller, *A History of American Education* (Macmillan, 1973), 31.

18  There was a major regional difference here: This summarizes parts of Sheldon Cohen, *A History of Colonial Education, 1607–1776* (John Wiley & Sons, 1974).

18  Washington never attended college: James Thomas Flexner, *George Washington: The Forge of Experience, 1732–1775* (Little, Brown and Company, 1965), 31.

18   "conspicuous by his absence": Richard Gummere, *The American Colonial Mind and the Classical Tradition* (Harvard University Press, 1963), 62.

18   among the decorations he ordered from London was a small bust of Caesar: "Enclosure: Invoice to Robert Cary & Company, 20 September 1759," Washington papers, *FO*.

18   "Homer, Virgil, Horace, Cicero": "Invoice from Robert Cary & Company, 15 March 1760," Washington Papers, *FO*.

18   eighteenth-century audiences expected lengthy declamations: Frederic Litto, "Addison's Cato in the Colonies," *William and Mary Quarterly* 23, no. 3 (July 1966), 432, 426.

19   Cato was the very embodiment of virtue: See Nathaniel Wolloch, "Cato the Younger in the Age of Enlightenment," *Modern Philology* 106, no. 1 (August 2008).

19   "Think Cato sees thee": "Poor Richard, 1741," Franklin Papers, *FO*.

19   He would know about the orator from the play: Meyer Reinhold, *Classica Americana: The Greek and Roman Heritage in the United States* (Wayne State University Press, 1984), 250.

19   "It is said of Cato": Plutarch, *The Lives of the Noble Romans and Grecians (The Dryden Translation)* (Encyclopaedia Britannica, 1952), 620.

19   "He undertook the service of the state": Plutarch, *Lives of the Noble Romans and Grecians*, 627.

20   "Caesar at this time had not done much": Anthony Trollope, *The Life of Cicero, Vol. 1* (Harper & Brothers, 1881), 216.

20   attainment of public virtue was the highest goal: Richard Jenkyns, "The Legacy of Rome" in *The Legacy of Rome: A New Appraisal*, ed. Richard Jenkyns (Oxford University Press, 1992), 22.

20   eighteenth-century "virtue" was essentially male: I wish this had occurred to me, but it did not. I saw it on p. 36 of Ann Fairfax Withington, *Toward a More Perfect Union: Virtue and the Formation of American Republics* (Oxford University Press, 1991).

21   "virtue" as "the love of the laws and of our country": Baron de Montesquieu, *The Spirit of Laws, Vol. 1* (J. Nourse and P. Vaillant, 1766), 48.

21   he would pursue "Honor and Reputation": "From George Washington to Robert Dinwiddie, 22 April 1756," *FO*.

21   "Justifying by virtue is a way of escaping hereditary control": Gordon Wood in conversation with author, 18 December 2017.

21   He read all his life: Harrison, *A Powerful Mind*, 81.

22   he owned a total of 2,315 acres: Chernow, *Washington*, 23.

23   "No frontiersman understood the Indians better": Douglas Southall Freeman, *George Washington: A Biography, Vol. 1, Young Washington* (Scribner's, 1948), 283.

24   "The Wine": "Journey to the French Commandant: Narrative," Washington Papers, *FO*.

25   "The Horses grew less able to travel": Ibid.

26   "The Cold was so extream severe": Ibid.

26   "As for the summons you send me to retire": Quoted in Freeman, *Washington, Vol. 1*, 325.

27   "The shabby and ragged appearance the French common Soldiers make": "From George Washington to Robert Dinwiddie, 7 March 1754," *FO*.

27   the First Peoples were inclined to support the French: David Preston, *Braddock's Defeat: The Battle of the Monongahela and the Road to Revolution* (Oxford University Press, 2015), 15.

28   "Nothing prevents their throwing down their commissions": "From George Washington to Robert Dinwiddie, 18 May 1754," *FO*.

29   "The *Indians* scalped the dead": "Expedition to the Ohio, 1754: Narrative," Washington Papers, *FO*.

29   "I heard Bulletts whistle": "From George Washington to John Augustine Washington, 31 May 1754," *FO*.

29   "He would not say so, if he had been used to hear many": Quoted in editor's note in *George Washington: Writings* (Library of America, 1997), 1096.

30   Louis Coulon de Villiers: "Coulon de Villiers, Louis," in *Dictionary of Canadian Biography, Vol. 3* (University of Toronto/Université Laval, 2003), accessed online.

31   "This was too degrading for G.W. to submit to": "Remarks, 1787–1788" [on David Humphreys' Biography of Washington, about 1787], *FO*.

31   "generous & disinterested": Ibid.

31   "he had too much self-confidence": Benjamin Franklin, *Benjamin Franklin: Autobiography, Poor Richard and Later Writings* (Library of America, 1997), 700–701.

32   "the greatest part [were] Virginians": Edward Braddock, "To Robert Napier," in *Military Affairs in North America, 1748–1765: Selected Documents from the Cumberland Papers in Windsor Castle*, ed. Stanley M. Pargellis (D. Appleton-Century Company, 1936), 84.

32   shot and scalped: Lee McCardell, *Ill-Starred General: Braddock of the Coldstream Guards* (University of Pittsburgh Press, 1958), 230.

32   "Shoot um down all one pigeon": Ibid., 243.

32   First, make a loud noise: Ben Gustafson, "Tips for Hunting Pigeons. Seriously," *North American Hunter*, July 2015, accessed online.

33   the largest First Peoples force ever assembled on behalf of the French: Preston, *Braddock's Defeat*, 149–50. From this paragraph on, my account of the battle relies heavily on Preston's fine book.

33    "As soon as the Enemys Indians perceiv'd our Grenadiers": Harry Gordon, "Gordon's Journal: Journal of Proceedings from Willes's Creek to the Mononga- hela," in *Military Affairs in North America*, ed. Pargellis, 106.

34    "Nothing afterwards was to Be Seen Amongst the Men But Confusion & Panick": Ibid.

34    "Experienced [tribal] war captains led their men": Preston, *Braddock's De- feat*, 235.

34    "broke and run as Sheep before Hounds": "From George Washington to Robert Dinwiddie, 18 July 1755," *FO*.

34    "the whole Body gave way": Gordon, "Gordon's Journal," 107–108.

35    about two-thirds were killed or wounded: Preston, *Braddock's Defeat*, 265.

35    "The shocking Scenes which presented themselves": "Remarks, 1787–1788" [on David Humphreys's Biography of Washington, about 1787], *FO*.

36    Their force had lost about twenty-five dead: Preston, *Braddock's Defeat*, 264.

36    "I am still in a weak and Feeble condn": "From George Washington to Mary Ball Washington, 18 July 1755," *FO*.

36    "it will meet with unbelief and indignation": "From George Washington to Robert Jackson, 2 August 1755," *FO*.

36    "I was employ'd to go a journey in the Winter": "George Washington to Augustine Washington, 2 August 1755," *FO*.

37    "Honor and Reputation in the Service": "From George Washington to Rob- ert Dinwiddie, 22 April 1756," *FO*.

37    "We want nothing but Commissions from His Majesty": "From George Washington to Robert Dinwiddie, 10 March 1757," *FO*.

37    "I see the growing Insolence of the Soldiers": "From George Washington to Robert Dinwiddie, 11–14 October 1755," *FO*.

37    "I am determined, if I can be justified in the proceeding, to hang two or three on it, as an example to others": "From George Washington to John Stanwix, 15 July 1757," *FO*.

37    ordering the executions of two deserters: "General Court-Martial, 25–26 July 1757," Washington Papers, *FO*. Description of Edwards is from footnote two on this document.

37    "They were proper objects to suffer": "From George Washington to Robert Dinwiddie, 3 August 1757," *FO*.

38    "of all sources of wealth, farming is the best": Cicero, "On Moral Duties," in *The Basic Works of Cicero*, ed. Moses Hadas (Modern Library, 1951), 56.

39    "the policy of the French is so subtle, that not a friendly Indian will we have on the continent": "George Washington to Adam Stephen, 23 October 1756," *FO*.

39   "We cannot suppose the French, who have their Scouts constantly out, can be so difficient in point of Intelligence": "From George Washington to Henry Bouquet, 2 August 1758," *FO*.

40   "Discipline is the soul of an army": "Instructions to Company Captains, 29 July 1757," Washington Papers, *FO*.

40   Washington "always understood power and how to use it": Gordon Wood, *Empire of Liberty: A History of the Early Republic, 1789–1815* (Oxford University Press, 2009), 86.

### Chapter 3: John Adams Aims to Become an American Cicero

42   "I did not love my Books half so well as my fowling-piece": "From John Adams to John Adams, 2 January 1820," Adams Papers, *FO*.

42   "I don't like my schoolmaster": John Adams, "From the Autobiography," in *John Adams: Revolutionary Writings, 1755–1775*, ed. Gordon Wood (Library of America, 2011), 617–618.

43   the first American college, and the one most connected to English traditions: George Marsden, *The Soul of the American University: From Protestant Establishment to Established Nonbelief* (Oxford University Press, 1994), 35. See also David Hackett Fischer, *Albion's Seed: Four British Folkways in America* (Oxford University Press, 1989), 39–40.

43   students there and at Yale were still ranked by their social standing: George Trevelyan, *American Revolution, Vol. 3* (Longmans, Green, 1915), 283. See also Gordon Wood, *The Radicalism of the American Revolution* (Vintage Books, 1993), 21.

43   This arrangement was manifested in writing: John Lord Taylor, *A Memoir of His Honor Samuel Phillips, LL.D.*(Congregational Publishing Society, 1856) 347. See also Henry Barnard, ed., *The American Journal of Education* 16 (March 1859), 67; and Franklin Bowditch Dexter, "On Some Social Distinctions at Harvard and Yale Before the Revolution," *Proceedings of the American Antiquarian Society* 9 (October 1893–October 1894), 55–56.

43   John Adams' class rank probably had more to do with the status of the family of his mother: Charles Francis Adams, "Life of John Adams," in *The Works of John Adams, Vol. 1* (Little, Brown and Company 1856), 14.

43   Rank determined, among other things, where one sat in the Commons for meals: Arthur Stanwood Pier, *The Story of Harvard* (Little, Brown and Company 1913), 75, 69. Reference to brewery, to the Saturday meal, and part of the breakfast information is from Samuel Eliot Morison, *Three Centuries of Harvard* (Harvard University Press, 1937), 116–17.

44   he grew accustomed to being greeted in the yard with "Contemptuous Noise & Hallowing": William Bentinck-Smith, ed., *The Harvard Book: Selections from Three Centuries* (Harvard University Press, 1982), 48–50.

44    "I soon perceived a growing Curiosity": "[Harvard College, 1751–1755], [from the Autobiography of John Adams]," *FO*.

44    "I have read him, for almost 70 years and seeme to have him almost by heart": "From John Adams to Elihu Marshall, 7 March 1820," *FO*.

45    "this distinction is entirely owing to Ciceros Letters and Orations": "From John Adams to Benjamin Rush, 4 December 1805," *FO*.

45    the son of a rustic "nobody": Anthony Trollope, *The Life of Cicero, Vol. 1* (Harper & Brothers, Franklin Square, 1881), 219.

45    his "quickness and readiness in learning": Plutarch, "Cicero," in *The Lives of the Noble Romans and Grecians (The Dryden Translation)* (Encyclopaedia Britannica, 1952), 704.

45    "He was always excessively pleased with his own praise": Ibid., 706.

46    Most young men of privilege were introduced to Cicero's works in secondary school: Robert Middlekauff, "A Persistent Tradition: The Classical Curriculum in Eighteenth-Century New England," *William and Mary Quarterly* 18, no. 1 (January 1961), 63.

46    "Catiline has plotted a dreadful and entire subversion of the Roman state": Plutarch, "Cicero," 628.

46    "How far wilt thou, O Catiline! abuse our patience": *The Orations of Marcus Tullius Cicero*, trans. William Guthrie (T. Waller, 1758), 2.

46    "men who are meditating the destruction of us all": Moses Hadas, ed., *The Basic Works of Cicero* (Modern Library, 1951), 265.

46    "You cannot possibly remain in our society any longer": Ibid., 266.

47    "Let the disloyal then withdraw": Ibid., 277.

47    he attacked Cicero's relatively low birth: Sallust, *Catiline's War, The Jugurthine War, Histories*, trans. A. J. Woodman (Penguin Books, 2007), 22.

47    "He is gone, he is vanished": *The Orations of Marcus Tullius Cicero*, trans. Guthrie, 39, 50.

47    "There is not any longer room for lenity": *The Orations of Marcus Tullius Cicero*, trans. C. D. Yonge (George Bell, 1877), 294.

47    "For on the one side are fighting modesty, on the other wantonness": Ibid., 301.

48    "Jupiter resisted them": Ibid., 313.

48    "I shall fall with a contented and prepared mind": Ibid., 319.

49    "You have a Consul, who, without Hesitation, will Obey your orders": *The Orations of Marcus Tullius Cicero*, trans. Guthrie, 121.

49    "Do you, then, still hesitate and doubt what to do with the enemies caught inside the walls?": Sallust, *Catiline's War*, 34–39.

49  "The fiery Soul abhor'd in Catiline": Alexander Pope, *Essay on Man* (William Bradford, 1747), 23.

50  Voltaire played the role of Cicero: Peter Gay, *The Enlightenment: An Interpretation: The Rise of Modern Paganism* (Alfred A. Knopf, 1966), 106.

50  Salieri wrote an opera about the Catiline war: Andrew Dyck, ed., *Cicero: Catilinarians* (Cambridge University Press, 2008), 14–15.

50  Cicero and Adams: My writing and conclusions in this section of this book were influenced by the discussion of Cicero in Peter Shaw's fine book *The Character of John Adams* (University of North Carolina Press, 1976), which should be better known.

50  "The Sweetness and Grandeur of his sounds": "Thursday [21 December 1758]," "From the Diary of John Adams," *FO*.

50  "the one man, above all others, who made the Romans feel how great a charm eloquence lends to what is good": Plutarch, "Cicero," 709, 713.

51  "but his using it to excess offended many": Ibid., 706, 713.

51  "[I have] the most ardent desire of being immediately distinguished in your glorious annals": Cicero, "To Lucius Lucceius," *Epistles, Elegant, Familiar & Instructive . . .* (Rivingtons, Longman, Law, Dodsley, etc., 1791), 71.

51  "Bob Paine is conceited": "[December 1758] [from the Diary of John Adams]," Adams papers, *FO*.

51  "Vanity I am sensible, is my cardinal Vice": "[May 1756] [from the Diary of John Adams]," *FO*.

52  "His genius was superb, but his soul was often common": Baron de Montesquieu, *Considerations on the Causes of the Greatness of the Romans and Their Decline* (Hackett Publishing, 1965), 166.

52  "I read it over and over": "1771. Wednesday June 5th. [from the Diary of John Adams]," Adams Papers, *FO*.

52  *The Preceptor* was a touchstone for his generation: Kevin Hayes, *George Washington: A Life in Books* (Oxford University Press, 2017), 126.

52  He began his life as a footman: Ian Crowe, *Patriotism and the Public Spirit: Edmund Burke and the Role of the Critics in Mid-Eighteenth-Century Britain* (Stanford University Press, 2012), 26.

52  To create his textbook, Dodsley drew up a twelve-part outline: Harry Solomon, *The Rise of Robert Dodsley: Creating the New Age of Print* (Southern Illinois University Press, 1996), 1–2, 123–125, 129; see also Austin Dobson, "At 'Tully's Head,'" *Scribner's Magazine* 15 (1894), 516–24.

53  "They never consider them as the Authors of Misery to thousands": Robert Dodsley, *The Preceptor: Containing a General Course of Education, Vol. 1*, 5th ed. (Dodsley, 1769), 269. First published in 1748.

53 "Could Rome have been saved from Slavery": Ibid., 309, 348–49.

54 "As the People are the Fountain of Power and Authority": Ibid., *Vol. 2*, 331.

54 Other eighteenth-century London bookstores boasted similarly classical names: Jacob Larwood and John Camden Hotten, *The History of Signboards: From the Earliest Times to the Present Day* (Chatto & Windus, 1875), 65.

55 a "fundamental irrelevance of religious revelation to the great issues of public life": Darren Staloff, *Hamilton, Adams, Jefferson: The Politics of Enlightenment and the American Founding* (Hill & Wang, 2005), 9.

55 from 1775 to 1815, religion had less influence in American life than it did in any later such forty-year period: Howard Mumford Jones, *O Strange New World: American Culture: The Formative Years* (Viking, 1964),341.

55 It is probably a mistake in emphasis to focus on the "ideas of the Enlightenment": See, for example, pp. 7 and 10, Bernard Bailyn, "The Central Themes of the American Revolution: An Interpretation," in *Essays on the American Revolution*, eds. Stephen Kurtz and James Hutson (W. W. Norton, 1973). See also Bernard Bailyn, *Faces of the Revolution: Personalities & Themes in the Struggle for Independence* (Vintage Books, 1992), 186.

55 "Only rarely did they develop ideas undreamed of in earlier generations": Robert Darnton, *George Washington's False Teeth: An Unconventional Guide to the Eighteenth Century* (W. W. Norton, 2003), 4.

55 the Enlightenment was more a process than a result: Robert Ferguson, "What Is Enlightenment?" in *The Cambridge History of American Literature, Vol. 1, 1590–1820* (Cambridge University Press, 1994), 371.

55 "true reform in ways of thinking": Quoted in Paul Giles, "Enlightenment Historiography and Cultural Civil Wars," in *The Atlantic Enlightenment*, eds. Susan Manning and Francis Cogliano (Ashgate, 2008), 19. See also Immanuel Kant, "What Is Enlightenment?" *Modern History Sourcebook*, accessed online.

55 "To be enlightened was to be filled with hope": Caroline Winterer, *American Enlightenments: Pursuing Happiness in the Age of Reason* (Yale University Press, 2016), 1.

55 "superstition, intolerance, tyranny": Carl Becker, *The Heavenly City of the Eighteenth-Century Philosophers* (Yale University Press, 1961), 105.

56 "What was most important and really new about the Age of Reason": William H. Goetzmann, *Beyond the Revolution: A History of American Thought from Paine to Pragmatism* (Basic Books, 2009), 28–29.

56 Montesquieu invented sociology in *The Spirit of Laws*: Peter Gay, *The Enlightenment: An Interpretation, Vol. 2: The Science of Freedom* (Alfred A. Knopf, 1969), 319.

56 Xenophon's *Oeconomicus*: Paul MacKendrick, "This Rich Source of Delight: The Classics and the Founding Fathers," *The Classical Journal* 72, no. 2 (December 1976–January 1977), 105.

57 "I liked them; they seemed rational": Quoted in William Tudor, *The Life of James Otis* (Wells and Lilly, 1823), 144–45.

57 "It is right that the people confer the political authority upon whomsoever they will": George Buchanan, *De Jure Regni Apud Scotos ("The Powers of the Crown in Scotland")*, trans. Charles Finn Arrowood (University of Texas Press, 1949), 52.

57 "Of pow'r THE PEOPLE are the source": Quoted in Michael Durey, *Transatlantic Radicals and the Early American Republic* (University Press of Kansas, 1997), 77.

58 the people "have the power to governe the Church": Roger Williams, *The Bloody Tenent* (no publisher listed, 1644), 249–50.

58 "no civil rules are to be obeyed": Jonathan Mayhew, "A discourse concerning the unlimited submission and non-resistance to the high powers, 1750," Founding.com.

58 "I read it, till the Substance of it was incorporated into my Nature": "John Adams to Thomas Jefferson, 18 July 1818," FO.

59 he became the teacher at the Center School: Elizabeth Porter Gould, *John Adams and Daniel Webster as Schoolmasters* (Palmer Company, 1903), 12–15.

59 He was lonely in Worcester: Page Smith, *John Adams, Vol. 1: 1735–1784* (Doubleday & McClure, 1962), 24.

59 "I have no Books, no Time, no Friends": "[April 1756], [from the Diary of John Adams]," Adams Papers, FO.

59 he had spent "a Clowdy morning" reading Charles Rollin's *Method of Teaching*: "March 8, 1754," Adams Papers, FO.

59 "a principal medium": William Gribbin, "Rollin's Histories and American Republicanism," *William and Mary Quarterly* 29, no. 4 (1972), 612.

60 "From Rollins I Suspect, Washington drew his Wisdom": "From John Adams to Benjamin Rush, September 1807," FO.

60 "I am very sick of your Gibbons's, Robertsons, Rollins the best of them": "To Thomas Jefferson from Ezra Stiles, 27 August 1790," FO.

60 Adams found Rollin's books "worth their weight in gold": "[March 1754], Adams diary," Adams Papers, FO.

60 "the Mischievous Tricks": "[10 June 1760], [from the Diary of John Adams]," FO.

60 a "meer Curiosity": "October 1758, From the Diary of John Adams," FO.

61 "Now I feel the Dissadvantages of Putnams Insociability": "Monday. December 18th. 1758, [from the Diary of John Adams]," Adams Papers, FO.

61 "Let no trifling Diversion or amuzement or Company decoy you from your Books": "Tuesday [January 1759], [from the Diary of John Adams]," FO.

61 "I know much less than I do of the Roman law": "[March 1759] [from the Diary of John Adams]," Adams Papers, FO.

61   the ancients looming much larger than did modern writers: Zoltan Haraszti, "John Adams Among his Books," *More Books: Bulletin of the Boston Public Library* 1 (1926), 6, 5.

62   *"Adams* flourishd in the second Century": "To John Adams from Jonathan Sewall, 13 February 1760," *FO*.

62   Gordon Wood suspects: Note from Gordon Wood to the author, 22 April 2019.

62   Adams "always wrote for the public as if he had a toga on": Jones, *O Strange New World*, 259.

62   Mayhew as "a clergyman equalled by a very few": John Adams, "To the Inhabitants of the Colony of Massachusetts-Bay, 6 February 1775," *FO*.

62   "An Awakening and a Revival of American Principles and Feelings": "From John Adams to Hezekiah Niles, 13 February 1818," *FO*.

63   "Cicero was a man thoroughly human": Trollope, *The Life of Cicero*, 33, 36.

### *Chapter 4:* Jefferson Blooms at William & Mary

65   "America's first great Romantic artist": Darren Staloff, *Hamilton, Adams, Jefferson: The Politics of Enlightenment and the American Founding* (Hill & Wang, 2005), 248.

65   "I am but a son of nature": "From Thomas Jefferson to Maria Cosway, 24 April 1788," *FO*. I first noticed this sentence when it was quoted by E. M. Halliday on p. 102 of his book, *Understanding Thomas Jefferson* (Harper Perennial, 2002).

65   "I like the dreams of the future better than the history of the past": "To John Adams from Thomas Jefferson, 1 August 1816," *FO*.

66   Jefferson "was more partial to the Greek than the Roman literature": Henry Randall, *The Life of Thomas Jefferson, Vol. 1* (Derby & Jackson, 1858), 27.

66   "begg'd me to learn him lattin": *The Journal and Letters of Philip Vickers Fithian, 1773–1774: A Plantation Tutor of the Old Dominion*, ed. Hunter Dickinson Farish (Colonial Williamsburg, 1965), 77.

67   dancing was treated as just as essential as reading books: For more on this value system, see David Tyack, *Turning Points in American Education* (Blaisdell Publishing, 1967), 28.

67   "Mr Douglas a clergyman from Scotland": Both quotations from "Thomas Jefferson: Autobiography, 6 Jan.–29 July 1821," *FO*.

67   such knowledge would enable "a Virginia gentleman": Quoted in Tyack, *Turning Points in American Education*, 37.

68   "the first master" of style: "Thomas Jefferson to John Adams, 5 July 1814," *FO*.

68   "Livy, Tacitus, Sallust, & most assuredly not in Cicero": "Thomas Jefferson to John Wayles Eppes, 17 January 1810", *FO*.

68 Colleges in the colonial era could be unruly: For background on Rowe, see Frederick Lewis Weis, *The Colonial Clergy of Virginia, North Carolina and South Carolina* (Clearfield, 1955), 44. For the previous faculty dismissal and for the issue of compensation, see Kevin J. Hayes, *The Road to Monticello: The Life and Mind of Thomas Jefferson* (Oxford University Press, 2008), 50. For the quotation on "scandalous and malicious," see Murray Rothbard, *Conceived in Liberty* (Ludwig von Mises Institute, 2011), 652.

68 a "castoff, a misfit, a drunk and a brawler": John K. Nelson, *A Blessed Company: Parishes, Parsons and Parishioners in Anglican Virginia, 1690–1776* (University of North Carolina Press, 2001), 90–91.

68 "remove himself and his effects at once from the college": Lyon G. Tyler, *The College of William and Mary in Virginia: Its History and Work, 1693–1907* (Whittet & Shepperson, 1907), 44. See also J. E. Morpugo, *Their Majesties' Royall Colledge: William and Mary in the Seventeenth and Eighteenth Centuries* (College of William & Mary, 1976), 124–25.

69 Conditions at the college at this time were, writes one historian, "pathetically absurd": Robert Polk Thomson, "The Reform of the College of William and Mary, 1763–1780," *Proceedings of the American Philosophical Society* 115, no. 3 (1971), 190.

69 Jefferson was taught almost exclusively by William Small: Dumas Malone, *Jefferson and His Time, Vol. 1: Jefferson the Virginian* (Little, Brown and Company 1948), 52–53.

69 "[Small] was appointed to fill it per interim": Thomas Jefferson, "The Autobiography," in *Jefferson* (Library of America, 1984), 4.

69 "the basic influence . . . of Hutcheson": Ralph Ketcham, *Presidents Above Party: The First American Presidency, 1789–1829* (University of North Carolina Press, 1984), 101.

70 This new church placed a strong emphasis on literacy: J.E.G. De Montmorency, *State Intervention in English Education: A Short History from the Earliest Times down to 1833* (Cambridge University Press, 1902), 116–17.

70 By 1750, according to some estimates, 75 percent of Scots could read: Arthur Herman, *How the Scots Invented the Modern World* (Three Rivers Press, 2001), 23.

70 Scotland's Enlightenment was university-based: Douglas Sloan, *The Scottish Enlightenment and the American College Ideal* (Teachers College Press, 1971), 14–15.

70 "a century of educational sleep": Montmorency, *State Intervention in English Education,* 107.

70 "I spent fourteen months" at Oxford: Edward Gibbon, *Memoirs of Edward Gibbon, Esq.* (Houghton, Mifflin, & Co., 1882), 79.

70 "given up altogether even the pretence of teaching": Adam Smith, *An Inquiry Into the Nature and Causes of the Wealth of Nations* (James Decker, 1801), 62.

70    "degenerated to a large extent": Howard Clive Barnard, *A Short History of English Education from 1760 to 1944* (University of London Press, 1947), 28.

70    Scottish institutions led the English-speaking world in having their faculty members specialize in one or two subjects: Frederick Rudolph, *Curriculum: A History of the American Undergraduate Course of Study Since 1636* (Jossey-Bass, 1981), 44.

71    work by Isaac Newton of Cambridge in mathematics and physics was taught in the Scottish universities: David Daiches, "The Scottish Enlightenment," in eds. Jean Jones, David Daiches, and Peter Jones, *A Hotbed of Genius: The Scottish Enlightenment 1730–1790*, 5. See also Winifred Bryan Horner, *Nineteenth-Century Scottish Rhetoric: The American Connection* (Southern Illinois University Press, 1993), 5.

71    "Edinburgh is a hot-bed of genius": Tobias Smollett, *The Expedition of Humphry Clinker, Vol. III* (W. Johnston, 1772), 4–5.

71    Scottish universities were relatively inexpensive: Herman, *How the Scots Invented the Modern World*, 26.

71    "Any boy who could do the work was welcome": Sloan, *The Scottish Enlightenment and the American College Ideal*, 15.

71    enrolled at Edinburgh just by walking eighty miles to the city and presenting himself: Horner, *Nineteenth-Century Scottish Rhetoric*, 4.

71    Scottish universities were remarkably cosmopolitan: Hilde de Ridder-Symgens, "Mobility," in Walter Ruegg, ed., *A History of the University in Europe, Vol. II: Universities in Early Modern Europe, 1500–1800* (Cambridge University Press, 1996), 438. See also R. M. Ogilvie, *Latin and Greek: A History of the Influence of the Classics on English Life from 1600 to 1918* (Routledge & Kegan Paul, 1964), xi.

71    French jurisprudence had its roots in ancient Rome: This paragraph relies heavily on the chapter on "Irnerius and the Civil Law Revival," in Hastings Rashdall, *The Universities of Europe in the Middle Ages, Vol. 1: Salerno, Bologna, Paris* (Clarendon, 1895). See also Robert Feenstra, "Law," in Richard Jenkyns, ed., *The Legacy of Rome: A New Appraisal* (Oxford University Press, 1992).

72    "Our law is grafted on that of Old Rome": Herman, *How the Scots Invented the Modern World*, 86–89. See also Ian Simpson Ross, *Lord Kames and the Scotland of His Day* (Clarendon Press, 1972), 22.

72    Jefferson would read extensively in Kames: Douglas Wilson, "Jefferson's Early Notebooks," *William and Mary Quarterly* 42, no. 5 (1985), 450.

72    "Virginia may rather be called a Scots than an English plantation": Daniel Defoe, *A Tour Through the Whole Island of Great Britain, Volume IV*, 7th ed. (J. and F. Rivington; Hawes, Clarke and Collins; J. Buckland; W. and J. Richardson, etc., 1769), 142, 144–45.

72    "Scotland's first global enterprise": T. M. Devine, *To the Ends of the Earth: Scotland's Global Diaspora, 1750–1810* (Smithsonian Books, 2011), 38.

72    Glasgow soon became a major trader in the American tobacco crop: Alan Karras, *Sojourners in the Sun: Scottish Migrants in Jamaica and the Chesapeake, 1740–1800* (Cornell University Press, 1992), 85. See also Herman, *How the Scots Invented the Modern World*, 162.

73    The Scottish merchants reexported almost all this tobacco: T. M. Devine, *The Tobacco Lords: A Study of the Tobacco Merchants of Glasgow and Their Trading Activities, c. 1740–90* (John Donald, 1975), 64–65.

73    shipping was faster to America by the route around northern Ireland to Scotland: Defoe, *A Tour Through the Whole Island of Great Britain,* 145.

73    Operating costs were lower in Glasgow than in London: Jacob Price, "Glasgow, the Tobacco Trade, and the Scottish Customs, 1707–1730: Some Commercial, Administrative and Political Implications of the Union," *The Scottish Historical Review* 63, no. 175 (April 1984), 1. See also T. C. Barker, "Smuggling in the Eighteenth Century: The Evidence of the Scottish Tobacco Trade," *The Virginia Magazine of History and Biography* 62, no. 4 (October 1954).

73    The Scots also modernized the business itself, buying whole shiploads in Virginia: Samuel Rosenblatt, "The Significance of Credit in the Tobacco Consignment Trade: A Study of John Norton and Sons, 1768–1775," *William and Mary Quarterly* 19, no. 3 (July 1962), 388. See also Devine, *The Tobacco Lords,* 68; Karras, *Sojourners in the Sun,* 84; and Henry Hamilton, *An Economic History of Scotland in the Eighteenth Century* (Clarendon Press, 1963), 259.

73    the Scots streamlined their banking system: Daiches, "The Scottish Enlightenment," in *A Hotbed of Genius,* 34.

73    a geological scale of time: Jean Jones, "James Hutton," in *A Hotbed of Genius,* 116.

73    "we find no vestige of a beginning,—no prospect of an end": James Hutton, "Theory of the Earth," *Transactions of the Royal Society of Edinburgh* 1, pt. II (1788), 304.

74    Hutton was the first "to perceive that the age of the Earth was so great": Gordon Davies, *The Earth in Decay: A History of British Geomorphology* (American Elsevier Publishing Company, 1969), 181.

74    "a bag of gravel is a history to me": George Bruce and Paul Scott, eds., *A Scottish Postbag: Eight Centuries of Scottish Letters* (The Saltire Society, 2002), 56.

74    big ideas provoke paradigm shifts: Thomas M. Allen, *A Republic in Time: Temporality and Social Imagination in Nineteenth-Century America* (University of North Carolina Press, 2008), 153–54.

74    Hutton's thinking about the age of the world: James Buchan, *Capital of the Mind: How Edinburgh Changed the World* (Murray Cards Ltd., 2003), 294.

74    Charles Darwin in turn: Stephen Jay Gould, *Time's Arrow, Time's Cycle: Myth and Metaphor in the Discovery of Geologic Time* (Harvard University Press, 1987), 7.

75  "Jefferson had a special interest in timepieces": Silvio Bedini, "Thomas Jefferson, Clock Designer," *Proceedings of the American Philosophical Society* 108, no. 3 (1964), 163.

75  control of time had moved from the church tower to inside the house: Hannah Spahn, *Thomas Jefferson, Time and History* (University of Virginia Press, 2011), 21, 31–32, 47. See also Mark Smith, *Mastered by the Clock: Time, Slavery and Freedom in the American South* (University of North Carolina Press, 1997).

75  Jefferson frequently represented Glasgow merchants: Jacob Price, "The Rise of Glasgow in the Chesapeake Tobacco Trade, 1707–1775," *William and Mary Quarterly* 11, no. 2 (1954): 179–99.

75  the country's infant mortality rates dropped during the eighteenth century: For the decline in Scottish infant mortality in the eighteenth century, see Devine, *To the Ends of the Earth*, 5.

75  twenty-six ships sailed every year: Karras, *Sojourners in the Sun,* 32.

75  That region received more graduates from Scottish institutions than from Oxford and Cambridge: James McLachlan, "Education," in *Scotland and the Americas, 1600 to 1800* (John Carter Brown Library, 1995), 66–67, 69.

75  "the custom heretofore to have all their Tutors, and Schoolmasters from Scotland": *The Journal and Letters of Philip Vickers Fithian, 1773–1774,* ed. Farish, 29.

76  "the Scots were the educators of eighteenth-century America": George Marsden, *The Soul of the American University: From Protestant Establishment to Established Nonbelief* (Oxford University Press, 1994), 59.

76  The Foulis brothers: John Ferguson, *The Brothers Foulis and Early Glasgow Printing* (Dryden Press, 1889), 11.

76  "the perfection of accuracy": "Thomas Jefferson to Wells & Lilly, 1 April 1818," *FO.*

76  the Scottish approach influenced late colonial America: Ned Landsman, *From Colonials to Provincials: American Thoughts and Culture, 1680–1760* (Cornell University Press, 1997), 24, 35.

76  "a practice unknown at contemporary Cambridge and Oxford": McLachlan, "Education," in *Scotland and the Americas, 1600 to 1800,* 65.

77  "The story of the rise of the Scottish Enlightenment and the transmission of its ideas to America is fundamental": William H. Goetzmann, *Beyond the Revolution: A History of American Thought from Paine to Pragmatism* (Basic Books, 2009), 54–55.

77  "I rid myself of the Pyrrhonisms": "From Thomas Jefferson to John Adams, 15 August 1820," *FO.*

77  George Wythe, a man of what Jefferson called "exalted virtue": "From Thomas Jefferson to John Sanderson, 31 August 1820," *FO.*

78  "one of the most fortunate events": "From Thomas Jefferson to Peter Carr, with Enclosure, 10 August 1787," *FO.*

78   "the Cato of his country": "Thomas Jefferson: Notes for the Biography of George Wythe., 31 August 1820," *FO*.

78   "Classical allusions were exceedingly rare in English courts": Carl J. Richard, *The Founders and the Classics: Greece, Rome, and the American Enlightenment* (Harvard University Press, 1994), 182.

78   "He carried his love of antiquity rather too far": William Wirt, *Sketches of the Life and Character of Patrick Henry* (Claxton, Remsen, and Haffelfinger, 1878), 66.

78   "He could hardly refrain from giving a line of Horace": Hugh Blair Grigsby, *The Virginia Convention of 1776* (J. W. Randolph, 1855), 129.

79   "his real education": Lawrence Cremin, *American Education: The Colonial Experience, 1607–1783* (Harper & Row, 1970), 552.

79   "The words of truth are simple": D. L. Wilson, ed., *Thomas Jefferson's Literary Commonplace Book* (Princeton University Press, 1989), 71.

79   The longest single set of extracts in the commonplace book: Wilson, ed. *Jefferson's Literary Commonplace Book*, 156.

79   "A system thus collected from the writings of ancient heathen moralists": Viscount Bolingbroke, "Concerning Authority in Matters of Religion," *The Philosophical Works of the late Right Honorable Henry St. John, Lord Viscount Bolingbroke*, Vol. II (no publisher, 1754), 306.

80   Jefferson would come to own some thirteen volumes by Bolingbroke: For "thirteen volumes," Richard Beale Davis, *A Colonial Southern Bookshelf: Reading in the Eighteenth Century* (University of Georgia Press, 1979), 61. For "highest order," see "From Thomas Jefferson to Francis Eppes, 19 January 1821," *FO*.

80   "I arose by the dawning of the day": "Diary," in *The Works of John Adams*, Vol. II, ed. Charles Francis Adams (Charles C. Little and James Brown, 1850), 105.

80   "His Ideas of the English Constitution are correct": "[Harvard and Worcester, 1751–1755] [from the Diary of John Adams]," *FO*.

80   "the law of nature is the law of God": Wilson, ed. *Jefferson's Literary Commonplace Book*, 40.

81   "Let us suppose a great prince governing": Ibid., 43.

81   Jefferson's reading of Shakespeare: Ibid., 113.

81   "Of Socrates we have nothing genuine but in the *Memorabilia* of Xenophon": "From Thomas Jefferson to William Short, 31 October 1819," *FO*.

81   The two accounts of Socrates: Jeffrey Henderson, introduction to Xenophon, *Memorabilia/Oeconomicus/Symposium/Apology* (Loeb Classical Library, 2013), xv.

81   "farming is the fairest, noblest, and most pleasant way to earn a living": Xenophon, *Oeconomicus* (Loeb Classical Library, 2013), 437.

82   He ordered a stack of books from T. Cadell: "To Thomas Jefferson from Perkins, Buchanan & Brown, 2 October 1769," *FO*.

82    the writings of Charles-Louis de Secondat, Baron de La Brède et de Montesquieu: *The Commonplace Book of Thomas Jefferson,* hereafter, *Legal Commonplace Book,* ed. Gilbert Chinard (Johns Hopkins University Press, 1926), 71, 31.

82    his first encounter: Marie Kimball, *Jefferson: The Road to Glory* (Coward-McCann, 1943), 210–11, 213.

82    Temple Stanyan's *Grecian History*: *Legal Commonplace Book,* 182.

83    then was reading Diogenes Laertius: Entry for March 16, 1767, "Memorandum Books, 1767," Jefferson papers, *FO.*

83    "Pleasure is the beginning and end of living happily": Diogenes Laertius, *The Lives and Opinions of Eminent Philosophers,* trans. C. D. Yonge (George Bell and Sons, 1901), 470–71.

83    few of Epicurus' actual words have survived: This paragraph draws on E. Zeller, *The Stoics, Epicureans and Sceptics,* trans. Oswald Reichel (Longmans, Green, 1880), 404–407, and also on Diskin Clay, "The Athenian Garden," in *The Cambridge Companion to Epicureanism,* ed. James Warren (Cambridge University Press, 2009), 13, 27.

84    "Happiness the aim of life": Enclosure in "From Thomas Jefferson to William Short, 31 October 1819," *FO.* In this letter he says he wrote this summary decades earlier.

84    "I too am an Epicurean": "From Thomas Jefferson to William Short," 31 October 1819, *FO.*

84    the "most rational system": "Thomas Jefferson to Charles Thomson, 9 January 1816," *FO.*

84    a "sensitized mind": Carl Becker, *The Heavenly City of the Eighteenth-Century Philosophers* (Yale University Press, 1961), 34.

85    Nor did he ever personally experience the American frontier: Malone, *Jefferson and His Time, Vol. 1,* 377. The point about Peter Jefferson traveling more than his son in Virginia was made to me in an interview with Susan Kern of William & Mary at her office on 30 April 2019.

85    "European to the bone": Peter Gay, *The Enlightenment: An Interpretation, Vol. 2: The Science of Freedom* (Alfred A. Knopf, 1969), 559.

85    "The art of life is the art of avoiding pain": "From Thomas Jefferson to Maria Cosway, 12 October 1786," *FO.*

85    he was forward thinking but not forward acting: For the formulation in these last six words, I am indebted to my daughter Molly Ricks.

## Chapter 5: Madison Breaks Away to Princeton
87    born into wealth: Ralph Ketcham, *James Madison: A Biography* (Macmillan, 1971), 3.

87    His first teachers: Irving Brant, *James Madison: The Virginia Revolutionist* (Bobbs-Merrill Company, 1941), 56.

87 emigrated to Virginia in the early 1750s: The precise date of his emigration is unclear. "King and Queen County: Economic and Social," *University of Virginia Record: Extension Series* 9 (1924), 91, has him arriving in Virginia in 1753, but the King and Queen Tavern Museum, which has studied Robertson's school, states that he left Scotland in 1752. "Donald Robertson's School," King and Queen Museum, accessed online.

87 "a man of great learning": "From James Madison to Joseph Delaplaine, September 1816," *FO*. There is a statement often attributed to Madison that has him say of Robertson, "All that I have been in life I owe largely to that man." Among the places this many-lived quotation appears are: Alfred Bagby, *King and Queen County, Virginia* (Neale Publishing Company, 1908), 86; Brant, *James Madison: The Virginia Revolutionist*, 60; Ketcham, *James Madison: A Biography*, 21; and James David Barber, *The Book of Democracy* (Prentice-Hall, 1995), 381. But the editors of the James Madison Papers have been unable to trace the quotation to Madison and so concluded that it "likely is apocryphal," leaving Robertson a somewhat murky figure. Email from Professor Tyson Reeder, assistant editor, Papers of James Madison, University of Virginia, 6 May 2019.

88 "the most influential writer of the eighteenth century": Peter Gay, *The Enlightenment: An Interpretation, Vol. 2: The Science of Freedom* (Alfred A. Knopf, 1969), 325, 332. See also Charles Camic, *Experience and Enlightenment: Socialization for Cultural Change in Eighteenth-Century Scotland* (University of Chicago Press, 1983), 98.

88 "advocated constitutionalism": Isaiah Berlin, *Against the Current: Essays in the History of Ideas* (Princeton University Press, 2013), 164–65.

89 "so agreeable a subject as ancient Rome": Baron de Montesquieu, *The Spirit of Laws, Vol. 1* (J. Nourse and P. Vaillant, 1766), 245.

89 "natural for a republic to have only a small territory": Ibid., 177.

89 "What makes free states last a shorter time than others": Baron de Montesquieu, *Considerations on the Causes of the Greatness of the Romans and Their Decline* (Hackett Publishing, 1965), 92.

90 "Montesquieu's spirit of laws is generally recommended": "From Thomas Jefferson to Thomas Mann Randolph, Jr., 30 May 1790," *FO*.

90 likely was irked by Montesquieu's conclusion: See, for example, Montesquieu, *Considerations on the Causes of the Greatness of the Romans and Their Decline*, 97.

90 a 1762 graduate: Brant, *James Madison: The Virginia Revolutionist*, states on p. 65 that Martin graduated in 1764, but according to the *Princeton Alumni Weekly* and other more recent sources, that date is incorrect. Frederic Fox, "Princetonia," *Princeton Alumni Weekly*, 2 March 1971, 5.

91 "an act of near-treason to Virginia": Brant, *James Madison: The Virginia Revolutionist*, 70.

*Notes*

91    "in a dissolute and unenviable state": Ketcham, *James Madison*, 23.

91    an act of loyalty to the Piedmont: I am indebted to Montpelier's Dr. Michael Dickens for his work mapping the "Princeton Invasion" of the Piedmont in late colonial times.

91    "I cannot think William and Mary College a desirable place": "From George Washington to Jonathan Boucher, 7 January 1773," FO.

92    the college was "in such confusion": *The Journal and Letters of Philip Vickers Fithian, 1773–1774: A Plantation Tutor of the Old Dominion*, ed. Hunter Dickinson Farish (Colonial Williamsburg, 1965), 65.

92    King's was the most Tory: David Robson, *Educating Republicans: The College in the Era of the American Revolution, 1750–1800* (Greenwood Press, 1985), 4.

92    Washington managed to take in a performance of *Hamlet*: Paul Leicester Ford, *Washington and the Theatre* (The Dunlap Society, 1899), 23. For its being Washington's first experience of a performance of Shakespeare, see Kevin Hayes, *George Washington: A Life in Books* (Oxford University Press, 2017), 128.

92    Madison was a far more diligent young man: Ketcham, *James Madison*, 23.

92    "a Seminary of Loyalty": Samuel Davies, *A Sermon Delivered at Nassau Hall, January 14, 1761* (R. Draper, Z. Fowle, S. Draper, 1761), 30.

92    "those of every religious Denomination may have free and equal Liberty": Samuel Blair, *An Account of the College of New-Jersey* (James Parker, 1754), 8.

92    the more sensual Thomas Jefferson: Jon Kukla has written a thoughtful volume on Jefferson's relations with women, several of them married, titled *Mr. Jefferson's Women* (Alfred A. Knopf, 2007). His summary of Jefferson's multiple aggressive passes in the 1760s at Elizabeth Moore Walker, the wife of a friend, is especially illuminating. Of Mrs. Walker, Jefferson later wrote, "I plead guilty to one of their charges, that when young & single I offered love to a handsome lady." "From Thomas Jefferson to Robert Smith, 1 July 1805," FO.

93    the colder Madison: Mary Sarah Bilder, *Madison's Hand: Revising the Constitutional Convention* (Harvard University Press, 2017), 10.

93    "Mr, Madison a gloomy, stiff creature": "Randolph and Tucker Letters," *The Virginia Magazine of History and Biography* 43, no. 1 (January 1935), 43.

93    the college "smoked with rebellion": Brant, *James Madison: The Virginia Revolutionist*, 73, 91, 101.

93    "the seedbed of sedition": Ketcham, *James Madison*, 44.

93    not as financially dependent on a provincial legislature: Robson, *Educating Republicans*, 19.

93    "conceived of as an integrative institution": Howard Miller, *The Revolutionary College: American Presbyterian Higher Education* (New York University Press, 1976), xx, 67.

93    Princeton by design drew from the entire Eastern Seaboard: Mark Noll, *Princeton and the Republic, 1768–1822* (Princeton University Press, 1989), 17.

93    also were students from Canada and the West Indies: Miller, *The Revolutionary College*, 67.

94    Madison's politicization: Edmund Morgan, *The Birth of the Republic, 1763–89* (University of Chicago Press, 2013), 40.

94    "articulated the radical position of the 1760s": Pauline Maier, *From Resistance to Revolution: Colonial Radicals and the Development of American Opposition to Britain, 1765–1776* (W. W. Norton, 1991), xix.

94    "a provincial carbon copy of Edinburgh": Douglass Adair, "'That Politics May Be Reduced to a Science': David Hume, James Madison, and the Tenth Federalist," *Huntington Library Quarterly* 20, no. 4 (August 1957), 346.

94    "outpost of the Scottish enlightenment": Jack Rakove, *James Madison and the Creation of the American Republic* (Pearson Longman, 2007), 3.

94    President Witherspoon is: Harold Dodds, *John Witherspoon 1723–1794* (Newcomen Society, 1944), 18.

95    he brought great energy to the college: Varnum Collins, *President Witherspoon, Vol. 1* (Princeton University Press, 1925), 103.

95    he managed simultaneously to upgrade admission standards: Noll, *Princeton and the Republic*, 30.

95    the college library grew to 1,500 volumes: Collins, *President Witherspoon, Vol. 1*, 106. See also Blair, *An Account of the College of New-Jersey*, 13.

95    "Witherspoon put the College of New Jersey at the head of higher education in America": Gilman Ostrander, *Republic of Letters: The American Intellectual Community, 1775–1865* (Madison House, 1999), 93.

95    Witherspoon steered by classical reference points: Jeffry Morrison, *John Witherspoon and the Founding of the American Republic* (University of Notre Dame Press, 2005), 105.

95    Epaminondas: Howard Mumford Jones, *O Strange New World: American Culture: The Formative Years* (Viking, 1964), 253.

95    the college's approach: Collins, *President Witherspoon, Vol. 1*, 147, 143.

96    "No correction by stripes is permitted": John Witherspoon, "Address in behalf of the College of New Jersey," in *The Works of the Rev. John Witherspoon, Vol. IV* (William Woodward, 1802), 194.

96    "All persons, young and old, love liberty": John Witherspoon, *Letters on the Education of Children, and on Marriage* (Flagg & Gould, 1817), 9.

96    the bust of Homer: Wayne Moss, "Witherspoon, Madison, Moral Philosophy, and the Constitution," *Princeton Alumni Weekly*, 23 April 2014, accessed online.

96    he spoke French with a Scottish brogue: Brant, *James Madison: The Virginia Revolutionist*, 64.

96    despite being pale, sickly, and small: Brant, *James Madison: The Virginia Revolutionist*, 73. Richard Brookhiser has him considerably smaller: "just over five feet tall, just over a hundred pounds." Richard Brookhiser, *James Madison* (Basic Books, 2011), 4.

96    "he is but a withered little apple-John": *The Life and Letters of Washington Irving, Vol. 1*, ed. Pierre Irving (Richard Bentley, 1862), 217.

96    "sudden attacks, somewhat resembling Epilepsy": "From James Madison to Joseph Delaplaine, September 1816," *FO*.

96    the two students who became his closest friends at Princeton: Brant, *James Madison: The Virginia Revolutionist*, 78.

97    studied far into the night: Collins, *President Witherspoon, Vol. 1*, 108.

97    "The general table-drink": Blair, *An Account of the College of New-Jersey*, 38.

97    "In the instruction of the youth": Blair, *An Account of the College of New-Jersey*, 28.

97    an ancient constitution that mandated equal rights and freedom of speech: Walter Miller, "Introduction," Xenophon, *Cyropaedia, Vol. 1* (Harvard University Press, 1914), xii.

97    allowed to skip that first year of studies: Ketcham, *James Madison*, 29.

97    "the sciences, geography, rhetoric, logic, and the mathematics": Blair, *An Account of the College of New-Jersey*, 24.

97    "to the Merchants in Philadelphia": "From James Madison to James Madison, Sr., 23 July 1770," *FO*. See also Thomas Wertenbaker, *Princeton, 1746–1896* (Princeton University Press, 1946), 56.

98    the obligation to resist a king who acts cruelly: Brant, *James Madison: The Virginia Revolutionist*, 94.

98    "moral philosophy": David Hume, *Essays and Treatises on Several Subjects* (T. Cadell; Bell & Bradfute; T. Duncan, 1793), 17.

98    "Ethics" and "Politics": Dennis Thompson, "The Education of a Founding Father: The Reading List for John Witherspoon's Course in Political Theory, as Taken by James Madison," *Political Theory* 4, no. 4 (November 1976), 523.

98    Today such a course might be considered something like an overview of political and social science: This sentence was inspired by the discussion of moral philosophy in Daniel Walker Howe, "European Sources of Political Ideas in Jeffersonian America," *Reviews in American History* 10, no. 4 (December 1982), 30.

98    the "problems of rights and obligations": Lawrence Cremin, *American Education: The Colonial Experience, 1607–1783* (Harper & Row, 1970), 465.

98    the need for civil liberty: Morrison, *John Witherspoon and the Founding of the American Republic*, 89.

98   "public law as something alive and growing": Brant, *James Madison: The Virginia Revolutionist*, 77.

99   "every good form of government must be complex, so that the one principle may check the other": John Witherspoon, *Lectures on Moral Philosophy*, ed. Varnum Lansing Collins (Princeton University Press, 1912), 29, 30, 94, 95.

99   senior year: Ketcham, *James Madison*, 51.

100   "it seems highly necessary that something shou'd be done": "From George Washington to George Mason, 5 April 1769," *FO*.

100   "Our All is at Stake": "To George Washington from George Mason, 5 April 1769," *FO*.

100   "each room invited just what was suited to it": Xenophon, *Oeconomicus* (Loeb Classical Library/Harvard University Press, 2013), 467.

100   A dome: Richard Jenkyns, "The Legacy of Rome," in Richard Jenkyns, ed., *The Legacy of Rome: A New Appraisal* (Oxford University Press, 1992), 9. Appropriately, the monument built to Jefferson in Washington, DC, during the presidency of Franklin Roosevelt is topped by a dome, as is the library of the University of Virginia, the major project of his old age.

101   "powerful in body and of shrewd intelligence": Cassius Deo, *Roman History* (Loeb Classical Library, 1925), 63.

101   "a land of liberty": Joseph Warren, "1772 Boston Massacre Oration," accessed online.

102   "from mutual Consent arose the Body politic": James Madison, "An Oration in Commemoration of the Founders of William and Mary College, August 15, 1772," *Bulletin of the College of William and Mary* 31, no. 7 (November 1937), 7.

102   "5 or 6 well meaning men": "From James Madison to William Bradford, 24 January 1774," Madison Papers, accessed online at *FO*.

103   "the rich resources of his luminous and discriminating mind": "Thomas Jefferson: Autobiography, 6 Jan.–29 July 1821, 6 January 1821," *FO*.

### Chapter 6: Adams and the Fuse of Rebellion

107   "Adams threw himself into Resistance to the Crown": Stanley Elkins and Eric McKitrick, *The Age of Federalism* (Oxford University Press, 1993), 531.

107   "What do We mean by the Revolution?": "From John Adams to Thomas Jefferson, 24 August 1815," John Adams papers, *FO*.

108   "Liberty, . . . which has never been enjoyd, in its full Perfection": Fragmentary Notes for "A Dissertation on the Canon and the Feudal Law," May–August 1765," John Adams papers, *FO*.

108   "the historians, orators, poets and philosophers of *Greece* and *Rome* were quite familiar": "'A Dissertation on the Canon and the Feudal Law,' No. 1, 12 August 1765," John Adams papers, *FO*. Adams' italics.

108    "They knew that government was a plain, simple, intelligible thing": "'A Dissertation on the Canon and the Feudal Law,' No. 2, 19 August 1765," John Adams papers, *FO*.

109    "Liberty must at all hazards be supported": "'A Dissertation on the Canon and the Feudal Law,' No. 3, 30 September 1765," John Adams papers, *FO*.

109    "Let us dare to read, think, speak and write": "VI. 'A Dissertation on the Canon and the Feudal Law,' No. 4, 21 October 1765," Adams papers, *FO*.

109    "it had an Effect upon the People": "From John Adams to Edmund Jenings, 20 April 1780," *FO*.

110    "Thirty Years of my Life are passed in Preparation for Business": "Braintree Decr. 18th. 1765. Wednesday," Adams papers, *FO*.

110    "a more obstinate War": "Anno Domini 1766: 1766. January 1st. Wednesday. [from the Diary of John Adams]," John Adams papers, *FO*.

111    "If this be treason, make the most of it": See John Ragosta, "'Caesar had his Brutus': What Did Patrick Henry Really Say?" *The Virginia Magazine of History and Biography* 26, no. 3 (2018).

111    "His manners had something of the coarseness of the society he had frequented": "Thomas Jefferson's Notes on Patrick Henry [before 12 April 1812]," and "Thomas Jefferson to William Wirt, 5 August 1815," *FO*. See also William Wirt, *Sketches of the Life and Character of Patrick Henry* (Claxton, Remsen, and Haffelfinger, 1878), 32.

111    "mr Henry's talents as a popular orator": "Thomas Jefferson: Autobiography, 6 Jan.–29 July 1821, 6 January 1821," *FO*.

111    "I well remember the cry of treason": "Thomas Jefferson to William Wirt, 14 August 1814," *FO*.

111    the impact of Henry's speech: Harlow Unger, *Lion of Liberty: Patrick Henry and the Call to a New Nation* (Da Capo, 2010), 42.

112    "he was the best humored man in society I almost ever knew": "From Thomas Jefferson to William Wirt, 4 August 1805," *FO*. His charge that Henry was "avaritious & rotten hearted" also appears in Wirt, *Sketches of the Life and Character of Patrick Henry*, 59. Jefferson confirms these exchanges with Wirt in his own autobiography. In 1795, Wirt represented Jefferson in a lawsuit involving the loss of two hogsheads of tobacco. They lost that case. Wirt later would be a prosecutor in the trial of Aaron Burr and then attorney general in the administration of James Monroe.

112    burdened by business problems: Richard Sheridan, "The British Credit Crisis of 1772 and the American Colonies," *The Journal of Economic History* 20, no. 2 (June 1960), 167.

112    they flooded the market with tobacco: Woody Holton, *Forced Founders: Indians, Debtors, Slaves, and the Making of the American Revolution in Virginia* (University

of North Carolina Press, 1999), 95. See also John Ferling, *A Leap in the Dark: The Struggle to Create the American Republic* (Oxford University Press, 2003), 95.

113    his written advice to Virginia's delegation heading to the Congress: "By a Native and Members of the House of Burgesses" in [Thomas Jefferson], *A Summary View of the Rights of British America* (Clementina Rind, 1774. Reprinted by G. Kearsly).

113    his words made a splash with his peers: Both this assessment and the purchase by Washington are from John Boles, *Jefferson: Architect of American Liberty* (Basic Books, 2017), 51.

113    "the Character of a fine Writer": "[In Congress, May–July 1776] [from the Diary of John Adams]," *FO*.

113    "Tacitus I consider as the first writer in the world": "From Thomas Jefferson to Anne Cary Randolph Bankhead, 8 December 1808," *FO*.

113    "left their native wilds": "Draft of Instructions to the Virginia Delegates in the Continental Congress (MS Text of A Summary View, &c.), [July 1774]," Thomas Jefferson papers, *FO*.

114    "*A Summary View* became the first sustained piece of American political writing that subjected the King's conduct to direct and pointed criticism": Pauline Maier, *American Scripture: Making the Declaration of Independence* (Alfred A. Knopf, 1997), 112.

114    "the god who gave us life, gave us liberty at the same time": "Draft of Instructions to the Virginia Delegates in the Continental Congress (MS Text of A Summary View, &c.), [July 1774]," Jefferson papers, *FO*.

114    "the first publication which carried the claim of our rights": "Thomas Jefferson to William Plumer, 31 January 1815," *FO*.

114    "the famous Mr. Jefferson": P. 506, "Note: Governor Ward's Opinion of Jefferson," *Magazine of American History, Vol. 1*, Part II, No. 8 (A. S. Barnes, August 1877), 506.

115    "swim or sink, live or die, survive or perish with my country": John Adams, *Novanglus and Massachusettensis* (Hews & Goss, 1819), vi.

115    Adams left Boston in mid-August 1774: John Howe Jr., *The Changing Political Thought of John Adams* (Princeton University Press, 1966), 51.

115    "the Virginians speak in Raptures": "August 1774, from the Diary of John Adams," *FO*.

115    "advisable as soon as possible to begin our defence": "From James Madison to William Bradford, 23 August 1774," *FO*.

115    "under the sacred ties of Virtue, Honour, and Love of our Country": "Continental Association, 20 October 1774," Jefferson papers, *FO*.

116    "the principles of Aristotle and Plato, of Livy and Cicero, of Sydney, Harrington and Lock": Adams, "To the Inhabitants of the Colony of Massachusetts-Bay, 23 January 1775," *FO*.

116    "The Greeks planted colonies": "VII. To the Inhabitants of the Colony of Massachusetts-Bay, 6 March 1775." *FO.*

116    "no nation or body of men can stand in preference to the general congress of Philadelphia": Basil Williams, *Life of William Pitt, Earl of Chatham, Vol. II* (Longmans, Green, 1914), 305.

117    "But can a virtuous Man hesitate in his choice?": "From George Washington to George William Fairfax, 31 May 1775," *FO.*

117    Adams proposed Washington to lead it: Douglas Southall Freeman, *George Washington: A Biography, Vol. 3, Planter and Patriot* (Scribner's, 1951), 435.

117    "I do not think my self equal to the Command I am honoured with": "Address to the Continental Congress, 16 June 1775," George Washington Papers, *FO.*

118    British redcoats charged up a slope against American militiamen: Robert Middlekauff, *The Glorious Cause: The American Revolution, 1763–1789* (Oxford University Press, 2005), 294.

118    "His whole life was a refutation of whites' basic justification for slavery": J. William Harris, *The Hanging of Thomas Jeremiah: A Free Black Man's Encounter with Liberty* (Yale University Press, 2009), 165. See also J. William Harris, "The Extraordinary Story of the Hanging of the Black Man Who Owned Slaves," *History News Network*, 3 January 2010.

119    "that is the only part in which this Colony is vulnerable": "From James Madison to William Bradford, 19 June 1775," *FO.*

119    "tipped the scales in favor of American independence": Jill Lepore, *These Truths: A History of the United States* (W. W. Norton, 2018), 94.

119    "Lord Dunmore, should be instantly crushd": "From George Washington to Lieutenant Colonel Joseph Reed, 15 December 1775," *FO.*

119    "open and avowed rebellion": "Proclamation of Rebellion," accessed online at DigitalHistory.Uh.edu.

119    "desperate conspiracy": "King George III's Address to Parliament, October 27, 1775," accessed online at Library of Congress.

119    "Virtue alone is or can be the Foundation": "From John Adams to William Tudor, 14 November 1775," *FO.*

119    "Public Virtue": "From John Adams to Mercy Otis Warren, 16 April 1776," *FO.*

## *Chapter 7:* Jefferson's Declaration of the "American Mind"

121    "The passage of the Patowmac": Thomas Jefferson, "Notes on the State of Virginia," in *Thomas Jefferson: Writings* (Library of America, 1984), 143. Kevin Hayes observes that in this passage, Jefferson was consciously echoing a descriptive passage in Herodotus. Kevin J. Hayes, *The Road to Monticello: The Life and Mind of Thomas Jefferson* (Oxford University Press, 2008), 264.

121    "Or the case may be likened to the ordinary one of a tenant for life": "Thomas Jefferson to John Wayles Eppes, 24 June 1813," FO.

122    "I have too good an opinion of their love of order": "From Thomas Jefferson to Patrick Henry, 27 March 1779," FO.

122    "to such a mind as yours, persuasion was idle & impertinent": "To George Washington from Thomas Jefferson, 23 May 1792," FO.

122    "The knell, the shroud, the mattock, and the grave": Quoted in D. L. Wilson, ed., *Thomas Jefferson's Literary Commonplace Book* (Princeton University Press, 1989), 102.

123    "Jefferson's literary tastes": Wilson, ed., *Jefferson's Literary Commonplace Book*, 13.

123    "this rude bard of the North the greatest Poet that has ever existed": "From Thomas Jefferson to Charles McPherson, 25 February 1773," FO.

123    Ossian was later revealed to be an invention: Wilson, ed., *Jefferson's Literary Commonplace Book*, 172.

123    Jefferson also disdained most novels: "Thomas Jefferson to Nathaniel Burwell, 14 March 1818," FO.

123    "perhaps the only piece of practical politics that is also theoretical politics and also great literature": G. K. Chesterton, *What I Saw in America* (Dodd, Mead & Co., 1923), 7.

124    "an appeal to the tribunal of the world": This and quotations from Jefferson in the following three paragraphs are from "From Thomas Jefferson to Henry Lee, 8 May 1825," FO.

124    he became more like Thomas Paine: Thomas Adams, *American Independence: The Growth of an Idea* (Brown University Press, 1965), xi.

124    "The birth-day of a new world is at hand": [Thomas Paine], *Common Sense* (W. and T. Bradford, 1776), 73, 87, 87–88.

124    Jefferson had received the pamphlet in the mail: "To Thomas Jefferson from Thomas Nelson, Jr., 4 February 1776," FO.

126    "profess faith in God the Father": "Constitution of Delaware 1776," Avalon Project Documents in Law, History and Diplomacy, Yale Law School Library, accessed online.

126    "the Declaration shimmers with a sublime optimism": Danielle Allen, *Our Declaration: A Reading of the Declaration of Independence in Defense of Equality* (W. W. Norton, 2014), 193.

126    "life, liberty and estate": Locke quotation is from John Locke, "Second Treatise on Civil Government," Chapter VII, Section 87–89, accessed online.

127    "The landless could no longer be regarded as either so marginal or so subordinate as in Locke": Jonathan Israel, *The Expanding Blaze: How the American*

*Revolution Ignited the World, 1775–1848* (Princeton University Press, 2017), 91. My assessment here also was influenced by David Post, "Jeffersonian Revisions of Locke: Education, Property-Rights, and Liberty," *Journal of the History of Ideas* 47, no. 1 (1986).

127   "Forms of Government may, and must, be occasionally changed": Quoted in Hayes, *The Road to Monticello*, 181.

127   "Liberty, like Power, is only good for those who possess it, when it is under the constant Direction of Virtue": George, Lord Lyttelton, *Dialogues of the Dead*, 4th edition, with additional dialogues 29–32 (W. Sandby, 1765), 403.

128   "it is their right, it is their duty, to throw off such a government": Quoted in Ronald Hamowy, "Jefferson and the Scottish Enlightenment: A Critique of Garry Wills's 'Inventing America: Jefferson's Declaration of Independence,'" *William and Mary Quarterly* 36, no. 4 (1979), 508.

128   "The ambiguity of the grievances": Stephen E. Lucas, "The Stylistic Artistry of the Declaration of Independence," National Archives, America's Founding Documents, https://www.archives.gov/founding-docs/stylistic-artistry-of-the-declaration.

129   that last phrase: Pauline Maier, *American Scripture: Making the Declaration of Independence* (Alfred A. Knopf, 1997), 148.

129   "Do you recollect the pensive and awful silence": "To John Adams from Benjamin Rush, 20 July 1811," *FO*.

130   Nineteen of the fifty-six signers of the Declaration were of Scottish or Ulster Scot extraction: Arthur Herman, *How the Scots Invented the Modern World* (Three Rivers Press, 2001), 253.

130   "a Purification from our Vices": "John Adams to Abigail Adams, 3 July 1776," FO.

130   "*independency* proclaimed under a triple volley": "From the *Saturday Evening Post*: Revolutionary Papers," *Atkinson's Casket: Gems of Literature, Wit and Sentiment* (Samuel Atkinson, 1836), 266.

130   pulling down the gilded statue of King George III: *Journal of Lieutenant Isaac Bangs, April 1 to July 29, 1776*, ed. Edward Bangs (J. Wilson and Son, 1890), 25, 57.

131   a present to the city: John Hazelton, *The Declaration of Independence: Its History* (Dodd, Mead, 1906), 253.

131   Washington admonished: "General Orders, 10 July 1776," George Washington papers, *FO*.

131   portions of the monarch's statue were melted down: Michael Kammen, *Colonial New York: A History* (Scribner's, 1975), 371.

131   "all men and women are created equal": Quoted in John Kasson, *Civilizing the Machine: Technology and Republican Values in America, 1776–1900* (Hill & Wang, 1999), 97.

132   "dedicated to the proposition that all men are created equal": "Gettysburg Address," Avalon Project Documents in Law, History and Diplomacy, Yale Law School Library.

132   a little leather-bound notebook: Maier, *American Scripture*, 203.

132   "this nation will rise up and live out the true meaning of its creed: 'We hold these truths to be self-evident, that *all* men are created equal'": Martin Luther King Jr., "I have a dream" speech, Avalon Project Documents in Law, History and Diplomacy, Yale Law School Library, accessed online. My italics, used to reflect King's emphasis in speaking.

132   "you cannot erase those words from the Declaration of Independence": Quoted, Hilary Parkinson, "Pieces of History," National Archives blog, 25 July 2013.

132   it's more about "what we ought to be": Maier, *American Scripture*, xix.

## Chapter 8: Washington: The Noblest Roman of Them All

133   "the most thoroughly classicized figure of his generation": Eran Shalev, *Rome Reborn on Western Shores: Historical Imagination and the Creation of the American Republic* (University of Virginia Press, 2009), 98.

133   two biographies of Washington published in America that were written in Latin: Edwin Miles, "The Young American Nation and the Classical World," *Journal of the History of Ideas* 35, no. 2 (1974), 269–70.

135   "kept them in continual alarm": Plutarch, "Fabius," in *The Lives of the Noble Romans and Grecians (The Dryden Translation)* (Encyclopaedia Britannica, 1952), 143.

135   "Latin books—14 volumes": Footnote on Washington's books, "From George Washington to Jonathan Boucher, 31 July 1768," FO.

135   "We are so bigoted to Thucidies": "From John Adams to Benjamin Waterhouse, 2 May 1821," FO.

135   owned a copy of *Plutarch's Lives*: "Appendix D. Inventory of the Books in the Estate, c.1759," Washington Papers, FO. For Washington's readings on abolishing slavery, see François Furstenberg, "Atlantic Slavery, Atlantic Freedoms: George Washington, Slavery, and Transatlantic Abolitionist Networks," in *William and Mary Quarterly* 68, no. 2 (2011), 247.

135   "set Forth to oppose Hannibal": Plutarch, "Fabius," 143.

135   "Fabius never won any set battle but that against the Ligurians": Plutarch, *Lives of the Noble Romans and Grecians*, 154.

136   "Washington had not achieved this kind of adulation as a result of battlefield brilliance": Fergus Bordewich, *Washington: The Making of the American Capital* (HarperCollins, 2008), 57, 97.

136   "making our resistance a war of posts": Alexander Graydon, *Memoirs of His Own Time* (Lindsay & Blakiston, 1846), 175.

136  "he must adapt a more defensive strategy and fight a 'War of Posts'": Joseph Ellis, *His Excellency: George Washington* (Vintage, 2004), 101.

136  "Washington's supposedly 'Fabian' view of warfare": Edward Lengel, *General George Washington: A Military Life* (Random House, 2007), 150.

138  "the tactical defeat proved an immense strategic gain": Lieutenant Commander Jason A. Fite, "Study the Past to Win Today," in *Proceedings of the U.S. Naval Institute*, December 2018, 61.

138  "partisan war": Mark Kwasny, *Washington's Partisan War, 1775–1783* (Kent State University Press, 1996), xii.

138  "It proved instead to be a popular war": R. Arthur Bowler, *Logistics and the Failure of the British Army in America, 1775–1783* (Princeton University Press, 1975), 239.

138  "In all your marches, at times, at least, even when there is no possible danger, move with front, rear, and flank guards": "From George Washington to Colonel William Woodford, 10 November 1775," *FO*.

139  "the most indifferent kind of People I ever saw": "From George Washington to Lund Washington, 20 August 1775," *FO*.

140  "willing and desirous of making the Assault": "From George Washington to John Hancock, 18–21 February 1776," *FO*. See also "Council of War, 16 January 1776," Washington papers, *FO*.

140  "publick Virtue & Honour": "From George Washington to Brigadier General John Thomas, 23 July 1775," *FO*.

140  costing the new Continental Army some five thousand troops: On Thomas, see Rufus Griswold et al., *Washington and the Generals of the American Revolution, Vol. II* (Carey & Hart, 1848), 202. On total American losses in Canada, see Alan Taylor, *American Revolutions: A Continental History, 1750–1804* (W. W. Norton, 2016), 153.

141  "my landed affairs on the Ohio": "From George Washington to Burwell Bassett, 28 February 1776," *FO*.

141  plunged into direct combat against the British: John Rhodehamel, *George Washington: The Wonder of the Age* (Yale University Press, 2017), 123.

141  "We live in daily Expectation": "John Adams to Abigail Adams, 3 August 1776," *FO*.

141  his men "running away in the most disgraceful and shamefull manner": "From George Washington to Nicholas Cooke, 17 September 1776," *FO*.

141  "Orders now issued, & the next moment reversed": "From John Haslet, 4 September 1776," in *Letters to and from Caesar Rodney, 1756–1784*, ed. George Ryden. (University of Pennsylvania Press, 1933), 112.

142  "avoid any considerable misfortune": "To George Washington from Major General Nathanael Greene, 5 September 1776," *FO*.

142    "we should on all occasions avoid a general Action": "From George Washington to John Hancock, 8 September 1776," FO.

142    "I never was in such an unhappy, divided state": "From George Washington to Lund Washington, 30 September 1776," FO.

143    "I am wearied almost to death": "From George Washington to John Augustine Washington, 6–19 November 1776," FO.

143    he used the word "misfortune" a lot that year: "From George Washington to John Hancock, 23 June 1776," FO.

143    "The defence of Long Island had been worse than futile": Douglas Southall Freeman, *George Washington: A Biography, Vol. 4, Leader of the Revolution* (Scribner's, 1951), 364.

145    "that fatal indecision of mind": Reed's letter to Lee as well as Lee's response are appended in a footnote to "From George Washington to Colonel Joseph Reed, 30 November 1776," FO.

145    "I opened it": "From George Washington to Colonel Joseph Reed, 30 November 1776," FO.

146    "censuring my Conduct to another was such an argument of disengenuity": "From George Washington to Joseph Reed, 11 June 1777," FO.

146    the British issued an amnesty offer: David Hackett Fischer, *Washington's Crossing* (Oxford University Press, 2004), 161, 163–65.

146    "Many a disguised tory has lately shewn his head": Thomas Paine, *The American Crisis* (R. Carlile, 1819), 12.

146    Northern New Jersey was the population center: Dave Richard Palmer, *The Way of the Fox: American Strategy in the War for America, 1775–1783* (Greenwood Press, 1975), 27.

146    "the spirits of the People . . . are quite sunk": "From George Washington to Jonathan Trumbull, Sr., 14 December 1776," FO.

146    3,000 men fit for duty: Fischer, *Washington's Crossing*, 381

146    "No Man, I believe, ever had a greater choice of difficulties": "From George Washington to Samuel Washington, 18 December 1776," FO.

147    "a certain great man is most damnably deficient": "General Charles Lee to General Horatio Gates, 13 December 1776" in *The Spirit of 'Seventy-Six: The Story of the American Revolution as Told by Participants*, eds. Henry Steele Commager and Richard Morris (Harper & Row, 1967), 500.

147    suspended operations at the college: Harold Dodds, *John Witherspoon 1723–1794* (Newcomen Society, 1944), 25.

147    the college's building, was made a jail: Fischer, *Washington's Crossing*, 163.

147    "they soon gutted the library": George Trevelyan, *The American Revolution, Vol. 3* (Longmans, Green, 1915), 31, 297.

147   "Old Weatherspoon has not escap'd their fury": "To Thomas Jefferson from Thomas Nelson, 2 January 1777," *FO.*

148   "use every means in your power to obtain a knowledge of the Enemys Numbers": "Orders to Brigadier General William Maxwell, 21 December 1776," Washington papers, *FO.*

148   Hamilton by many accounts directed his battery of cannon to fire at the college chapel: Trevelyan, *American Revolution, Vol. 3*, 137. But Michael Newton maintains that Hamilton's presence is not clearly proven, because one artillery unit had remained at Trenton. See Michael Newton, *Alexander Hamilton: The Formative Years* (Eleftheria Publishing, 2015), 182.

149   "the subsequent skirmishes in the Jersey . . . blasted the agreeable prospect of a speedy settlement": T. M. Devine, ed. *A Scottish Firm in Virginia, 1767–1777* (Scottish History Society, 1984), 237.

150   "abandoned the strategy of a war of posts": Kwasny, *Washington's Partisan War*, 112, 223.

150   "I am sure they can never be brought fairly up to an attack": "From George Washington to Joseph Reed, 15 January 1777," *FO.*

150   militia commanders had absconded with a good deal of the British supplies: See a militia colonel's response to Washington, "To George Washington from Colonel David Chambers, 9 February 1777," *FO.*

150   "we should learn to estimate them rightly": "From George Washington to The States, 18 October 1780," *FO.*

151   One militia tactic was to leave cattle out in the open: Murray letter and cattle tactics are in Kwasny, *Washington's Partisan War*, 114–115.

152   They might lose two men one day, ten the next: Kwasny, *Washington's Partisan War*, 126.

152   "they are now become a formidable enemy": "Colonel William Harcourt to his father Earl Harcourt," quoted in *The Spirit of 'Seventy-Six*, eds. Commager and Morris, 524.

152   "General How has invareably pursued the Maxims of an invader": "To John Adams from Nathanael Greene, 3 March 1777," *FO.*

152   "both a Fabius and a Camillus": "To Sir Horace Mann, April 3, 1777," *The Letters of Horace Walpole, Fourth Earl of Orford, Vol. 6* (John Grant, 1906), 424.

153   "Time for Us to abandon this execrable defensive Plan": "From John Adams to Nathanael Greene, 13 April 1777," *FO.*

153   "Howe is no Sylla": "From John Adams to Nathanael Greene, 24 May 1777," *FO.*

154   "Our business then is to avoid a General engagement": Both quotations are in "From Alexander Hamilton to Robert R. Livingston, 28 June 1777," *FO.*

154   he probably was born in 1755: See Ron Chernow, *Alexander Hamilton* (Penguin Press, 2004), 16–17.

154   "better policy, to harass and exhaust the soldiery": "'The Farmer Refuted, &c., [23 February] 1775," Hamilton papers, *FO*.

155   "both one's learning and one's experience may be used instrumentally": Stanley Elkins and Eric McKitrick, *The Age of Federalism* (Oxford University Press, 1993), 97.

155   "the Militia assembled in the most spirited manner": "From George Washington to John Hancock, 20 June 1777," *FO*.

155   "A tolerable Body of Men": Both quotations in this paragraph are "From George Washington to George Clinton, 16 August 1777," *FO*.

156   "The strategic key was the Continental Army": Joseph Ellis, *Founding Brothers: The Revolutionary Generation* (Vintage, 2002), 130–31.

156   "consumed in fruitless maneuverings": Rhodehamel, *George Washington*, 147.

156   a strong strategic parallel between the circumstances of the ancient Roman situation and the American Revolution: For this observation I am indebted to Thomas Nelson Winter's essay on "The Strategy That Gave Independence to the U.S.," *The Classical Bulletin* 53 (November 1976).

156   the small bookshelf of the military instruction manuals: Kevin Hayes, *George Washington: A Life in Books* (Oxford University Press, 2017), 182–83.

156   "I am sick of Fabian Systems": "John Adams to Abigail Adams, 2 September 1777," *FO*.

157   "Howe is a wild General": "John Adams to Abigail Adams, 20 August 1777," *FO*.

157   "a Man of no enterprize": "From George Washington to John Augustine Washington, 24 February 1777," *FO*.

157   "No military Connection": "[Notes on Relations with France, March–April 1776.] [from the Diary of John Adams]," *FO*.

157   "You slept away your time in the field": Thomas Paine, "Letter to George Washington," in *The Writings of Thomas Paine, Vol. 3*, ed. Moncure Conway (G. P. Putnam's, 1895), 247, 217, 249.

158   "He was a fighter": Marcus Cunliffe, *George Washington: Man and Monument* (New American Library, 1958), 83.

158   "incumbent upon him to risk a battle": Sir William Howe testimony, "Proceedings in the Commons relating to the Enquiry into the Conduct of the American War," *The Parliamentary History of England, Vol. XX, December 1778–February 1780* (Hansard, 1814), 692.

158   an inexplicable military blunder: Freeman, *George Washington, Vol. 4*, 484.

158   years earlier had given an eloquent address: Irving Brant, *James Madison: The Virginia Revolutionist* (Bobbs-Merrill Company, 1941), 94.

158  "outgenerald and twice beated": "To John Adams from Benjamin Rush, 21 October 1777," FO.

158  "any considerable loss sustained by the army could not speedily, or easily be repaired": Howe testimony, "Enquiry into the Conduct of the American War," *Parliamentary History of England, Vol. XX,* 679.

159  "the centre of gravity": Piers Mackesy, *The War for America, 1775–1783* (University of Nebraska Press, 1993), 159.

159  "A General Action is by all means to be avoided": "Major General John Sullivan's Opinion, 29 October 1777," FO.

159  "Stupid men": "To George Washington from Major General Lafayette, 30 December 1777," FO.

159  "the less Shewy but regulated Conduct of Fabius": "To George Washington from Major General Arthur St. Clair, 5 January 1778," FO.

160  "he had found a way": Nathaniel Philbrick, *In the Hurricane's Eye: The Genius of George Washington and the Victory at Yorktown* (Viking, 2018), 156.

160  "I Saw great Fabius Come in state": "To George Washington from Annis-Boudinot Stockton, 13 March 1789," FO.

160  "Le Fabius de l'amérique": "To George Washington from Charles François Guéniot, 19 April 1783," FO.

160  "succeeded in our Revolutionary War": "From John Quincy Adams to Abigail Smith Adams, 31 December 1812," FO.

160  "execute promptly & vigorously": "From George Washington to James McHenry, 13 July 1796," FO.

## Chapter 9: The War Strains the Classical Model

161  "nothing but virtue has kept our army together": *The Spirit of 'Seventy-Six: The Story of the American Revolution as Told by Participants,* ed. Henry Steele Commager and Richard Morris (Harper & Row, 1967), 648.

161  "interest is the governing principle": "From George Washington to a Continental Congress Camp Committee, 29 January 1778," FO.

162  "they may talk of patriotism": "From George Washington to John Banister, 21 April 1778," FO.

163  "virtue must always be tied to interest": Glenn Phelps, "The Republican General," in *George Washington Reconsidered,* ed. Don Higginbotham (University Press of Virginia, 2001), 166, 171.

163  "The Want of public Virtue": "Elbridge Gerry to John Wendell, 11 November 1776," *Letters of Delegates of Congress, Vol. 5, August 16–December 31, 1776,* ed. Paul Smith (Library of Congress, 1979), 471.

163  "return a little more to first principles": "From George Washington to James Warren, 31 March 1779," FO.

163    "that decay of public virtue": "From George Washington to John Augustine Washington, 12 May 1779," *FO*.

164    entry of the French into the war changed the British strategic view: Piers Mackesy, *The War for America, 1775–1783* (University of Nebraska Press, 1993), 216.

164    the British decision to leave the city: John M. Coleman, "Joseph Galloway and the British Occupation of Philadelphia," *Pennsylvania History: A Journal of Mid-Atlantic Studies* 30, no. 3 (July 1963), 288. See also Robert Calhoun, "Loyalism and Neutrality," in *The Blackwell Encyclopedia of the American Revolution*, eds. Jack Greene and J. R. Pole (Blackwell, 1994), 252.

164    "the friends of government were dismayed": Sir William Howe testimony, "Proceedings in the Commons Relating to the Enquiry into the Conduct of the American War," *The Parliamentary History of England, Vol. XX, December 1778–February 1780* (Hansard, 1814), 705.

164    "left to wander like Cain upon the Earth": Edward Tatum Jr., ed., *The American Journal of Ambrose Serle* (Huntington Library, 1940), 295–96.

165    "could no longer be manipulated by British policies": John Shy, *A People Numerous & Armed: Reflections on the Military Struggle for American Independence* (University of Michigan Press, 1990), 234.

165    "All your secret intrigues shall be exposed": [Joseph Galloway], *Letters from Cicero to Catiline the Second* (J. Bew, 1781), 13, 18. This early edition was published anonymously.

166    "I rely on your activity": "From George Washington to Major General Philemon Dickinson, 18 June 1778," *FO*.

166    "seen these maneuvers carried out better": Robert Selig, "Light Infantry Lessons from America? Johann Ewald's Experiences in the American Revolutionary War as Depicted in His *Abhandlung über den Kleinen Krieg* (1785)," *Studies in Eighteenth-Century Culture* 23 (1994), 119.

166    "Bygone heroes could not have had more hardships": Johann [von] Ewald, *Diary of the American War: A Hessian Journal* (Yale University Press, 1979), 139. See also Mark Lendler, "The Politics of Battle: Washington, the Army and the Monmouth Campaign," in *A Companion to George Washington*, ed. Edward Lengel (Blackwell, 2012), 226.

166    their baggage train: Mark Kwasny, *Washington's Partisan War, 1775–1783* (Kent State University Press, 1996), 205.

167    "a precipitate retreat": "Tarleton Recalls His Raid on Charlottesville," in *The Spirit of 'Seventy-Six,* eds. Commager and Morris, 1207.

167    "the Carter-Mountain hero": Thomas Green Fessenden, *Democracy Unveiled* (David Carlisle, 1805), 95, 102.

167    "unprepared by his line of life": "I. Diary of Arnold's Invasion and Notes on Subsequent Events in 1781: Versions of 1796?, 1805, and 1816," Jefferson papers, *FO*.

168   "the swift concentration that proved decisive": Douglas Southall Freeman, *George Washington: A Biography, Vol. 5, Victory with the Help of France* (Scribner's, 1952), 480.

168   "This sink of nastiness": James Tilton, *Economical Observations on Military Hospitals* (J. Wilson, 1813), 64.

170   "some matters of delicacy and importance": "From Alexander Hamilton to George Washington, [13 February 1783]," *FO*.

170   Hamilton was telling fellow members of Congress: "Notes on Debates, 20 February 1783," Madison papers, *FO*.

170   "there are dangerous combinations in the Army": "To George Washington from Joseph Jones, 27 February 1783," *FO*.

170   "anxious to know": "From Alexander Hamilton to George Washington, [5 March 1783]," *FO*.

170   "I shall pursue the same steady line of conduct": "To Alexander Hamilton from George Washington, 4 March 1783," *FO*.

171   "Awake—attend to your Situation": A copy of the letter was enclosed in a notice Washington sent to Congress. "From George Washington to Elias Boudinot, 12 March 1783," *FO*.

171   "such disorderly proceedings": "General Orders, 11 March 1783," Washington Papers, *FO*.

172   "something very misterious in this business": "From George Washington to Alexander Hamilton, 12 March 1783," *FO*.

172   "my indignation has arisen": "From George Washington to Officers of the Army, 15 March 1783" (also known as "The Newburgh Address"), *FO*.

172   "astonishment and indignation": "From George Washington to William Heath, 26 September 1780," *FO*.

172   "The Storm . . . is dispersed": "From George Washington to Joseph Jones, 18 March 1783," *FO*.

172   "The Virtue, & patient forbearance of the Army": Both quotes are in "From George Washington to Lund Washington, 19 March 1783," *FO*.

173   "It must submit to its hard fate": "From Alexander Hamilton to George Washington, 25 March 1783," *FO*.

173   "I read your private letter of the 25th. with pain": "To Alexander Hamilton from George Washington, 4 April 1783," *FO*.

174   "principal & most confidential aid": "From George Washington to John Adams, 25 September 1798," *FO*.

175   "whether the Revolution must ultimately be considered as a blessing or a curse": "From George Washington to The States, 8 June 1783," *FO*.

175 Oliver Cromwell: "To George Washington from Lund Washington, 23 July 1783," *FO*; "Commonplace Book, 1759–1772," Madison papers, *FO*; "From John Adams to Unknown, 27 April 1777," *FO*.

175 "I retire from the great theatre of Action": "From George Washington to United States Congress, 23 December 1783," *FO*.

176 "the approbation of good & virtuous Men": "From George Washington to Thomas Jefferson, 10 February 1783," *FO*.

176 "proceed to Virginy": "To George Washington from François-Jean de Beauvoir, marquis de Chastellux, 23 August 1783," *FO*.

176 "I shall not rest contented": "From George Washington to François-Jean de Beauvoir, marquis de Chastellux, 12 October 1783," *FO*.

176 "a tour thro' all the Eastern States": "From George Washington to Marie-Joseph-Paul-Yves-Roch-Gilbert du Motier, marquis de Lafayette, 12 October 1783," *FO*.

177 he wanted a Frenchman to accompany him: I am indebted to Nathaniel Philbrick for noticing these two passages and quoting them: Nathaniel Philbrick, *In the Hurricane's Eye: The Genius of George Washington and the Victory at Yorktown* (Viking, 2018), 256.

177 "the best Actor of Presidency": "From John Adams to Benjamin Rush, 21 June 1811," *FO*.

178 "absolutely out of his Senses": "From Benjamin Franklin to Robert R. Livingston, 22[–26] July 1783," *FO*.

### Chapter 10: From a Difficult War to an Uneasy Peace

179 "as strong as any similar republican confederation": Gordon Wood, *The American Revolution* (Modern Library, 2002), 72.

179 "a much faster and better job of reconstruction": Edmund Morgan, *The Birth of the Republic, 1763–89* (University of Chicago Press, 2013), 121.

180 "men in a free state who are bold in war and timid in peace": Baron de Montesquieu, *Considerations on the Causes of the Greatness of the Romans and Their Decline* (Hackett Publishing, 1965), 93.

180 "it is the institutions that form the leaders": Montesquieu, *Considerations on the Causes of the Greatness of the Roman and Their Decline*, 25.

181 "do dishonorary injustice to ourselves": Thomas Paine, *The American Crisis* (James Watson, 1835), 61, 141.

181 "The confederation itself is defective": "From Alexander Hamilton to James Duane [3 September 1780]," *FO*.

182 "ridiculous to seek for models in the simple ages of Greece and Rome": "The Continentalist No. VI [4 July 1782]," *FO*.

182    "Neither the manners nor the genius of Rome are suited to the republic": "New York Assembly. Remarks on an Act Acknowledging the Independence of Vermont [28 March 1787]," Hamilton papers, *FO*.

182    "the necessity of a reform in our present Confederation": "To Alexander Hamilton from George Washington, 31 March 1783," *FO*.

183    an enslaved man named Billey: Elizabeth Dowling Taylor, *A Slave in the White House: Paul Jennings and the Madisons* (Palgrave Macmillan, 2012), 28.

183    "most prudent not to force Billey back to Va.": "From James Madison to James Madison Sr., 8 September 1783," *FO*.

183    Madison had him deliver a plow for Thomas Jefferson's farm: "From James Madison to Thomas Jefferson, 17 June 1793," *FO*.

183    his widow, Henrietta, became Jefferson's laundress: "From Thomas Jefferson to John Barnes, 24 February 1800," *FO*.

183    the fragile condition of the United States: "Notes on Ancient and Modern Confederacies, [April–June?] 1786," Madison papers, *FO*.

184    Madison's document was unprecedented: Noah Feldman, *The Three Lives of James Madison: Genius, Partisan, President* (Random House, 2017), 75.

184    "the occasional purchase of rare & valuable books": "From James Madison to Thomas Jefferson, 16 March 1784," *FO*.

185    "What has become of the subterraneous City discovered in Siberia?": "From James Madison to Thomas Jefferson, 27 April 1785," *FO*.

185    trunks full of books for Madison's "course of reading": Kevin J. Hayes, *The Road to Monticello: The Life and Mind of Thomas Jefferson* (Oxford University Press, 2008), 282. "Make free use" is from "To James Madison from Thomas Jefferson, 20 February 1784," *FO*.

185    "the danger of having the same *game played on our confederacy*": "From James Madison to Thomas Jefferson, 18 March 1786," *FO*.

186    "a mixture of monarchy, aristocracy, and democracy": John Adams, *A Defence of the Constitutions of Government of the United States* (C. Dilly, in the Poultry, 1787), 216.

186    "The best constitution": Polybius, *Histories*, trans. Evelyn S. Shuckburgh (Macmillan, 1889), book 6, chapter 1, chapter 11, chapter 3.

186    "no government of laws, without a balance": Adams, *A Defence of the Constitutions*, 224.

187    "Human Passions are all unlimited and insatiable": "From John Adams to Louis Alexandre, Duc de La Rochefoucauld d'Anville," circa 1788, *FO*.

187    "the happiness of nations": Adams, *A Defence of the Constitutions*, 322.

187    "Montesquieu had never study'd a free Democracy": William Vans Murray, *Political Sketches* (C. Dilly, in the Poultry, 1787), 28, 14.

188   "A Man without Education—But not without Abilities": "Samuel Osgood to John Adams, 14 Nov. 1786," Adams papers, *FO*.

188   unable to pay his debts: Richard Morris, *Witnesses at the Creation: Hamilton, Madison, Jay, and the Constitution* (Henry Holt, 1985), 170. However, some recent scholarship argues that the protests were more against taxes than against debt. See, for example, Robert Gross, "A Yankee Rebellion? The Regulators, New England, and the New Nation," *The New England Quarterly* 82, no. 1 (March 2009).

188   hundreds of its members sided with the insurgents: Leonard Richards, *Shays's Rebellion: The American Revolution's Final Battle* (University of Pennsylvania Press, 2002), 12.

188   A volley of grapeshot: This paragraph relies on the account in David Stewart, *The Summer of 1787: The Men Who Invented the Constitution* (Simon & Schuster, 2007), 12–14.

189   "The flames of internal insurrection": Jonathan Elliot, *The Debates, Resolutions and Other Proceedings in Convention . . . , Volume III, Containing the Debates in the States of North Carolina and Pennsylvania* (self-published, 1830), 305.

189   "stepping over fires smouldering": Horace, *Odes II: Vatis Amici,* trans. and ed. David West (Clarendon Press, 1998), 3.

189   "great commotions are prevailing in Massts.": "From James Madison to James Madison Sr., 1 November 1786," *FO*.

189   "this rebellion jolted American political reflections": John T. Agresto, "Liberty, Virtue, and Republicanism: 1776–1787," *The Review of Politics* 39, no. 4 (October 1977), 488.

190   "Perfection falls not to the share of mortals": "From George Washington to John Jay, 15 August 1786," *FO*.

190   "insignificant & wretched fragments of Empire": "From George Washington to Henry Lee, Jr., 22 September 1788," *FO*. I am indebted to Peter Onuf for pointing out this quotation to me.

190   "a general Degeneracy": "From John Adams to James Warren, 9 January 1787," *FO*.

190   "Our Governments want Energy": "To Thomas Jefferson from John Jay, 9 February 1787," Jefferson papers, *FO*.

190   "Our Government is unequal to the Task": "To John Adams from John Jay, 21 February 1787," *FO*.

190   "mere partisans & satellites": "Thomas Jefferson's Explanations of the Three Volumes Bound in Marbled Paper (the "Anas"), 4 February 1818," *FO*.

191   "fed up with the Articles": Daniel Walker Howe, "Why the Scottish Enlightenment Was Useful to the Framers of the American Constitution," *Comparative Studies in Society and History* 31, no. 3 (July 1989), 585.

191    "a report calling for a national convention": Richard Brookhiser letter to the author, 15 May 2019.

191    "Political foes who underrated James Madison did so at their peril": Ron Chernow, *Alexander Hamilton* (Penguin Press, 2004), 517.

191    "the present System neither has nor deserves advocates": "From James Madison to Edmund Pendleton, 24 February 1787," *FO*.

192    "All civilized societies are divided": "Vices of the Political System of the United States, April 1787," Madison papers, *FO*.

192    "systematic change": "From James Madison to Edmund Randolph, 8 April 1787," *FO*.

192    "ratification must be obtained from the people": "To George Washington from James Madison, 16 April 1787," *FO*.

192    "Madison was the most astute, profound, and original political theorist among the founding fathers": Gordon Wood, "The Founding Realist," *The New York Review of Books*, 19 October 1995, accessed online.

### Chapter 11: Madison and the Constitution: Balancing Vice with Vice

193    Enlightenment thinkers: Donald Lutz, "The Relative Influence of European Writers on Late Eighteenth-Century American Political Thought," *The American Political Science Review* 78, no. 1 (March 1984), 192, 190.

193    "a new basis of republican government": John T. Agresto, "Liberty, Virtue, and Republicanism: 1776–1787," *The Review of Politics* 39, no. 4 (October 1977), 504. For a dissenting view that holds that public virtue remained central during the writing and ratification of the Constitution, see David Hendrickson, *Peace Pact: The Lost World of the American Founding* (University Press of Kansas, 2003), 250.

194    "an exact account of what might pass": "James Madison: Origin of the Constitutional Convention, December 1835," *FO*.

194    "Madison was not only serving the muse of history": Richard Brookhiser, *James Madison* (Basic Books, 2011), 59.

195    Madison fiddled with his notes on the Constitution all his life: See especially Mary Sarah Bilder, *Madison's Hand: Revising the Constitutional Convention* (Harvard University Press, 2017), 67.

195    "by the people": "The Virginia Plan, 29 May 1787," Madison papers, *FO*.

195    "Why might not a Cataline or a Cromwell arise": June 4, 1787, James Madison, *The Debates in the Federal Convention of 1787 Which Framed the Constitution of the United States of America*, eds. Gaillard Hunt and James Scott (Oxford University Press, 1920), 53.

195    "the example of Solon": June 5, 1787, Madison, *Debates in the Federal Convention*, 61.

196    "Three will contend among themselves": June 16, 1787, Madison, *Debates in the Federal Convention*, 109.

196    He was not even a notable writer: This sentence is a paraphrase of one on p. 62 of Irving Brant, *James Madison: The Virginia Revolutionist* (Bobbs-Merrill Company, 1941).

196    "the best-informed man": Brant, *James Madison: The Virginia Revolutionist*, 78.

196    "The only remedy is to enlarge the sphere": June 6, 1878, Madison, *Debates in the Federal Convention*, 64, 65, 65.

197    "their number was augmented": June 7, 1787, Madison, *Debates in the Federal Convention*, 71.

197    "the greater tendency in such systems to anarchy": June 21, 1787, Madison, *Debates in the Federal Convention*, 141.

197    "Carthage & Rome tore one another to pieces": June 28, 1787, Madison, *Debates in the Federal Convention*, 178–79.

198    "Every Person seems to acknowledge his greatness": *Records of the Federal Convention of 1781, Vol. I*, ed. Max Farrand (Yale University Press, 1911), 94–95, 110.

198    the league: See, for example, Rufus Davis, *The Federal Principle: A Journey Through Time in Quest of a Meaning* (University of California Press, 1978), 13.

198    "a parallel used almost *ad nauseam*": Richard Gummere, *The American Colonial Mind and the Classical Tradition* (Harvard University Press, 1963), 101.

199    "In the Amphictyonic confederation": *Records of the Federal Convention of 1787, Vol. III*, ed. Max Farrand (Yale University Press, 1911), 184.

199    Rollin's *Ancient History*: Epaminondas Panagopoulos, *Essays on the History and Meaning of Checks and Balances* (University Press of America, 1985), 113.

199    "the fittest model for that form of Government": June 30, 1787, Madison, *Debates in the Federal Convention*, 194.

199    "the great pervading principle": June 8, 1787, Madison, *Debates in the Federal Convention*, 76.

199    "The great division of interests in the U. States": June 30, 1787, Madison, *Debates in the Federal Convention*, 195.

200    "the energies of James Madison were involved in continental rather than state problems": Stanley Elkins and Eric McKitrick, *The Founding Fathers: Young Men of the Revolution* (American Historical Association, 1962), 24.

200    resonated with the eight other delegates: Mark Noll, *Princeton and the Republic, 1768–1822* (Princeton University Press, 1989), 91. For their being more of them than from any other college, see Ron Chernow, *Alexander Hamilton* (Penguin Press, 2004), 47.

201 "their situation is distinct from either the people of Greece or Rome": Monday, June 25, 1787, Madison, *Debates in the Federal Convention*, 159.

201 "want of political wisdom": June 28, 1787, Madison, *Debates in the Federal Convention*, 181.

201 "The want of some provision": "From James Madison to Thomas Jefferson, 24 October 1787," Madison papers, *FO*.

201 a kind of peace treaty between the states: This idea appears in Hendrickson, *Peace Pact*. He notes on p. 285 that in taking this approach he is walking in the neglected footsteps of James Brown Scott, who argued in 1918 that the Constitution took the form of "an international conference."

202 "In all ages one half mankind had been slaves": August 22, 1787, Madison, *Debates in the Federal Convention*, 444. See also Mark Kaplanoff, "Charles Pinckney and the American Republican Tradition," in *Intellectual Life in Antebellum Charleston*, eds. Michael O'Brien and David Moltke-Hansen (University of Tennessee Press, 1986).

202 "impossible for us to suppose these creatures to be men": Baron de Montesquieu, *The Spirit of Laws, Vol. 1* (J. Nourse and P. Vaillant, 1766), 352.

202 "helped undo some of the wrongs he had helped to create": Holly Brewer, "Slavery, Sovereignty, and 'Inheritable Blood': Reconsidering John Locke and the Origins of American Slavery," *The American Historical Review* 122, no. 4 (October 2017), 1075.

202 admitted two free blacks to Princeton: Jeffry Morrison, *John Witherspoon and the Founding of the American Republic* (University of Notre Dame Press, 2005), 76.

203 "the censorial power is in the people": "House Address to the President, [27 November] 1794," *FO*.

203 "his justice cannot sleep forever": Thomas Jefferson, "Notes on the State of Virginia," *Thomas Jefferson: Writings* (Library of America, 1984), 289.

203 "those of his planter brethren": Douglas Egerton, "Review of *Master of the Mountain: Thomas Jefferson and His Slaves*. By Henry Wiencek." *Journal of the Early Republic* 33, no. 3 (Fall 2013), 559.

203 "No body here reads them": "From Thomas Jefferson to James Madison, with a List of Books, 1 September 1785," *FO*.

204 "I have been nourished with the remains of Roman grandeur": "From Thomas Jefferson to Madame de Tessé, 20 March 1787," *FO*.

204 "he became responsible for making America's public buildings resemble Roman temples": Gordon Wood, *The Idea of America: Reflections on the Birth of the United States* (Penguin, 2011), 75.

204 "vain irritable and a bad calculator of the force and probable effect of the motives which govern men": "To James Madison from Thomas Jefferson, 30 January 1787," *FO*.

204     "The tree of liberty must be refreshed from time to time with the blood of patriots and tyrants": "From Thomas Jefferson to William Stephens Smith, 13 November 1787," *FO*.

205     "I shall concur in it chearfully": "From Thomas Jefferson to James Madison, 20 December 1787," *FO*.

205     not enough states would ratify it: "From Thomas Jefferson to Richard Price, 8 January 1789," *FO*.

205     "rather be exposed to the inconveniencies attending too much liberty": "From Thomas Jefferson to Archibald Stuart, 23 December 1791," *FO*.

206     "the most characteristic product of the American Enlightenment": Peter Gay, "The Enlightenment," in *The Comparative Approach to American History*, ed. C. Van Woodward (Basic Books, 1968), 43.

206     published under the pen name Publius: Gummere, *The American Colonial Mind and the Classical Tradition*, 220.

206     twice as many references to Greeks as to Romans: George Kennedy, "Classical Influences on *The Federalist*," in *Classical Traditions in Early America*, ed. John Eadie (Center for the Coordination of Ancient and Modern Studies, University of Michigan, 1976), 121.

206     "it is not safe to trust to the virtue of any people": "From Alexander Hamilton to John Jay, 26 November 1775," Hamilton papers, *FO*.

206     "the source of many of our errors": June 22, 1787, Madison, *Debates in the Federal Convention*,150.

206     the pillar of "virtue" has fallen": This observation is made in Ruth H. Bloch, "The Gendered Meanings of Virtue in Revolutionary America," *Signs: Journal of Women in Culture and Society*, 13, no. 1 (Autumn 1987), 54.

207     "a nation of philosophers is as little to be expected as the philosophical race of kings": "The Federalist Number 49, [2 February] 1788," Madison papers, *FO*. See also his remarks at the Virginia Ratifying Convention, 20 June 1788, at which he rejected the two extremes of having unlimited confidence in the people or in considering them to be devoid of virtue.

207     "self Interest is more powerfull than publick virtue": "Abigail Adams to Mercy Otis Warren, 22 January 1779," *FO*.

207     "Sordid self-Interest": "From Benjamin Franklin to John Paul Jones, 27 May 1778," *FO*.

207     "The *causes* of faction cannot be removed": This and the quotations in the next three paragraphs are from "The Federalist Number 10, [22 November] 1787," Madison papers, *FO*. Madison's italics.

208     Madison's most innovative thinking: See Roy Branson, "James Madison and the Scottish Enlightenment," *Journal of the History of Ideas* 40, no. 2 (1979).

208     "power should be a check to power": Montesquieu, *The Spirit of Laws* (1766), 220.

208 "a blind veneration for antiquity": "The Federalist Number 14, [30 November] 1787," Madison papers, *FO*.

209 "attention to the dead languages": Noah Webster, "On the Education of Youth in America," in *A Collection of Essays and Fugitiv Writings on Moral, Political and Literary Subjects* (I. Thomas and E. T. Andrews, 1790), 23, 3–4.

210 "the tendency of federal bodies, rather to anarchy among the members than to tyranny in the head": James Madison, "The Federalist Number 18, [7 December] 1787," *FO*.

210 eighteen to twenty members of the ratification meeting there were in fact veterans of Shays' Rebellion: "To James Madison from Nathaniel Gorham, 27 January 1788," *FO*.

210 Madison gloomily passed the word to George Washington: "From James Madison to George Washington, 3 February 1788," *FO*.

210 "Never perhaps was a state more divided than Virginia is on the new Constitution": "To James Madison from John Dawson, 18 February 1788," *FO*.

210 the largest of the state conventions: Pauline Maier, *Ratification: The People Debate the Constitution, 1787–1788* (Simon & Schuster, 2011), 165–66.

210 "A democracy is a volcano": "Speech in the Convention of Massachusetts on Biennial Elections," in *The Works of Fisher Ames* (T. B. Wait, 1809), 24.

211 "they will swallow up all us little folks": Jonathan Elliott, ed., *The Debates in the Several State Conventions on the Adoption of the Federal Constitution, Vol. 2* (J. B. Lippincott, 1901), 102.

211 "I have known the worth of a good government by the want of it": Elliott, ed., *The Debates in the Several State Conventions, Vol. 2*, 108.

211 "The quoting of ancient history was no more to the purpose": Elliott, ed., *The Debates in the Several State Conventions, Vol. 2*, 68–69.

211 192 against and only 144 in support: Maier, *Ratification*, 186.

212 twenty-three essays: Madison, "The Federalist, Number 38, [12 January] 1788," *FO*.

212 "the liberties of Rome proved the final victim to her military triumphs": James Madison, "The Federalist Number 41, [19 January] 1788," *FO*.

212 "Ambition must be made to counteract ambition": "The Federalist Number 51, [6 February] 1788," *FO*.

212 "History informs us of no long lived republic which had not a senate": James Madison, "The Federalist No. 63, [1 March 1788]," *FO*.

213 "half-lettered": "From Thomas Jefferson to Pierre Samuel Du Pont de Nemours, 18 January 1802," *FO*.

213 "Sparta was little better than a well regulated camp": "The Federalist No. 6, [14 November 1787]," *FO*.

213   "men of heroic virtue": Meyer Reinhold, *Classica Americana: The Greek and Roman Heritage in the United States* (Wayne State University Press, 1984), 157.

213   "the situation of your state is critical": "From Alexander Hamilton to James Madison, [19 May 1788]," *FO*. Hamilton's italics.

213   "pray for his death": "From Thomas Jefferson to James Madison, 8 December 1784," *FO*.

214   *"We, the people . . .* instead of We, the states?" Hugh Grigsby, *The History of the Virginia Federal Convention of 1788* (Virginia Historical Society, 1890), 81.

214   "Something must be done to preserve your liberty and mine": "Speech of Patrick Henry (June 5, 1788)," *Anti-Federalist Papers*, accessed online.

214   "turbulence, violence and abuse of power": James Madison, "General Defense of the Constitution, [6 June] 1788," *FO*.

214   "the fervid declamation of Mr. Henry": "Thomas Jefferson: Autobiography, 6 Jan.–29 July 1821, 6 January 1821," *FO*.

215   "The great and wise State of Massachusetts has taken this step": Bernard Bailyn, ed., *Debate on the Constitution: Federalist and Antifederalist Speeches, Articles, and Letters During the Struggle over Ratification, Part Two* (Library of America, 1990), 750.

215   "men who had seen hard military service": Hugh Blair Grigsby, *History of the Virginia Federal Convention of 1788* (Da Capo Press, 1969), 339.

215   perhaps one dead: On p. 246 in *Witnesses at the Creation: Hamilton, Madison, Jay, and the Constitution* (Henry Holt, 1985), Richard Morris has one dead, but on p. 274 of *Ratification*, Maier has none.

215   "a disturbance in the City of Albany": "From Alexander Hamilton to James Madison, [8 July 1788]," *FO*.

216   "Faction was virtue's opposite": John Howe Jr., "Republican Thought and the Political Violence of the 1790s," *American Quarterly* 19, pt. 1 (Summer 1967), 158.

216   "none but the most disinterested, able and virtuous men may be appointed to either house of Congress": "From George Washington to Benjamin Fishbourn, 23 December 1788," *FO*.

216   "Our party killed one Indian": "From George Washington to John Stanwix, 8 October 1757," *FO*.

### *Part III:* Americanization
217   "a radical shift in discourse": John Shields, *The American Aeneas: Classical Origins of the American Self* (University of Tennessee Press, 2001), 258.

### *Chapter 12:* The Classical Vision Smashes Into American Reality
219   Brackenridge and Madison had been friendly at the college: Ralph Ketcham, *James Madison: A Biography* (Macmillan, 1971), 34.

220    "The great mischief in democracy is party": H. H. Brackenridge, *Modern Chivalry: Containing the Adventures of a Captain and Teague O'Reagan, His Servant, Vol. I* (Johnson & Warner, 1815), 2, 2, 57, 65–66.

221    "There are no scholars amongst us, save a Latin schoolmaster": H. H. Brackenridge, *Modern Chivalry, or the Adventures of Captain Farrago and Teague O'Regan, Vol. III* (J. T. Shryock, 1853), 154–55, 132, 216, 40.

221    "unique, revolutionary, pluralistic, changing, progressive nation": Meyer Reinhold, *Classica Americana: The Greek and Roman Heritage in the United States* (Wayne State University Press, 1984), 175.

221    "the experiment entrusted to the hands of the American people": "First Inaugural Address: Final Version, 30 April 1789," *FO*.

221    "Madison wrote the House's response, and Washington's answer to the House's response": Richard Brookhiser, *James Madison* (Basic Books, 2011), 79.

221    a good part of early American history consists of such instances of Madison talking to himself: Professor Allen credits her father with this insightful quip. Danielle Allen, *Our Declaration: A Reading of the Declaration of Independence in Defense of Equality* (W. W. Norton, 2014), 103.

222    "His Majesty's Opposition": Archibald Foord, *His Majesty's Opposition, 1714–1830* (Oxford University Press, 1964), 1.

222    "loyal opposition": This discussion is influenced by Joyce Appleby's insights on p. 20 of *Inheriting the Revolution: The First Generation of Americans* (Harvard University Press, 2001).

222    "The Federalists never saw themselves as a party": Gordon Wood, *Revolutionary Characters: What Made the Founders Different* (Penguin Press, 2006), 55.

222    The classical mindset would prove a poor framework in which to view the emerging politics of the 1790s: This sentence paraphrases the observations on p. 3 of James Roger Sharp, *American Politics in the Early Republic: The Nation in Crisis* (Yale University Press, 1993).

222    "Publick virtue, and the love of their country, . . . were extinct": Edward Wortley Montagu, *Reflections on the Rise and Fall of the Antient Republicks* (A. Millar, 1759), 269.

223    "luxury, effeminacy and corruption": Montagu, *Reflections on the Rise and Fall of the Antient Republicks*, 280, 270, 371.

223    "faction was the ruin of Carthage, and riches probably were the cause of faction": J. Burgh, *Political Disquisitions; Or, An Enquiry Into Public Errors, Defects, and Abuses, Vol. 3* (Edward and Charles Dilly, 1775), 67.

223    "The spirit of liberty was dead, and the spirit of faction had taken its place on both sides": Lord Bolingbroke, "Letter 2, Remarks on the History of England," in *Lord Bolingbroke, Historical Writings*, ed. Isaac Kramnick (University of Chicago Press, 1972), 167.

223    to be politically aligned: Marshall Smelser, "The Federalist Period as an Age of Passion," *American Quarterly* 10, no. 4 (Winter 1958), 395–96.

224    "If I could not go to heaven but with a party, I would not go there at all": "From Thomas Jefferson to Francis Hopkinson, 13 March 1789," *FO*.

224    "I found a state of things which, of all I had ever contemplated, I the least expected": "The Anas," *Thomas Jefferson: Writings* (Library of America, 1984), 665–66.

224    "whenever I Use the Word Republick, with approbation I mean a Government": "From John Adams to Samuel Adams, Sr., 18 October 1790," *FO*.

224    "Is not the *whole* sovereignty, my friend, essentially in the People? [Samuel Adams' italics]": "John Adams from Samuel Adams, Sr., 25 November 1790," *FO*.

225    "stock jobbers and King-jobbers": "From Thomas Jefferson to Lafayette, 16 June 1792," *FO*.

225    Washington would dwell on questions of land: George Washington, "Diary Entry: 29 June 1791," *FO*. See also William Seale, *The President's House, Vol. 1* (White House Historical Association, 1986), 14.

225    "The Federal City on the Potomac": Stanley Elkins and Eric McKitrick, *The Age of Federalism* (Oxford University Press, 1993), 169–70.

226    "grain . . . as fine as that of our best earthen ware": "From Thomas Jefferson to Thomas Johnson, 8 March 1792," *FO*.

226    "the first temple dedicated to the sovereignty of the people": "Thomas Jefferson to Benjamin Henry Latrobe, 12 July 1812," *FO*.

226    Thus was set the neoclassical style of American official buildings, especially courts and state capitol buildings: This sentence paraphrases p. 19, Jean Matthews, *Toward a New Society: American Thought and Culture, 1800–1830* (Twayne, 1991).

226    "the City of Magnificent Intentions": Charles Dickens, *American Notes for General Circulation, Vol. 1* (Wilson & Company, 1842), 21.

226    "the speculators and Tories": "To Thomas Jefferson from James Madison, 1 May 1791," *FO*.

226    "parties are unavoidable": "For the National Gazette, [ca. 23 January] 1792," Madison papers, *FO*.

227    an outlet for anti-Hamilton views: This paraphrases p. 42, Richard McCormick, *The Presidential Game: The Origins of American Presidential Politics* (Oxford University Press, 1982).

227    "Party is a monster who devours the common good": William Wyche, *Party Spirit: An Oration. . . .* (T. & J. Swords, 1794), 15–16. Information about Wyche from Robert Emery, "William Wyche," *The Yale Biographical Dictionary of American Law*, ed. Roger Newman (Yale University Press, 2009), 605.

227    "Mr. Madison cooperating with Mr. Jefferson": "From Alexander Hamilton to Edward Carrington, 26 May 1792," *FO*.

228 "I did not expect that truth, honor and virtue would so soon have been trampled": "From John Adams to Henry Marchant, 3 March 1792," *FO.*

228 "rending the Union asunder": "From George Washington to Edmund Randolph, 26 August 1792," *FO.*

228 "if we have an embryo-Cæsar in the United States 'tis Burr": "From Alexander Hamilton to–, 26 September 1792." Hamilton papers, *FO.*

228 "the Catilines and the Cæsars of the community": "Catullus No. III, 29 September 1792," *FO.* Hamilton's italics.

229 "the greatest man that ever lived": Conversation from era of Washington presidency recounted in "Thomas Jefferson to Benjamin Rush, 16 January 1811," *FO.*

229 "bent upon my subversion": "From Alexander Hamilton to George Washington, 9 September 1792," *FO.*

229 "a shillyshally thing of mere milk & water": "The Anas," *Thomas Jefferson: Writings* (Library of America, 1984), 692.

229 "daring to call the republican party a *faction*": "From Thomas Jefferson to James Madison, 29 June 1792,"*FO.*

229 "There is not a Jacobin in France more devoted to Faction": "John Adams to Abigail Adams, 28 December 1792," *FO.*

230 Democratic Societies: Elkins and McKitrick, *The Age of Federalism,* 456–57.

230 "be prepared to defend the Rights of Man": Quoted in Eugene Link, *Democratic-Republican Societies, 1790–1800* (Columbia University Press, 1942), 79.

230 "The President is not well": "From Thomas Jefferson to James Madison, 9 June 1793," *FO.*

231 "The Presidt. was much inflamed": Thomas Jefferson papers, "Notes of Cabinet Meeting on Edmond Charles Genet, 2 August 1793," *FO.* Jefferson's italics.

231 "His soul is poisoned with Ambition": "John Adams to Abigail Adams, 26 December 1793," *FO.*

231 "Jefferson went off Yesterday": "John Adams to Abigail Adams, 6 January 1794," *FO.*

232 "I am become too lazy, with the pen": "From Thomas Jefferson to George Wythe, 18 April 1795," *FO.*

232 "to feed every animal on my farm except my negroes": "From Thomas Jefferson to John Taylor, 29 December 1794," *FO.*

232 "the federalists got unchecked hold of Genl. Washington": "The Anas," *Thomas Jefferson: Writings* (Library of America, 1984), 673.

232 "I long to see you": "From Thomas Jefferson to James Madison, 27 April 1795," *FO.*

233 the tax resistance movement: Link, *Democratic-Republican Societies,* 147.

233    "Shall the general will prevail, or the will of a faction?": "Tully No. II, [26 August 1794]," Hamilton papers, *FO*.

233    "How long, ye Catilines, will you abuse our patience": "Tully No. III, [28 August 1794]," Hamilton papers, *FO*.

233    "Meetings of Malcontent persons": "To George Washington from Alexander Hamilton, 5 August 1794," *FO*.

233    "There simply had to be a plot": Smelser, "The Federalist Period as an Age of Passion," *American Quarterly*, 398.

234    "a curse on his virtues, they've undone his country": "To James Madison from Thomas Jefferson, 27 March 1796," *FO*.

234    if the nation broke up, he would go with the North: "Notes of a Conversation with Edmund Randolph, [after 1795]," *FO*.

234    "you should properly estimate the immense value of your national Union": "Farewell Address, 19 September 1796," *FO*.

235    He reacted to it eccentrically: The instructive word "eccentricities" is used on p. 247 of Peter Shaw, *The Character of John Adams* (University of North Carolina Press, 1976). For a contrary view of Adams, one which I think is erroneous, see pp. 192–94 in C. Bradley Thompson, *John Adams and the Spirit of Liberty* (University Press of Kansas, 2002).

235    "Mausoleums, Statues, Monuments will never be erected to me": "From John Adams to William Sumner, 28 March 1809," *FO*.

235    John Adams, coming from New England, had seen more of democracy in practice than had Thomas Jefferson of aristocratic Virginia: This paraphrases a comment made by Wood in conversation with the author, Providence, R.I., 18 December 2017.

235    "I like a little rebellion now and then": "From Thomas Jefferson to Abigail Adams, 22 February 1787," *FO*.

236    "the nation has been awaked": "From Thomas Jefferson to George Washington, 4 December 1788," *FO*.

236    "I look with great anxiety for the firm establishment of the new government in France": "From Thomas Jefferson to George Mason, 4 February 1791," *FO*.

237    "Terror is the order of the Day": "To George Washington from Gouverneur Morris, 18 October 1793," *FO*.

237    "the basis of popular government during a revolution is both virtue and terror": Marissa Linton, *The Politics of Virtue in Enlightenment France* (Palgrave, 2001), 1.

237    "the disgusting spectacle of the French revolution": Hamilton papers, "The Stand No. III, [7 April 1798]," *FO*.

237    "Our vessel is moored at such a distance": "From Thomas Jefferson to John Breckinridge, 29 January 1800," *FO*.

238    "a conspiracy of vice against virtue": "Printed Version of the 'Reynolds Pamphlet, 1797,'" Alexander Hamilton papers, *FO.*

239    "an Opinion that Hamilton was the Writer of Washingtons best Letters": "From John Adams to Benjamin Rush, 23 August 1805," *FO.*

239    "Their Emissaries are scatterd through all parts": "Abigail Adams to Mercy Otis Warren, 25 April 1798," *FO.*

239    "a little patience and we shall see the reign of witches pass over": "From Thomas Jefferson to John Taylor, 4 June 1798," *FO.*

239    "nothing was more important than the maintenance of the established order": Moses Hadas, ed., *The Basic Works of Cicero* (Modern Library, 1951), x.

239    "a temperamental conservative caught in the nets of revolution": Anthony Everitt, *Cicero: The Life and Times of Rome's Greatest Politician* (Random House, 2001), 322.

239    worried that the new nation would drift toward factionalism: See, for example, "From John Adams to Benjamin Rush, 9 June 1789," Adams papers, *FO.*

240    "the capstone of the new Federalist system": Leonard Levy, *Emergence of a Free Press* (Oxford University Press, 1985), 300.

240    the number of newspapers published in the United States more than doubled: Robert Shalhope, *The Roots of Democracy: American Thought and Culture, 1760–1800* (Rowman & Littlefield, 1990), 139.

240    the majority of newspapers were Federalist: David Hackett Fischer, *The Revolution of American Conservativism: The Federalist Party in the Era of Jeffersonian Democracy* (Harper & Row, 1965), 131.

240    "operated as if the law of seditious libel did not exist": Levy, *Emergence of a Free Press*, x.

240    "the nation's enduring source of political stability, was forged in—and, fair to say, created by—the nation's newspapers": Jill Lepore, *These Truths: A History of the United States* (W. W. Norton, 2018), 145.

241    voter turnout sometimes exceeding 100 percent: Charles Sellers, *The Market Revolution: Jacksonian America, 1815–1846* (Oxford University Press, 1991), 37.

241    the party in power cracking down on the opposition press: Terri Diane Halperin, *The Alien and Sedition Acts of 1798: Testing the Constitution* (Johns Hopkins University Press, 2016), 73.

241    involved Thomas Cooper: Jonathan Israel, *The Expanding Blaze: How the American Revolution Ignited the World, 1775–1848* (Princeton University Press, 2017), 352–53.

241    "being a wicked and malicious person": Alfred Young, Gary Nash, and Ray Raphael, eds, *Revolutionary Founders: Rebels, Radicals and Reformers in the Making of the Nation* (Vintage, 2012), 371.

241  "the bullying speech of your president and the stupid answer of your senate": J. Fairfax McLaughlin, *Matthew Lyon: The Hampden of Congress* (Wynkoop Hallenbeck Crawford, 1900), 369.

241  the median price of an American house was $614: Lee Soltow, "The Distribution of Income in the United States in 1798: Estimates Based on the Federal Housing Inventory," *The Review of Economics and Statistics* 69, no. 1 (February 1987), 182.

241  imprisoned a Vermont newspaper editor: Charles Slack, *Liberty's First Crisis: Adams, Jefferson, and the Misfits Who Saved Free Speech* (Atlantic Monthly Press, 2015), 199.

242  "Every defendant was a Republican": Smelser, "The Federalist Period as an Age of Passion," *American Quarterly*, 412.

242  "combinations or conspiracies to raise insurrections against government": Cushing's remarks are quoted in a footnote to "To Thomas Jefferson from John Taylor, 15 February 1799," *FO*.

242  Jedediah Peck: Elkins and McKitrick, *The Age of Federalism*, 705. "In irons" is from Gordon Wood, *Empire of Liberty: A History of the Early Republic, 1789–1815* (Oxford University Press, 2009), 262.

242  "a regular conspiracy to overturn the government": "From Alexander Hamilton to Theodore Sedgwick, 2 February 1799," *FO*.

242  "take with you copies": "From Alexander Hamilton to Timothy Pickering, [14 May 1800]," *FO*.

242  "political espionage": Daniel Sisson, *The American Revolution of 1800* (Alfred A. Knopf, 1974), 375.

243  "Let that party set up a broomstick": "From George Washington to Jonathan Trumbull, Jr., 21 July 1799," *FO*.

243  "moving by hasty strides to some awful crisis": "From George Washington to James McHenry, 17 November 1799," *FO*.

243  "His last scene corresponded with the whole tenor of his life": "To John Adams from Tobias Lear, 15 December 1799," *FO*.

243  "every countanance is coverd with Gloom": "From Abigail Smith Adams to Mary Smith Cranch, 18 December 1799," *FO*.

244  "His Name may be still a rampart": "Inaugural Address, 4 March 1797," Adams papers, *FO*.

244  "Our guide, our Washington's no more": Samuel Griswold Goodrich, *Recollections of a Lifetime: Or Men and Things I Have Seen* (Miller, Orton and Mulligan, 1856), 107–108.

244  "the President will be fretted, perplexed, and tormented": "From William Stephens Smith to Abigail Amelia Adams Smith, 22 December 1799," *FO*.

244 "Washington never assumed the Character of perpetual Dictator—. That Pretension was reserved for one of his Aids": "From John Adams to Alexander Hamilton, 1800," *FO*. It is not clear that this letter was sent.

245 "The object of this party is to destroy ancient systems": David Daggett, "Sun-Beams May Be Extracted from Cucumbers, But the Process Is Tedious," in *The Rising Glory of America, 1760–1820*, ed. Gordon Wood. (Northeastern University Press, 1990), 214.

245 partly by working as a butler: "Sketch of the Life and Character of the Hon. David Daggett," Connecticut State Library, accessed online.

246 "the unreasonable demands & desires of the few": "William Manning's *The Key of Libberty*," ed. Samuel Eliot Morison, *William and Mary Quarterly* 13, no. 2 (April 1956), 211, 212, 214, 220, 205.

246 "he sought to counteract social disruption and reestablish the deferential world order": Richard Rollins, "Words as Social Control: Noah Webster and the Creation of the *American Dictionary*," *American Quarterly* 28, no. 4 (Autumn 1976), 416. My discussion here also was influenced by a reading of David Simpson, *The Politics of American English, 1776–1850* (Oxford University Press, 1986).

246 "angrily secluded" at his home: Gordon Wood, *Empire of Liberty*, 273.

246 "a final dissolution of all bonds": "From Thomas Jefferson to Benjamin Hawkins," 18 February 1803," *FO*.

247 "the most serious and formidable conspiracy": "To Thomas Jefferson from James Monroe, 15 September 1800," *FO*.

247 "Nothing is talked of here but the recent conspiracy of negroes": "To Thomas Jefferson from James Thomson Callender, 13 September 1800," *FO*.

## Chapter 13: The Revolution of 1800: The People, Not the Plebes

249 "eternal hostility against every form of tyranny": "From Thomas Jefferson to Benjamin Rush, 23 September 1800," *FO*.

249 "it is better to get a friend to forward it by some of the boats": "From Thomas Jefferson to John Breckinridge, 29 January 1800," *FO*.

249 "as true a *Cataline* as ever met in midnight conclave": "From Alexander Hamilton to James A. Bayard, 6 August 1800," *FO*. Hamilton's italics.

249 "He is truly the *Cataline* of America": "From Alexander Hamilton to Oliver Wolcott, Junior, 16 December 1800," *FO*. Hamilton's italics.

249 "It is too late for me to become his apologist": "From Alexander Hamilton to James A. Bayard, 16 January 1801," *FO*.

250 "he does not possess the talents adapted to the *Administration* of Government": "Letter from Alexander Hamilton, Concerning the Public Conduct and Character of John Adams, Esq. President of the United States, [24 October 1800]," *FO*. Hamilton's italics.

250　might have violated the Sedition Act: Charles Slack makes this point on p. 219 of *Liberty's First Crisis: Adams, Jefferson, and the Misfits Who Saved Free Speech* (Atlantic Monthly Press, 2015).

250　"all the Vanity and Timidity of Cicero": "From John Adams to François Adriaan Van der Kemp, 25 April 1808," *FO.*

250　"bastard brat of a Scotch Pedler": "From John Adams to Benjamin Rush, 25 January 1806," and "John Adams to Thomas Jefferson, 12 July 1813," FO. In the letter to Jefferson, Adams spelled the word "bratt."

250　"a damn'd Rascall and a Devil": "From John Adams to Boston Patriot, 1809," *FO.*

250　"only capable of, enormous wickedness": Abbe Claude Millot, *Elements of General History, Vol. 2 of Ancient History* (James Watson, 1811), 69.

251　"equated parties with factions and considered them unmitigated evils": Bruce Ackerman, *The Failure of the Founding Fathers: Jefferson, Marshall and the Rise of Presidential Democracy* (Belknap/Harvard University Press, 2005), 3–5.

251　"The revolution of 1800": "From Thomas Jefferson to Spencer Roane, 6 September 1819," *FO.*

252　"foundation of the overthrow of the federal party": "From John Adams to Boston Patriot, 29 May 1809," *FO.*

252　"resources of wisdom, of virtue, of zeal": Thomas Jefferson papers, "First Inaugural Address, 4 March 1801," *FO.*

253　Jefferson pardoned Callender: "Pardon for James Thomson Callender, 16 March 1801," *FO.*

253　"he was in possession of things which he could & would make use of": "From Thomas Jefferson to James Monroe, 29 May 1801," *FO.*

253　"a striking though sable resemblance to those of the President himself": Quoted on p. 158, Michael Durey, *With the Hammer of Truth: James Thomson Callender and America's Early National Heroes* (University Press of Virginia, 1990).

253　Callender's corpse would be found: Michael Durey, *Transatlantic Radicals and the Early American Republic* (University Press of Kansas, 1997), 62, 207, 245–46.

253　a bill to establish the U.S. Military Academy at West Point: See Peter Onuf, *The Mind of Thomas Jefferson* (University of Virginia Press, 2007), 196.

253　one path toward nonclassical higher education: Theodore Crackel, *West Point: A Bicentennial History* (University Press of Kansas, 2002), 96–97.

253　"the West Point engineers doubled the capacity of the little American army": Henry Adams, *History of the United States of America During the Administrations of James Madison* (Library of America, 1986), 1342.

253　"I was turned out of Office": "From John Adams to James Lloyd, 31 March 1815," *FO.*

254    catching the early coach to Baltimore: David McCullough, *John Adams* (Touchstone, 2002), 564.

254    "I thought I had made a good exchange . . . of honors & virtues, for manure": "From John Adams to Samuel Dexter, 23 March 1801," *FO*.

254    "The Virtue and good Sense of Americans": "From John Adams to François Adriaan Van der Kemp, 24 July 1802," *FO*.

254    "It behoves all men": "From John Adams to John Rogers, 6 February 1801," Adams papers, *FO*.

254    "a proof of the falsehood of that Mass of odious Abuse of my Character": "John Adams from the Autobiography of John Adams," 5 October 1802. Adams papers, *FO*.

254    "the torment of a perpetual Vulcano of Slander": "[1768–1770], [from the Autobiography of John Adams]," *FO*.

255    "Jefferson is not a Roman": "From John Adams to Benjamin Rush, 19 September 1806," *FO*.

255    "could not long refrain from abusing me": "From John Adams to Benjamin Rush, 23 June 1807," *FO*.

255    "a Secret and deliberate design": "From John Adams to Abiel Holmes, 6 May 1807," *FO*.

255    "Change the Names and every Anecdote will be applicable to Us": "From John Adams to Benjamin Rush, 4 December 1805," *FO*.

255    "Poor Cicero": "From John Adams to Benjamin Rush, 18 January 1808," *FO*.

255    "Cicero was libelled, Slandered insulted by all Parties": "From John Adams to William Sumner, 28 March 1809," *FO*.

256    "The Last Roman": Linda Kerber, *Federalists in Dissent: Imagery and Ideology in Jeffersonian America* (Cornell University Press, 1970), 122.

256    "How many Martyrdoms must I Suffer?": "From John Adams to Thomas Jefferson, 12 July 1813," *FO*.

256    "his last appointments to office as personally unkind": "From Thomas Jefferson to Abigail Smith Adams, 13 June 1804," *FO*.

256    "scenes of midnight appointment": "Thomas Jefferson to Benjamin Rush, 16 January 1811," *FO*.

257    "the reign of terror is no more": Abraham Bishop, *Oration Delivered in Wallingford, On the 11th of March 1801, Before the Republicans of the State of Connecticut, at Their General Thanksgiving, For the Election Of Thomas Jefferson to the Presidency, And of Aaron Burr to the Vice-Presidency, Of the United States of America* (William Morse, 1801), 97.

257    Aaron Burr wrote to Jefferson about who should get it: "To Thomas Jefferson from Aaron Burr, 21 April 1801," *FO*.

257 "the best political plum in Connecticut": Dumas Malone, *Jefferson the President: First Term, 1801–1805* (Little, Brown and Company 1970), 70, 75. See also Samuel Griswold Goodrich, *Recollections of a Lifetime: Or Men and Things I Have Seen* (Miller, Orton and Mulligan, 1856), 125.

257 Theodore Dwight, brother of the president of Yale College, penned a satire: "Tribes of faction" is quoted on p. 483, Lynde Harrison, "History of Political Parties," in *History of the City of New Haven to the Present Time*, ed. Edward Atwater (W. W. Munsell & Co., 1887). The couplet is quoted on p. 209, Richard Purcell, *Connecticut in Transition: 1775–1818* (Wesleyan University Press, 1963).

257 the politicization of the customs office: "Remonstrance of the New Haven Merchants, [18 June 1801]," Jefferson papers, *FO*.

257 the first statement written by a president expressly as a leader of a political party: Malone, *Jefferson the President: First Term*, 79.

257 Did you Federalists think you held a monopoly on government jobs?: "From Thomas Jefferson to the New Haven Merchants, 12 July 1801," *FO*.

257 "the whole herd have squealed out": "From Thomas Jefferson to Pierre Samuel Du Pont de Nemours, 18 January 1802," *FO*.

258 "have not snored through four years at Princeton": Alfred Young, "The Mechanics and the Jeffersonians: New York, 1789–1801," in *The Labor History Reader*, ed. Daniel Leab (University of Illinois Press, 1985), 93.

258 "We have striven to be faultless, and neglected to be natural": Edmund Trowbridge Dana, "The Powers of Genius," *The Monthly Anthology and Boston Review* II, no. 10 (October 1805), 531–32.

259 "And CATO liv'd again—in WASHINGTON": no author listed, "Occasional Prologue to Cato's Tragedy," *The Monthly Anthology and Boston Review* II, no. 10 (October 1805), 586.

259 the Federalist shelf was bare: This and the following two paragraphs draw on the work of Linda Kerber in *Federalists in Dissent*.

259 "The Roman historians are the best that ever existed": no author listed, "Is the Study of Latin and Greek Languages Useful?" *New England Quarterly Magazine*, July–September 1802, 125.

259 the Jeffersonians were "wretches [who] announce hostility": Thomas Green Fessenden, *Democracy Unveiled* (David Carlisle, 1805), 121, 6, 80, 129, 198, 202.

260 "the aristocracy of virtue is destroyed": Quoted in Paul L. Ford, Review of "The Life and Correspondence of Rufus King," *The American Historical Review* 3 (October 1897–July 1898), 564.

260 Washington Benevolent Society: Information on the number of chapters is from Richard Buel and Jeffers Lennox, *Historical Dictionary of the Early American Republic* (Rowman & Littlefield, 2017), 366.

260     "ostensibly charitable organizations but in reality arms of the party": Gordon Wood, *Empire of Liberty: A History of the Early Republic, 1789–1815* (Oxford University Press, 2009), 306–307.

260     "rank and condition" affected the degree of injury caused by act: Christopher Clark, *Social Change in America from the Revolution Through the Civil War* (Ivan R. Dee, 2006), 110.

261     "Hamilton seems to be literally Mad": "To Thomas Jefferson from Aaron Burr, 21 April 1801," *FO*.

261     "this American world was not made for me": "From Alexander Hamilton to Gouverneur Morris, [29 February 1802]," *FO*.

261     "He was indiscreet, vain and opinionated": "The Funeral, [14 July 1804]," Alexander Hamilton papers, *FO*, where the quotation from the Morris diary is appended.

262     "virtue so rare, so bold": Fisher Ames, "Sketch of the Character of Alexander Hamilton," *The Works of Fisher Ames, Volume II*, ed. Seth Ames (Little, Brown and Company, 1854), 259, 261, 262.

262     "Our country is too big for union": Letter of 26 October 1803, *The Works of Fisher Ames* (T. B. Wait, 1809), 483.

262     "as to any harm": "Notes on Aaron Burr, 15 April 1806," Jefferson papers, *FO*.

263     Burr's efforts to somehow establish an independent nation in the Ohio River Valley: "From Thomas Jefferson to United States Congress, 22 January 1807," *FO*.

263     "His conspiracy has been one of the most flagitious": "From Thomas Jefferson to Marie-Joseph-Paul-Yves-Roch-Gilbert du Motier, marquis de Lafayette, 14 July 1807," *FO*.

263     "immune to the ideology and values of the Revolution": Gordon Wood, *Revolutionary Characters: What Made the Founders Different* (Penguin Press, 2006), 229, 235, 239.

263     "our Cataline": Jefferson refers to Burr thusly in two letters—"From Thomas Jefferson to Caesar Augustus Rodney, 5 December 1806," and "From Thomas Jefferson to John Langdon, 22 December 1806," both in *FO*.

263     "a free and virtuous nation": "First Inaugural Address, [4 March] 1809," Madison papers, *FO*.

264     "a brave, a free, a virtuous, and an intelligent people": "Second Inaugural Address, [4 March] 1813," Madison papers, *FO*.

264     More than fifty-seven American towns and counties are named for him: Wood, *Empire of Liberty*, 699.

264     "his Administration has acquired more glory": "From John Adams to Thomas Jefferson, 2 February 1817," *FO*.

264   "He went over to the works of Eschylus, Sophocles and Euripides": D. L. Wilson, ed., *Thomas Jefferson's Literary Commonplace Book* (Princeton University Press, 1989), 163.

264   *"Vive, vale, et siquid novisti rectius istis"*: "Thomas Jefferson to James Madison, 13 May 1810," *FO*.

264   "Live: be happy": Christopher Smart, *The Works of Horace, Volume 2* (Stirling & Slade, 1819), 173.

265   "I think little of them, and say less": "To John Adams from Thomas Jefferson, 21 January 1812," *FO*.

*Chapter* 14: The End of American Classicism

267   "a great tobacco planter, who had herds of black slaves": [Josiah Quincy], "Climenole, No. 1," *The Port-Folio*, 28 January 1804, 27.

267   "sexual connection with all women—matrimonial alliances with none": [Josiah Quincy], "Cimenole, No. 3," *The Port-Folio*, 11 February 1804, 42.

267   "friendship with all nations, entangling alliances with none": Thomas Jefferson papers, " First Inaugural Address, 4 March 1801," *FO*.

268   "would endanger our union": "Second Inaugural Address," *Thomas Jefferson: Writings* (Library of America, 1984), 519.

268   "Civil War is preferable to Slavery": "From John Adams to Benjamin Rush, 23 March 1809," *FO*.

268   "If the Nation will not read them": "From John Adams to Samuel Perley, 18 April 1809," *FO*.

268   He considered the great Greek philosopher an obscure mystic: See "Thomas Jefferson to Benjamin Waterhouse, 13 October 1815," *FO*.

268   "I amused myself with reading Plato's republic": "Thomas Jefferson to John Adams, 5 July 1814," *FO*.

269   "undertake a regular course of history & poetry in both languages": "From Thomas Jefferson to Francis Eppes, 6 October 1820," *FO*.

269   "infidel philosophy": Quoting Cyrus King, in William Dawson Johnston, *History of the Library of Congress, Vol. 1, 1800–1864* (Government Printing Office, 1904), 86.

269   "wholly unintelligible": Quoted in Kevin J. Hayes, *The Road to Monticello: The Life and Mind of Thomas Jefferson* (Oxford University Press, 2008), 553.

270   "This mementous question, like a fire bell in the night, awakened and filled me with terror": "From Thomas Jefferson to John Holmes, 22 April 1820," *FO*.

270   "come home to roost": Darren Staloff, *Hamilton, Adams, Jefferson: The Politics of Enlightenment and the American Founding* (Hill & Wang, 2005), 352.

270   "are we then to see again Athenian and Lacedemonian confederacies?": "From Thomas Jefferson to John Adams, 22 January 1821," *FO*.

271   "No human efforts can ever abolish slavery": "Admission of Maine and Missouri," February 1820, *Annals of the Congress of the United States, 16th Congress, 1st Session* (Gales and Seaton, 1855), 328–29, 355–57, 382.

271   seventy violent incidents: Joanne Freeman, *The Field of Blood: Violence in Congress and the Road to Civil War* (Farrar, Straus and Giroux, 2018), 5.

271   On Jefferson's bedside table: Carl J. Richard, *The Founders and the Classics: Greece, Rome, and the American Enlightenment* (Harvard University Press, 1994), 276.

272   "the Union of the States be cherished & perpetuated": "James Madison: Advice to my Country," 1830–1836, *FO*.

272   "almost the last of the Romans": "From the Correspondent of the Portland Advertiser: Visit to Mr. Madison," *Niles' Register*, 17 August 1833, 409–10. Elizabeth Dowling Taylor quotes part of this report in *A Slave in the White House: Paul Jennings and the Madisons* (Palgrave Macmillan, 2012), 126.

272   "care little about what happened in Rome and Athens": Alexis de Tocqueville, *Democracy in America*, trans. Arthur Goldhammer (Library of America, 2004), 564.

272   failed in classics: George Wilson Pierson, *Tocqueville in America* (Johns Hopkins University Press, 1996), 17.

273   Greek Revival: "Sacred city" is quoted by R. M. Ogilvie in *Latin and Greek: A History of the Influence of the Classics on English Life from 1600 to 1918* (Routledge & Kegan Paul, 1964), 79. He lists the Romantic poets and discusses their various inclinations. The first four words of the Shelley quotation are quoted on p. 82 of Ogilvie. The complete quotation is at pp. viii–ix, Percy Bysshe Shelley, Preface, *Hellas* (Charles and James Ollier, 1822).

273   horror at the ancients' acceptance of homosexuality: The quotation about "crime against nature" is from p. 283 and the one about "not fit to be named . . ." is from p. 291, in Mark Kann, "Sexual Desire, Crime, and Punishment in the Early Republic," in *Long Before Stonewall: Histories of Same-Sex Sexuality in Early America*, ed. Thomas Foster (New York University Press, 2007).

273   homosexuality "cannot operate here": Edward Livingston, *A System of Penal Law for the State of Louisiana* (James Kay, Jun. & Co., 1833), 17. This paragraph draws from the discussions on pp. 260 and 252 in Charles Sellers, *The Market Revolution: Jacksonian America, 1815–1846* (Oxford University Press, 1991). Sellers quotes the passage quoted from Livingston.

274   "Our Federal Union. It must be preserved": This account is from Martin Van Buren, *The Autobiography of Martin Van Buren*, ed. John Fitzpatrick (Annual Report of the American Historical Association, Vol. 2/Government Printing Office, 1920), 415–16.

274   "a government, not a league": "President Jackson's Proclamation Regarding Nullification, December 10, 1832," Avalon Project Documents in Law, History and Diplomacy, Yale Law School Library.

274    "the people have twice decided this man knows enough": William Bentinck-Smith, ed., *The Harvard Book: Selections from Three Centuries* (Harvard University Press, 1982), 277.

274    "a barbarian who could not write a sentence of grammar": *The Memoirs of John Quincy Adams, Vol. VIII*, ed. Charles Francis Adams (J.B. Lippincott, 1876), 546.

275    "political parties are inseparable from free government": Van Buren, *Autobiography*, 125.

275    "You pays your money and you takes your choice!": Mark Twain, *Adventures of Huckleberry Finn* (Charles L. Webster, 1885), 249.

276    "A fair and generous competition among the different denominations of christians": Samuel Stanhope Smith, "The Divine Goodness of the United States of America," *The Analytical Review* XXII, July–December 1795 (J. Johnson, 1796), 417–18. The London magazine that carried this excerpt of Smith's sermon would be shuttered a few years later, in part because the publisher, Joseph Johnson, was jailed for seditious libel.

276    "bawling, itinerant, field and barn preachers": Thomas Green Fessenden, *Democracy Unveiled* (David Carlisle, 1805), 184–86.

276    "Direct access to divine grace and revelation": Sellers, *The Market Revolution*, 30.

277    the Constitution and the Scriptures: Gordon Wood, *Empire of Liberty: A History of the Early Republic, 1789–1815* (Oxford University Press, 2009), 611, 614.

277    "eternal felicity in the next world": Tocqueville, *Democracy in America*, trans. Lawrence, 530.

277    These new Americans would turn not to the ancient world but to themselves for guidance through belief systems leading to a plethora of cults and movements in nineteenth-century America: This sentence is influenced by the overview provided by Alice Felt Tyler in *Freedom's Ferment: Phases of American Social History to 1860* (University of Minnesota Press, 1944).

277    "this new democratic society was the very opposite of the one the revolutionary leaders had envisaged": Gordon Wood, *The Radicalism of the American Revolution* (Vintage Books, 1993), 230, 368.

277    abandoned the rationalist secularism: Alan Taylor, *American Revolutions: A Continental History, 1750–1804* (W. W. Norton, 2016), 451.

277    a third of Americans were members of churches: Daniel Walker Howe, *What Hath God Wrought: The Transformation of America, 1815–1848* (Oxford University Press, 2007), 186.

277    "In God We Trust": Howard Mumford Jones, *O Strange New World: American Culture: The Formative Years* (Viking, 1964), 230.

278    An "Age of Fun": Quoted in Alan Nourie and Barbara Nourie, eds., *American Mass-Market Magazines* (Greenwood Press, 1990), 184.

278 "the almighty dollar": Washington Irving, "The Creole Village," in *The Works of Washington Irving, Vol. 19* (G.P. Putnam's Sons, 1895), 294. I first saw this fact noted in Joyce Appleby, *Inheriting the Revolution: The First Generation of Americans* (Harvard University Press, 2001), 252.

278 "the era of Trade": Ralph Waldo Emerson, "Journal XXVII, 1836," in *The Emerson Digital Archive*, 137–38. I am indebted for this to Joseph Ellis, who quotes Emerson about the "era of Trade" in *After the Revolution: Profiles of Early American Culture* (W. W. Norton, 1979), 218.

278 was "virtue": Richard Rollins, "Words as Social Control: Noah Webster and the Creation of the *American Dictionary*," *American Quarterly* 28, no. 4 (Autumn 1976), 415.

278 "the predominant signification of *virtus* among the Romans": No page number, "Vir to Vis" page, Noah Webster, *An American Dictionary of the English Language, Vol. II* (S. Converse, 1828). Note: I owe this notice of Webster's definition to p. 212 in Ellis, *After the Revolution*.

278 "little more than female chastity": Wood, *Radicalism of the American Revolution*, 357. See also Ruth H. Bloch, "The Gendered Meanings of Virtue in Revolutionary America," *Signs: Journal of Women in Culture and Society* 13, no. 1 (1987).

279 "Had I the time, I could say much about Cato and Brutus": Peter Parley, [Samuel Griswold Goodrich], *Tales About Rome and Modern Italy* (Thomas Tegg, 1839), 213–24.

279 depicting George Washington as a bare-chested Roman: John Crawford, "The Classical Tradition in American Sculpture: Structure and Surface," *The American Art Journal* 11, no. 3 (July 1979), 40.

279 "They have a Roman gown on him": David Crockett, *Life of Col. David Crockett, Written By Himself* (G. G. Evans, 1860), 205. I first saw Crockett's comment in Crawford, "The Classical Tradition in American Sculpture."

279 "warfare against common sense": Ralph Waldo Emerson, "New England Reformers," in *Essays: Second Series* (Phillips, Sampson & Co., 1850), 250.

279 "the style of Pope, of Johnson, of Gibbon, looks cold and pedantic": Ralph Waldo Emerson, *The American Scholar* (Laurentian Press, 1901), 52.

280 "A man can be a man of education without being drilled through college": *Appendix to the Congressional Globe*, 33rd Congress, 1st Session, May 19, 1854 (John C. Rives, 1854), 1223. I first saw part of this quotation in Edwin Miles, "The Young American Nation and the Classical World," *Journal of the History of Ideas* 35, no. 2 (1974), 267.

281 "Athens . . . when her sons, under Miltiades, won liberty for mankind": Charles Sumner, *The Crime Against Kansas* (John P. Jewett & Co., 1856), 4, 22–23, 92–95.

281   "a far greater influence on nineteenth century America": David Wiesen, "The Contribution of Antiquity to American Racial Thought," in *Classical Traditions in Early America*, ed. John Eadie (Center for the Coordination of Ancient and Modern Studies, University of Michigan, 1976), 197.

281   "barbarians . . . have never yet risen to the rank of men": *Aristotle's Ethics and Politics, Vol. II*, trans. John Gillies (A. Strahan, 1797), 20, 33.

281   "virtually a sectional American hero": Wiesen, "The Contribution of Antiquity to American Racial Thought," 210–11.

281   "slavery is unfavorable to a republican spirit": Harvey Wish, "Aristotle, Plato, and the Mason-Dixon Line," *Journal of the History of Ideas* 10, no. 2 (April 1949), 260–62.

282   "not one single passage at all calculated to disturb the conscience of an honest slaveholder": Thomas Dew quoted in Susan Ford Wiltshire, "Jefferson, Calhoun and the Slavery Debate: The Classics and the Two Minds of the South," *Southern Humanities Review* 11, no. 1 (1977), 37, 34.

282   the power of steam: Sellers, *The Market Revolution*, 132.

282   reduced the prices: John Larson, *The Market Revolution in America: Liberty, Ambition, and the Eclipse of the Common Good* (Cambridge University Press, 2010), 31.

282   steamboats operating on "western" rivers: George Rogers Taylor, *The Transportation Revolution 1815–1860* (Routledge, 1977), 63–64.

282   laid the first stone: [W. P. Smith], *A History and Description of the Baltimore and Ohio Rail Road* (John Murphy & Co., 1853). I first learned of this groundbreaking ceremony from Pauline Maier, *American Scripture: Making the Declaration of Independence* (Alfred A. Knopf, 1997), 178.

283   "so much more to know than ever before": Russel Blaine Nye, *The Cultural Life of the New Nation* (Harper & Row, 1960), 192.

283   "A steamer is a mightier epic than the *Iliad*": Leo Marx, *The Machine in the Garden: Technology and the Pastoral Ideal in America* (Oxford University Press, 1964), 199, 212, 203.

284   "the philosophers of Scottish Realism vanished": Perry Miller, *American Thought: Civil War to World War I* (Holt, Rinehart and Winston, 1961), ix.

284   "The whole career of Latin and Greek": Louis Franklin Snow, *The College Curriculum in the United States*. Ph.D. dissertation, Columbia University, 1907, 15–16.

284   a requirement that all students pass a basic Latin examination: Meyer Reinhold, *Classica Americana: The Greek and Roman Heritage in the United States* (Wayne State University Press, 1984), 332.

284   Harvard stopped issuing diplomas inscribed in Latin: Jones, *O Strange New World*, 232.

## *Epilogue:* What We Can Do

286 "Property monopolized or in the Possession of a few is a Curse to Mankind": "I. Fragmentary Notes for 'A Dissertation on the Canon and the Feudal Law,' May–August 1765," John Adams papers, *FO.*

286 "Enlightened statesmen will not always be at the helm": "'The Federalist Number 10, [22 November] 1787," *FO.* I am indebted to a conversation in May 2019 with Elizabeth Chew, Christian Cotz, and Michael Dickens of the Montpelier organization for reminding me of this quotation.

286 "bad men will sometimes get in": "From Thomas Jefferson to Moses Robinson, 23 March 1801," *FO.*

286 He has tried to introduce a retrogressive personal form of rule: This sentence was inspired by the discussion of "primitive and personalized forms of authority" on p. 64 of Akhil Reed Amar, *America's Constitution: A Biography* (Random House, 2005).

286 the majority of Americans surveyed said they think they are living at the lowest point in American history: Rebecca Savransky, "Poll: Most Say This Is the Lowest Point They Can Remember for US," *The Hill*, 1 November 2017, accessed online.

287 "three epochs in history signalized by the total extinction of national morality": "Autobiography," *Thomas Jefferson: Writings* (Library of America, 1984), 93.

287 Seven of the thirty-nine people who signed the Constitution: Amar, *America's Constitution*, 164.

287 corporate campaign spending the essence of political corruption: See especially chapter 13, "Citizens United," of Zephyr Teachout, *Corruption in America: From Benjamin Franklin's Snuff Box to Citizens United* (Harvard University Press), 2014.

287 *"salus populi suprema lex esto"*: Cicero, *De Legibus (On the Laws)*, Book 3, Part 3:8, accessed online at LatinLibrary.Com.

287 Salus was the Roman goddess: William Smith, *A Smaller Classical Dictionary* (Harper & Brothers, 1886), 343.

287 John Adams wrote in 1766: "Saturday. Jany. 18th. 1766. [from the Diary of John Adams]," Adams Papers, *FO.*

288 As the social philosopher Michael Sandel: Quoted, Christina Pazzanese, "'People Want Politics to be About Big Things': Michael Sandel's Passion for Justice," *Harvard Gazette*, 5 April 2016, accessed online.

289 "If Congress can make canals, they can with more propriety emancipate": no author listed, "Literary Notes," *North Carolina University Magazine* 18, no. 4 (April 1901), 200.

289 "raise the negroes to a social and political equality": Quoted in Daniel Walker Howe, *What Hath God Wrought: The Transformation of America, 1815–1848* (Oxford University Press, 2007), 480.

289   "willing to block the modernization of the whole country's economy": Howe, *What Hath God Wrought*, 222.

290   One of the hallmarks of oligarchy is a legislature that is elected but tame: This sentence paraphrases p. 125 in Matthew Simonton, *Classical Greek Oligarchy: A Political History* (Princeton University Press, 2017). On the fusion of democracy and oligarchy, see also Jeffrey Winters and Benjamin Page, "Oligarchy in the United States?" *Perspectives in Politics* 7, no. 4 (December 2009).

# Index

Page numbers followed by n and nn indicate notes.

# About the Author

THOMAS E. RICKS is the military history columnist for the *New York Times Book Review* and a visiting fellow in history at Bowdoin College. Ricks has covered the US military for the *Washington Post* and the *Wall Street Journal*, where he was a reporter for seventeen years. He received two Pulitzer Prizes as part of reporting teams at those newspapers. Ricks is the author of seven books, including the Pulitzer Prize finalist *Fiasco: The American Military Adventure in Iraq*. His most recent book, *Churchill and Orwell: The Fight for Freedom*, was his fourth consecutive *New York Times* bestseller. Born in Massachusetts, Ricks grew up in New York and Afghanistan, and graduated from Yale University. He is married to Mary Catherine Ricks, the author of *Escape on the Pearl*, with whom he shares two grown children.